Healey

Healey

Compiled by Peter Garnier F.R.S.A.
from the archives of

TEMPLE PRESS

TEMPLE · PRESS

NEWNES·BOOKS

Published by Temple Press
an imprint of Newnes Books
Astronaut House, Feltham, Middlesex, England
and distributed for them by
The Hamlyn Publishing Group Limited
Rushden, Northants, England.

© Transport Press 1983

First published 1983
ISBN 0 600 35025 8
Printed in Great Britain

For the additional illustrations the Publisher wishes
to thank the following: Geoffrey Goddard;
National Motor Museum; and *Thoroughbred and Classic Cars*.

Contents

Progress by Proving

By Peter Garnier

The Second World War was not long over; most people were struggling on with their pre-war cars, cursing the continuing petrol rationing and looking enviously – and somewhat curiously – at the unaccustomed styling of the few post-war models which, in one jump, had advanced six years. It made little difference, however, which of them a hopeful customer ordered; the Government decreed that he gave a list of preferences; if the first choice was not available, he got the second best . . . or the third or fourth. In any case, the waiting list was very, very long. Motoring was struggling back into existence like a bedraggled fly emerging from a pot of glue.

In October 1945, within months of the end of the war in Japan, Donald Healey unveiled the prototype (and the only example in existence) of the 2.4-litre Riley-based sports saloon – and quickly followed it with the lovely open roadster. With bodywork designed by Ben Bowden, these two cars were breathtaking, so were the orders that rolled in from both sides of the Atlantic. Donald Healey's long and successful competition record, and his wealth of experience in sports car design, meant that performance and handling were in keeping with the cars' looks, too. Outstanding at the time was the soft, comfortable ride made possible by an extremely rigid chassis frame.

No tyro at attracting public attention either, Donald Healey was quick to demonstrate the performance of the new cars, covering the flying quarter-mile on the Como-Milan *autostrade* at an officially timed 104·65 mph in 1946, and following it up with the flying mile and five miles at 110·8 and 107·8 mph respectively the following year – using a saloon version for all these figures. Very soon, too, the cars were entered for major international events, with a roadster driven by the late Tommy Wisdom winning its class in the 1947 Alpine. Clearly, these essentially road-going sports cars had competition-winning performance as well as looks.

These early Healeys were the work of a very small and dedicated team consisting of: Donald Healey; A. C. Sampiero – ex-Alfa Romeo, Maserati and Thomson and Taylor – who designed the suspension; B. G. Bowden, MSAE, MIAE, stylist, ex-Farina; James Watt, salesman, whom Healey had met at Humber; and Mr Ireland, who designed the chassis. Peter Skelton, another Humber link as their Hereford distributor, gave a helping hand by making the frames, bodies and other parts, and providing floor-space in his Westland Garage at Hereford; and, in a corner of a concrete-mixer factory at The Cape, Warwick, 'production' began, with Victor Leverett of Riley supplying the engines and transmissions.

Peter Skelton could not manage the saloon bodies as well as the roadsters, so the saloons were farmed out to Elliotts at Reading, with an initial order for 50 – thus the cars became known as the Westland Roadster and the Elliott Saloon, the chassis of these two continuing virtually unaltered until 1954.

With the Government-imposed export quota, and the blind doubling of Purchase Tax on the more expensive cars, the saloon was priced at £1,250 plus £347 19s 5d tax, and the roadster at £1,225 plus £341 0s 7d. In consequence, very few were reaching British customers. However, with the chassis price at £900, Ian Duncan's coachbuilding firm in Norfolk set about building a stark, door-less, hood-less two-seater which dodged the double Purchase Tax and put the Healey into the hands of British enthusiasts. Other specialist coachbuilders, too, got to work on the Healey chassis, but nothing they produced had the

This fully streamlined Silverstone Healey, fitted with an American 3.8-litre Nash engine and overdrive transmission, took fourth place in the 1950 Le Mans with Tony Rolt (seen here) and Duncan Hamilton.

Members of the Sports Car Club of America's Central Board stand by a newly imported Healey Silverstone.

looks of the two standard production cars. Two years later, in 1949, came the Silverstone, with a 450 lbs weight saving on the standard car – which is surprising since the much starker Duncan Healey, at 2,150 lbs, was 84 lbs heavier than the Silverstone.

Following Tommy Wisdom's Alpine success in 1947, the cars were entered for such events as the Targa Florio, Mille Miglia, Spa 24 Hours and the Alpine during the following couple of years, with the Silverstone making its competition début in the 1949 Alpine, driven by Donald Healey and Ian Appleyard. As with the previous appearances in international events, this Healey, too, proved extremely successful, finishing second overall and first in its class – a wonderful début for any car, but more so for the fact that it cost under £1,000 (without Purchase Tax). Only 105 were made, but they did their share of international rallies, though often seeming to be dogged by ill-fortune when particularly well placed. Peter Riley's private entry in the Liège-Rome-Liège of 1951, with Bill Lamb, was more fortunate, however. The car won the 3-litre GT class from strong Lancia opposition and finished eighth overall. Peter's name was later to become closely associated with success after success in this and other events, driving the works 'big Healeys'.

At the end of 1949, in response to American demands for something larger than the 2.4-litre Riley engine, Healey came to an agreement with Nash Motors in the States to use their 3.8-litre unit. This was installed in a modified Silverstone chassis early in 1950 – and given an encouraging try-out in the Mille Miglia, followed by Le Mans in which Tony Rolt and Duncan Hamilton finishing fourth overall. The export-only Nash-Healey went into production, making its début at the Chicago Show in February 1951. After that, orders came pouring in and ten cars a week were exported to the States. Cars were run again in the Mille Miglia, with Donald and Geoffrey Healey taking fourth place in their class, and at Le Mans, where Rolt and Hamilton finished sixth overall. A larger-engined (4,138 cc) version was introduced in 1952 and again the cars ran in these two major sports car events. This time, Leslie Johnson and Bill McKenzie finished eighth overall in the Mille Miglia whilst Johnson and Tommy Wisdom were third overall and first in class at Le Mans.

These continuing competition successes by the works cars – notably in six consecutive Mille Miglias – gave lustre to the name. There were also the essentially road-going cars for the sporting driver, among them the Sportsmobile, the Tickford- and Abbott-bodied cars, and the 3-litre Alvis-engined Sports Convertible. The latter, introduced at the London Motor Show in 1951, gave the British public something approaching the Nash-engined export cars, with a similar body style and very luxurious specification.

All this was very long ago, but few cars can have come to the fore, or made such a name for themselves, as quickly as the early Healeys. Inevitably, though, in writing a potted history of the marque, one tends to hurry through these cars in anticipation of getting to the 'real' Healeys, which started with the sensational Healey 100 making its bow at Earls Court in 1952. So 'right' did this simple, clean-lined car look that even now, 27 years later, it still looks modern. It took the Press and the public by storm; no words were adequate to describe this styling *tour de force* by Gerry Coker, nor the simple, straightforward chassis design by Geoffrey Healey and Barrie Bilbie. This brand new concept was prompted largely by the 'drying-up' of 2½-litre Riley parts and engines, and the need for a new source of power units. Naturally enough, Donald Healey had long been associated with Sir Leonard Lord, chairman of Austin at Longbridge, so it was no surprise that he should turn to the 4-cylinder Austin A90 Atlantic engine.

Demand for the car was enormous, orders for 3,000-plus being quickly received. Because the Show car, and one other, were all that existed, and the Warwick factory was in no way large enough for this scale of production, things must have become very worrying indeed. At this stage, Sir Leonard Lord stepped in, offering to take over production of what was to become the Austin-Healey. With the resources of Longbridge behind it, and large-scale production assured, the new car was immediately a winner. International competition activities remained the responsibility of the Warwick factory – as did the design of the cars right through to the end; and Donald Healey, maintaining his policy of 'progress by proving', embarked on a competition programme.

Naturally this included the Mille Miglia of 1953 for

Donald Healey, with drivers Stirling Moss and Lance Macklin (right), celebrates coming sixth in the Sebring 12 Hour at Florida in March 1955.

which two cars were entered (Hadley and Mercer; Lockett and Reid), but the new cars were beset by teething troubles, largely due to oil in the clutches. At Le Mans – despite one of the cars being involved in an accident on the day before the race – they gave a faultless demonstration of reliability, the Gatsonides and Lockett car finishing 12th and the Becquart and Wilkins 14th. The 1953 season ended with a record-breaking trip to Utah where, with no modifications permitted, a standard but carefully prepared car took all American records from five to 3,000 miles and up to 24 hours, during which it averaged 104 mph. Subsequently, a tuned version covered the flying mile at 142.6 mph. The Austin-Healey's future in the States was assured.

In 1954, Donald Healey developed a lightweight competition version of the production cars, and entered one for the Sebring 12 Hour race driven by Macklin and Huntoon. The car did remarkably well, lying third behind Moss's almost brakeless Osca and an ailing Lancia in the closing stages. Macklin's gallant effort to take the lead resulted in the car going on to three cylinders with a broken rocker-arm, but it finished third overall and first in class. This version was subsequently marketed as the 100S, along with the 100M, to 1953 Le Mans specification.

Just before the 1954 Le Mans race, however, and thoroughly disillusioned by the fact that European sports car racing had developed into a battle-ground for very thinly disguised racing cars, built in extremely small numbers with the express intention of winning races, Donald Healey decided to withdraw from works participation in such events. There was little point in running production sports cars, however reliable, against such highly specialised machinery. Record-breaking, however, continued and in August two cars were sent out to Utah – the 1953 record-breaker modified to Sebring specification, and a special super-charged car with a beautiful aerodynamic body. Among a host of other records, the standard car took the 12 Hours at 132.5 mph and the 24 Hours at 132.3 mph. The blown car covered the flying mile at an astonishing 192.6 mph.

The following year – 1955 – was a disastrous one for sports car racing. Early in the season, 100S cars came first, second and third in the Series Production Sports class at Sebring in March. Cars were entered for Le Mans and the Tourist Trophy by the newly set-up B.M.C. Competitions Department – the famous 'Comp Shop' at Abingdon, under Marcus Chambers – the decision having been taken by B.M.C. to re-enter international races and rallies. In both the Le Mans and T.T. events, serious accidents took place involving Healeys – through no fault of their drivers, since the accidents had already started before they arrived on the scene.

With the Austin A90 engine now outdated and beginning to be out-performed, it was decided in 1956 to turn to the 2,639 cc Austin Westminster engine – the six-cylinder Series C – and thus came about the Austin-Healey 100-Six, produced as a two-seater and an 'occasional four'. The car made its début at the 1956 Earls Court Show, but not before two versions had been taken to Utah for the annual outing, both streamlined, one using a six-port head and the other supercharged. The more-or-less standard prototype of the 100-Six achieved a further host of records, including 500 miles at 153.14 mph – while the blown version did an absolutely staggering 203 mph! Thus, the 'big Healey' made its début with the most impressive background, and to back it up the streamlined car was on show at Earls Court.

For the best part of the next ten years, the competition performances of these cars – and the 3000 that followed them in 1959 – were to become legendary. There was very little they did not win in the European rallies: Pat Moss and Ann Wisdom's outright win in the 1960 Liège-Rome-Liège, the toughest and longest 'road race' in the European calendar; Pat Moss's endless *Coupe des Dames* wins, and her three European Ladies' Championship victories; the 'Morley twins' two consecutive Alpine Rally outright wins in 1961 and 1962; Aaltonen and Ambrose's Liège-Sofia-Liège victory in 1964; and Timo Makinen's inspired performances (mostly sideways). There were team prizes and class wins galore, and a host of second and third places overall.

Somehow, the scarlet team cars with their white hardtops will always be associated with the mountains, hurtling up goat tracks like the Gavia and

A 'big Healey' in its element: Timo Makinen drives through a typical forest section during the 1964 R.A.C. Rally. Timo and his co-driver Don Barrow came first in the G.T. category and second overall.

Vivione, their raucous exhausts bellowing out ahead of the nearside rear wheel and echoing round the snow-covered peaks (and keeping the co-driver's seat uncomfortably warm sometimes). It was a glorious period, with names like Seigle-Morris, Sears, Gott, Riley, Hopkirk, Aaltonen and many others – apart from those already mentioned – becoming household names in the world of rallying. It is doubtful if the combination of British cars and drivers will ever again achieve such a period of rally successes; more is the pity that British crowds could not watch our products at work, as they can Grand Prix cars, for the Healeys achieved their many successes in wild, distant places, and often at night. It is a source of considerable pride and pleasure to me to have been associated with these great years, as a member of the Marcus Chambers team, co-driving with Jack Sears in these events, including the Liège-Sofia-Liège.

Had the Sprite flown the Austin-Healey flag on its own, it would probably have received the same sort of acclaim as its larger brother – but inevitably its performances, impressive though they were, became overshadowed. Intended to provide its owners with a competitive sports car in a smaller, cheaper category, the Mark I was introduced in 1958, based – naturally enough – on the 948 cc Austin 35 engine and transmission. As with the bigger Healeys, it passed through a series of engine-size increases. The Mark II, introduced in 1962, had its engine-size increased to 1,098 cc by enlarging the bores and lengthening the stroke; the Mark III, launched in March 1964, had various improvements to increase the general comfort; and the Mark IV, introduced at the 1966 London Motor Show, was fitted with the Mini Cooper 1,275 cc unit.

It must have been almost before the first cars were completed that a team of three was entered for the 1958 Alpine – taking first, second and third places in their class ... John Sprinzel, who will for ever be associated with racing and rallying successes in Sprites, drove the winning car. Driving a privately-entered car in 1959, he won his class in the Liège, finishing eighth overall. The same year, a special streamlined, supercharged Sprite was built at Abingdon and taken to Utah, where it averaged 138.75 mph for 12 hours and 146.95 mph for the hour.

It was beginning to look like the Austin-Healey story all over again. With Sebring and Le Mans their special tramping ground, Sprites won their class at Sebring in 1965, 1966 and 1967, and at Le Mans in 1960 (averaging 85.6 mph) and 1965. In 1967 and 1968 they took 15th position at Le Mans – the best-placed British cars. As a result of the Sebring successes, the 995 cc Sebring Sprite special competition car went into production, with an extra-lightweight version scaling just over 1,200 lbs.

In sales terms, the success of the Austin-Healeys owed a great deal to the North American market, and by the late 1960s B.M.C. was becoming nervous about sports car prospects in the face of infringing US legislation. Production of the 3000 tailed off in 1967, although a handful of cars were completed in 1968, and although various projects were developed to the prototype stage a successor was not put into production. The Sprite continued until the link between British Leyland and Healey was broken in 1970, although some Sprites were produced as Austins into the following year.

Donald and Geoffrey Healey were soon involved in another sports car programme, with Jensen. In 1970 control of that company had fallen into the hands of a group headed by Kjell Quale, a prominent US West Coast sports car distributor. The Jensen plant was obviously too large for the low rate of production – around a dozen cars a week – and the company naturally looked to an expansion of the range to take up the slack. The appointment of the Healeys to the Jensen board, with Donald Healey as Chairman, naturally encouraged enthusiasts to expect a 'Healey 3000 replacement'.

The Jensen-Healey was obviously viewed in that light when it was unveiled at the 1972 Geneva Motor Show. It proved to be an open two-seater, using bought-in components from several sources, including the Lotus twin-cam engine. A GT version followed in 1976, but by that time the Jensen company was struggling to survive. The end came that year, when the factory equipment was auctioned in the summer.

This effectively ended the line of Healey sports cars, which had been an essential part of the British sporting scene for almost three decades.

SPECIFICAT

Designing a Car for the Enthusiast:

JUDGING by what one reads in the motoring Press and by the fervour displayed when the enthusiasts get together, there is an increasingly lively interest in the special kind of car usually known as the sports type, a subject over which I have worked and dreamed and worked again.

It will be granted that the first requisite of an " enthusiast's," or " sports," car, as it is commonly termed, is performance. Performance in the broadest sense is signified, meaning that this ideal car must be capable of covering the kind of road on which it is intended to travel in a better, far better, style than the orthodox car. Furthermore it must give to its driver an unusual sense of gratification by reason of its absolute obedience to his skill.

Getting down to a definition, the chief requirements of a sports car are that :—

(a) It must be much more readily controllable than the usual car by a reasonably expert driver, even if to obtain this quality may mean that a novice will find the car " difficult."

(b) It must have a high cruising speed, and enough power in reserve at such a speed to have an acceleration in the order of 5ft. per sec. per sec. This calls for an engine which gives plenty of power where required, and carefully chosen gear ratios. Top gear performance at 10 m.p.h. is not an essential.

In order to satisfy requirement (a) the various components of the car must be maintained in their proper position and alignment under all conditions. We all know how badly a car behaves after it has been " bent " in a crash, and not straightened out properly. Moreover, it is not difficult to imagine what happens when a frame weaves, twists and bends at high speed, or when springs and radius arms deform and allow the wheels to take up whatever positions they like.

A Rigid Main Frame

The most important single component of a car, and especially so of a fast car, is the main frame, and unless this is really rigid in all directions it is not much use trying to design suitable springing and steering, for the model will be vicious and liable to " pile up " only too often.

Many people understand why a frame must be torsionally rigid, but very few know how rigid a frame should be in a horizontal plane. Yet it is easy to see that centrifugal force, acting at the centre of gravity, tends to bend the frame like a bow, bringing the inner wheels together, and causing perhaps a serious tendency to " over-steer." A number of well-known drivers came to grief because of this ; it was a marked fault of a number of Grand Prix cars up to about 1934.

I would put a correct, quick and sensitive steering as the second essential ; steering connections must be rigid ; flimsy steering arms, bent track or push and pull rods and badly supported boxes have no business in a fast car. Some designers mask faults of steering geometry by introducing springiness or sponginess in the connections—such people cannot have had any experience of fast driving.

The steering geometry must be such that a slight " understeer " is present. It must be borne in mind that in order to have a side thrust the wheels must be turned a fraction, and that the tyres will deform like a spring, and tend to " straighten back," so too much under-steering is undesirable. About the best compromise is to have a slight over-steer at low speeds and large locks, and a slight under-steer at high speeds and small locks.

Springing and Steering

What must on all accounts be avoided is the reverse ; a car that over-steers at high speeds is tiring to its driver, and dangerous. A number of such cars have been produced, and will probably still be produced, not all of them across the Atlantic. When discussing steering the rear wheels must be remembered ; a badly located back axle or an indifferent rear independent springing will spoil the best steering.

Springing and wheel location are so bound up with steering that it is impossible to discuss one subject without the other. The amount of control which can be applied through a wheel is limited to the tangential force that the said wheel can exert, i.e., the product of the coefficient of friction between tyre and ground, and the load supported by the wheel. The coefficient of friction may be between 0.6 and 0.8 ; the load is the static weight plus or minus the variation in load of the spring.

The variation in load of the spring may be the result of centrifugal force, positive or negative acceleration, aerodynamic effects, brake or power torque reaction, and, of course, unevenness of the road surface. It is apparent that every endeavour should be made to minimise these variations of loading, by accurate weight distribution, use of body shapes with zero lift coefficient, suitable spring linkages, and the use of soft springs, properly damped to minimise the effect of road unevenness. The hard suspension associated with sports cars will not be tolerated in the future.

On the subject of the various spring linkages : since each one has been chosen by some manufacturer for specific reasons it would not be fair to criticise. However, it can be pointed out that a linkage which tilts the wheels or alters the track, or inter-

The author at the wheel of the low-chassis 4½-litre Invicta with which he won the Monte Carlo Rally in 1931, starting from Stavanger.

[I]ON for *PERFORMANCE*

Propositions and Contentions Based on Practical Experience

—By DONALD HEALEY, M.S.A.E.—

Enthusiasts for sport and sports cars will find a great deal to interest them in these personal views expressed by Mr. Donald Healey, who was well known before the war for his many successes in international events, which included winning both categories in the Monte Carlo Rally and eight premier awards in nine Alpine Trials. Besides being a practical motorist he has been associated with the design of a number of successful cars.

feres with the steering geometry can be satisfactory only if the springs are fairly rigid, thus defeating the requirement of "soft springing." These bad features also have been responsible for the excessive tyre wear which is so general with independent front suspension.

It can also be pointed out that the car which has the best "cornering capacity," the 1,500 c.c. G.P. Alfa-Romeo, has fore and aft links on its front wheels, and that is about the only system which permits the use of soft springs without introducing tyre scrub and gyroscopic effects or steering interference. This has also been used with torsion bars by Auto-Union, but the coil system has many advantages.

The rear wheels should be just as well located as the front, but as the rear springs need not be quite so soft as the front ones (this can easily be demonstrated, but the equations required would be out of place in this article), independent springing does not give quite the same improvement on the rear as on the front wheels. A light rear axle, located by a torque tube and a side strut, with coil springs to decrease unsprung weight, may easily be considered a very useful compromise between the best theoretical layout and practical simplicity.

Shock Absorbers Important

Whenever springing is being discussed, dampers, or shock absorbers, should not be forgotten. Shock absorbers have nearly as much to do with the good or bad suspension of a car as the springs themselves. On a fast car they should be well up to their job to prevent "fade" on a long run; the levered piston variety of the hydraulic type with pressure recuperation is about the best for the vehicles under consideration, but in some cases additional friction types may be useful. It is worth while to remember that a good and well-proportioned hydraulic damper with pressure recuperation is very nearly self-adjusting, but a frictional shock absorber is nothing of the sort, and whilst the former can be fitted, adjusted and left, the second requires some means of adjustment by the driver, such as Telecontrol.

Having outlined a car which will really hold the road, be comfortable to its driver, and go where its driver desires we can start to think how to push it along, and then how to stop it.

The total power required at the wheels is divided into:

(1) Air resistance

$$\frac{H.P.}{\text{air resistance}} = \frac{A \times V^3}{374} \times k$$

Where k is a coefficient = 0.0018 for an open car of the old sports car type; = 0.0008 for a very well streamlined saloon; and = 0.0004 for a good records attempt car.

A is the frontal area of the vehicle in sq. ft.

V is the speed in m.p.h.

(2) The power to overcome rolling resistance (rr), given by

$$\frac{H.P.}{rr} = \frac{V \times W}{p^a \times 1520}\left(245.6\frac{V^b}{397} \times p^{1.44}\right)$$

V = speed of car in m.p.h.

W = weight of car as tested in lb.

p = tyre pressure in lb. per sq. in.

a and b are determined by the design of the tyre and road surface.

Up to a few years ago the rolling resistance was assumed as independent of speed, say 40 lb. per ton on good roads, and therefore the power required to overcome rolling resistance was assumed to be merely proportional to speed. For low speed and with high pressure tyres it is nearly so, but at higher speeds with fairly soft tyres the equation given above should be used. This equation was determined after tedious work for racing tyres as used before the war; tyres with nylon cords, artificial rubber, or of materially different design may show marked variations.

(3) The reserve of power, which will give life to a car. The force required to produce an acceleration a is equal to

$$a \times \frac{w}{g};$$

and the corresponding power at a speed V

$$H.P. = \frac{a\,wv}{370g}$$

where a is the acceleration in feet/sec./sec.

w is the weight of the car as tested.

v is the speed at which the acceleration is considered.

g is the gravitational constant.

In order to have an acceleration of 5 feet/sec./sec. at 10 m.p.h. with a car weighing 2,500 lb. when tested 10.5 b.h.p. is required at the wheels as the necessary reserve of power to produce it. In order to have the same acceleration at 80 m.p.h. the reserve of power at that speed must be 84 b.h.p. Further, whilst the air resistance b.h.p. is only 0.07 at 10 m.p.h., at 80 m.p.h. this increases to 36 b.h.p., in both cases with a car having $k = 0.0018$ and a frontal area of 14 sq. ft. The power required by the rolling resistance will be 2 b.h.p. and 25 b.h.p. respectively, using tyres of pre-war pattern, pumped at 20 lb. per sq. in., so that we shall have :—

	10 m.p.h.	80 m.p.h.
Power required at wheels at		
To overcome air resistance	0.07 b.h.p.	36 b.h.p.
To overcome rolling resistance	2 b.h.p.	25 b.h.p.
Reserve of power required to give an acceleration of 5ft. per sec. per sec.	10.50 b.h.p.	84 b.h.p.
Total power required at the wheels	12.57 b.h.p.	145 b.h.p.

Transmission Losses

The engine has to develop 10 or 20 per cent. more power to take account of transmission losses. It is clear that the engine must develop a lot of power at r.p.m. corresponding to high road speeds; this explains why cars developed as sports cars by firms without previous experience are sometimes disappointing. In order to have a good bottom end performance on top gear the car is undergeared, the engine strangled so that it cannot breathe at higher r.p.m., the moving parts are so heavy that pumping and frictional horse-power increase out of all proportion, and the car, whilst fairly lively up to about 50 m.p.h., becomes more and more sluggish at higher speeds, and more or less dies on one at 60 m.p.h., even if eventually capable of 75 m.p.h. Wear and tear at high speed are high and fuel consumption is ridiculous—quite a high price to pay for that 10 m.p.h. top gear performance.

A good portion of our power is used up by air resistance. With a well-streamlined saloon we may have to face an increase of frontal area to, say, 15 sq. ft., but if we can reduce our k to 0.0008, the air power at 80 m.p.h. will be decreased to 17 b.h.p., the total power to arrive at 80 m.p.h. will be reduced from 61 to 42 b.h.p., and, given the same weight and the same acceleration of 5 feet/sec./sec., the total power will be reduced from 145 to 126 b.h.p.

To save the same amount of power by weight reduction would entail pruning away 300 lb., thus having a complete vehicle weighing 2,200 lb. It is impossible to have high speed performance without proper streamlining, but I mean streamlining, not addition of chromium " motifs " and chromium strips along the waist line.

The design of the engine, whether supercharged or not, cannot be discussed here in detail, but I would say:

(a) The crankshaft should be as short, rigid and light as possible.
(b) The crankcase should be a really rigid structure.
(c) Valves should be as large as possible, ports well shaped and cooled, and valve gear light and rigid.

Unless (a) and (b) are satisfied the engine will not be capable of running for long periods at high speed and high loads ; its main and connecting rod bearings will see to that. Unless (c) is satisfied—and the best solution is to use a hemispherical head—with two valves the engine will not breathe easily at high r.p.m. and the power will thus be limited.

An engine of this type must work at high b.m.e.p. and high maximum pressure. To avoid blown gaskets, deformations and chewed valves, the cylinder head and top deck of the block must be rigid, and the studs well distributed and " waisted." The use of a fixed head is to be deprecated, as it puts a limit on the valve size when using a hemispherical head.

Little doubt can be entertained on the comparative efficiencies of various shapes of head. Figures obtained in racing engines and in aero engines prove the hemisphere to be the best shape beyond all doubt, even if poor designs resulting from the conversion of side-valve units " roughen up " some engines which cannot stand the additional power. The main design of a hemispherical head is so simple, and gas and water passages are so clean, that the production side cannot grumble, and Riley's have shown for many a year what a good job it can be even in a relatively inexpensive design.

The number of cylinders is, of course, related to the power of the engine. The lightest engine for a given power is not the one with the largest number of very small cylinders, even if the maximum power for a given capacity may be developed by the engine with the most cylinders. We must bear in mind that the capacity of a cylinder increases as the third power of the linear dimensions, whilst the area of the cylinder increases only as the second power.

Stroke-bore Ratio

The power developed per cycle is, within limits, proportional to the capacity, heat losses to cooling water, and friction losses caused by oil shear between piston and cylinder. Whilst the power developed increases as the third power of a linear dimension (say the cylinder bore), a very substantial part of the losses increases only as the second power. The large cylinder will therefore be more efficient.

With the fuels to be expected for the immediate future about the best compromise is 25–40 b.h.p. per cylinder. Aircraft engine cylinders develop up to and over 160 b.h.p. each, but they have to work over a narrow range of speed, and thus vibrations are in a fairly narrow range.

A lot can be said about stroke-bore ratio ; the square engine is lighter, but with modern fuels and high com-

SPECIFICATION

for

PERFORMANCE

Continued

pression ratios a square engine loses more as the result of difficulties with combustion space shape than is otherwise gained. If the engine is supercharged matters are different but the value of the stroke-bore ratio should be chosen according to the compression ratio of the engine. I would choose a four-cylinder engine of 2 to 2½ litres having a stroke-bore ratio of 1 : 1.3.

Regarding transmission, I think that good synchromesh with remote control in the right position will satisfy the requirements of the sports car for a long time yet, although I have driven some excellent examples with the Cotal electrically controlled gear box.

Brakes should be powerful, progressive and more than anything else *consistent*. To have consistency the drums should be really rigid, the shoes well supported, and good cooling means should be provided. Fins outside the drum are of material help to increase rigidity, but not much good as dissipators ; air scoops are much better.

The front brakes will do over 70 per cent. of the work, and must therefore be bigger and better cooled than the rear. A lot can be said for all brake operating systems ; personally, I think that hydraulic is the best, provided that the " plumbing " is carefully installed, and kept away from the exhaust pipes. Air brakes or " spoilers " may be quite useful on streamlined cars, and materially ease the life of the main brakes.

Just before the war it was obvious that the sports car as a type was due for considerable further development. There were not very many of these machines that possessed so much more performance than the ordinary touring car as to justify their special appeal and price. Furthermore it is obvious that the sports car has to keep pace with the racing car ; that is, it has to resemble the very latest type of racing car, whereas most sports cars of the date in question owed much of their appearance to the Grand Prix cars before 1926—cars broadly distinguished by the fact that their radiators were well behind the front axle. Again, a number of these cars handled well, but they did not handle so much better than their rivals in the touring class as to be outstanding, and unless the sports car is outstanding the query inevitably arises as to whether it is worth its price.

Sports Car *v.* Ordinary Car

It is, perhaps, invidious to mention names, but there is just one example of what I mean ; the Riley Brooklands model was one of the very few sports cars within my experience which had a modern outline and a performance which stood out.

Then there was another thing : the sports car should shine in the big international rallies, apart from racing. There again it was gradually becoming apparent before the war that the ordinary car, or some slight modification of the ordinary car, had such a high performance as to be almost, if not quite, on equal terms with its rival. In its day the 4½-litre Invicta could meet Continental competitors and beat them on their own ground, in the Coupe des Alpes and the Monte Carlo Rally, for example. But later rallies showed the evolution of touring cars with a very high performance indeed.

It was, perhaps, not unnatural that a great number of sports cars developed out of touring cars and that the process involved undesirable compromises here and there, but if one thing is more certain than another it is that a sports car must have its own personality, and it must be a machine of which every part has a definite relation to the purpose of the design. It may be that certain components of the ordinary touring car can fit into that design, but a very great deal depends upon the result being a logical whole and not an obvious adaptation.

For Enthusiasts—

The 2.4-litre HEALEY

DONALD HEALEY, the well-known and highly successful driver in international trials, rallies, and other competitions, has designed and is about to put on the market a car of his own. It will attract the immediate attention of enthusiasts the world over, because its construction meets so many points which could only be understood by people who have handled fast cars in the major sporting events.

Personal experience has shown Donald Healey that a fast car is not really a fast car unless it holds the road. Holding the road means that the car is completely stable and will invariably obey the control of the driver at all speeds of which it is capable, and under all road conditions.

Power-Weight Ratio

Having secured the road holding the next point is the performance. That can be obtained only by having a good power-weight ratio—in the order of 100 b.h.p. and 20 cwt.

In those desiderata are the makings of a good fast car. They are conditions which are not at all easily satisfied. At this point the reader is invited to study the specification of the Healey car (on page 16), and thereafter the reasons underlying the details of the design will be outlined. Two styles of complete car will be made, a saloon and a roadster. The saloon is one of the most graceful and individual designs yet seen.

As the engine is a descendant of the excellent 16 h.p. Riley, already well known and well proven—concerning which a separate review in connection with a forthcoming Riley model will appear in due course—it is not proposed to describe it in detail on this occasion. Suffice it to say that the engine used in the Healey car has a special arrangement of twin carburettors, and special exhaust manifolding.

Now to examine the design in the light of the special factors which determined it: To secure road holding the first need is an extremely rigid frame, and the second is a comparatively soft suspension. The Healey frame is of 6in. deep section, though

British Design to Compete on Every Count with the Best of Continental Sports Cars

reasonably light in gauge, and is built up of a "top hat" section with a closing flange welded across the brim. Across the front is a large tube backed up by a box section cross-member, so as to give stiffness against "lozenge" stressing, and provide adequate rigidity for the support of the independent front suspension. Towards the middle is a short stiff cruciform, the centre of which carries the mounting of the torque tube. Further bracing is provided by a deep centre cross-member carrying a tunnel which surrounds the propeller-shaft. At the apex of the wheel arches is yet another deep cross-member, and the after part of the frame is further stiffened by steel underpanning. It is only necessary to look at this frame to realise that it is remarkably rigid. Yet it is not heavy—as shown in the illustration it weighs 160 lb.

Now the suspension: The first point has been to reduce unsprung weight to the lowest possible point, which has been done by eliminating comparatively heavy half-elliptic leaf springs and replacing them by coil springs, also by using wheels of relatively small diameter. It is surprising how the weight of a wheel and tyre goes up with a small increase in diameter, and therefore how much can be saved by decreasing diameter. In turn the next need is to provide a suspension which has as little friction as possible, but at the same time allows for a considerable deflection without causing an alteration of the track. That is why the trailing link arrangement has been adopted, for rise and fall of the wheels do not cause them to move out of their plane of rotation, and so is

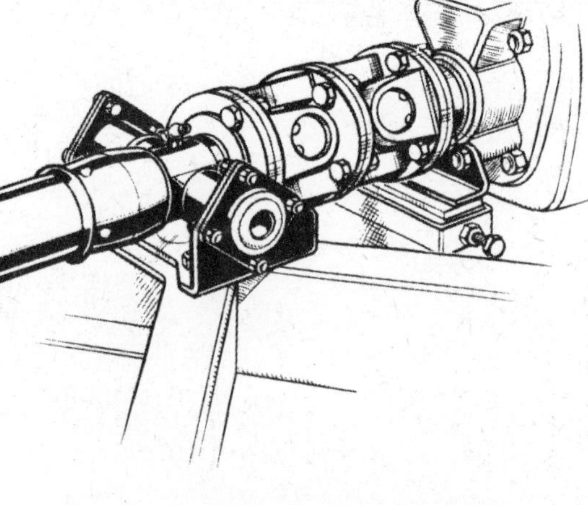

*Showing the rubber=bush=mounted trun=
nion for the forward end of the torque
tube, and the compounded needle=bearing
universal joints which ensure constant
velocity drive.*

The 2.4-litre Healey

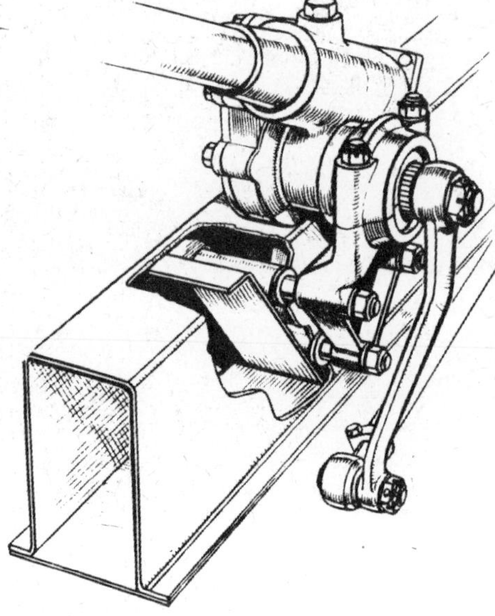

*This sketch illustrates not only the deep
box section of the frame, the lower flange
of which is welded on, but also the interior
stiffening which gives special rigidity to
the steering gear box.*

avoided the kind of wheel flap which
may arise from the reactions of gyroscopic forces. The Healey front suspension allows for a maximum deflection of 3 inches up and 3½ inches down,
which would have been considered in-
credible on a fast car of older days,
when stiff springs allowing 1 inch up
and 1½ inches down would have been
about usual.

Because the design of the suspension
aims at rigidity it looks more complicated than it really is. Welded to the
outer ends of the front cross tube of
the frame are large sheet-steel boxes,
which incline rearward at the top to
provide the upper abutments for the
coil springs. Spigoted into the lower
extremity of each box is the housing
for the fulcrum shaft of the trailing
link member, the shaft being carried
on needle roller bearings and provided
with ball thrusts. The bearings are
few in number and large in size in
order to reduce friction to its lowest
point. The assembly is packed with
lubricant, which should suffice for a
long period of use. Attached to the
rear end of the trailing link is a yoke

piece carrying the steering swivel and
stub axle assembly. Plain thrust bearings are used for the swivel pins. The
upper end of the yoke is hinged to the
end of a second link which forms the
actuation arm of a specially designed
Luvax-Girling self-recuperating piston-type hydraulic damper, which is
bolted to the steel box member. In
this way a parallel link motion is
secured, which avoids alteration of
caster angle with deflection, as well
as avoiding wheel plane deflection.

The upper extremity of the large
coil spring is secured to the underside
of the steel box member, and the
lower end bears down upon the trailing link. This trailing link is made of

a high duty light alloy and is designed to be rigid without being
heavy. Thus it will be seen that
the unsprung weight of this suspension is reduced to a minimum by
material as well as by design.

Another very interesting aspect
of the suspension is that the choice
of relatively small diameter wheels
on a fast car has given food for
thought in the matter of tyre equipment, especially with synthetic tyres,
which are apt to be sensitive to the
effect of increased heat arising from
high speed. Careful experiment and
testing were carried out, and it was
found that synthetic tyres did not
reach undesirable temperatures on this
car, because, it is considered, of the
absence of wheelspin.

This fact brings into prominence
another feature of the design. Because the tyres keep good contact with
the road the braking is unusually efficient. Hence no specialised design of
braking has been found necessary, and
normal Lockheed hydraulic brakes are
used. The equipment adopted after
experiment employs 11in. drums with
1½in. operating cylinders on the front
wheels, and 10in. drums with 1¼in.

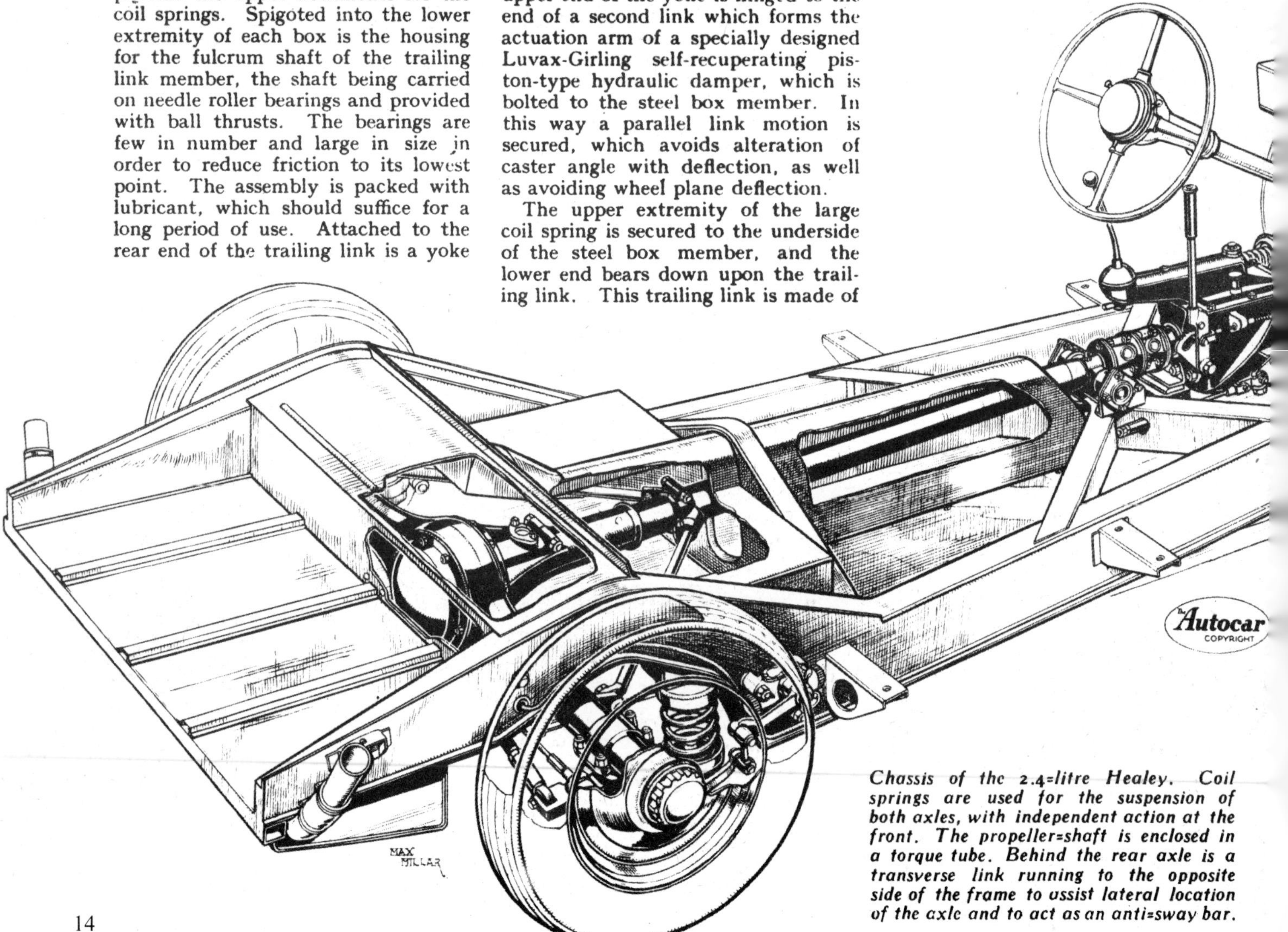

*Chassis of the 2.4=litre Healey. Coil
springs are used for the suspension of
both axles, with independent action at the
front. The propeller=shaft is enclosed in
a torque tube. Behind the rear axle is a
transverse link running to the opposite
side of the frame to assist lateral location
of the axle and to act as an anti=sway bar.*

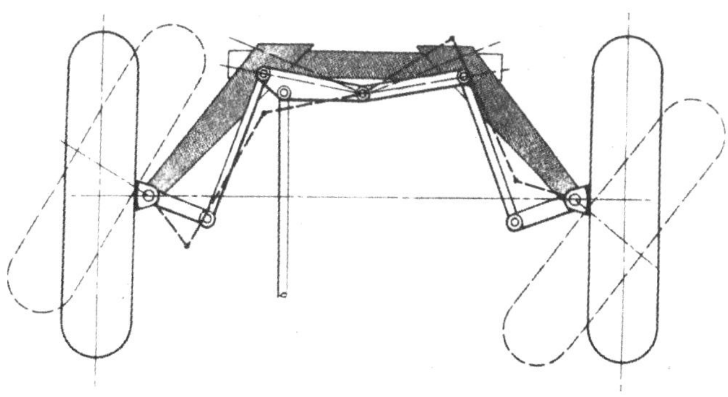

cylinders on the rear wheels. Again, the use of brake drums of reasonable diameter conserves the unsprung weight and helps in the all-important matter of maintaining wheels in contact with the ground. This arrangement gives a braking ratio of approximately 70 per cent. front and 30 per cent. rear, and is in accordance with the transference of weight distribution during heavy braking at high speeds. It has been worked out by experience so as to ensure that rear wheels will not lock under heavy braking, for, as every fast driver knows, the instant a wheel is locked the full arresting power of brakes is lost. The car as a whole has been designed with a slightly forward weight distribution; approximately 55 per cent. front and 45 per cent. rear. This distribution not only gives excellent braking characteristics, but also has been found to provide remarkable stability on corners.

The Healey car has an unusual but not untried system of rear suspension. The rear axle casing is of the normal pressed steel banjo type, but the propeller-shaft is enclosed in a torque tube, the head of which is anchored on rubber-bushed trunnions to the centre of the cruciform of the frame. The rear axle as a whole is therefore located by the trunnion. In the transverse plane, however, further location is provided by a lateral link, or "sway bar," which is anchored at one end close to one hub of the axle and at the other to a bracket on the opposite side of the frame. The exact location of this frame bracket has a considerable influence upon the effectiveness of the sway bar. Since the rear axle is positively located by these means, it becomes possible to abandon rear half-elliptic springs, and substitute for them coil springs, thus saving unsprung weight and avoiding friction. Luvax-Girling hydraulic dampers again provide the exact and unvarying degree of damping which is sought.

Before leaving the coil spring suspension used at both ends of the car one should note that rubber, too, plays a part. Within the coils of each spring, at the top and pointing downwards, is a sharp "pear" of rubber. When a spring is compressed a short distance the point of each rubber pear, or "snubber," contacts the housing at the base of the spring, which commences to compress the rubber; and the rate of resistance of the rubber increases the further it is compressed owing to its shape.

Not the least interesting part of this very interesting car is the steering, which, again, has been very carefully thought out with certain ends in view. Basically, of course, the chief source of trouble in steering is that the road wheels may be bouncing up and down over road inequalities all the time that they are being steered, to overcome which needs an exactness in geometry, rigidity, and other details. On the Healey car the steering gear, which is a "high efficiency" type, is rigidly secured to a rigid frame with gusset plates inside to maintain the stiffness at the point of attachment. The drag link of this gear proceeds, not to a steering arm on a stub axle, but to a swivel beam, the centre of which is carried below the front cross-member of the frame. From the ends of this beam track links run diagonally backwards to the steering arms on the stub axles. Thus there is no rise and fall at the end of the drag link, and the rise and fall of the outer ends of the track links are cancelled by the fact that their effective length rearwards from the ends of the beam is the same as the length of the suspension trailing link from fulcrum to swivel pins. The exact arrangement of this steering linkage and an indication of how the Ackerman principle of correct tangent on corners is obtained can be seen in the illustration below.

"Centrifugally Assisted" Clutch

There are certain other features in the design which call for attention. Between the Riley-built engine and the gear box is a special form of dry single-plate clutch, which is "centrifugally assisted." Instead of there being a complete ring of pressure springs for engagement, a series of the springs is replaced by small bell-crank bob-weights.

As the speed of the engine rises these bob-weights are influenced by centrifugal force to exert increasing pressure, forcing the clutch back plate to grip the spinning member more and more strongly. At the same time, as the pressure springs are fewer, the pedal pressure to disengage the clutch is less than usual at normal speeds or when starting from rest. The net result is a light-operating clutch with a powerful grip when grip is needed.

The gear box is a perfectly normal four speed with synchromesh on second, third, and top, of robust pro-

Underneath view of the Healey steering linkage, showing how the drag link is completely unaffected by up and down wheel movement, and also how the Ackerman angles are maintained to give true radii on curves.

The Healey body style obeys aerodynamic principles as far as modern taste in design will allow.

HEALEY SPECIFICATION

Engine.—Manufactured by Riley (Coventry), Ltd. 16 h.p., four cylinders, 80.5×120 mm. (2,443 c.c.). Overhead valves at 90 degrees operated by twin camshafts, short push-rods and rockers, in machined hemispherical combustion chambers, with straight-through machined ports. Compression ratio 6.5 to 1. Maximum b.h.p.: 100 at 4,600 r.p.m. B.M.E.P.: 125 lb. per sq. in. Monobloc construction with crankcase, Counterbalanced crankshaft in three large bearings. Steel connecting rods, machined and balanced. Aluminium alloy pistons, with four compression and one scraper rings, and large-diameter gudgeon pins. Twin large-size S.U. carburettors with air silencers. High-capacity oil pump draws oil from a large cooled sump and delivers under pressure through a large filter to all main bearings. Pressure-sealed water cooling system with pump, and cross flow to valve seats.

Transmission.—Centrifugally assisted dry single-plate clutch. Four-speed remote control gear box, synchromesh on second, third and top. Overall ratios: top 3.5, third 4.96, second 7.54, first 12.75 to 1. Constant velocity duplex universal joint, enclosed propeller-shaft, and spiral bevel rear axle.

Frame.—Straight-sided deep box-section of great stiffness.

Suspension.—Independent front suspension on trailing link principle with coil springs. Coil spring rear suspension with lateral locating link.

Steering.—High-efficiency type with special linkage geometry.

Brakes.—Lockheed hydraulic with 11in. front and 10in. rear drums.

Fuel capacity.—16-gallon light alloy rear tank with twin electric pumps and 2 gallons in reserve.

Wheels and tyres.—Dunlop 5.75×15 tyres on wide-base rims. Bolt-on five-stud disc wheels with Ace easy-clean discs.

Electrical Equipment. — Lucas specialised 12-volt with 63 amp.-hour battery, and automatic voltage control. Concealed inbuilt head lamps, flush-fitting side lamps, inbuilt pass and fog lamps.

Main Dimensions. — Wheelbase: 8ft. 6in. Track: (front) 4ft. 6in.; (rear) 4ft. 5in. Overall length (saloon): 14ft. 1½in., width 5ft. 5½in., height 4ft. 10in. Ground clearance 7in. Turning circle 35ft. Dry weight: 20 cwt. (approx.).

portions, and having a remote lever mounted upon a rearward-projecting tunnel. But behind the gear box is a special feature. Instead of a single needle-bearing universal joint there is a compound joint, effected by combining two similar joints. The purpose of this arrangement is to cancel out the variation in angular velocity which would occur with a single joint. It is a very simple method of securing a constant velocity joint.

Another point is the use of pressure cooling for the water circulation. This system is sealed, to release at a pressure of 15 lb. per sq. in. The purpose is to raise the boiling point so that the cooling system is not affected when the car is used in high altitudes, such as the Alps. The header tank is not part of the radiator assembly, but is mounted separately at the back of the engine. The object here is to keep the bonnet line low and narrow, and thus to secure good visibility for the driver as well as a slender frontal appearance.

At the time of writing the first of the saloons was not quite completed. The illustrations have been made from a quite beautiful scale model, which has been constructed primarily for air resistance tests in an aerodynamic wind tunnel. The first chassis has been built and sedulously tested, and before these lines appear will have been finished off as a roadster. Under these conditions a comprehensive description of the coachwork of the two models, saloon and roadster, is not possible, although a clear indication of the major points can be given. The body design has been carried out by Mr. B. G. Bowden, M.S.A.E., M.I.A.E., B.I.B.C.A.M., M.R.D.

Of the appearance of the two-door saloon it is not necessary to say much beyond emphasising the exceedingly graceful and modern lines. There is one point that does not show up in the side views, namely that the wings have a sharp Gothic arch cross-section, which gives them a spine along their length. To reduce wind resistance the head lamps are completely concealed in the front wings, and when they are switched on a trapdoor in front of each rises to expose the lenses.

Below the neat grille of the radiator

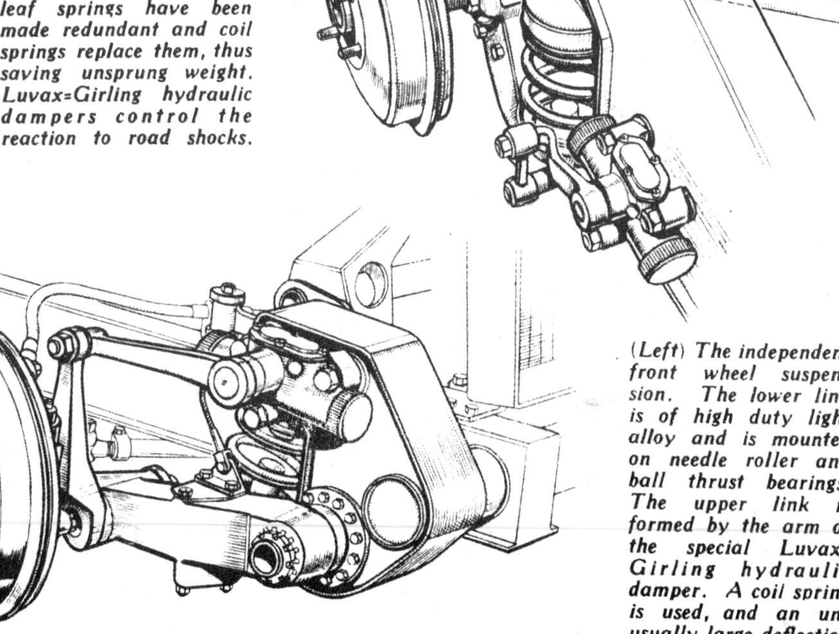

is arranged an inbuilt number plate, with the numerals mounted on a slotted surface which permits air to pass to cool the oil sump. At the sides of this assembly are inbuilt pass and fog lamps. Another good feature is that the "alligator" type of bonnet is hinged at the front end and opens at the rear, the reverse of usual procedure. The point of this arrangement is that this bonnet, even if improperly secured, cannot possibly blow open and blot out the driver's vision. It is also possible to leave the bonnet open a short way in order to let warm air from the engine play on the windscreen to prevent ice formation in severe winter conditions. One more point is that the drop windows have curved glasses.

TALKING OF SPORTS CARS

"THE SPIV"

Experiences of the Prototype Healey-Duncan Competition Two-seater

The original "Spiv"—prototype of the Healey-Duncan light sports two-seater, with the wide front first adopted, now modified on the production version.

GREAT interest has been aroused by the 2½-litre Healey among those attracted by high performance, but owing to current conditions the car is as yet unfortunately less well known among actual owners in this country than it deserves to be. The export quota and an inevitably high price have combined to put it out of the reach of many who would wish to own a car of such outstanding capabilities, based as it is on the highly potent 2½-litre Riley, which even in standard form is fast enough to satisfy the really keen driver.

There will be additional interest in a development even of the Healey, itself developed from the Riley. This is the Healey-Duncan, a lightweight competition car using the standard Healey chassis but carrying a sketchy two-seater open body. Experiences with the prototype car of this type are described by Gordon Wilkins, who has had connections with its development by Ian Duncan, of the Norfolk specialist bodybuilding firm bearing his name, whose products during the past year or so have been mentioned in *The Autocar*. Wilkins drove this car at one of the Bo'ness hillclimbs last year. VIZOR.

"I NEVER cease to admire the people who try to run businesses and build up new enterprises under the present régime" (writes Gordon Wilkins). "There are still people who refuse to slip into the licensed lethargy and organized apathy of the planners' State.

"The blind decision to double purchase tax on the more expensive cars was particularly hard on makes of high technical merit and high prestige value such as the Healey. It cut off a large part of the home market at a time when life was made difficult enough by material scarcities, rising costs and the inevitable technical problems involved in producing 100 m.p.h. cars with no adequate road or track test facilities nearer than Belgium. So thought Ian Duncan, an unquenchable spirit who builds bodywork in a centuries' old building in Norfolk that has served variously as theatre, barracks and boiler works. Last autumn he decided that some way must be found to cut costs drastically if Healey performance was to be enjoyed by any appreciable number of enthusi-

asts in this island. He therefore evolved a really simple light competition car that would give maximum performance at minimum cost. And in three weeks to the day—less time than it takes a government department to answer a letter—the first Healey-Duncan two-seater was on the road. It was not perfect and it was not pretty, but it provided the experience for an improved type now being delivered to private owners.

"The basis was the standard Healey chassis, but the extension beyond the rear axle was removed and the petrol tank moved forward to a position over the axle to keep down weight and overall length. A light frame was built up from welded steel angle section and to this the aluminium panelling was fixed by riveting locally and rolling over at the edges. Single-curvature panelling was used wherever possible and the only double-curvature hand-beaten panels were on the nose and the tail. Radiator grille and louvres were merged into a continuous structure bent to shape.

Simple Seating

"The seats were built on the sound principle that a good shape is worth more than an elaborate structure. The basis is a simple curved sheet of light alloy rolled well upwards for full support under the knees. This is covered with a layer of sponge rubber and pleasingly upholstered in P.V.C. A deeply rounded squab, also on a sheet metal foundation, completes the ensemble. In practice it has the merits of the exceptionally hard and astonishingly comfortable seats on the 328 Frazer Nash-B.M.W. and is rather less spartan. I have found it entirely adequate for distances up to 500 miles in a day, without developing any of the local stresses which often impose limits on ones' sedentary endurance.

"There are no doors because their omission made it easier to obtain a simple and rigid structure. Wings are a simple cycle-type curved high at the front to accommodate the 7½in travel of the i.f.s. They are easily removable for racing, and so are the head lamps, mounted low on a bar before the grille. Without petrol, but ready for the road, the car weighs 19¼ cwt, which shows a

considerable reduction on the standard saloon and roadster, neither of which is unduly adipose.

"Throughout the European competition world there is growing support for the principle of taking care of the pounds and letting the drag take care of itself. The restricted nature of contemporary sporting events places the emphasis on acceleration rather than a high maximum, and the new Healey-Duncan lines up with the growing practice of Snipping for Victory.

"With its gaudy colouring, square shoulders and general air of unabashed enterprise, the car inevitably came to be known as 'The Spiv' and this name has stuck to it. As streamlined as a bulldozer, as functional as a steam-roller, the car looks as though it means business and it is certainly no slouch in action. To drive it for hundreds of miles provides an interesting comparison with the various other Healeys, carrying British and Continental coachwork, which I have sampled at various times. Standstill to 50 m.p.h. takes 7.2 sec, as far as can be checked with present facilities, and 0-70 m.p.h. takes 14.6 sec, representing improvements of about 1 sec and 3 sec on the standard saloon, which does not loiter unduly. Like all Healeys 'The Spiv' wears a deceptively modest air in the lower speed ranges, but seems to take a second wind at 60 m.p.h. and from there soars right on regardless.

"On this particular car valve bounce seems to set in at a few over 5,000 r.p.m., but no accurate checks on the rev counter have been made so far. The corresponding figures in m.p.h. on the gears would be first 31, second 52, third 79 and top 113 m.p.h. The top gear figure, as S. C. H. Davis recently pointed out, is subject to a slight minus correction for wheelspin, and probably a rather larger plus correction for the increase of effective tyre diameter resulting from centrifugal force. The full 5,000 r.p.m. has once been clocked on top, and 4,800-4,900 can be held for miles when circumstances permit. 4,400 r.p.m., giving the theoretical 100, comes up rapidly on quite short stretches of road. The instruments may be a little optimistic but the general level of performance will occasion no surprise in view of the known capabilities of the Healey product.

"Transcribed into practical terms,

Another view of the car in its original form. The bodywork is obviously of spartan character but entirely in line with the ideas of those who cling to notions of the "real" sports car.

these figures indicate a road car which for practical purposes is faster than an aircraft over distances up to 200 miles and often beyond. Having motored in Healeys in several countries, I will not encourage controversy by specifying the location, but I recall one fast night trip of nearly 400 miles at a running average of well over 50 m.p.h. which included a familiar stretch of 20 miles covered in some 16¼ minutes, giving an average of about 74 m.p.h.

"Night motoring of that order is best done in an open car. There is a subtle sense of extra awareness which comes with the absence of a roof, and it puts 5 m.p.h. on the cruising speed which can be maintained without strain. One is grateful, too, for the big old-style head lamps.

Front-wheel Fascination

"The low weight permitted a sort of floating sensation at the front of the car at first, but it has been found possible to eliminate this by the use of stiffer dampers. When cruising fast it is fascinating to watch the front wheels rising and falling at the ends of the long trailing arms without feeling any corresponding effect on the motion of the car. It adds to the unhurried air of devouring miles in seven-league boots which has been the subject of comment by many people who have driven Healeys. High-speed swerves provoke some front-end roll, which is all the more easily observed as the wheels are exposed for all to see. When cornering at the limit of adhesion to win its class at the autumn Bo'ness hill-climb, the car may have appeared to 'Heal Duncanly,' as one wit remarked, but the effect is more apparent to the spectator than to the driver. On other Healeys, with greater structure weight, I have experienced an understeer reminiscent of the V12 Lagonda, but it is not noticeable on 'The Spiv.'

"Apart from the fascination it offers of watching a really good i.f.s. at work the spartan Duncan front provides excellent cooling for brakes and tyres. The standard braking system employs anti-fade linings, which have a moderate coefficient of friction, but with 'The Spiv' it would appear possible to use linings with a higher coefficient at the front, which should nicely reduce pedal pressures and eliminate a tendency to lock the rear wheels which exists with the very light bodywork.

"Seen approaching at high speed in a cloud of spray, the broad-shouldered 'Spiv' looks as grimly efficient as a landing barge full of Commandos. The chassis, being schemed primarily for modern all-enveloping coachwork, and having a low, wide radiator, does not readily accommodate a slim nose without using a fair amount of overhang, which would increase the weight.

"The drag coefficient must be considerably higher than that for the standard saloon, but the low frontal area and weight are compensating factors, and 'The Spiv's' appetite for fuel contrasts happily with its tendency to devour the miles. On a trip of nearly 1,000 miles at running averages of over 50 m.p.h. the fuel consumption worked out at the very favourable figure of 24 m.p.g.

"Naturally this is a car with an appeal for the sportsman who puts performance before personal comfort. It is strictly a surrey with no fringe on the top; indeed, a hood would be an embarrassment in the absence of doors. Getting into 'The Spiv' as it first emerged was rather like putting on a tin sarong, and luggage space was slight; there was just room for a pair of pyjamas provided that you wore them under your overcoat.

"The car has now covered 10,000 miles and has proved a remarkably reliable and husky high-speed conveyance. Maintenance has been at a minimum and running repairs have consisted of adding a few split pins here and there, and curing an hydraulics union leakage. Geographical conditions, and the exigencies of business have caused it to spend an abnormal proportion of its running mileage at speeds of 100 and over, and in the circumstances it is not surprising that tyres can be worn out in 4,000 miles. In my experience this order of mileage is to be expected on cars in the performance bracket of a Healey-Duncan, if driven really hard.

"After all, these were racing speeds a few years ago, and it is an achievement to make the tyres stand the racket at all. Before the war it was not unknown for a Southern entrant to wear out a new set of tyres on the Scottish Rally if he included some high-speed cruising on the trip to Scotland and back. Inevitably there is speculation on the effect of the 15in wheels on tyre wear. They obviously do more revs per mile than 16in tyres of the same section, and they fall farther into the holes.

"On the other hand, the saving in unsprung weight offered by small wheels is a factor contributing to the fine suspension and steering characteristics of the Healey chassis. Moreover, it is worth noting in passing that recent tests in America showed that, on tyres of the same section, a reduction of rim size from 16 to 15in effected a saving in power consumption of 5 to 10 per cent. Another factor which has been found to have an important effect on high-speed handling is the Panhard rod location. If the rod is set at too acute an angle it can produce a slight and baffling tendency to pull to the right.

In Production Form

"'The Spiv' provided a lot of fun and useful information which has been used in the design of a more comfortable production type, known almost inevitably as 'The Drone.' On this the bonnet louvres are horizontal instead of sloped and the wings afford rather more protection. A folding screen is fitted and the accommodation is more commodious. It comes on the B-type chassis, which incorporates various minor improvements, and the fuel tank is left in the standard position to allow space for a luggage locker behind the seats. Doors are now fitted, but the basic principle of obtaining maximum performance at minimum cost by simplicity and lightness has been maintained. To offset the weight of doors and other equipment the framework is now built up from light alloy extrusions instead of steel.

"No attempt has been made to obtain more power from the engine, but with previous experience of engines on the Riley general layout there appears to be plenty of scope, and possibilities are being investigated by various owners. The crankshaft is a handsome robust job, and with perhaps four carburettors and separate exhaust pipes, allied to suitable detail work, it should be possible to achieve a vehicle offering 120 b.h.p. per ton without undue sacrifice of tractability or reliability.

"Meanwhile the Duncan enterprise is laying further plans in the old-world surroundings of North Walsham."

Above: Production version of the Healey-Duncan two-seater with hood, four doors and a slimmer nose than the prototype, also horizontal instead of sloping bonnet louvres. This car has been dubbed "The Drone." Right: "The Drone" being sampled during the Geneva Salon by Roger Barlow, a well-known American correspondent of *The Autocar* and enthusiast for European "performance" cars, while on a recent visit from the U.S.

The Mille Miglia

New 2-litre Ferrari Wins Italy's Greatest Sports Car Race : Meritorious Performance by British Healeys Driven by Donald Healey and by Count Lurani

TWO comparatively new makes of car, using motor racing to establish their reputations, succeeded last week-end when the fifteenth Mille Miglia was run off over slightly more than 1,000 miles of Italy's main roads.

The race was won outright by a coupé-bodied 2-litre unsupercharged Ferrari, made in Modena, Italy, and driven by that fine and veteran Italian driver Clemente Biondetti, who has twice won this race before. Following this result, which is called the general classification of the race, there is the touring category and it is pleasant to be able to record that this proved a victory, for the first time, for a British car, the 2½-litre Healey saloon driven by Count Lurani, the same car which won its class in the recent Tour of Sicily. The latter event was described by Lurani in a special article last week, and it is hoped to include a further edition of his personal experiences in the Mille Miglia in an early issue. Last week-end he changed his spare driver and was accompanied by Sandri.

Several Healeys had been entered for the race but only three competed, those driven by Lurani, by Donald Healey himself, and by Haines, the Healey agent from Belgium. Donald Healey did very well to finish as high as ninth in the general classification, Lurani being thirteenth. The vast majority of the starters, which numbered well over one hundred, were Fiats, and this make was second and third in the general classification with streamlined saloons of only 1,100 c.c., an exceptional performance.

The Mille Miglia is an extremely confusing race to follow because, as explained in the special article last week ("A High-Speed Rally"), when nearly 200 cars set off over 1,000 miles right across Italy and have to make time checks at various points, the event as a whole becomes more like a high-speed rally. Thus the first car actually to

Donald Healey, with his son as co-driver, awaits the fall of the starter's flag last Saturday night. This Roadster model Healey finished ninth in the whole race.

finish at Brescia was Lurani's Healey but he was not, of course, the race winner. There had been no massed start, cars leaving Brescia on Saturday night at short intervals and returning to Brescia on Sunday afternoon in very scattered groups, after anything between fifteen and nearly twenty hours' driving.

Naturally it must be some time before the results of such a vast event can be properly collated and judged. The timing system in itself is complex, there are usually protests to be dealt with—especially as to whether cars really complied with the touring category regulations—and it is difficult to ascertain the exact reasons for failures. And so there has been in the daily press—rightly elated at the British successes—a certain amount of variation in the reports, which can be understood in the circumstances. But although Lurani's win in the touring category must not be confused or compared with Biondetti's victory in the race proper, it is none the less an historic achievement for the new British make from Warwick. Any car which goes the whole distance at a respectable average in the Mille Miglia must be a good car, and it usually takes an Italian driver who knows more than most about the huge course to get the best out of a particular car. The more credit, then, to Donald Healey, who can hardly have had the opportunity for any practice at all, for finishing so high in the final race list.

The umbrellas testify to the wretched weather conditions, as Sandri, with Lurani, drives the Healey saloon which won the touring category into Brescia at the finish.

MILLE MIGLIA RESULTS

General Classification: 1, Biondetti and Troubetzkoy (Ferrari), 15 hr 5 min 44 sec, 121.23 k.p.h. (75.8 m.p.h.); 2, Comirato and Dumas (Fiat), 110.56 k.p.h. (69.1 m.p.h.); 3, Apruzzi and Apruzzi (Fiat), 108.3 k.p.h. (67.25 m.p.h.).

Touring Category: 1, Lurani and (Healey), 17 hr 32 min 12 sec, 104.17 k.p.h. (65.1 m.p.h.); 2, M. Bornignia and F. Bornignia (Lancia Aprilia); 3, Bracco (Lancia Aprilia).

Touring Class Wins.—Over 1,100 c.c.: Lurani and (Healey). **Under 1,100 c.c.:** Capelli and Veronelli (Fiat).

Sports Class Wins.—Over 2,000 c.c.: Bianchetti (Alfa-Romeo), 107.0 k.p.h. (66.45 m.p.h.); **2,000 c.c.:** Biondetti and Troubetzkoy (Ferrari), 121.23 k.p.h. (75.28 m.p.h.). **1,100 c.c.:** Comirato and Dumas (Fiat), 110.56 k.p.h. (m.p.h.).

Special Sports Class Prize.—Under 750 c.c.: Fiorio and Avalle (Fiat 500).

2.4-LITRE
HEALEY
ROADSTER

Autocar ROAD TESTS

DATA FOR THE DRIVER

2.4-LITRE HEALEY

PRICE, with Roadster body, £1,500, plus £834 16s 8d British purchase tax. Total (in Great Britain), £2,334 16s 8d.

RATING : 16 h.p., four cylinders, overhead valves, 80.5 × 120 mm, 2,443 c.c.

TAX (in Great Britain), £10.

BRAKE HORSE-POWER : 104 at 4,500 r.p.m. **COMPRESSION RATIO** : 6.9 to 1.

WEIGHT, without passengers : 23 cwt 0 qr 14 lb. **LB per C.C.** : 1.06.

TYRE SIZE : 5.75 × 15in on bolt-on steel disc wheels.

LIGHTING SET : 12-volt. Automatic voltage control.

TANK CAPACITY : 13½ gallons : approx. fuel consumption range, 22–28 m.p.g.

TURNING CIRCLE : 34ft (L and R). **MINIMUM GROUND CLEARANCE** : 7in.

MAIN DIMENSIONS : Wheelbase, 8ft 6in. Track, 4ft 6in (front) ; 4ft 5in (rear). Overall length, 14ft 0in ; width, 5ft 5½in ; height, 4ft 7in.

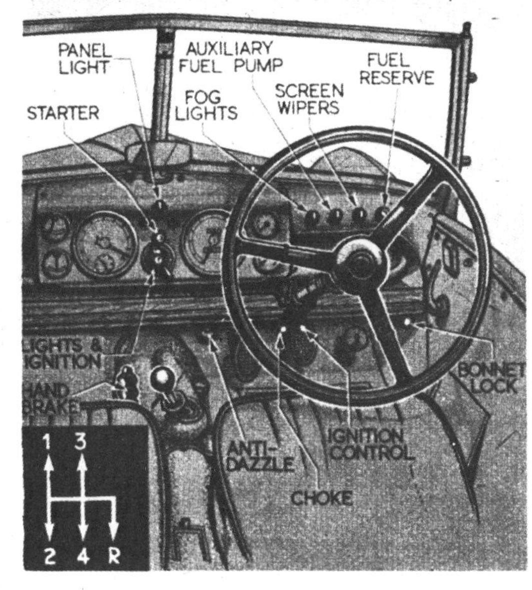

Described in " The Autocar " of January 4, 1946.

ACCELERATION

Overall gear ratios	From steady m.p.h. of		
	10 to 30	20 to 40	30 to 50
3.50 to 1	10.3 sec.	10.2 sec.	10.4 sec.
4.96 to 1	7.0 sec.	7.1 sec.	7.2 sec.
7.54 to 1	4.7 sec.	4.9 sec.	5.4 sec.
12.76 to 1	4.1 sec.		

From rest through gears to :—

30 m.p.h.,	4.3 sec.	70 m.p.h.,	19.2 sec.
50 m.p.h.,	10.2 sec.	80 m.p.h.,	28.3 sec.
60 m.p.h.,	14.7 sec.	90 m.p.h.,	46.3 sec.

Steering wheel movement from lock to lock : 2½ turns.

Speedometer correction by Electric Speedometer (conversions on kilometre-calibrated instrument) :—

Car Speedometer	Electric Speedometer	Car Speedometer	Electric Speedometer
10	= 10	40	= 38
20	= 19.75	70	= 66
30	= 30	80	= 76

Speeds attainable on gears (by Electric Speedometer)

	M.p.h. (normal and max.)
1st	25—30
2nd	44—50
3rd	65—76
Top (with hood down)..	100/102

WEATHER : Dry, warm ; wind light.

Acceleration figures are the means of several runs in opposite directions.

I N an existence which has been purely post-war the Healey has put itself on the motoring map in a position where it is recognized as offering one of the highest all-round performances currently available in production cars. An extensive test which has recently been carried out by *The Autocar* has enabled a proper appreciation to be obtained of just what nature of performance this remarkable newcomer offers. The occasion has been all the more interesting because the car provided for testing was the actual machine with which Donald Healey himself competed so successfully in the recent Italian Mille Miglia race, in which it finished ninth in the general classification at nearly 66 m.p.h. average, a very fine performance indeed, pointing as clearly as anything possibly can to the merits of the car in high-speed endurance. This achievement, it will be remembered, was in addition to that of a saloon model finishing first in the touring classification of the same race.

Some ten days after the Roadster's return to England from a trip which, including the race, had totalled some 3,000 miles, *The Autocar* took it over for testing, and in the meantime it had covered appreciable further mileage. It was understood that, except for repair of a front wing which had been damaged by hitting a dog in the race, the car was in the same trim as in the Mille Miglia and that it had not even had the tappets adjusted.

Prepared initially, as one is, for very high performance indeed from this car, one realizes within a short space of time that here is a sports car *par excellence* in modern form. Descendant it is of the true sports car one has known in limited numbers throughout the years, but with the difference as compared with, say, fifteen years ago, that the engine is of a type easily giving more power per litre than was then considered creditable for a sports model, and, above all, with the difference that the suspension is of a soft type, affording real riding comfort as well as the essential lateral stability. The heart of the Healey car is, of course, the Riley-built 2.4-litre twin high-camshaft overhead-valve four-cylinder engine, and a very fine engine this is for power and for reliability under the hardest use. The chassis, of course, is individually Healey, with a rigid but light box-section frame and coil spring suspension at front and rear, independent in front, and the car runs on decidedly high gear ratios.

Just what the maximum speed of such a car may be is not regarded as being so important within 5 or even 10 m.p.h. as some people would make out, for there are many other qualities of an ultra-fast car which assume greater importance. Chief among these are acceleration up to speeds which can frequently be used on British roads, say, 80 m.p.h., also the range of speed which is the natural cruising rate of the car, and its general handling. There is none the less a certain satisfaction as well as a certain practical significance in the knowledge that a car will top 100 m.p.h. given suitable conditions, the practical significance being that at such speeds as 80-90, normally to be regarded as very fast, such a car still possesses a definite margin of reserve. The testing carried out by *The Autocar* has enabled the maximum of this particular Roadster in open form to be put down as between 100 and 102 m.p.h. on level ground. The makers state that it is some 4 m.p.h. faster with the hood erected, which may well be credited, as in turn the saloon model is faster still.

"Four-five on Top"

Data-recording conditions on this occasion were not helped by the fitting of a kilometre-calibrated speedometer for purposes of the Italian race, the needle of which was not regular in behaviour and prevented a proper check of its readings being made at some speeds. A top reading of 4,500 r.p.m. on the rev counter was seen on top gear, and thus as 1,000 r.p.m. corresponds almost exactly to 24 m.p.h., theoretically this should represent 108 m.p.h., but various factors enter into the matter at very high speeds.

The next outstanding question with such a car concerns the average speeds which can be achieved with it. In this country, of course, traffic has a considerable influence, and the Healey had the benefit of the last few days of roads abnormally clear by reason of the private motoring ban and, therefore, more nearly corresponding on certain routes to Continental conditions than are likely, one hopes, to be seen again in this country. It is perhaps sufficient indication in this direction to record that in one particular hour during the test the Healey recorded 58 miles without touching maximum speed.

There is no cruising speed which can be specially assigned to it, for much more than with most cars, even high-performance examples, it can be driven on its high ratio, exceptional today in being in the "three-point-something" category, as fast as the road permits and the driver chooses, without feeling stressed mechanically. The average stretch of road available in England is just not sufficient to let this car right out to full maximum; 80 is seen with consummate ease and 90, approximately 4,000

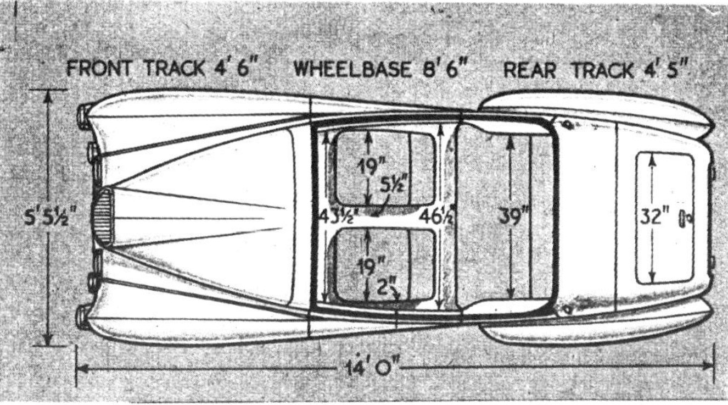

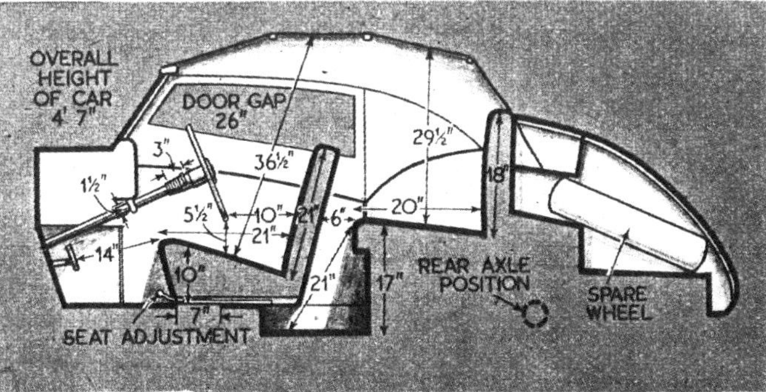

Measurements are taken with the driving seat in the central position of fore and aft adjustment. These body diagrams are to scale.

r.p.m., becomes almost a commonplace on a favourable route, but obviously a somewhat exceptional stretch is required for the magic hundred and over in safety, although the car gets there quickly given the space.

It will be noticed that an unusual range of through-the-gears acceleration figures has been recorded and it is a very striking commentary on the performance that 90 m.p.h. can be reached from rest in a mean time of 46.3 seconds. When accelerating for test purposes in this style it is possible to make the rear tyres leave long black power marks from wheelspin on a dry surface during the getaway on a wide throttle opening. Results such as these are obtained without appearing to stress the car unduly. With a light-alloy body the power-weight ratio is exceptional, the car carrying, in full running trim as tested, only fractionally more than 1 lb per c.c. of engine size.

All told, it will be realized that, as expected, the performance is tremendous. Few cars could live with the Healey on a journey if its driver were trying, and it hardly needs to be said that gradients scarcely exist for it. Main road slopes present opportunities for accelerating safely into the eighties. A more considerable slope may bring the pace down to a point where, for amusement value, it may be worth using a third which offers a genuine 76 m.p.h. maximum. Steeper stuff such as the 1 in 6½ hill often used in these tests gives the opportunity for almost a Shelsley-type climb, bringing in a second on which 50 m.p.h. is obtained within a 5,000 r.p.m. limit.

If the picture has been given of a 100 m.p.h.-maximum

Showing the seating and instruments. The telescopically adjustable spring-spoked steering wheel is taped to suit Mr. Healey's personal ideas in a long-distance event. The switch seen on the left of the facia board is for an additional horn fitted for the race. The angle of the front seat back rests can easily be adjusted.

A useful "grab" rail, which has a structural usefulness, extends across the driving compartment. Although the rear seat is comfortably upholstered and has foot wells, it will be seen that it is of strictly "occasional" nature. It is chiefly useful as luggage space, for the rear locker houses the spare wheel, side-screens, tools, and twin petrol pumps.

The Healey Roadster from various viewpoints, and still carrying its Italian Mille Miglia race numbers and the B.A.R.C. and B.R.D.C. badges fitted by Mr. Donald Healey, who drove this car in the race. This car attains a thoroughly modern and aerodynamically efficient shape, the test of which aesthetically is that it is readily acceptable even by a motorist who inclines towards a " diehard " outlook over car appearance, besides which this Healey looks " right " from any angle, including the view over the bonnet from the driving seat. Perhaps, however, here the dead front view is the most pleasing. The car is seen also to be still sightly with the hood up.

car which achieves its performance without fuss, without noise which in itself would cause the passer-by to look round, and of a car which can achieve quite startling point-to-point averages, then sufficient has probably been said about the sheer performance aspect.

Not so much expected are the tractability and flexibility of the car, its near-silence, and its comfort. It will potter through a town on the high top gear, and can even be made to pull round a right-angle corner on top gear, although with some pinking on the present Pool petrol when pulling away unless the pull-and-push ignition control mounted near the steering column is retarded. On going into a speed limit one throttles back from high speed and runs through the area without noise or ostentation. In traffic, third and second suffice except for actual starting and both gears are virtually dead silent. There is some exhaust note on accelerating hard, but not of a strident kind that booms in the ears.

As to comfort, the car is again a surprise. It is quite softly sprung, with considerable amplitude of spring movement, and poor surfaces are scarcely noticed, yet at the same time one can do with this car on corners just what one wishes to do with a fast car. As so often applies to modern fast cars with i.f.s., there is little guidance in the feel of the car as to the correct and safe speed for open bends, but at all events there is some suggestion of the tail tending to slide first with excess of zeal, which is as one prefers.

The steering—which is not of rack and pinion type, as on a number of modern cars—gives accurate handling at speed on the straight and for placing the car in corners. It has strong castor action and is quite high geared; it is on the heavy side for low-speed turning and manœuvring. The Lockheed hydraulic brakes are given a big job of work to cope with on such a car as this, and they cope satisfactorily. The short remote-control gear lever is admirably placed, but the hand-brake lever, to the left of it, could be within easier reach. It is effective, however. The gear change is a delight to use, with excellent synchromesh on second, third and top. The clutch action is smooth for starting and there is adequate room for the left foot beside the

pedal. One obtains a first-rate driving position, and driving vision is capital, with a full view of both wings—a most desirable attribute of such a machine.

The concealed hood is quite easy to put up and down and there are good side screens easily attached and removed. Points of detail have been considered in the provision of a shelf for oddments under the instrument board and roomy compartments with flap lids in the thickness of the wide but light doors. The instruments include an engine water thermometer. A reserve petrol supply is obtained simply by pressing a switch on the instrument board, when an auxiliary electric fuel pump comes into operation, together with a reminder light on the instrument board; the auxiliary pump is also available for sustained Alpine climbing. Instant starting from cold was obtained with very brief use of the choke.

A good light for medium speeds is given by the built-in fog lamps, which incorporate parking bulbs, and the main head lamp beam is adequate for speeds in the eighties. For such a car the horn note could certainly be stronger. The oil consumption was very low under conditions of sustained hard driving.

Engine view when the one-piece bonnet is lifted ; it is released by a remote control inside the bonnet and guarded against unwanted opening by a robust safety catch. Twin S.U. carburettors without air cleaners will be noticed, also the radiator filler and the steam-valve-protected vent pipe. The sparking plugs are accessible between the valve gear covers and the oil filler is convenient on the left side.

Clean front of the Healey Sportsmobile, with its substantial bumper. The small grilles feed air through ducts to the front brakes.

SPORTMOBILE IS HEALEY'S LATEST

Striking Drop-head Coupé

A SMART and practical foursome convertible, to be called the Sportsmobile, is now added to the Healey range. It is planned for fast and comfortable long-distance motoring. Interior width is four inches more than in the standard saloon, and passengers sit low in the car, well protected from the wind.

In front is a bench-type seat with split squab which tilts forward to give access to the rear seats. The cushions are in Dunlopillo, covered in leather. The luggage boot is really big and extends out to the full width of the car inside

On the instrument panel are rev counter, speedometer, oil and petrol gauges, ammeter and water thermometer. On the left are the ignition and light switches. Other switches and controls are grouped below.

Left : This view shows the sleek lines and the neat tail, which houses a luggage boot of exceptional size. Both front wings are visible from the driving seat.

Below : The lines are long and low but the sides are high enough to give good protection to the passengers. Door handles are flush fitting.

the rear wings. Construction is all metal, with aluminium alloy for outer panels, and the weight is approximately 2,750lb.

Interior trim is bold and original. Above the main instrument casing is a strip containing indicator lights, hooded to prevent dazzle. These comprise warnings for Trafficators, pilot lights for the auxiliary alpine fuel pump and main head lamp beam, and the usual ignition warning. On one end of the case is the ignition and light switch and on the other end is the Trafficator switch. Remote controls for bonnet and boot locks are placed inside, so that, when the cubby hole is locked, neither can be opened.

The hood is very easily erected and is secured by three quick-release toggles above the windscreen. It has a zip-fastened panel at the rear which can be opened for ventilation in hot weather.

The price, including radio, is £1,850, plus British purchase tax £1,029 5s 6d, total £2,879 5s 6d.

The Healey Silverstone

Fog lamps may be fitted as extras, as on this car for the Alpine Trial. Head lamps are set high behind the Healey front grille.

AN APTLY NAMED NEW MODEL FOR THE SPORTS CAR RACING ENTHUSIAST

SPECIFICATION

Engine.—4 cyl, 80.5×120 mm, 2,443 c.c. Overhead valves in hemispherical combustion chambers and driven by twin camshafts. Counterbalanced crankshaft. Two carburettors. Sealed pressure cooling by pump and thermosyphon.

Transmission.—Borg and Beck single-plate clutch. Four-speed gear box with synchromesh on second, third and top. Rear axle ratio: 3.5 to 1, with alternative ratios of 3.25 and 3 to 1.

Frame.—Box-section throughout with straight side members and 6in cross-members.

Suspension.—Front: independent with coil springs and hydraulic dampers. Rear: vertical coil springs and telescopic dampers.

Brakes.—Lockheed hydraulic, with two-leading shoes in front in 11in drums. 10in rear drums. Cable hand brake to rear.

Wheels and Tyres.—Dunlop disc wheels, wide base. All balanced. Dunlop s.l.p. tyres, 5.50 by 15in or 5.75 by 15in.

Electrical Equipment.—12-volt. Coil ignition, automatic voltage control. 63 ampère-hour battery.

Dimensions.—Wheelbase 8ft 6in; track (front) 4ft 6in, (rear) 4ft 5in. Overall length 14ft, width 5ft 3in, height 4ft 6in.

ANY addition to the sports car ranks, though at the present time their numbers hardly constitute even one rank, will be certain to meet with a warm reception. With this will be combined a keen sense of expectation when such a contribution is made by Healey.

Without more ado then, consider the design of the Healey Silverstone, as this newcomer is named. Obviously, the underlying motives have been to reduce weight to the bare minimum, the elimination of any kind of frills and, indeed, of everything not having a clearly defined job to do. Back to function, in fact.

This results in a clean-cut, sturdy car, meant to stand up to really hard work, with an absence of any features susceptible to damage and needing costly replacement. Having pleasant curves moulded into it, the single shell light alloy body is constructed on stressed skin principles, thus reducing the amount of internal framework.

The nose is carried far enough for-ward to enclose the head lamps side by side beneath a slightly larger grille than before of the familiar Healey shape, hinged at its lower edge to give access for adjustment or cleaning glasses. There is no bonnet in the ordinary sense; instead, a large, quickly detachable, hatch cover is provided, well louvred for ventilation, and pierced for the radiator cap, which is nearly flush with the surface.

On the present car a well-raked fold-flat screen is fitted but later models will have the glass arranged to retract into a well in the scuttle, leaving enough upstanding to form a low racing screen. Fasteners are provided to enable the cockpit to be enclosed when parking the car or partly enclosed if no passenger is being carried. Those at the rear are also used for securing the hood, which stows away behind the seat squab. Seats are set low with the torque tube casing running between, whilst the floor is covered by smart rubber matting having a smooth upper surface and "aerated" beneath. A tail just large

Healey Silverstone

enough, but no larger than is necessary, to house the 17-gallon tank and spare wheel terminates in a horizontal slot through which the rearmost part of the tyre tread protrudes, creating at once a neat yet business-like air. Narrow wings of dome section, with the suspicion of a spine and faired off at the rear, are carried on detachable brackets for removal in events which allow for this. Both wings and body conform with F.I.A. regulations. Small side lamps are mounted on the front wings, and the wings at the rear have narrow valances.

An overall weight of 18½ cwt calls for smaller section tyres of 15 × 5.50in, and direct acting spring dampers on the rear axle, otherwise the chassis specification remains as before, with all the well-known Healey features. Standard axle ratio is 3.5, but final drives giving 3.25 and 3.0 to 1 are available as extras.

Driving Position

Unlike its circuit namesake, getting in and out of this Silverstone is easy through the two shallow, stoutly hung doors with catches on the inside, no external handles being necessary. The driver sits well back from the steering wheel in true Grand Prix fashion and its modest 16in diameter allows it to be set low down. A full view forward allows accurate placing of the car on the road.

A fully remote gear lever is not necessary since the direct box-to-hand lever is quite short; yet it brings the knob in just the right place and, having no trace of spring, permits precise, clean changing.

Instruments are well placed and easily seen. Nearest to the left hand is the ignition timing knob, alongside which are mixture and starting controls. Above these is the main lighting and ignition switch, flanked by panel light and wiper switches; the anti-dazzle switch is on the instrument board to the right.

On the road the steering is direct yet pleasantly light, without being lively. Cornering revealed a gentle lateral flexibility, much to be preferred on a fast car to an absolute rigidity so productive of slides. It is a refreshing change to be able, from the driving seat, to " see the wheels go round " and also to see them beat up and down; it is also refreshing to reflect that in the old type of sports car with "solid" suspension the driver would take the beating!

The price of the Healey Silverstone is £975, plus £271 11s 8d British purchase tax; it may be supplied in pale green or blue metallic finish or red cellulose with red or beige upholstery. It is predicted that this model will soon become known as the Quicksilverstone!

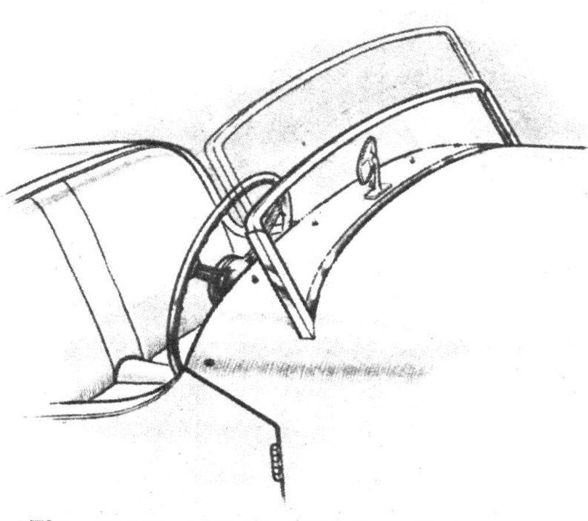

The screen retracts into a well to provide a low racing windshield. This screen was not fitted to the car photographed.

The modern trend to frontal overhang allows the head lamps to be recessed behind the grille.

Better half, not " better half." Mrs. Mortimer habitually turns Goodwood faster than her husband in OPA 2 and holds the unofficial ladies' lap record—1 min 53⅖ sec.

SILVERSTONE HEALEY

SATISFYING AND ECONOMICAL COMPETITION, SPORTS AND EVERY-DAY ROAD CAR

FOR those who would fain motor race and still practise what the late Lucius Seneca called "the science of avoiding unnecessary expenditure," the Silverstone Healey is a sovereign tool. It looked that way to Charles Mortimer when he bought OPA 2 in December, 1949, and it looks no different now that he and his wife have a crowded season of combined operations behind them. So, wotting well that racing budgets, so far from making sense, seldom even make nonsense beyond about their third month, Mortimer is writing a book on this one of his, and much m.e.p. to his elbow.

OPA 2, the second Silverstone ever built, started out as a works car and in that capacity ran in the 1949 B.R.D.C. production car race, driven by Rolt. When the Mortimers acquired it the Healey had done about a thousand miles. In the way that early samples of a series have, the car lacked a few of the furnishings afterwards standardized. It had, for example, no speedometer.

Total mileage is currently 4,000, of which only a small fraction has been racing miles. Between whiles the car plays the ordinary unspectacular roles common to every family's daily round—shopping and getting around generally; plays them with credit, too, the day having gone when vehicles of the sports-racing persuasion threw temperaments all over the place. "I go, I come back," as that chap used to say in the Handley show.

This Healey, as revealed by its public performances, is rather swifter than the regular run of Silverstoneware. Precisely what gives it its bigger bangs is Charles Mortimer's business, and, understandably, he won't talk in detail. "When we bought it we had the engine all apart and put it back again very carefully," is the noncommittal way he tells it.

The success of these molestations is best measured by the progressive rigour of the handicappers' attitude to OPA 2 and its operators, for although the car piled up a satisfying number of places during the 1950 season it never won a race. At Goodwood in August, for instance, Jean Mortimer found herself in flattering solitude on the scratch mark for a five-lap handicap, and even then finished fifth, lapping in the process in 1min 53 2/5sec; officially, no such thing as a ladies' record existed, but that time was faster than any scored before or since by a memsahib, and I believe there is talk of giving it official record status. At the same meeting she came third in a scratch five-lapper up to three litres, behind the phenomenal Connaught of Kenneth McAlpine and Peacock's Le Mans Replica Frazer-Nash.

Mama Knows Best

In the early Goodwood meetings, Charles, in the "papa knows best" spirit natural to papas, entered himself for the scratch races and his wife for the handicaps, but as time wore on and the stopwatch evidence became more and more face-reddening (for him) he ruefully vice versa'd the roles. The Healey did, however, console him with one Goodwood "second"—in the June club meeting.

In club affrays at Silverstone, too, the appearance of the device kindled a gleam in the handicapper's eye, as witness the time when Jean, under Midland M.E.C. auspices there, was called upon to give long starts to male drivers of 3½-litre Jaguars and the rest of the Silverstone Healeys. There was nothing much that could be done about that, but OPA 2 was placed third, again with the wife and mother at the stick, in a five-lap scratch race the same afternoon. And in another Silverstone clubfest, viz., the Maidstone and Mid-Kent's, Mrs. Mortimer ranked second and fourth respectively in sports *and racing* scratch races, *libre* c.c.

There are two varieties of piston for Silverstone Healeys, high ones giving 7.2 to 1 compression, low ones at 6.9 to 1. The car had and still has the low type, but the first time it gave best to another Silverstone Healey was in the B.R.D.C. production car race at Silverstone in August, the Mortimers' ninth meeting on this car, when, with C.K.M. up, it ran fifth in its class, averaging 76.61 m.p.h. against the 79.92 set by the class-winning Healey of Duncan Hamilton. The Hamilton car had the high pistons.

This model, it will be remembered, was in a sense built down to a price, expressly to beat the double purchase tax, but a strenuous season of mixed motoring, competitive and otherwise, on the sample in question, has revealed only one small weakness which might be attributed to pricebound workmanship. Inside the 17-gallon fuel tank are two vertical pipes, one for the normal supply, the other for reserve. During practice for the opening Goodwood meeting, both these pipes parted at their common attachment point, enforcing a non-start.

For Mortimer, in common with most other competing *tipos*, the rain-lashed Tourist Trophy in September is something best forgotten, but, as he doesn't

Offside view of the Healey shows the perforated disc wheels, affording good brake cooling, and the retractable windscreen in the full-drop position.

Charles Mortimer hugging the grass on the ascent to Cuckoo Corner in the Blandford production car race last Whitsun, in which his Silverstone Healey finished third at 72.61 m.p.h.

SILVERSTONE HEALEY

have to read this, we will recall it just the same, if only because his Dundrod experience points a moral which may save others woe.

Immediately before the practice period, OPA 2's brakes were relined. By some mischance they were lined with a non-standard material leaving practically everything to be desired. After the first training séance, during which Homeric pedal pressures begat negligible retardation, they were relined again with the right stuff—but, warned the expert anchorites, the brakes would need several hundreds of miles' bedding-in. Time did not permit, and consequently for Charles the T.T. resolved itself into one bad pull-up for carmen after another. What with being ten-tenths brakeless and soaked to the protoplasm, he was feeling altogether pretty uncalled-for by the end, though, creditably enough, the Healey did average 66.48 m.p.h. and finished fourteenth out of 27 survivors.

It being the owner's intention, as mentioned in my opening, to dash into print at some length himself on the pounds, shillings and pice of limited-scale sports car racing, I will refrain from going into detail regarding the costs of OPA 2's 1950 season, but it can anyway be said that these were most moderate. During most inter-meeting lulls, nothing was done to the car at all, apart from greasing. The cylinder head was not lifted between the initial teardown and close of play in September. For the T.T., the services of a Riley works mechanic were laid on (Correct, Reader Proudfoot, the Healey has a Riley engine and gear box), more as a precautionary measure than anything, in view of the long lines of communication involved.

Moderately compressioned for a sports engine, this Riley unit puts a good face on Pool. Routine maintenance jobs are much facilitated by the divorcement of the wings from the slim body, allowing a really close-up approach to the bonnet's contents. Although light, the body structure as a whole, consisting of a stressed shell of 16-gauge light alloy on channel-section framework, stands a lot of bashing without developing rattles; and cretins in car parks are continually frustrated by the spare wheel, which, being slotted horizontally into the tail, just at the point of maximum sabotage, serves the important secondary purpose of an impregnable bumper.

It is, of course, no secret that the Silverstone model has a lower maximum than the saloon, for obvious aerodynamic reasons, but for owners who can take some climate on the chin the open Healey has it all over the closed one for really fast touring. Its high power-weight ratio —104 horse, $18\frac{1}{2}$ cwt dry—gives it a beaut of a pick-up to the sort of speeds— eighty and some—at which it will cruise all day. The absence of metallic lingerie around the wheels, moreover, affords as good brake cooling as we were accustomed to twenty years back, before all this Progress broke out, and the brakes in consequence, when lined with the right linings and properly bedded down, are immune from fade under anything but the most relentless pedalling.

OPA 2, according to Mortimer, has a top speed of just about 105. On the Lavant Straight at Goodwood, which isn't long enough for the revs to stop building up in top gear, he gets an r.p.m. reading just equivalent to the "ton." As for acceleration, over the standing-start kilometre in the West Essex club's speed trials at Chelmsford last spring, Jean Mortimer put up 33.16 sec, which was fastest ladies' time and second fastest time regardless (Matthews' $3\frac{1}{2}$-litre Jaguar beat her for top place by a decimal).

About seven times out of ten, it seems, one finds oneself quoting Brighton performances as accelerative criteria, but although OPA 2 ran there we perhaps never will know how fast this car can cover the Madeira Drive. First, Charles arrived after his class had been run off. Second, the class he had entered turned out to be the wrong one. Third, when he did run—rather swiftly—the timing gear didn't register. Fourth, when he tried again it was to return a time of such sloth that they nearly reopened the road on him. . . .

Sustained consumptions as good as 22 m.p.g. are normal under fast highway conditions, while in the T.T.—it will be remembered that the regulations permitted non-standard carburettor settings— the average was just better than 8 to the gallon.

All in all, looking at the matter from a cost-performance point of view—which is exactly how these combined operators intended all along to look at it—the conclusion formed from OPA 2's first competition season is that a Silverstone Healey has an all-round raceability which it would be hard to beat at the price, and which consistently places it close on the heels of costlier opponents. It is easy to tend, hard to break, by no means hoodlum in exhaust note and very passably tourable provided you don't wish to hump rafts of baggage; you can't have it both ways, of course, and the ability to carry seventeen gallons of fuel has to be paid for in terms of luggage room; the goods department between the seat squab and the petrol tank mightn't impress Messrs. Carter Paterson but it serves well enough for a one- or two-night stand by an unexacting twosome on the laughing side of forty—I mean thirty in Jean's case.

The Mortimers, as a matter of fact, are unexacting to the point that they don't even erect the hood, no matter what, and sidescreens have they none, although such screens are regular equipment on later and fully standard examples. The windscreen, which slides up and down in a trough instead of folding, leaving six inches protruding at full retract, is neat and rattle-proof and shrugs the airblast accurately over the driver's head in its lowest position.

By the time this appears in print, the Silverstone may have gone to a new home. If it hasn't, it will be seen some more in '51 around the circuits and sprint venues of old England and peradventure Ireland. In that case they will put in a set of the taller pistons and perhaps amend the body contours here and there to relieve drag a piece.

Dennis May.

Acceleration duel between the Healey, farthest from camera, and a Connaught, at Goodwood, where the Healey scored a number of places but no outright wins during 1950.

The Nash - engined Healey

An example of Anglo-American co-operation with far-reaching implications, the Nash-Healey combines British-built chassis and coachwork with American engine, transmission and rear axle, and will be exported for sale through the vast Nash organization in the United States. The engine is a six-cylinder of 3.8 litres with twin carburettors and other modifications which raise the power to about 140 b.h.p.

OCTOBER 12, 1951

New 3-litre Healey: ALVIS ENGINE IN CONVERTIBLE

A HIGH-PERFORMANCE highlight at the London Show will be a new 3-litre Healey along the general lines of the export only Nash-Healey. It will be remembered that the Nash-Healey was introduced last year as a Healey car, less engine, to be exported across the Atlantic, where Nash engines would be fitted and Nash service widely available.

The 3-litre car uses the current Alvis six-cylinder engine with a bore and stroke of 84 and 90mm respectively. Two S.U. horizontal carburettors are used and the unit gives 106 b.h.p. at 4,200 r.p.m. Maximum torque is 150lb ft at 2,000 r.p.m., and the compression ratio is 7 to 1. This rugged unit has a robust seven-bearing crankshaft, the transmission being through a 10in Borg and Beck clutch, a four-speed gear box with synchromesh on second, third and top, and a hypoid rear axle giving a 3.77 to 1 top gear ratio.

The suspension is the Healey trailing link type with coil springs, Girling dampers and an anti-roll bar. At the rear trailing links are also used, with coil springs surrounding the dampers. A stabilizer bar is fitted for sideways location.

Standard equipment includes a heater, radio and Lucas long-range head lamps. The price is not yet settled.

Below: The Alvis engine as used in the Healey. Push-rods operate the overhead valves, fed by twin S.U. carburettors.

The sleek lines of the new Nash-Healey are accentuated by the sloping curved screen and a bonnet which dips below the front wings. The coachwork is built by Pinin Farina.

Nash-Healey with Pinin Farina Body

ANGLO—U.S.—ITALIAN MODEL WITH BIGGER ENGINE

THE Nash-Healey sports car, a pioneer example of international collaboration in sports car production, becomes a tripartite Anglo-American-Italian enterprise with the appearance of the 1952 model. This was revealed at the Chicago Automobile Show which opened last Saturday. Engines and transmission units made in America are installed in chassis built by the Donald Healey Motor Co., Ltd., of The Cape, Warwick, England, in which Nash Motors of America are now substantial shareholders. The chassis are then shipped to Italy, where they are fitted with hand-built open two-seater bodies at the Turin works of Pinin Farina. Completed cars finally go to the United States, purchase being reserved for customers with dollars to spend.

The Farina body has more sleek and flowing lines than the previous Nash-Healey. The head lamps are incorporated in the radiator air intake, instead of being mounted in the wings, and the tail treatment is styled to suit the current American fashion by the introduction of small fins in the line of the rear wings. The doors are wide and set farther forward, making it easier to enter the car, and a single-piece curved screen is used, in place of the V screen with triangular side panels.

The power unit is an improved version of the Nash Ambassador, a six-cylinder overhead-valve push-rod unit. The cylinder bore has been increased to bring it up to 88.9mm and the stroke is 111mm. This raises the swept volume to 4,141 c.c. as against 3,847 c.c. for the engine used in the previous series. The former engine gave 125 b.h.p. on a compression ratio of 8 to 1, but the modified power unit gives more power, and an appreciable improvement in torque, resulting in better acceleration from low speeds. The new output figures have not yet been released.

The engine has an aluminium cylinder head and an oversize built-in manifold fed by two British S.U. horizontal carburettors. It has a seven-bearing counter-balanced crankshaft.

Transmission is through a three-speed gear box with automatic overdrive. Front suspension is the standard Healey layout with trailing arms, coil springs and an anti-roll bar. Rear suspension is by coil springs, and the propeller-shaft is enclosed in a torque tube.

Deliveries to the American public are expected to start in the late spring of this year. Meanwhile, the British Healey organization continues independently with the production of two other models, the Riley-engined chassis which is fitted with saloon coachwork by Tickford, and the open three-seater convertible, which is powered by the 3-litre Alvis engine. These, fortunately, are still available in non-dollar markets.

Head lamps incorporated in the radiator grille and a bonnet motif emerging from the carburettor air intake characterize the front end. On the scuttle is the intake for the heating system.

A neat hood folds away completely when not required and can be supplemented by side screens fitted to the doors.

The Tickford saloon has a smooth, modern form. A long sweep of the front wings eliminates any suspicion of slab-sidedness. Screw-on hub caps are fitted to the perforated-disc wheels.

HEALEY TICKFORD SALOON

THE Healey company is one of the very few organizations of its kind to be formed since the war for the purpose of building motor cars. This in itself is no mean achievement in times of restrictions and shortages, when any new venture is bound to be beset with difficulties, especially a small company with relatively limited resources. Even more credit is due when it is realized that a whole range of models has been designed and produced, all of them in the high-performance class.

Since the original Riley-engined model was produced several other makes of engines have been used to suit the particular requirements of the various models. Perhaps the best-known example is the Nash-engined Healey, which in its latest form is dressed by Pinin Farina. Truly an international car. It is, however, available only for export at the moment. The home market is catered for by the 3-litre Alvis-engined two-seater and the Riley-engined model with a Tickford convertible or saloon body, and it is this last-named version that has recently been tested.

A close-coupled four-seater coachbuilt saloon, built on a sports car chassis and powered by a well-designed twin high-camshaft and push rod 2½-litre engine, looks on paper to be a car with very desirable qualities. After driving it for over a thousand miles for test purposes, both in this country and in Belgium, where the performance figures were recorded, there is no doubt in the minds of those concerned that this car has a definite appeal. It is one for the specialist driver who requires high-speed transport and at the same time closed-car convenience. The passenger space is comfortable for two persons and quite a lot of luggage, yet four persons can be carried, although it must be admitted that

---

DATA

PRICE (basic), with saloon body, **£1,600.**
British purchase tax, £890 7s 9d.
Total (in Great Britain), £2,490 7s 9d.
Extras : Radio £59 7s 9d. Heater £21 0s 0d.

ENGINE : Capacity : 2,443 c.c. (149.0 cu. in.)
Number of cylinders : 4.
Bore and stroke : 80.5 × 120 mm. (3.139 × 4.680in).
Valve gear : o.h.v. twin camshaft, push rods and rockers.
Compression ratio : 6.85 to 1.
B.H.P. : 106 at 4,800 r.p.m. (60.3 B.H.P. per ton laden).
Torque : 136 lb ft at 3,000 r.p.m.
M.P.H. per 1,000 r.p.m. on top gear, 20.6.

WEIGHT (with 5 galls fuel), 26½ cwt. (2,961 lb)
Weight distribution (per cent) : 50.6 F ; 49.4 R.
Laden as tested : 30¼ cwt. (3,375 lb).
Lb. per c.c. (laden) : 1.38.

TYRES : 6.40—15in.
Pressures (lb per sq in) : 22 F ; 24 R

TANK CAPACITY : 16 Imp. gallons.
Oil sump, 14 pints.
Cooling system, 24 pints (plus 2 pints if heater is fitted).

TURNING CIRCLE : 34ft 0in (L and R)
Steering wheel turns (lock to lock) : 2¼.

DIMENSIONS : Wheelbase 8ft 6in.
Track : 4ft 6in (F) ; 4ft 7in (R).
Length (overall) : 14ft 9in.
Height : 4ft 7in.
Width : 5ft 7in.
Ground clearance : 7in.
Frontal area : 21.2 sq ft (approx.).

ELECTRICAL SYSTEM : 12-volt 63 ampère-hour battery.
Head lights : Double dip, 48/48 watt.

SUSPENSION : Front, coil springs, trailing links.
Rear, coil springs, trailing arms, Panhard rod.

PERFORMANCE

HEALEY TICKFORD SALOON

ACCELERATION : from constant speeds. Speed, Gear Ratios and time in sec.

M.P.H.	3.77 to 1	5.33 to 1	8.11 to 1	13.72 to 1
10—30	10.3	7.2	5.1	—
20—40	9.8	6.7	4.9	—
30—50	10.7	7.4	10.8	—
40—60	10.8	7.9	—	—
50—70	12.7	9.1	—	—

From rest through gears to :

M.P.H.	sec
30	5.0
50	10.5
60	14.6
70	19.6
80	28.3

Standing quarter mile, 19.3 sec.

SPEEDS ON GEARS :

Gear		M.P.H. (normal and max.)	K.P.H. (normal and max.)
Top	(mean)	102	164
	(best)	104.6	168
3rd		65—75	105—121
2nd		40—50	64—80
1st		18—29	29—47

SPEEDOMETER CORRECTION : M.P.H.

Car speedometer	10	20	30	40	50	60	70	80	90	100	108
True speed	11.5	21	30	39	48	57	66.5	77	87	97	104.6

TRACTIVE RESISTANCE : 28.8 lb per ton at 10 M.P.H.

TRACTIVE EFFORT :

	Pull (lb per ton)	Equivalent Gradient
Top	210	1 in 11
Third	318	1 in 7
Second	454	1 in 4.8

BRAKES :

Efficiency	Pedal Pressure (lb)
92 per cent	165
65 per cent	100
36 per cent	50

FUEL CONSUMPTION :
22 m.p.g. overall for 418 miles. (12.8 litres per 100 km.)
Approximate normal range 22-26 m.p.g. (12.8-10.8 litres per 100 km.)
Fuel, British Pool.

WEATHER : Dry surface. Wind negligible. Air temperature 46 degrees F.

Acceleration figures are the means of several runs in opposite directions.

Tractive effort and resistance obtained by Tapley meter.

A neat, simple main grille blends well into the smooth curves of the front of the car. Separate side lamps are mounted below the head lamps.

Smooth lines at the rear are broken only by the plated fittings. A useful protective plate is fitted to the leading edge of the rear wings.

ROAD TEST · · · · · · · · · · · ·

The two wide doors contain useful deep pockets. Rear-seat passengers are adequately accommodated for a car of the high-performance character of the Healey.

gear, while third will deal with most of the steeper variety; second gear is valuable for gradients steeper than 1 in 6. More important perhaps than the ability to travel at well over a hundred miles an hour is the safe feel of the car when it is doing so.

The suspension, unusual in that it has trailing arms all round, provides a means of really glueing the car to the road. This, together with the low build of the body, results in a very stable vehicle. Directional stability is further improved by understeer characteristics. Slightly more castor action in the steering would be an advantage, but this can very easily be obtained as this is one of the few modern cars on which such an adjustment is provided for. The damper arms which form the top links of the suspension are fitted with eccentric bushes at the outer pivot point, and if these are turned the alteration in effective arm length varies the castor angle.

Individual seats, adjustable for angle, are in keeping with the sporting nature of the Healey. The interior reveals a practical and well-finished simplicity.

the rear seats are somewhat cramped. However, for this type of car this disadvantage is offset by the fact that the reduction of interior space permits a car of low overall height, which, coupled with a body of low drag characteristics, results in a car that is very economical on petrol, even at high speed. For example, even during performance testing the fuel consumption did not fall below 22 m.p.g.

The Healey, too, is one of the few cars tested by *The Autocar* that has a mean maximum speed of over 100 m.p.h. It is therefore not surprising that high average speeds are obtained without its giving the impression that it is being overworked, average speeds nearer fifty than forty miles to the hour being common. Although the big four-cylinder engine is quite flexible it shows a definite tendency to pink on Pool petrol if it is allowed to slog, or even at fairly high speeds when accelerating hard. However, with improved fuel obtainable abroad pinking is eliminated. Intake noise or power roar is noticeable, but the degree of silence sacrificed is directly beneficial in the increase of power obtained. Also, wind noise is very low and above 60 m.p.h. the overall noise level is distinctly lower than average, conversation being quite easy even at 100 miles an hour.

Normal main road hills can be climbed fast on top

Briefly, this is a car that stays on course at all times, and has that firm, positive feel on corners that inspires confidence. All this is achieved at the expense of a ride that is a little hard by present-day standards, but not unduly so. There is almost no roll on corners, and the riding is not too hard for comfort on rough surfaces.

Retardation by means of Girling hydraulically operated brakes (with two leading shoes at the front) is very effective, although the pedal pressure required to obtain maximum efficiency is higher than usual. The brakes did not show any signs of fade during the severe conditions of performance testing, and they did not require any adjustment to restore balance or reduce pedal travel after a very substantial mileage had been covered.

Sitting-up

When sitting in the Healey the driver does not get the impression that the car is as low as it really is. This is because the seating arrangements do not place him in an uncomfortable position an inch or so from the floor, but reasonably high up in a position where control can be easily directed. Both front seats are adjustable for leg length, and the angle of the seat backs can be varied by means of an adjusting screw for each, though these do not enable the back rests to be positioned as near to the vertical as is desired by some people. The steering wheel is well placed and mounted on an adjustable column; it has a pleasingly shaped rim and is comfortable to hold. The horn button and direction indicators control are mounted on the wheel hub. It would be an advantage if the spring under the horn

Spare wheel and tools are carried beneath the luggage locker floor. There is decidedly reasonable stowage space.

button were a little stronger, as it apt to be operated inadvertently by the back of the driving seat when this is pivoted forward to gain access to the rear seats via the wide door.

All the pedals are well placed and there is room for the driver's left foot between the tunnel and the clutch pedal, a very desirable feature. The clutch is smooth and the pedal pleasant to operate. The organ-type throttle pedal, too, is arranged to give a nice action, and is correctly positioned to permit heel-and-toe gear changing if desired. The central remote-control gear change is very positive and does not vibrate. The lever is short and rigid and nicely positioned; because of its cranked shape the movement is more up and down than backwards and forwards, which tends to make its operation feel a little heavy, and also its shape causes it to get in the way, in reverse position, of the hand brake lever placed conveniently between the seats.

Minor controls and switches are arranged in two groups, one in the centre of the facia and the other on the right-hand side below the radio controls if such equipment is fitted. To enable the best performance to be obtained with different types of fuel a hand-operated overriding ignition control is provided on the facia. Another very useful provision is a reserve petrol supply, brought into operation by a switch

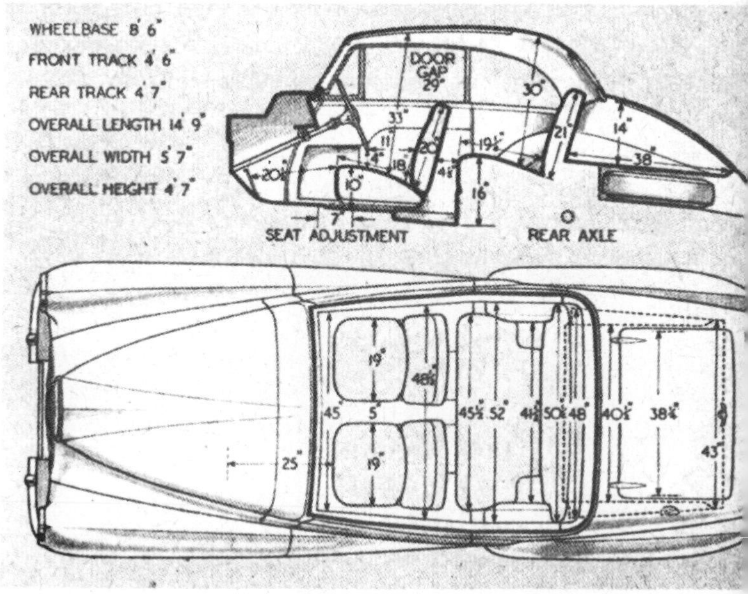

Measurements in these ¼in to 1ft scale body diagrams are taken with the driving seat in the central position of fore and aft adjustment and with the seat cushions uncompressed.

on the facia, which also illuminates a warning light showing that the reserve supply is being used.

From the driving seat forward visibility is very good and both front wings can be clearly seen; the windscreen pillars are nicely shaped and slender, with the result that blind spots are reduced to a minimum. The rear view mirror is well placed, but better rear vision would be obtained if the rear window were larger.

General finish, both of the inside and of the exterior, is much above average—as, of course, must be recognized is the price also. In particular the hardwood facia is very well polished. Circular instruments are spaced across it, not closely grouped in front of the driver, but this arrangement does prevent windscreen reflections in front of the driver's eyes when the instrument lights are on.

The head lights are quite definitely in keeping with the rest of the car; they are powerful and have a good range as well as a useful spread—the kind of lights, in fact, that make night driving a pleasure. The twin horns have a pleasing note, yet for a car of this type a more powerful warning system would be advantageous. Starting from cold was quick and little use of the choke was required.

The Healey is a car with a very definite appeal to the driver who requires high-speed quality transport with an accent also on good petrol consumption, two very desirable qualities that do not usually go together. Also it has saloon car comforts and protection. Briefly, it looks and feels right.

The pipe communicating with the air cleaner extracts oil mist from the valve rocker covers. The air cleaner for the twin S.U. carburettors is of unusual shape to fit into the available space under a well-filled bonnet.

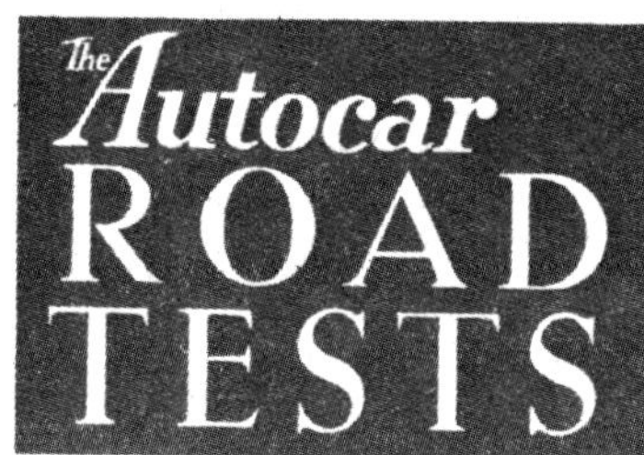

The Healey has long, low, rakish lines and smooth contours. Open semi-circular wheel arches are used both at the front and at the rear.

3-LITRE HEALEY SPORTS CONVERTIBLE

AS mentioned in the March 14 issue of this journal, the Alvis-engined open two-three-seater is available in this country as an alternative to the Riley-engined Healeys. An early version of this car has recently been tested both in this country and on the Continent, where the performance figures were obtained. The 3-litre is no ordinary stark open sports car, but a sports convertible—a car fully equipped and both snug and lockable in the closed position, yet one that can be completely open without any visible sign that a hood is being carried.

Mounted on the well-known Healey chassis, the shell for this all-enveloping body is produced by Panelcraft, of Birmingham, and trimmed at the Healey works at Warwick. The six-cylinder engine used to power this model develops the same maximum power output (106 b.h.p.) as the 2½-litre Riley engine used in some of the other models, but at a lower speed—4,200 compared with 4,800 r.p.m.; also the maximum torque occurs at a very much lower speed in the larger engine, although the actual torque figure is only 4 lb ft greater. This difference in engine characteristics, together with a slight decrease in weight, results in a gain in the acceleration figures, yet the ultimate maximum speed of around the hundred mark is a little less than that recorded by *The Autocar* for the saloon model. The axle ratio, giving a road speed of 20.6 m.p.h. per 1,000 r.p.m., results in a road speed of 86.5 m.p.h. at maximum power output, so that for the ultimate maximum speed the engine is well past its peak. However, this is a speed seldom used under normal road conditions, whereas the acceleration qualities are sampled whenever the car is driven.

The Healey is a car that seems to thrive on high-speed cruising and is quite happy at around the 80 mark. The limiting factors are usually road conditions;

PERFORMANCE

3-LITRE HEALEY SPORTS CONVERTIBLE

ACCELERATION : from constant speeds. Speed, Gear Ratios and time in sec.

M.P.H.	3.77 to 1	5.01 to 1	7.28 to 1	11.20 to 1
10—30 ..	9.2	7.0	4.5	3.6
20—40 ..	8.6	6.2	4.5	—
30—50 ..	8.3	6.6	5.2	—
40—60 ..	9.3	7.1	—	—
50—70 ..	9.7	8.4	—	—
60—80 ..	11.7	11.8	—	—
70—90 ..	17.4	—	—	—

From rest through gears to :

M.P.H.	sec.
30	4.4
50	9.7
60	13.5
70	18.8
80	26.6

Standing quarter mile, 19.9 sec.

SPEED ON GEARS :

Gear		M.P.H. (normal and max.)	K.P.H. (normal and max.)
Top ..	(mean)	99	159
	(best)	100	161
3rd		70—80	113—129
2nd		40—55	64—89
1st		25—34	40—55

TRACTIVE RESISTANCE : 11.7 lb per ton at 10 M.P.H.

TRACTIVE EFFORT :

	Pull (lb per ton)	Equivalent Gradient
Top	239	1 in 9.5
Third ..	324	1 in 6.9
Second.. ..	450	1 in 4.9

BRAKES :

Efficiency	Pedal Pressure (lb)
90 per cent	185
60 per cent	100
30 per cent	50

FUEL CONSUMPTION :
23.8 m.p.g. overall for 233 miles. (11.9 litres per 100 km.)
Approximate normal range 20—24 m.p.g. (14.1—11.8 litres per 100 km.)
Fuel : Belgian premium grade, approximately 80 octane.

WEATHER : Dry surface, wind light.
Air temperature 70 degrees F.
Acceleration figures are the means of several runs in opposite directions.
Tractive effort and resistance obtained by Tapley meter.
Engine described in *The Autocar* of March 17, 1950.

SPEEDOMETER CORRECTION : M.P.H.

Car speedometer	10	20	30	40	50	60	70	80	90	99
True speed	13	21	30	40	49	59	69	79	89	100

DATA

PRICE (basic), with sports convertible body, £1,600.
British purchase tax, £890 7s 9d.
Total (in Great Britain), £2,490 7s 9d.
Extras : Radio and heater fitted as standard.

ENGINE : Capacity : 2,993 c.c. (182.6 cu in).
Number of cylinders : 6.
Bore and stroke : 84 × 90 mm (3.31 × 3.54in).
Valve gear : o.h.v., push rods and rockers.
Compression ratio : 7 to 1.
B.H.P. : 106 at 4,200 r.p.m. (74.5 B.H.P. per ton laden).
Torque : 140 lb ft at 2,000 r.p.m.
M.P.H. per 1,000 r.p.m. on top gear, 20.6.

WEIGHT (with 5 galls fuel), 25 cwt (2,783 lb).
Weight distribution (per cent) 51.5 F ; 48.5 R.
Laden as tested : 28¼ cwt (3,197 lb).
Lb per c.c. (laden) : 1.07.

BRAKES : Type : F, two leading shoe ; R, leading and trailing shoe.
Method of operation : F, hydraulic ; R, hydraulic.
Drum dimensions : F, 11in diameter, 1¾in wide ; R, 11in diameter, 1¾in wide.
Lining area : F, 85 sq in. R, 85 sq in (119 sq in per ton laden).

TYRES : 6.40-15in.
Pressures (lb per sq in) : 22 F ; 24 R (for high speed 26 F, 28 R).

TANK CAPACITY : 16 Imperial gallons.
Reserve : 1½ gallons.
Oil sump, 12 pints.
Cooling system, 28 pints.

TURNING CIRCLE : 34ft 0in (L and R).
Steering wheel turns (lock to lock) : 2½.

DIMENSIONS : Wheelbase 8ft 6in.
Track : 4ft 5in (F) ; 4ft 7in (R).
Length (overall) : 14ft 6in.
Height : 4ft 8in.
Width : 5ft 5in.
Ground clearance : 7in.
Frontal area : 22.3 sq ft (approx.).

ELECTRICAL SYSTEM : 12-volt ; two 6-volt 63 ampère-hour batteries.
Head lights : Double dip, 48 watt.

SUSPENSION : Front, independent, coil springs and trailing links with anti-roll bar.
Rear, coil springs and trailing links.

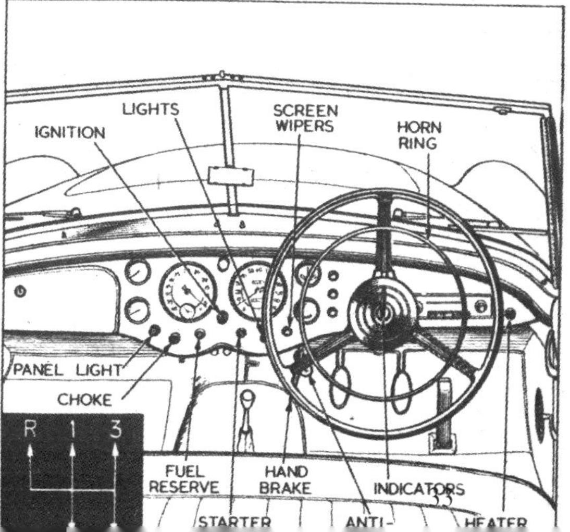

The small, oval-shaped radiator grille blends neatly into the front of the car. Narrow horizontal strips are placed between the large rectangles formed by the main grille pressing. Separate side lamps are mounted below the main built-in head lamps.

An exceptionally large plastic rear window is fitted into the hood. The gracefully sloping tail contains a useful luggage locker which must be opened to gain access to the fuel tank. Direction indicators are built into the body, just behind the doors.

ROAD TEST . . . . .

the way the driver feels and how much of a hurry he may be in. Under favourable conditions averages of well over 40 m.p.h. for quite long periods are quite possible. The smooth six-cylinder engine purrs away in a very willing manner, with no suspicion of fuss or over-work. There was slight pinking on Pool fuel of approximately 72 octane, though on 80 octane, on which the performance testing was carried out, pinking was negligible. Driven in a leisurely way, the Healey is very much a top gear car. On the other hand, if the driver wishes, the car is ready and willing for really fast motoring, and then the gears can be freely used. The gear ratios enable relatively high speeds to be obtained on both second and third gears without over-revving the engine.

The gear change is particularly pleasant and quick, the centrally placed remote control lever is short and positive with just about the right amount of travel from gear to gear. A slice up from third to top when the car is speeding to the upper seventies is a particularly pleasant manœuvre; the car seems to enter into the spirit of the exercise, too. One criticism of the gear box is that it is stiff to engage first gear when the car is at rest, but once on the move the box

leaves little to be desired as regards its changing qualities, although the gears are a little more audible than some. This is perhaps justifiable on a car of this type, where extra sound-deadening material would only increase the weight and adversely affect performance.

A quick change down to third results in hills of the order of 1 in 6 being climbed at over 40 m.p.h., leaving two lower gears in hand for the really steep ones! The less steep main road slopes normally require no change down at all.

No matter what type of body it is fitted with, the Healey chassis gives the car a controlled, taut feel. The ride is a little hard, perhaps by present-day standards, but a softening of the suspension would be warranted on this type of car

The neatly fitting hood provides good protection and blends nicely with the general lines of the car.

Fixed triangular panels mounted on the doors form a neat and draughtproof joint with the side of the V windscreen. Useful pockets are arranged in the trim on both of the wide doors, and large rubber mats protect the carpet on both sides of the gear box cover.

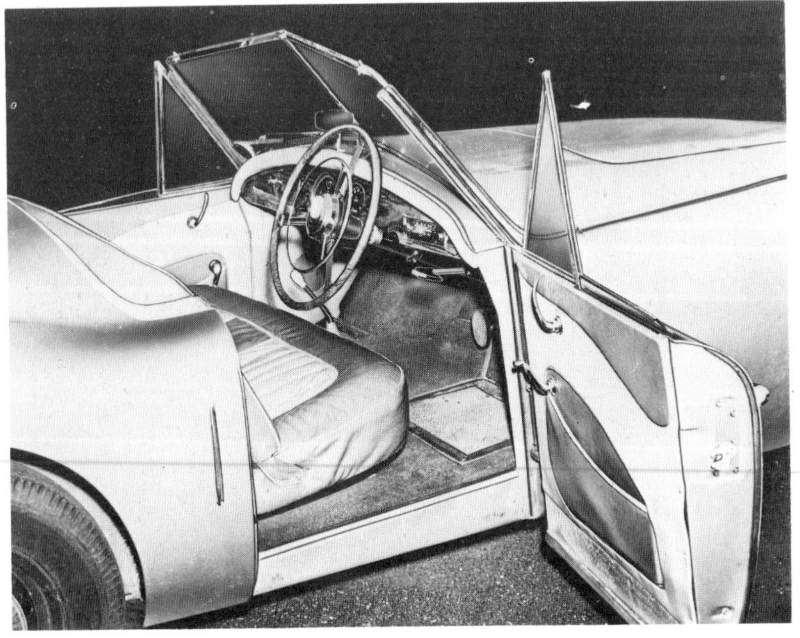

only if it could be achieved without prejudicing its general handling qualities. There is that comforting feeling that the car is "all in one piece," and intends to stay on the road, pointing in the right direction, too. The steering, with two and a half turns from lock to lock, is fairly heavy, especially with the tyres set at the lower pressures recommended for normal use. It is very positive and has a sense of precision bettered by few. The definite understeer characteristics of the car as a whole further inspire confidence in this very controllable car. A certain amount of tyre squeal is noticeable on both cornering and braking, but this is not excessive and applies more particularly when the car is driven with the lower tyre pressures.

Eleven-inch diameter brakes are fitted to both the front and the rear wheels and the hydraulically operated brakes have two leading shoes at the front. Under maximum braking conditions a very good efficiency figure was recorded, but to obtain it a very high pedal pressure was necessary. Under the severe conditions of performance testing no brake fade was experienced.

The driving position in the Healey is, generally speaking, very good. The one-piece seat is adjustable for leg length and the back rest can be adjusted for angle by means of two screw adjusters. The seat cushion gives good support to the driver's legs, but it would be advantageous for some drivers if it were a little longer and, for some, a little higher, and also if it could be moved a little farther forward. The seat itself is well sprung and effectively insulates the driver from minor road shocks, though on a long journey a certain amount of discomfort was experienced from the bottom of the back rest being a trifle hard. A wide folding arm rest effectively divides the seat when only two persons are carried. Three-abreast seating is possible, although it is rather cramped for anything but short journeys.

The steering wheel can be adjusted by means of a telescopic column with the normal screw type of locking

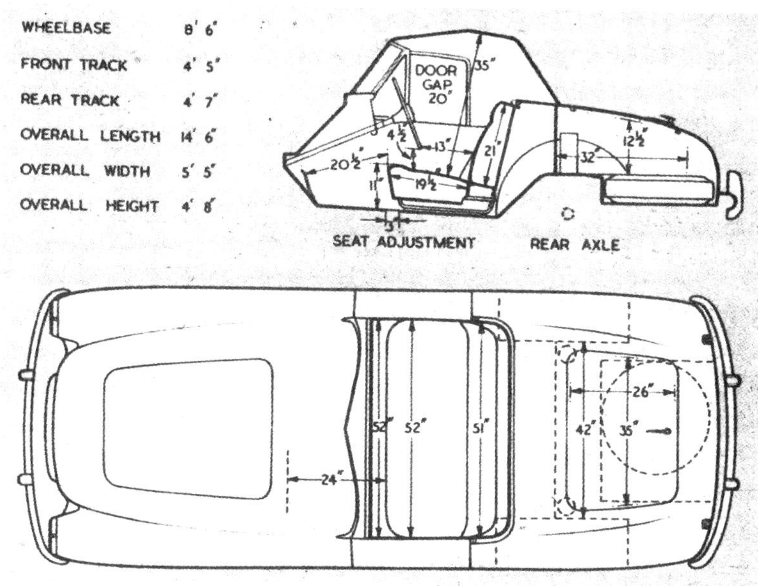

Measurements in these ¼in to 1ft scale body diagrams are taken with the driving seat in the central position of fore and aft adjustment and with the seat cushions uncompressed.

The luggage locker also contains the spare wheel and tools and is fitted with a flush-fitting lid, which has a self-locking support strut. The whole of its interior is nicely trimmed with carpet. The housings of the vertically mounted telescopic dampers are seen in the forward corners of the compartment.

The luggage locker is of ample proportions for a car of this seating capacity and this, too, is lockable. The fuel filler cap is placed inside the luggage locker. Built-in head lamps mounted in the front wings are powerful and have a good range. Yet it would be better for fast night driving if still more powerful lights could be fitted.

The horn, controlled by a ring on the steering wheel, has a pleasing note but the control is a little stiff to operate. Starting from cold, with the aid of the manually operated electrically controlled starting device, was very good. There is the valuable feature of a reserve petrol supply, brought into use by a facia switch.

The 3-litre Healey offers a combination of both open and closed car motoring at high speed, coupled with good petrol economy.

arrangement. All the pedals are well placed and there is plenty of room for the driver's left foot when it is not operating the clutch pedal. The organ pedal type of throttle control is smooth to operate, but its position relative to the brake pedal could be improved to facilitate the heel-and-toe type of gear changing.

The dip switch, mounted to the left of the clutch pedal, is conveniently placed for quick operation. The minor controls on the car tested were conveniently ranged in two groups, one on either side of the instruments. On future production cars extra instruments will be included and the switches arranged in a row below the speedometer and tachometer units, while a radio control panel and heater fan switch, both auxiliaries being standard equipment, are fitted on the facia on the right of the steering column. A useful locker with lockable lid is fitted in the left of the facia.

From the driving seat the forward visibility is very good and the windscreen pillars are particularly slender, especially in view of the fact that a separate yet fixed triangular light is fitted. With the hood in the raised position the unusually large rear window produces a very light interior. The material from which it is made is not, however, quite as transparent as could be desired; consequently, the mirror view is somewhat indistinct. This is particularly so at night and in rain or when the sun is shining on the back of the car.

The hood mechanism, which is completely enclosed when the hood is in the lowered position, is very simple to operate and can be very quickly erected, although it is first helpful to slide the seat forward so that the back rest can be hinged forward to gain access to the hood compartment. Glass winding side windows are used, and it is possible to lock the car—a very desirable feature, but one seldom found on an open sports car.

The engine usefully fills the available space under the one-piece bonnet, which is unusual in that it is hinged at the front. The twin S.U. carburettors are fitted with individual air cleaners, and the fuel is supplied by a mechanical pump on the right side of the engine.

SPECIAL-BODIED HEALEY

A FEW years ago I built an aero-dynamic H.R.G. coupé. This was a first attempt by a complete amateur and did, in fact, turn out to be surprisingly satisfactory. Its history is fairly well known, but, to recapitulate, it was approximately 2 sec faster over the standing kilometre than normal H.R.G.s, it held the Goodwood 1½-litre sports record for a time, and was placed third in 1948 and second in 1949 in the Belgian 24-hour races. Apart from this competition work, it was used every day for business purposes, including London travel, putting up about 30,000 miles.

During all this time no welded joints parted and very little structural work had to be done. All the same, I decided that something equivalent, but far more comfortable, would be worth constructing. As a preliminary therefore, I will summarize my objections to the H.R.G.

Hard Ride

The brakes, power-weight ratio and reliability were thoroughly satisfactory; the steering was far too vague at high speeds, although perfectly usable; and the springing quite impossible. The bodywork, the seating, colour (British racing green, which never appears to fade), the basic shape, special light door construction, the use of Perspex windows, the lack of external handles and the absence of squeaks, were all really satisfactory. The screen was too steeply sloped (this demanded a beetle-browed shape in order to get a good streamlining); the metal floorboards transmitted too much heat; the accessibility was unsatisfactory; pneumatic seat backs were not up to the standard of the rest of the seats; the doors were too narrow and carried down too far, so that they hit against kerbs when opened; the undershield was a pest, and the cockpit ventilation unsatisfactory.

I decided that in the new car the cost of the chassis was not to be considered in view of the amount of work I was going to put in, and I examined carefully every worthwhile type, finally selecting a Healey as possessing the best combination. Subsequent use has not modified this opinion.

Basically, the shape was to be an improved version of the H.R.G. using the same principle of thin steel tubes covered with felt, with aluminium sheet laid on them and gripped at the edges only, the floors and various other parts to be rigidly fixed to the chassis and flexibly mounted to the body.

The data from which I worked are as follows: (a) The distance from the pedals to the bottom of the rear of driving seat; (b) The position of the eyes above this point; (c) The position of the wheel in order to give clearance from the lap of the seated driver, with reasonable arm room; (d) The position of the screen, sloped in this case at 45 deg in order to be as close to the eye as is possible and still to leave adequate clearance from the hands at the top of the wheel. (This point is vital. If the screen can be got within 12in of the eyes, practically no side obstructions such as pillars matter.)

The screen length was taken as 15in, as being the maximum practical size with this slope, and the eye line was taken just above the centre. The slope was a compromise; more slope gives trouble with reflections and needs a larger glass area, but gives a better streamline over the roof. The highest portion of the roof will probably be immediately above the driver's head, and this is determined by reasonable clearance (e.g., 4in) over the top of his head. A real streamline demands, in any case, a *rise* after the top of the windscreen, to fill the vacuum caused by the air accelerated from the top of the screen.

Completing the Plan

The maximum permissible rear overhang, and the position of the radiator and engine top, are also fixed points. It remains only to sketch in the best streamline shape from these fixed points, and the first exterior design is completed.

With regard to seating, my wife and I have always found from various cars which we have driven long distances that we arrive less tired when the feet are well raised, even up to the actual level of the hips. The seats have therefore been designed so that the cushion thickness when compressed is not more than 1in above floor level; real comfort can be obtained with Float-on-Air cushions even with this small clearance. The seat backs, however, have proved more successful with ultra-soft Dunlopillo of 1in thickness.

It is found in practice that springiness is not required in a seat back at all, but firmness without any hard spots is ideal. (They must have enough "give" to accept the back trouser buttons comfortably!)

The seat cushions, therefore, sit right on the floorboards and are held in position by a light surround, and the back hinges from the floorboards. It can be of very light construction because all strains are taken by a strap which passes round the centre of the back and then down on both sides to brackets on the floor, near the *front* of the seats; this makes the back angle readily adjustable and gives lateral support in cornering.

Plywood Floor

It was decided this time to make all the floor and the scuttle of thin waterproof plywood, "doped" heavily with chlorinated rubber solution in order to achieve minimum heat transmission; this was covered with thin aluminium sheet where the heat was greatest. The perpetual problem of the flexible cover for the gear box was solved by using a fabricated assembly of sail canvas next to the box, then ⅛in of Fibreglass sheet, and then rubber-backed matting. This has proved outstandingly successful, completely eliminating gear box heat from the interior without too much weight.

When the chassis had been received I immediately bent up and welded the structures in the shape desired. With the type of construction used the panelwork takes the curve of the tubing and rests on it, so that it is imperative that these tubes should carry the correct shape from the first. This means that the bending of the tubes running up the corners of the windscreen had to be correct in three dimensions, with some very complicated curves, and, in fact, they took 3½ hours each to prepare, with a maximum error of less than ⅛in. Apart from this, the rest of the work is relatively simple.

The bonnet is a completely separate assembly; I felt that it was so important that everything under the bonnet should be accessible that I planned a rather unusual layout, hinging the assembly on a trunnion which I fitted into the Healey front cross-tube. For a "one-off" production it is not easy to give this type of construction rigidity while maintaining quick opening, and I finally decided that I dare not have any form of snap fastener.

The bonnet assembly hinges down on to rubber pads on welded brackets, supported from the scuttle stiffeners, and steel tommy bars are screwed down to lock bonnet to scuttle rigidly. These two $\frac{1}{4}$in B.S.F. bolts are the only connections, except for two rubber-mounted stops in V-blocks at the bottom of each wing to prevent them from vibrating. It is a distinctly light construction, but has stood up very well to hard driving and racing abroad, and I can only say that light construction, properly designed, seems quite safe. For instance, the whole front of the H.R.G. construction was held up by four 2 B.A. steel bolts, and these never gave any trouble at any time. It is merely a question of distributing the loads sensibly.

The front scuttle hoop and the rear door support hoop are carried right across the car, and give a considerable increase in general rigidity when the whole assembly is welded together. As a matter of fact, it is most amusing to discover how the rigidity increases as each piece is welded into position. If any one of the parts is removed the whole assembly can be shaken fairly freely. I think this proves that there are no redundant parts —every part is hopelessly weak on its own, but if they are tied together and covered with a reasonably strong aluminium skin, the strength is quite up to normal standards (as I proved, unwittingly, when sliding the front end into a post during one of the Swiss hill-climbs).

The doors were increased in length over those of the H.R.G., but despite this the construction (which consists of a few pieces of bent 22-gauge sheet steel welded together and covered with 16-gauge aluminium) is adequately strong, and they weigh approximately 15 lb each.

Body Weight

All the panelling below waist level is in 16-gauge aluminium, and the roof in 18-gauge; the total weight of all bodywork, seating, floor, lamps, tools, and so on, comes to $3\frac{1}{4}$ cwt. I think it will be agreed that it is considerably lighter than the normal method of construction, for a car which gives such very large internal space. The spare wheel has been mounted very far out at the back, as in the Healey Silverstone. This seemed a very good idea to me, as one can mount the wheel on expendable brackets, and use it as a bumper to give warning of over-backing.

I have again used the extractor method for lowering the under-bonnet temperatures, as this was extremely satisfactory on the H.R.G. I think that the one continuous length looks neat and it does, of course, give tremendous assistance in demisting the windscreen, apart from keeping under-bonnet temperatures down. It is interesting to point out that one of the biggest aircraft experimental establishments, who were doing work on air extraction, said that, of all methods of extracting air, louvres were the only complete failures! Apparently a set functions no better than any one single louvre, the first louvre blanketing the rest. This extractor type is the recommended system, and certainly lowered the water temperature of the H.R.G. by 15-20 deg C.

The windows consist of Perspex front triangles hinged at the front edge, and then vertical sliding Perspex windows. It was felt that three positions for these would be adequate, and they can be locked shut, 1in open, 2in open or fully open by means of a removable peg inside the car.

The mounting of the windscreen and rear windows is also of interest, as I was able to avoid the very costly manufacture of the usual type of windscreen by employing the new Claytonrite rubber. The

During the course of construction : as the panelling rests on the tubing and follows its curves, very accurate bending and welding were essential.

openings of the windows are cut directly in the aluminium, filed exactly to shape, and the glass or Perspex is also cut to the same shape but $\frac{3}{16}$in smaller all round. The Claytonrite rubber is then fitted with its special removable expanding member and makes a perfect pressure-tight seal without straining the glass. Incidentally, the large rear Perspex window is curved in both directions to match the body, and took hours of soaking in the bath with kettles of boiling water, and then stretching over a towel.

The method of sealing all the joints between the floor and the body, and the inside of the mudguards and body, involved cutting the floor to have 1in clearance or so from the body, and then fitting a fillet of heavy-grade Rexine by the use of Boscoprene adhesive.

I have retained the original Silverstone Healey grille for the head lights, which caused a lot of controversy; it is true that the side illumination of the left-hand kerb is vital for cornering at night, but this is easily arranged by cutting the centre out of the grille, and then using the right-hand head lamp to illuminate the left-hand side, and vice versa; i.e., the head lamps shine slightly cross-eyed.

The most controversial aspect has been the fins. On all the ultra-streamlined cars there appears to be a tendency for instability at high speed with high cross-winds. When you have once tried to drive 300 or 400 miles across France with a 50 m.p.h. side wind this point becomes important, and the aerodynamic people at the aircraft research wind tunnels assured me that some rear fin area was really essential. Thus the fins are purely functional and represent the biggest extra side area which we thought could be used without looking grotesque. The shape, in fact, was drawn out by my partner, rather in imitation of the Hawker aircraft fin, and I think it will be agreed that they do blend in with the car as far as anything of this type can.

It now remains to sum up what we have got. The aim was to produce an exceptionally comfortable, fast, long-distance touring car, which could be used for certain mild racing; and it seems to me that we have achieved what we set out to do. On the M.I.R.A. tests it equalled the normal XK120 performance, and beat the normal Silverstone Healey performance quite handsomely, while in two Swiss hill-climbs it just beat the normal XK120 on a fast course, but was beaten by them on a very "hair-pinny" course, where the Jaguar second gear is so useful.

Results of the Shape

As the total weight is $20\frac{3}{4}$ cwt with water and oil, it is obvious that some of this performance must come from the streamlining, and, in fact, the cruising speed is really high. The car goes straight up to an accurate 115 m.p.h. where the engine peaks, and there is no doubt that much more would be available with a higher top gear. It appeared likely to be at least 15 m.p.h. faster than the top speed of the Silverstone Healey, given the higher gearing, which it can easily pull. On a run of 3,000 miles across the Continent, including several Alpine climbs, and cruising normally at a genuine 70-80, the petrol consumption was 28 m.p.g. and in England it is normally between 30 and 32, and I think we must owe a good deal of this to the streamlining also.

Some of these exceptional results are certainly owed, however, to the engine tuning, very sportingly carried out by H.R.G., which seemed to produce quite a herd of new horses. Finally, I want to make it plain that while I did the actual tube bending, fitting and most of the special work, the bee-utiful smoothness and shapeliness are the painstaking spare-time work of Arthur Monroe and his friend, who never allowed anything to be too difficult—not even the fins !

R. BROCK.

Some rear fin area was considered essential—the fins successfully blend in with the clean lines of the car.

NEW CARS DESCRIBED

The new Healey Hundred has an extremely pleasing appearance with sleek lines. The short chromium strip just behind the front wheel on each side covers an engine compartment ventilator. Right : a modified form of the familiar Healey radiator grille is used on this model. The windscreen is shown lowered ; it is arranged to swing forward from the bottom and downward so that it acts the part of a sloping wind deflector.

THE HEALEY HUNDRED

AUSTIN-POWERED SPORTS CAR WITH OPTIONAL OVERDRIVE

IN a relatively short space of time the products of the Donald Healey Motor Company have built up a reputation for high performance and first-class road manners. Several models have been introduced, and in each case the car has been powered by a proprietary unit of either British or American design. These power units have in some cases been quite large; for example, the Nash engine is just under 4-litre capacity. Of medium size is the 2½-litre Riley unit.

The latest addition to the range is an extremely pretty open two-seater known as the Healey Hundred. This latest model is powered by the well-known Austin A.90 engine, and it has a completely new chassis layout which is both more simple in design and less expensive to produce than the previous models. The car is,

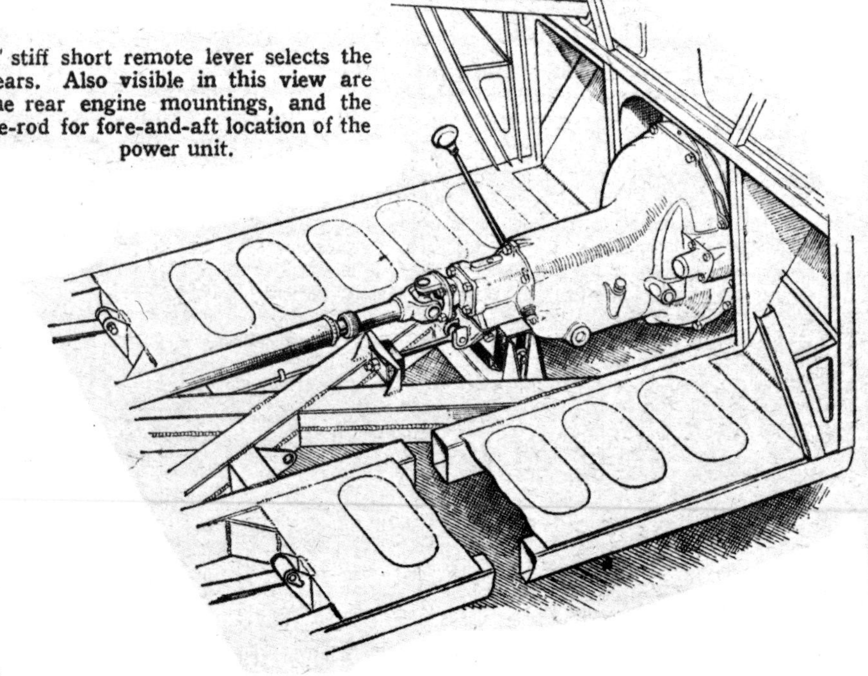

A stiff short remote lever selects the gears. Also visible in this view are the rear engine mountings, and the tie-rod for fore-and-aft location of the power unit.

in fact, designed with a view to filling a gap that exists in the sports car market, particularly in dollar areas where the would-be purchaser is given little to choose from in the range of cars with a maximum speed of around 100 m.p.h.

The engine is very well known and consequently will not be described in detail. It is of orthodox design with a stiff cylinder block and crankcase which extends well below the crankshaft centre line. A three-bearing crankshaft runs in steel-backed white metal bearings, and this pattern is also employed for the connecting rod big-end bearings. The gudgeon pin is held in place in the little-end by means of a pinch bolt. Water passages extend the entire length of the bore, and ample water spaces are also provided around the ports and cylinder head.

The combustion chamber is of a somewhat unusual shape, and the design of this part of the engine was carried out in collaboration with Weslake and Co., Ltd. Fuel is delivered by twin S.U. carburettors, and, on the Healey, these are fitted with small circular air cleaners. The gear box, also of Austin design, is fitted with a central remote control change mechanism. Also as an optional extra, provision is made for the attachment of a Laycock de Normanville overdrive unit. From the gear box a short propeller-shaft transmits power to the spiral bevel final drive, for which two gear ratios are available. A 3.66 to 1 ratio is used as standard, or, if an overdrive unit is fitted, a 4.125 to 1 ratio is used.

Perhaps the most interesting feature of the chassis is the design of the frame structure, and here several requirements have to be fulfilled. First, the structure must be rigid to ensure good handling characteristics; it must also be light in weight, simple to produce, and have sufficient rigidity to enable special coachbuilt bodywork to be fitted if desired, although the standard production body does contribute a certain amount of extra stiffness to the frame.

Basically, the frame structure consists of two straight 3in square box section members placed 17in apart and running the entire length of the frame. A box section cross member is attached some 13in from the front of the frame, and to this, as well as to the side members, the suspension brackets are attached. The centre of the frame is stiffened by a box section cruciform, and at the rear another cross member is attached, also of box section but projecting out from the side members, on both sides, to form anchorage points for the rear springs, which are placed approximately 38½in apart.

Outriggers are also provided for the scuttle mounting attachment points and the front mounting points for the rear leaf springs; the latter are continued through, and are attached to the rear legs of the cruciform. A cross member is also fitted between the front members of the cruciform bracing to support the rear end of the power unit.

Scuttle Stiffness

One design problem associated with open cars is that of scuttle rigidity, as, of course, no stiffness can be provided by windscreen pillars and roof panels, as in a saloon body. With the Healey this problem has been tackled by building the scuttle structure as part of the frame; a built-up bulkhead unit is, in fact, welded to the body mounting supports. It is also stiffened by means of a triangulation formed by attaching from the top of the bulkhead a strut which runs forwards and downwards to the front of the chassis frame. The floor pressings are also attached to the chassis frame, and further stiffness is provided by the body frame members, which are also welded to the main frame structure.

The body shell, which is attached to the body frame, is a composite structure; the main panels are produced from 16-gauge aluminium, whereas the wings and doors are produced from steel. This method is adopted to facilitate servicing in the event of damage, and is particularly suitable for overseas requirements.

Unlike other Healey models, which employ a trailing link system of front suspension and coil springs at the rear, the Healey Hundred suspension is by wishbones and coil springs at the front with suspension dampers arranged to form the upper wishbone unit. Steering is by a Burman steering box and operates in conjunction with a slave lever mounted on the opposite side of the frame and a normal three-piece track rod arrangement. An anti-roll bar is also fitted at the front. Rear suspension is orthodox in that the axle casing tubes are attached by means of U-bolts to the two half-elliptic rear springs. The chassis frame runs underneath the rear axle, and transverse axle location is provided by a Panhard rod. Piston type spring dampers are bolted to the frame side members in front of the rear axle.

The driving compartment is well appointed, but, of course, with this type of car the accent is on performance and utility, and unnecessary frills are avoided. The facia panel is of painted aluminium, and a small plated instrument panel is mounted centrally about the steering column. The instruments include a 120 m.p.h. speedometer, rev counter, fuel gauge and combined oil pressure and water temperature gauge. Individual Dunlopillo seats trimmed with leather are used, and there are large pockets in both doors. All-weather equipment includes a fully disappearing hood which is fitted with a large Vinylite rear window. Partially framed Perspex side screens are dowelled to the tops of the doors, and there is a signalling flap in the corner of the hood. Luggage accommodation is provided by an external locker, which also contains the spare wheel and the fuel filler.

SPECIFICATION

Engine.—4 cyl, 87.3×111.1 mm (2,662 c.c.). Compression ratio 7.5 to 1. 90 b.h.p. at 4,000 r.p.m. Torque 144 lb ft at 2,000 r.p.m. Three-bearing crankshaft. Heart-shaped combustion chambers. Side camshaft, operating vertical overhead valves by push rods and rockers.

Clutch.—Borg and Beck dry single-plate, 10in diameter; six-spring. Carbon thrust withdrawal mechanism.

Gear Box.—4 forward speeds with synchromesh on top, third and second. Overall ratios: top 3.62, third 5.2, second 8.25, first 13.2, reverse 18.26 to 1. Overall ratios with overdrive fitted; top 3.12, fourth 4.125, third 5.83, second 9.28, first 14.83, reverse 20.5 to 1. Central remote control lever.

Final Drive.—Spiral bevel. Ratio 3.67 to 1 (9 : 33); or, with overdrive, 4.125 to 1 (8 : 33).

Suspension.—Front, independent by coil springs and wishbones. Piston-type dampers and anti-roll bar. Rear, half-elliptic leaf springs. Piston-type dampers and Panhard rod. Suspension rate (at the wheel), front 75 lb per in; rear 92 lb per in. Static deflection, front 6⅛in; rear 5¼in.

Brakes.—Girling hydraulically operated two-leading shoe front, leading and trailing rear. Drums $10 \times 1\frac{3}{4}$in front and rear. Total lining area 135 sq in (70 sq in front).

Wheels and Tyres.—5.50—16in on 4-stud perforated steel disc wheels.

Electrical Equipment.—12-volt 63 ampère-hour battery. Head lamps double dip, 48-48 watt bulbs.

Fuel System.—10½-gallon tank. Oil capacity 13 pints.

Main Dimensions.—Wheelbase 7ft 6in. Track, front 4ft 0¾in, rear 4ft 1½in. Overall length 12ft 2in. Width 5 ft. Height (in running trim with hood erect), 4ft 1in. Ground clearance 7in. Frontal area 16.7 sq ft approx. (hood up). Turning circle 30ft. Weight (in running trim with 5 gallons fuel), 17½cwt (1,960lb).

Price.—£850. With British purchase tax, £1,323 14s 5d.

This view shows the chassis in a partly completed form. Note the rigid bulkhead and scuttle structure welded to the main chassis frame. Twin six-volt batteries are mounted on each side of the frame just in front of the rear axle.

The perforated brake drums can be seen behind the centre-lock wire wheels. Leather straps and hinges supplement the steel bonnet hinges mounted inside and on the front of the bonnet.

NASH-HEALEY for LE MANS

FURTHER DEVELOPMENT OF 4.1-LITRE MODEL, TO BE DRIVEN BY JOHN FITCH

Twin side-draught Carter carburettors meter fuel to the engine, and the three exhaust pipes, seen below the carburettors, feed into a tail pipe which finishes in front of the left rear wheel. The light alloy radiator is fitted with a pressure cap.

DESIGNED to compete in the Mille Miglia (reported elsewhere in this issue) and in the forthcoming Le Mans Twenty-four Hour Race, the latest car to leave the Healey works at Warwick is a modified form of the well-known Nash-Healey. It will be remembered that the production version of the car is the result of a three-country combination—British chassis, American engine, and Italian body. Mechanically, the engine and chassis specification is similar to that of the production car. In American terms, the power is supplied by a "Nash Ambassador Le Mans Dual Jet-fire" engine, which, translated, means a six-cylinder 4,138 c.c. engine with a bore and stroke of 88.983 × 111.12mm (3.5 × 4.375in), running on an 8 to 1 compression ratio and fitted with twin Carter carburettors. A Laycock-de Normanville overdrive unit is fitted to the three-speed gear box and is arranged so that overdrive can be obtained on second as well as top gear. This results in a total of five forward ratios, although it is necessary to operate two controls when changing from overdrive second to direct drive top, or vice versa. The overall ratios are top 3.54, second 5.39, and first 9.1 to 1. With the overdrive in operation the two additional ratios are overdrive top 2.48 and overdrive second 3.77 to 1. It will be seen that the overdrive second gear ratio is quite close to that of direct drive top.

The two-seater body consists of a light alloy shell attached to a lightweight steel frame which is welded to the main chassis frame unit. With a car of this type it is necessary to reduce the drag to a minimum, but with some all-enveloping bodies it is difficult to cool the brakes. On this design there is an undershield running almost the whole length of the body, but to increase the air flow around the brakes and rear wheels the sides of the body are swept in with a reverse curve between the wheels, while at the front the wing pressing is cut back just below the head lamps. A curved plastic wind deflector is used in place of a normal windscreen; this is shown somewhat larger than it will be

when the car is racing; it will be tailored to suit the requirements of driver John Fitch.

SPECIFICATION

Engine.—Six cylinders, 88.983 × 111.12 mm (4,138 c.c.) 8 to 1 compression ratio. Overhead valves operated by pushrods and rockers.

Clutch.—10in diameter dry single-plate; ball race withdrawal mechanism.

Gear Box.—Three-speed with Laycock-de Normanville overdrive. Overall ratios: Overdrive top 2.48; normal top 3.54; overdrive second 3.77; normal second 5.39; first 9.1 to 1. Central gear change.

Final Drive.—Torque tube. Rear axle ratio 3.54 to 1.

Suspension.—Front, independent with coil springs and trailing links. Rear, coil springs.

Brakes.—Girling hydraulic two-leading-shoe front; drums 11in diameter, 2¼in wide, front and rear.

Wheels and Tyres.—Dunlop 6.00-16in on centre-lock wire wheels.

Electrical Equipment.—12-volt battery. Head lamps, 48-48 watt bulbs.

Fuel System.—45-gallon tank.

Main Dimensions.—Wheelbase 8ft 6in. Track, front, 4ft 6in; rear, 4ft 5in. Overall length 15ft. Width 5ft 5in.

Large air scoops are fitted to the front brake drums.

The facia panel and instruments are finished in a dull black to prevent reflections. A 45-gallon fuel tank is below the rear panel.

The Healey Silverstone was an aptly named car for the
sporting enthusiast. Shown is the Silverstone D, of
1949, which could have fog lamps fitted as an extra.

Right and previous pages. The unmistakeable styling of the 'frog-eyed' Sprite, which was produced as an economical two-seater sports car to complement the Austin-Healey 3000.
Below. The less distinctive but still popular Mark II Sprite.

AUSTIN-HEALEY HUNDRED
TWO-SEATER

In this view of the Austin-Healey Hundred the windscreen is seen lowered and the tonneau cover completely enclosing the cockpit.

The *Autocar* ROAD TESTS

WHEN it was introduced at the London Show last year there was little doubt that the Healey Hundred, as it was called then, had really got something. This trim two-seater sports car with a 2.6-litre engine, having a speed well over the magic three-figure mark and initially priced at £850, was certainly a car to be reckoned with. During the Show it was announced that the Austin Motor Company (their A.90 engine is used to power the car) were to take over the production of the model, which would in future be known as the Austin-Healey Hundred. The combination of the sporting background of the Donald Healey Motor Company with the production "know-how" of the Austin company assured the success of what looked to be a most promising sports car and provided a moderately priced model midway between established sports cars of both small and large capacity.

Of the very small number of standard production cars in the over-110 m.p.h. maximum speed class there are very few indeed that can compete in price with the Austin-Healey, which, for its current basic figure of £750—a reduction of £100 from the original price—includes items such as a Laycock-de Normanville overdrive, a heater and centre-lock wire wheels, often optional extras on cars of much higher price. Yet in spite of its high maximum speed the Austin-Healey is not one of those cars in which everything is sacrificed in order to make it go fast. It is roomy, comfortable to ride in, and its general road behaviour and handling qualities are of a very high order. A very good power-to-weight ratio, combined with carefully chosen gears, results in a car with a very high cruising speed; just how high will,

Showing the hood up : the centre-lock wire wheels are completely exposed, front and rear, and the length of the car is emphasized by a crease in the body panels.

of course, depend on road conditions. But perhaps even more important is the fact that this car is of the type that will get from place to place very quickly without needing to be driven very fast.

In addition to maximum speed being recorded in the normal way with the weather equipment in position, it was recorded with the driver only and an aero screen fitted in place of the normal full-size windscreen. The results obtained produced a mean speed of 111 m.p.h. with one up, while with hood and sidescreens plus the added weight of an extra person the mean maximum speed was 103 m.p.h., with best speeds in one direction only of 119 and 108 m.p.h. respectively in the two sets of conditions, a very good performance, particularly, again, considering the price of the car.

The transmission consists of a conventional plate clutch, a three-speed gear box and an electrically operated Laycock-de Normanville overdrive unit arranged so that it can be operated on both second and top gears. This, in effect, means that the car has five forward speeds, although it is necessary to operate two controls if it is desired to change from overdrive second to direct top gear, for example. From rest the car is driven normally in first gear and a change to second gear is made in the usual way. To obtain overdrive second it is necessary only to move the overdrive switch. To change from overdrive second to normal top gear the switch as well as the gear lever must be operated. On the other hand it is possible to change from overdrive second to overdrive top gear simply by operating the normal gear lever.

A propeller-shaft-actuated governor prevents the overdrive from coming into operation until a road speed of 35 m.p.h. is reached. To prevent jerk and shock to the transmission when a change down from overdrive to direct top or second gears is made there is a throttle switch, and, even if the

The four-cylinder engine is housed neatly under the bonnet. Its twin S.U. carburettors are supplied with cool air from a forward-facing duct. The coil is mounted on the side of the engine close to the distributor. The water and oil filler caps are readily accessible.

The radiator grille is neat and simple, and blends well with the general lines of the body. Separate side lights are mounted below the head lamps, and two additional driving lamps (not standard equipment) are seen on the example tested. The anti-roll bar can just be seen below the front number plate. Right: The tonneau cover can be used to enclose the hood. The wing pressings are detachable and the joints for the rear wings can be seen from this angle. Full-width bumpers and over-riders provide useful protection at the rear. The exhaust tail pipe is swept up at the back to provide increased ground clearance.

ROAD TEST . . .

overdrive switch is operated the actual change down will not occur until the throttle is opened and the car is accelerated. The remote control gear lever is centrally placed; it is very positive to operate and has a convenient amount of movement from gear to gear. The layout of the gate is a little unusual, as instead of reverse gear being placed opposite first gear, as is often done with a three-speed box, it is placed at the far side of the gate to the right of top gear position. This arrangement can be seen in the diagram of the controls and instruments. Both clutch and gear controls are well positioned, robust and well able to cope with fast gear changes when necessary.

All the Healey cars possess fine handling qualities and the latest model follows this tradition. The suspension provides a comfortable yet well-controlled ride that is suitable for fast driving and at the same time is sufficiently soft to deal with rough road surfaces without shaking the car and occupants. With $2\frac{1}{2}$ turns from lock to lock, the steering is very positive and the car can be placed with precision, yet in spite of the small number of turns it is also pleasantly light and has good self-centring action. It has a well-balanced layout that does not feel dead and at the same time does not transmit road shocks back through the wheel.

In its handling qualities as a whole the Austin-Healey feels very safe and has a satisfactory amount of understeer, a combination of qualities that results in a car that is very pleasant to drive and one that quickly inspires confidence. The 11in diameter hydraulically operated brakes are well up to the high performance of the car. No fade was experienced under fast driving on the open road or during the specialized conditions of the performance testing. The pedal pressure required for maximum braking is also relatively light, although for normal check braking the

pressure is perhaps a little higher than is usual. No brake adjustment was required even after many hundreds of miles of fast driving.

In the interests of performance there is a limit to the weight that can be added in the form of sound-insulating material, and in consequence some noise can be heard from the engine compartment, while a certain amount of heat is also noticed in the cockpit, particularly with the hood and sidescreens in position. Otherwise, apart from a certain amount of transmission noise from the indirect gears, the car is quite quiet, although if it is driven very fast with hood and sidescreens in position some noise is caused by wind pressure deflecting the Perspex sidescreens. Road noise can be heard inside the car, but this is not excessive.

Perhaps the outstanding thing about the bodywork of the Austin-Healey is the surprising amount of room inside the car. The general layout is so well arranged that in spite of the low overall height the driver is in no way cramped. The steering wheel is telescopically adjustable on its column and is nicely placed in relation to the pedals. Both seats are adjustable by means of bolts and cage nuts, involving the use of a spanner; this not altogether convenient arrangement if more than one person is handling the car is adopted to reduce the height that would be required for a conventional sliding seat mechanism. The seats themselves are well upholstered and give good support, although they might be even more comfortable to some tastes, and sizes of drivers in particular, if the cushion length were increased slightly. There is enough room for the driver's left foot when it is not operating the clutch pedal, and the dip switch is positioned so that it forms a footrest. All the minor controls are conveniently placed around the facia panel; on the car tested the overdrive switch was fitted on a steering wheel spoke, although on present production models this is placed in the centre of the facia above the gear lever.

From the driving seat there is good all-round visibility

Large pockets are provided in both doors, and the right-hand door handle can be seen inside the pocket, a little to the right of the steering wheel. A grab handle is fitted on the passenger side. A bright strip is fitted round the edge of the cockpit and along the tops of the doors. The overdrive control was fitted on the steering wheel on the car tested, but has been moved to the facia on later production cars.

The top of the fuel tank forms the main floor of the luggage locker. A separate compartment at the top of the locker houses the spare wheel, while a small compartment alongside this holds the tools.

and the thin windscreen pillars do not cause any obstruction. With the full weather protection in position general visibility is also good, as a large plastic rear window is fitted. Both front wings can be easily seen from the driving seat. The instruments are grouped around the steering column, where they can be easily seen by the driver. The instrument lighting is effective but it does cause some reflection in the screen at night. A bad reflection is also caused by a chromium-plated strip running right across the body, above the facia, as also can arise in daylight from the same source with the hood down in bright sunshine. The windscreen wipers cover a wide area and are quite effective.

Large doors provide easy access and it is not difficult to enter the car even with the hood up, although the overall height is low—4ft 1in to the top of the hood. Besides the comfortable layout for the driving seat, already mentioned, the passenger compartment is also roomy. The facia panel is swept up to give extra knee room, and a large parcel tray is built on to the bulkhead. The plastic material hood is simple to operate and folds down behind the seats. A full-length tonneau cover is supplied and this can be used for covering the hood when it is down. As well as being completely detachable, the windscreen can be lowered to form a deflector. The curved Perspex sidescreens fit in nicely with the contours of the car, but it is not possible to give hand signals when both the hood and the driver's sidescreen are in position. The fuel tank filler cap is placed inside the luggage locker. It is large and the tank can be filled quickly without blowing back. Double-dip head lamps provide a satisfactory beam and spread of light in both positions. The horns have a particularly powerful and penetrating note. Twenty-one chassis lubrication points require attention with a grease gun, 14 of them at intervals of 500 miles.

AUSTIN-HEALEY HUNDRED TWO-SEATER

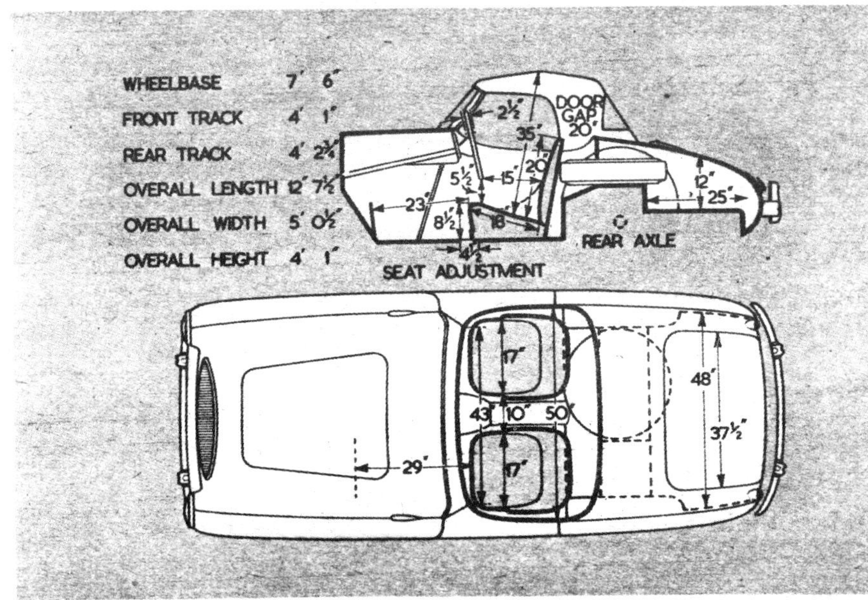

Measurements in these ¼in to 1ft scale body diagrams are taken with the driving seat in the central position of fore and aft adjustment and with the seat cushions uncompressed.

DATA

PRICE (basic), with open two-seater body, £750.
British purchase tax, £313 12s 6d.
Total (in Great Britain), £1,063 12s 6d.
Extras: Heater, standard equipment.

ENGINE: Capacity: 2,660 c.c. (162.2 cu in).
Number of cylinders: 4.
Bore and stoke: 87.3 × 111.1 mm (3.438 × 4.375in).
Valve gear: Overhead, push rods.
Compression ratio: 7.5 to 1.
B.H.P.: 90 at 4,000 r.p.m. (B.H.P. per ton laden 79.6).
Torque: 144 lb ft at 2,500 r.p.m.
M.P.H. per 1,000 r.p.m. on top gear, 18; on overdrive 23.8.

WEIGHT (with 5 gals fuel), 18¾ cwt (2,100 lb).
Weight distribution (per cent) 50 F; 50 R.
Laden as tested: 22⅜ cwt (2,500 lb).
Lb per c.c. (laden): 0.94.

BRAKES: Type: F, Two-leading shoe. R, Leading and trailing.
Method of operation: F, Hydraulic. R, Hydraulic.
Drum dimensions: F, 11in diameter; 1¾in wide. R, 11in diameter, 1¾in wide.
Lining area: F, 72.6 sq in. R, 72.6 sq in (130 sq in per ton laden).

TYRES: 5.90 — 15in.
Pressures (lb per sq in): 22 F; 24 R (normal). 35 F; 36 R (for fast driving).

TANK CAPACITY: 12 Imperial gallons.
Oil sump, 12 pints.
Cooling system, 28 pints.

TURNING CIRCLE: 30ft 0in (L and R).
Steering wheel turns (lock to lock): 2¼.

DIMENSIONS: Wheelbase 7ft 6in.
Track: (F) 4ft 0½in; (R) 4ft 2¼in.
Length (overall): 12ft 7½in.
Height: 4ft 1in.
Width: 5ft 0½in.
Ground clearance: 6in.
Frontal area: 16.6 sq ft (approximately) with hood up.

ELECTRICAL SYSTEM: 12-volt; 63 ampère-hour battery.
Head lights: Double dip, 48–42 watt.

SUSPENSION: Front, Coil springs and wishbones; anti-roll bar.
Rear, Half-elliptic springs.

PERFORMANCE

ACCELERATION: from constant speeds. Speed, Gear Ratios and time in sec.

M.P.H.	3.12 to 1	4.125 to 1	4.42 to 1	5.85 to 1	9.28 to 1
10—30	—	7.5	—	4.6	3.3
20—40	—	7.0	—	4.4	—
30—50	8.5	6.8	5.2	4.5	—
40—60	8.9	7.0	5.8	5.3	—
50—70	9.5	7.6	6.9	—	—
60—80	10.9	9.3	—	—	—
70—90	14.9	12.9	—	—	—

From rest through gears to:

M.P.H.	sec
30	3.3
50	7.6
60	10.3
70	13.4
80	18.0
90	25.6

Standing quarter mile, 17.5 sec.

SPEED ON GEARS:

Gear		M.P.H. (normal and max.)	K.P.H. (normal and max.)
Top	(mean)	111	177.02
	(best)	119	191.51
Overdrive 2nd		70—76	113—122
2nd		52—60	84—97
1st		30—39	48—63

TRACTIVE RESISTANCE: 26 lb per ton at 10 M.P.H.

TRACTIVE EFFORT:

	Pull (lb per ton)	Equivalent Gradient
Overdrive Top	245	1 in 9.1
Top	318	1 in 6.9
Overdrive Second	453	1 in 4.9
Second	495	1 in 4.5

BRAKES:

Efficiency	Pedal Pressure (lb)
75 per cent	100
71 per cent	80
46 per cent	60

FUEL CONSUMPTION:
24.5 m.p.g. overall for 471 miles (11.5 litres per 100 km).
Approximate normal range 24–27 m.p.g. (11.8–10.5 litres per 100 km).
Fuel, First grade.

WEATHER: Fine, dry surface; slight wind. Air temperature, 72 degrees F.
Acceleration figures are the means of several runs in opposite directions.
Tractive effort and resistance obtained by Tapley meter.
Model described in *The Autocar* of October 24, 1952.

SPEEDOMETER CORRECTION: M.P.H.

Car speedometer	10	20	30	40	50	60	70	80	90	100	110	117
True speed	12	21	30	41	51	61	71	80	90	103	113	119

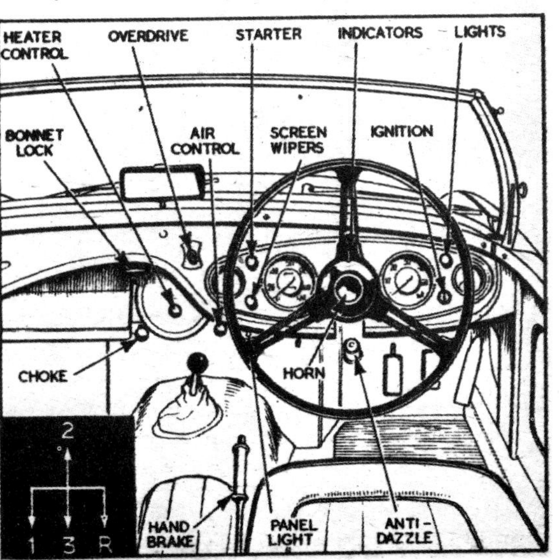

Sports Car Racing

The Austin-Healey Withdrawal from European Events

[65675.]—As there has been considerable comment and some criticism of the statement issued last week by the Austin Motor Company and myself, I feel that as the entrant of the team at Le Mans I should amplify the brief statement issued.

The French sporting journal, *l'Equipe*, stated that the Austin-Healey cars entered were prototypes and themselves bear no resemblance to production cars of this make. I can only repeat that the Austin-Healeys are basically production cars and that all such cars which have run in any race or record attempt since their introduction have been such.

Last year the two cars which performed so well at Le Mans were completely standard chassis and bodies, and the few modifications carried out on the engine, change of axle ratios and so on, have all been made available to the public, and have since been supplied in large quantities to owners.

The majority of the cars admitted to the Mille Miglia in the sports category were literally racing cars. Less than three weeks before the race the regulations were changed to allow single-seaters, to suit the designs of one Italian manufacturer. The descriptions of some of the cars being specially built for Le Mans are of a type which could never be made and sold to the public on a production basis—owing to their elaborate design and prohibitive cost—and bear not the slightest resemblance to cars sold. They certainly will provide a great race spectacle for the racing public and advertisement material for their makers.

These cars are permitted to enter the Le Mans race as prototypes, but the entry form is accompanied by a letter from the Society of Motor Manufacturers and Traders which states: "The Society accepts your assurance that the . . . cars you propose to enter for the above will be prototypes of cars you intend to put in production." Is this august body happy that its members make these promises year after year without any intention of keeping their word?

The Austin-Healey cars under preparation for this year's event were basically production models, but if we were to keep pace with our competitors I found they would have to have such radical alterations as special high-compression cylinder heads and multiple non-British carburettors, multi-pad type disc brakes with complicated servo system and special wheels to suit, close-ratio gear boxes and ratios quite unsuitable for normal use. The bodies would have to be converted to virtually single-seater shells. The resulting car would bear no resemblance to our production model with its expensive specification—brakes alone would cost more than a complete production car. Would our assurance to the S.M.M.T. be worth much?

I therefore decided to stop their preparation and to withdraw my entry as a protest against regulations which admit such changes and virtually change a great sports car endurance test into a race of hand-built prototype racing cars.

My withdrawal from the race was done in ample time to allow the organizers to admit their reserve entries; this will at least admit a few genuine private entries who have been on the reserve list. My deposit is forfeited and I ignore the assertion of "unfair play." I have competed in French events for thirty years and in the past five years my little company has spent more than £30,000 in the preparation and running of cars in this event! I feel I am fully entitled to make a decision of this kind, which is made with the one idea of trying to bring sports car racing back to a more realistic basis.

Motor sport in America is often criticized owing to their comparatively short experience of it, but they do try to control the cars admitted in sports car races so that the genuine private owner has a chance. For instance, in the S.C.C.A. airfield races a production car must be as catalogued and cannot even be run "modified" until the club has proof that the manufacturer has sold 500 such modification kits. Stock cars for record attempts are selected from random agent's stocks by the A.A.A. and only running-in and adjustments are allowed under very strict supervision.

We sell sports cars to the buying public which have to be suitable for everyday use, but they are *sports* cars and the owner is entitled to expect them to be eligible for sports car races; he often wants to compete in such events but is frightened off by the manufacturer's entry which he knows will be to an entirely different specification.

Warwick, June 1, 1954.   D. M. HEALEY.

[The Mille Miglia regulations were amended to allow drivers to travel alone in the cars; the normal two seats were still obligatory (although a cover was permitted on the passenger side) and this point was checked during scrutineering.—ED.]

One of two new Austin-Healeys which made its first appearance at the Le Mans circuit in 1953, with M. Becquart and G. Wilkins driving. This car finished fourteenth whilst the other Healey came twelfth.

NEW CARS AT EARLS COURT

With its low, Perspex deflector screen and louvred bonnet, the new Healey has a very rakish appearance. The large racing type fuel filler cap runs into a 20-gallon fuel tank in the luggage locker. There are no hood and sidescreens but the car is provided with a tonneau cover.

PLUS A HUNDRED

AUSTIN-HEALEY PRODUCE A SEBRING MODEL—THE 100 S

BASED on the well-known Austin-Healey 100, a new competition car has recently emerged from Warwick called the 100S—the S stands for Sebring, the car being developed from those used for that race—at present available for export only. Compared with the standard car, the 100S has a more powerful engine and a different gear box; the chassis has improved dampers and Dunlop disc brakes, and in place of steel, light alloy is used for the bodywork.

The four-cylinder Austin A.90 engine has been redesigned. Distributor and drive have been moved from the right to the left-hand side; all the crankshaft bearing surfaces are nitride hardened, and indium-coated lead-bronze bearings are used for both mains and big ends. The pistons have solid skirts and two upper rings are for compression control, the third being an oil-control ring. The pistons are flat-topped and work in conjunction with a heart-shaped combustion chamber similar to that used on other Austin engines.

Separate Porting

A new cylinder head is cast in light alloy, and in place of siamesed ports for the inlets and numbers two and three exhaust ports, separate porting is now provided for all valves; because of the cylinder-head material, valve seat inserts are used. The new engine has inlet and exhaust valves of $1\frac{13}{16}$ and $1\frac{5}{8}$in diameter respectively, the corresponding throat sizes being $1\frac{9}{16}$ and $1\frac{1}{8}$in. The exhaust valves are produced from KE.965 steel. The mixture is supplied by twin horizontal S.U. carburettors fed with fuel by twin pumps, and there is a dual exhaust layout. The compression ratio is 8.3 to 1.

A new camshaft provides a valve lift of 0.435in and the valve timing overlap has been increased so that the inlet valves now open 10 deg before top dead centre and close 50 deg after bottom dead centre, and the exhaust valves open 45 deg before bottom dead centre and close 15 deg after top dead centre. These modifications result in a very worthwhile increase in power output, the engine now producing 132 b.h.p. at 4,700 r.p.m. compared with 90 b.h.p. at 4,000 r.p.m. for the standard unit.

To increase reliability under arduous operating conditions the lubrication system includes an oil cooler of finned cylindrical light alloy casting placed across the front of the car; this unit also contains a full-flow filter.

A specially designed steel flywheel is attached to the crankshaft and from this the drive is continued via a racing-type dry single-plate clutch to the Healey version of the new B.M.C. gear box. This has four forward ratios, with synchromesh on top, third and second gears. The gear box casing is in cast iron and has a side cover plate, and for the Healey this contains the gear change selector mechanism, a short remote control type of lever being built straight into the box side cover. The standard rear axle ratio is 2.92 to 1, but alternative ratios of 3.66, 4.125 and 2.69 to 1 are also available.

The basic structure of the new Healey is very similar to that of the standard production model, but front end modifications have been made primarily to withstand the possible increase in reaction forces that might be brought about by the use of disc brakes. The suspension springs have been modified to suit the new car and improved damping is provided by the use of double-acting Armstrong RXP spring dampers.

As mentioned previously, the car has Dunlop disc brakes, with one pair of pads per wheel and no servo assistance, the distribution of braking between front and rear wheels being obtained by varying the diameters of the wheel cylinders. The discs are $11\frac{1}{2}$in in diameter, the pads $2\frac{1}{4}$in.

Light alloy is used in place of steel for all panels and structural body members. To improve the streamlining the nose of the car has been restyled, so that it extends slightly forward and has a rather more pleasing contour. The air intake grille is smaller and lower down, but still retains a slightly modified version of the familiar Austin-Healey radiator grille. To assist ventilation of the engine compartment, louvres are cut in the top of the bonnet, and in place of a remote control catch, which might prove embarrassing if the cable broke in the middle of a race, the bonnet is held in place by a leather strap and two simple but effective external catches. Because of the layout of the rear of the car—the petrol tank takes pride of place in the luggage compartment—the spare wheel is housed underneath the rear deck just behind the passenger seat, the rear end projecting into the luggage compartment.

The cockpit is very well laid out; there is a racing type of steering wheel with light alloy spokes and a slender wooden rim, and the bucket seats are light in weight but comfortable. Slots are cut in the seat backs to improve ventilation.

The 100S has independent front suspension with wishbones and coil springs, the arms of the upper wishbones being attached to Armstrong RXP dampers. The combined oil filter and cooler can be seen in the background. Dunlop disc brakes, with one pair of pads per disc, are used.

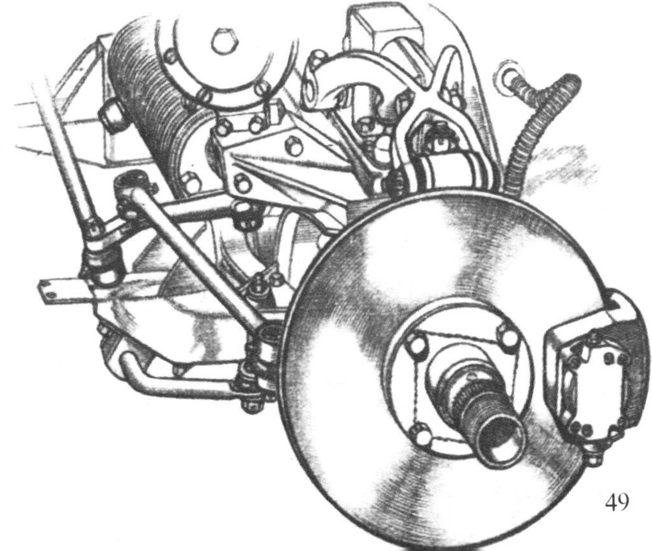

ON THE ROAD WITH THE 100S

With its leather bonnet strap and Perspex deflector screen the Austin-Healey 100S has a very sporting appearance. The use of two-tone paintwork gives the impression of increased length and on this car it was carried out in blue and white, the American racing colours

IMPRESSIONS OF A NEW COMPETITION AUSTIN-HEALEY, NOW IN PRODUCTION

ON Thursday, February 10, the first six 100S cars to come off the production racing car lines of the Donald Healey Motor Company started the first stage of their journey to America, where they will be privately entered in the Sebring Grand Prix. They are to go to Jackie Cooper and Briggs Cunningham in New York, Bob Fergus in Ohio, Fred Allen of Pennsylvania, Dr. Fenner of Dallas, and Mr. Ferguson of Toronto. In addition, Lance Macklin and Stirling Moss, from Britain, will also be driving the 100S. This competition car was described in *The Autocar* of October 22, 1954. It is based on the well-known Austin-Healey 100, it has a light alloy body, specially tuned engine, and Dunlop disc brakes.

Trial Run

After we had inspected the production lines earlier this week—approximately 20 cars a month will be built—Donald Healey invited me to sample one of these cars, the run being in the nature of an *apéritif* before a full-scale road test. It was raining when the arrangements were made, but fortunately, by the time a set of "slave" tyres had been fitted, the sun was shining and the roads were drying. So in the space of a short run it was possible to sample the handling qualities of this car on both wet and dry surfaces.

Once at the wheel the driver immediately feels at home. The general layout of the controls is first-rate, and the seat, complete with ventilated squab, is particularly comfortable. To comply with the regulations, a safety belt is fitted, and with this in place the driver becomes part of the car. If the red line on the tachometer is treated with respect, the Healey accelerates briskly up to an indicated 80 m.p.h. in second gear, and will top the three-figure mark in third. On normal roads there was no opportunity for trying the all-out maximum speed, but on several short stretches of road an indicated 110 was reached very quickly indeed. The 100S has extremely good acceleration. Indeed, it is probable that the stopwatch and controlled conditions would reveal some quite exceptional figures.

Braking is also exceptional. Although no servo system is used (as with some disc brake applications) the pedal pres-

To fit the front and rear suspension units the body shells are placed on waist-high trestles and after these components have been assembled the cars are transferred to another line for the installation of the power unit

ON THE ROAD WITH THE 100S . . .

sure is not excessive, and a number of stops from high speed were made without any noticeable deterioration in braking efficiency. Further, the car stops in a dead straight line.

Perfect Balance

This Austin-Healey has fine handling qualities, fully in keeping with the improved peformance possessed by the 100S. The car has perfect balance and responds well to any cornering technique that the driver may wish to use, from a touring turn to a four-wheel drift. The suspension is very well damped but at the same time it is sufficiently flexible to provide a comfortable ride on second-rate roads. Two small points which could be criticized are a slight stiffness in the gear change mechanism, particularly between the first and second gears, and the throttle pedal position, which, although comfortable for normal driving, made heel and toe gear changing a little difficult. However, it should be mentioned that the car was relatively new, and the gear change mechanism would no doubt free off with increased mileage.

The brief experience made me feel that the new Healey 100S is an outstanding car, particularly if one bears in mind its performance in relation to price. It should certainly please American owners. JOHN RABSON.

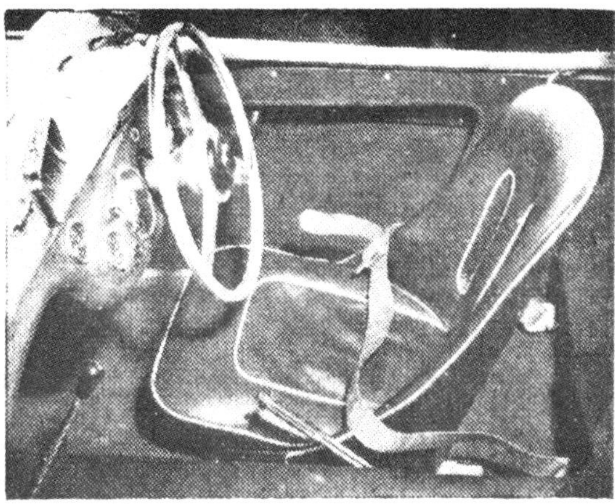

A quick-release safety strap is provided for the driver and this is securely anchored to the main structure of the car. Note the wooden steering wheel rim

Austin-Healey Records

MORE records have been set up on the Bonneville salt flats in Utah, U.S.A., this time by an Austin-Healey Hundred, driven by Mr. Donald Healey and Capt. G. E. T. Eyston. Most impressive result was the astonishing speed of 142.636 m.p.h. over a mile, the highest speed yet recorded in an official record run by a basically production car.

Other new figures for production cars of any size which were set up by Mr. Healey included many for flying and standing starts over distances of up to ten miles. Some flying start speeds were 109.390 m.p.h. for five kilometres, 109.243 m.p.h. for five miles, 109.173 m.p.h. for ten kilometres and 108.788 m.p.h. for ten miles.

As *The Autocar* closed for press, the first 1,000 kilometres of a 24-hour run had been covered at an average speed of 127 m.p.h. On the conclusion of their attack on international records, the drivers started last Wednesday their attempts on American stock car records.

A Road Test of the Austin-Healey appeared in *The Autocar* last week.

Mr. Donald Healey at speed in the Austin-Healey Hundred at Bonneville, U.S.A., where he set up a number of new figures for production cars of any size. He covered a mile at over 142 m.p.h.

J. G. Benett, one of the drivers of the 'stock' Austin Healey Hundreds at Bonneville in 1953, talks to Geoffrey Healey (centre) and A. C. Pilsbury, an official of the American Automobile Association. The car took scores of records, including a 5,000-kilometre endurance run at no less than 103.94 m.p.h.

A SPORTING CAR FOR THE YOUNG AND FOR THE YOUNG IN HEART

Since its introduction the Austin-Healey has set a standard in sports car styling, with its pure and unflamboyant lines

By
S. C. H. DAVIS

PROFILE:

A well-matched pair; "Sammy" Davis, with familiar beret and duffel-coat, in the car

IF you analyse the reasons why a friend buys a car which he has selected you often find that the decision has rested on characteristics that were not only unappealing to you but also anything but obvious.

Now the Austin-Healey appealed to me because I had had a fast run of over 300 miles in one which suggested the possession of two things I particularly value. It was comfortable and it was quiet—or rather it could be driven quietly in spite of its performance. Once in the driving seat I felt comfortably secure; felt that I could place the car just where I wanted it to go; decided that the machine would jump to it when I wanted to overtake a string of merchant vehicles. The run proved that it could put fifty in the hour and I liked the quality of the cruising at 60-70 m.p.h. Little things interested once the premier requirements were established.

Now all of us who have had years of experience testing every kind and type of car retain the fear that the impression left after a test may not be fully confirmed if you subsequently buy the car. Not even a week of testing will disclose whether the machine will or will not develop those irritating defects whose elimination can cost a mint of money. Still, it seemed to me that any firm as big as the British Motor Corporation was unlikely to sponsor a car which was unreliable, while I knew that their spares and service system was good (which, as far as I am concerned, is a decisive factor in selection). Finally the cost was of vital importance, for although one might like a Bentley Continental or a Mercedes 300SL, one can have only what one can afford, particularly when the hell-hounds of Inland Revenue help themselves to so much of one's hard-earned money. Summing everything up, I liked a host of things. Some I was doubtful about: the electrically-operated change into overdrive on second and top, for example, and the odd position of the gear lever.

A few I did not like: for instance, the fuel filler within

Unobstructed vision, clear road ahead and a well laid-out instrument panel—the ingredients of amusing motoring

1954 AUSTIN-HEALEY

the luggage locker, the absence of starting handle, ammeter and clock—and the darned old-fashioned hydraulic jack.

So there we were, and when the opportunity arose to acquire that very car then came also the chance to see how right or wrong the original opinion had been.

First there were two matters of importance: inspection of the doubtless-well-substantiated cost of certain spares for my youngster's Healey led to a panic enquiry as to Austin-Healey costs and, secondly, inspection of the beautiful little low-built green car when delivered disclosed only one fault. Now I have had a great deal to do with inspection, therefore am probably pernickety; but in the first of my post-war cars there were eight faults and in the second five. Moreover, the fault this time was only that the spare wheel tyre was not inflated, so this was encouraging.

Next came fitting out: this consisted of mounting a clock and ammeter on the facia board, adjusting the throttle pedal until it was possible to "toe and heel," providing a socket for an inspection lamp, collecting a spare part pack from Lucas (including yellow head lamp bulbs), fitting the St. Christopher badge I have had for years and also a badge

With the hood up and the rigid sidescreens in position, the car is proof against the winter and does not lose any of its good looks

PROFILE : 1954 AUSTIN-HEALEY . . . .

bar. On this bar were arranged a Lucas "flame thrower" lamp of the smaller size, companioned, at that firm's suggestion, by a flat-topped beam fog lamp. As to badges, the car will normally wear two, but for full-dress can take six, varying according to the job in hand or the country. Covering the tail pipe was a chromium plate addition, rusty pipes being unsightly. A GB plate and an attachment for towing "Beelzebub" were added. ("Beelzebub" is the author's 1897 Léon Bollée tricycle.—ED.) Tool kit, a fire extinguisher, and so forth were then put aboard and the task was finished. Well, there we were, and I must say the car is a little peach for my work, which is mostly solo, usually entails 100 miles to a run—often 200 and sometimes 400—as a rule in a certain hurry. At the end of 400 miles there is no sense of fatigue, which is the best testimonial to a car I know. We can express *joie de vivre* on curves safely, no screech coming from the tyres, and it seems difficult *not* to put over 40 miles

into an hour. The brakes are fine—even the hand brake— the steering light but certain; you and the car are one. With the aid of the high ridges above the front wheels the width is easy to judge in the awkward entrance to my garage and I now like the gear lever position and movement. There is plenty of room in the cockpit, which is unusual for a sports car on racing lines, and though it is awkward for passengers to get in or out, that troubles me not at all! I know how it should be done.

Five speeds are amusing, though I am still experimenting to see how to make the overdrive change absolutely smooth. The fore and aft visibility is first class, so that no "hostile" vehicle can take station on the quarter unnoticed (though several have tried in 30 limits). Opened, and with the screen down in its racing position, I can get all the fresh air I want; closed it is snug by reason of a most efficient heater. The view astern is magnificent as the rear window is very wide indeed. Of all the cars I have ever owned this is the easiest to wash, including, funnily enough, the wire wheels of which I was doubtful.

There is room for plenty of luggage, again an unusual point for this type of car; the hood and side curtains are quickly stowed or erected, and though it hasn't happened *yet* I know that the locker will be flooded with fuel one day as a result of overflow from the internal filler. Except for the propeller-shaft joint nipples it is easy enough to service the car and carry out regular maintenance and that goes for the engine auxiliaries as well. There is more room for maps, guide books, and the paraphernalia I carry than on any other car of the kind I have had, but—though this is an advantage—less

Room for plenty of luggage, though the locker could be flooded by an overflow from the filler

room for the dog. I still want a starting handle, having been almost caught when the battery was a bit down after three weeks' rest while I was away, and I still dislike having to grovel if the jack has to be used.

Petrol consumption at the speed at which I drive is a gallon to 24 miles, less when pottering about. For an ash tray which can be used for a pipe (rare accessory) I am duly grateful.

Now, you may notice that some things so often considered to be of vital importance have not been mentioned. Maximum speed for example, and time taken to reach

Towing attachment for Beelzebub, the author's 1897 Léon Bollée tricycle: and a shiny tail pipe

Guardian of a succession of fast cars through the years; the author's St. Christopher badge

60 m.p.h. from a standstill. Well, maximum speed interests me very little, though I know this car can attain 110. What I want is miles *in* an hour, not miles per hour for a moment, and as to acceleration from a standstill the bare idea seems horrific and expensive, let alone the fact that we are always left at the post in getting away from traffic lights, having a preference for starting only on the green (not that we are tail-end Charlie a few seconds afterwards).

Efforts by drivers of other, often smaller, sports cars to take the Mickey out of the Austin-Healey cause amusement, because at the end of 100 miles they may or may not be there, and mostly aren't ahead. After all, many years of racing make one disinclined to " dice " on unclear roads.

Tyre pressures are important; you can bring the tail round with the throttle nicely, and inexperience might find that the curve ahead was being taken at 70 m.p.h. instead of the estimated 40, wherein lies danger. On ice and snow you can have a lot of fun and the long straights in France are just the job for this type of car; also the head lamps are good enough for the speed, which is something.

Finally—though this is just naughty pride—the car attracts attention wherever it goes, which means that you have to drive more carefully and keep thoroughly awake, for any error, however slight, will result in, " look at that lunatic with a racing car; oughtn't to be allowed," and so on. I don't say there are not more exciting cars if you have £3,000 or more to spend, but I do say that this car suits me for the particular kind of drives I prefer, and certainly it is an enjoyable car to drive for the sake of driving which, after all, is the purpose for which it was built. And it is amusing to note that the opinions formed during the original test are, in the main, confirmed, even if experience has proved that some things thought to be difficult to handle turned out to be much easier on longer acquaintance.

And, by way of epilogue, it is good to recall that this car would never have been born, or might have had a different name, had it not been for the perfervid enthusiasm of a youngster with a garage at Perranporth, in Cornwall, who became involved in high adventure with those fantastic two-cylinder, air-cooled, A.B.C. cars; who subsequently won the Monte Carlo Rally with the kind of car no normal person would dream of going to the Riviera in, then ran into foreign trains and generally learned the hard way to make a car for himself. Or for the violent obstinacy of a delightful engineer who spent much time trying to design an egg - poaching machine but lived to gain a knighthood, ruling the huge works known by his name.

Donald Healey and Sir Herbert Austin.

And if it hadn't been for the fairy godfather quality of one Sir Leonard Lord, the car might not be in my garage at this moment.

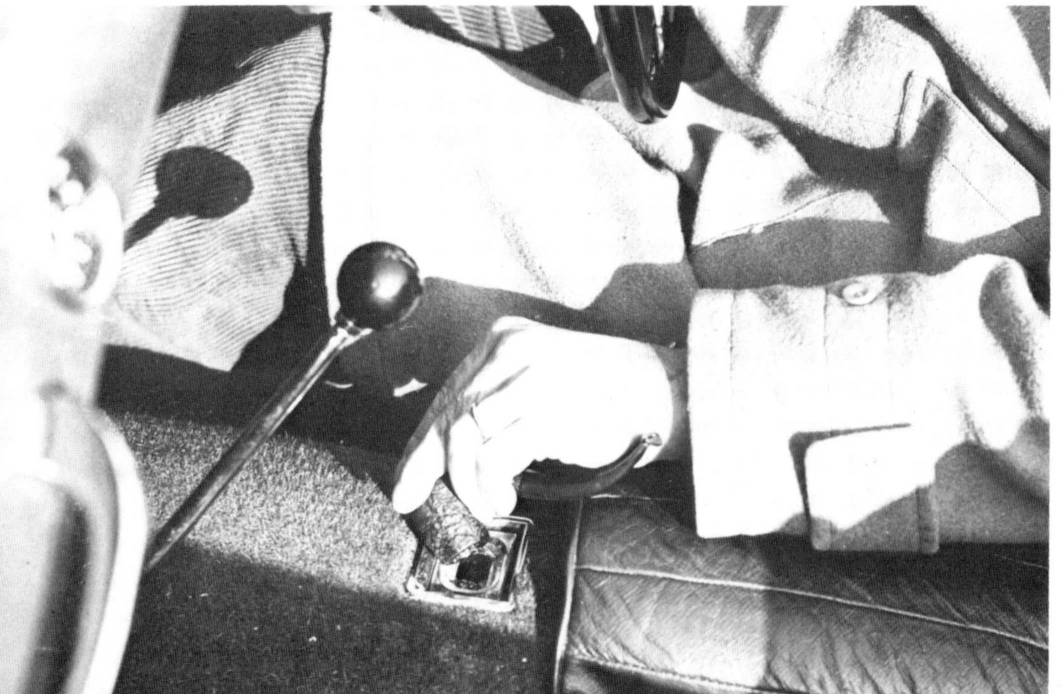

The familiar pipe indicates attention to detail—an ashtray on the shaft tunnel

Six Cylinder Austin-Healey

MORE POWER, MORE SEATS IN REVISED MODEL

PROOF of a sound and successful design is indicated when it remains virtually unchanged for a number of years and, when eventually it is revised in even major details, the basic outline and character are still preserved. In the years since its original introduction at Earls Court in 1952, the Austin-Healey has not only won its spurs in the competition world, but also endeared itself to countless private owners the world over—among them many of mature years who wanted a robust and long-legged touring two-seater rather than a 100 m.p.h. greyhound.

The new Austin-Healey 100 Six is a logical successor, and in both lines and character is still very much a Healey. It is now powered by the B.M.C. "C" series six-cylinder, 2,639 c.c. engine, tuned to the same degree as that fitted in the Austin A.105. Thus it has high-compression pistons to give it a ratio of 8.25 to 1, and the power output of 102 b.h.p., at the comparatively low crankshaft speed of 4,600 r.p.m., represents an 11 per cent increase over the previous model in standard trim.

The same four-speed gear box as was installed in the later four-cylinder cars, and is also used in the Austin Westminster, is fitted; the new car has, too, the Westminster's rear axle, which has resulted in a fractional reduction in the rear track to 4ft 2in. In other mechanical respects the 100 Six remains little changed in design from its predecessor, although a slight increase in weight and an alteration in its distribution between front and rear axles has necessitated minor changes in such details as road spring rates.

In standard form the Austin-Healey will be supplied with ventilated steel disc wheels and tubeless tyres, but such items as centre-lock wire wheels, Dunlop Road Speed tyres, heater and Laycock-de Normanville electrically controlled overdrive are listed at extra cost. When the overdrive is fitted, the rear axle ratio is raised from 3.91 to 1 to 4.1 to 1 (i.e., the gearing is lowered), the equivalent road speeds at 1,000 r.p.m. being 18.9 m.p.h. on the low axle ratio top, 23.2 m.p.h. on the high ratio axle overdrive. Thus the overdrive version reaches approximately 107 m.p.h. at the peak of the engine power curve.

The new model can be distinguished, from the front, by a modification of its grille, which is of reduced area and now has a corrugated, horizontal chromed mesh relieved by widely spaced vertical strips. An additional air intake, serving also to provide clearance for the radiator header tank, is incorporated in the rear-hinged bonnet. The windscreen pillars are no longer so curvaceous, and the screen is a fixture—it will be remembered that the former one could be lowered along the scuttle.

The most fundamental change in the bodywork, however, is in the space allocated to the passengers, whereby the volume of the luggage locker has been reduced to make room for two children behind the two main bucket seats.

For this purpose the open cockpit has

A snug and well-tailored hood covers the increased seating. New for 1957 are the external fuel filler cap, outside door handles and faired-in reflectors

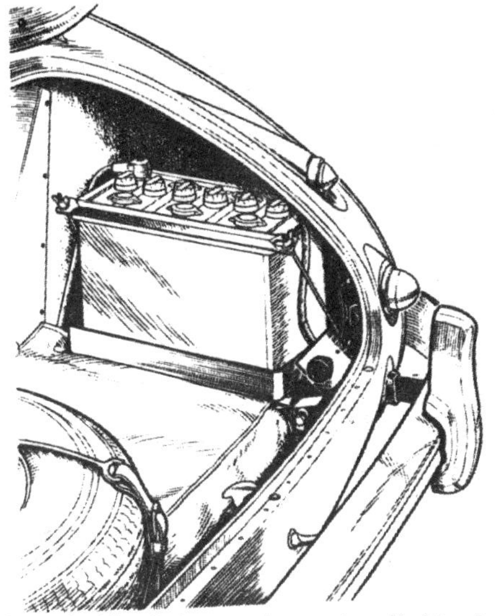

A single 12-volt battery is now installed in the luggage boot with a master switch. Note the position of the spare wheel, and the streamlined fairing enclosing the regulation reflector

is a large rear window of flexible plastic material, and the hood it attached to the rear panel by a series of quick-action fasteners. It stows away out of sight behind the rear seat when not required.

The front doors now have external handles and can be locked. The telescopic steering column will be appreciated. The dashboard is covered in leather-cloth to match the real hide of the bucket seats, and the upper edge of the scuttle has a sponge rubber backing, also covered in leathercloth—perhaps less sightly, but certainly safer than the aluminium strip it replaces. A more elaborate heating and ventilation system is installed—at extra cost—which includes demisting ducts and a booster for fresh air.

The fuel filler is now mounted externally on the right. Reflectors are streamlined into the tail above the combined rear lamps, brake and direction signals. Whereas formerly two six-volt batteries were supplied, and mounted rather inaccessibly behind the seats, there is now a single 12-volt one in the luggage boot, behind the right rear wheel arches. Here it keeps clean and cool, can be

In this view the handsome new grille and additional seating accommodation are clearly shown. Rigid side screens each have a sliding panel, and an aluminium beading surrounds the cockpit. The windscreen is now a fixture

SPECIFICATION

ENGINE

No. of cylinders and arrangement ...	...	6—in line
Bore and stroke	...	79.4 x 89 mm (3.125 x 3.5in)
Displacement ...	...	2,639 c.c. (161 cu in)
Valve position	...	Push rod o.h.v.
Compression ratio	...	8.25 to 1
Max. b.h.p. ...	...	102 at 4,600 r.p.m.
Max. b.m.e.p. ...	...	141 lb sq in at 2,400 r.p.m.
Max. torque ...	...	142 lb ft at 2,400 r.p.m.
Carburettors ...	...	Two S.U. horizontal, H.4
Fuel pump ...	...	S.U. electric, type H.P.
Tank capacity ...	...	12 Imp. gals (54.55 litres)
Sump capacity ...	...	12 pints (6.82 litres)
Oil filter ...	...	Full flow
Cooling system	...	Fan and water pump
Battery	...	12 volt, 51 amp. hr

TRANSMISSION

Clutch ...	...	Single dry plate, 9in dia
Gear box ...	...	4 forward speeds; 1 reverse. Central change
Overall gear ratios	...	Top 3.91, 3rd 5.21, 2nd 7.48, 1st 12.03. Rev. 16.33
Overall gear ratios, with overdrive ...	...	O top 3.19; top 4.1; O.D. 3rd 4.25; 3rd 5.47; 2nd 7.84; 1st 12.61; Rev. 17.12
Final drive, normal	...	Hypoid (3.91 to 1)
Overdrive ...	...	Hypoid (4.1 to 1)

CHASSIS

Brakes ...	...	Girling hydraulic. F: 2 L.S.; R: L. and T.
Drum size ...	...	11in dia x 2¼in wide
Suspension ...	...	F: Independent, coil springs and wishbones, stabilizer bar. R: Live axle, half-elliptic springs, Panhard rod
Dampers ...	...	Lever type, hydraulic
Wheels ...	...	Ventilated steel disc, 5 studs
Tyre size...	...	5.90 x 15, tubeless
Steering ...	...	Cam and peg.
Steering wheel	...	3 spring spokes, 16½in dia. 2¾ turns lock to lock

DIMENSIONS

Wheelbase ...	...	7ft 8in (2.336m)
Track ...	...	F: 4ft 0⅞in (1.238m). R: 4ft 2in (1.27m)
Overall length ...	...	13ft 1½in (4m)
Overall width ...	...	5ft 0½in (1.536m)
Overall height (hood up)	...	4ft 1in (1.244 m)
(hood down)	...	3ft 10in (1.168m)
Ground clearance	...	5⅛in (.014m)
Turning circle ...	...	35ft (10.668m)
Kerb weight ...	...	21¾ cwt (1,105 kg)

PERFORMANCE DATA

Top gear m.p.h. at 1,000 r.p.m. (3.91 axle) ...		18.9 m.p.h.
Top gear m.p.h. at 1,000 r.p.m. (4.1 axle)		18 m.p.h.
O.D. top gear m.p.h. at 1,000 r.p.m. (4.1 axle)		23.2 m.p.h.
Torque, lb ft per cu in engine capacity		0.882
Brake surface area swept by linings ...	...	312 sq in

been extended farther aft, and two upholstered, horseshoe-shaped cushions and a common backrest provide comfortable perches for a growing family. One adult could travel over a short distance in this rear compartment, even with the hood raised, but he would not be able to sit upright. When not otherwise occupied, this space can be used for additional luggage; there is a really efficient tonneau cover, with built-in longitudinal stiffening ribs and supported on a rigid, detachable cross-tube, to protect it when no rear passengers are carried.

Weather protection has received a lot of thought and the improvement is very marked. The new, fixed screen has eliminated one source of possible leakage of wind and rain, and there are now rigid-framed sidescreens, each with one fixed and one sliding panel of transparent plastic. The frames are of extruded aluminium, very neatly made and finished, and form a good seal with the leathercloth hood. This mates ingeniously with the top bar of the windscreen frame, lapping over it throughout its length, and is locked down by two over-centre clamps. There

Heart of the Austin-Healey 100 Six is the 102 b.h.p., six-cylinder B.M.C. unit of 2,639 c.c. In this installation it is fed by two horizontal S.U./H.4 carburettors, and is in unit with a four-speed synchromesh gear box with central change. The Laycock-de Normanville overdrive unit in this picture is an extra fitting

A pleasing and comfortable leather-trimmed interior with space for two in front with long legs, and two behind with short ones. The passenger seat does not adjust, but the driver can alter both seat and steering wheel positions

Six Cylinder Austin-Healey . . .

reached easily for servicing, and has a master switch beside it for use in emergency or when laying the car up. The spare wheel lies horizontally on the left of the boot, which is lined with a plastic material.

The 100 Six is available in a variety of attractive single or two-tone colour schemes, and has a well-balanced, purposeful look from any angle. The recent exploits of a basically similar car, which covered 1,000 kilometres on the Utah salt flats in America at an average speed of over 150 m.p.h., is further proof of the soundness of its conception, and the briefest glance at the unusually substantial boxed-section chassis will convince the engineer of the worth beneath its skin.

On the road, one's impression is that the flexibility of the car is outstanding; the Austin six-cylinder engine is very tractable indeed, and the combination of comparative light weight (22 cwt unladen), a high axle ratio and good power-to-weight ratio provide the essentials for fast motoring with fuel economy. The gear box is pleasant to use, and we formed a good opinion of steering and brakes.

Performance includes a maximum of well over 100 m.p.h., a standing quarter in around 18 sec, and acceleration to 60 m.p.h. from rest through the gears in about 12 sec. Fuel consumption for a journey was 23/24 m.p.g.

Basic price of the occasional four-seat Austin-Healey Six is £762. With purchase tax of £382 7s this makes a total of £1,144 7s. Extras, inclusive of purchase tax, are: Heater—£23 5s, Overdrive—£69 15s, wire wheels with Road Speed tyres—£46 10s.

●●●●●●●●●●●●●●●●●●

The 1954 'streamlined' Austin-Healey at speed on the Salt Flats at Utah during its record-breaking run. It achieved 192.74 m.p.h. over a flying kilometre and later took sixteen US National or International Class D records.

A good-looking car from all angles. When dismantled the hood and supports fold completely away behind the back seat rest

The Autocar ROAD TESTS

AUSTIN-HEALEY 100 SIX

SEVERAL quantity-production sports cars are made today by the larger firms, and they incorporate power and transmission units similar to those used in their more sedate products. They have performance equal to that of pre-war specialist cars, but their price remains reasonable. The new Austin-Healey 100 Six, a logical development of its popular predecessor, falls into this category. The 2.6-litre four-cylinder engine has been replaced by the C series, 102 b.h.p., six-cylinder unit of fractionally smaller capacity, as fitted in the Austin A.105 saloon, and there are two additional forward-facing occasional seats for children.

Externally there is little noticeable difference between the old and the new—a sure indication of good basic design. The air inlet on the bonnet top and re-styled radiator grille —rather more ornate than in the past—bearing the unmistakable imprint of Longbridge, distinguish the 100 Six from the former Hundred at a quick glance. The wheelbase has been extended by 2in to 7ft 8in, and this extra length sensibly has been incorporated in the door opening, thereby making for easier entry and exit. A fixed windscreen, neatly shaped and of quite large area, is now fitted.

The Austin engine is exceptionally smooth, and its useful torque range extends to very low crankshaft speeds. Thus the revised Austin-Healey is even more tractable than its predecessor, and is as much at home pottering about on a shopping expedition as speeding along *routes nationales* and *autobahnen*. For purely experimental purposes, one can move off from a standstill in top gear and accelerate in this ratio to over 100 m.p.h. without protest from engine or transmission.

The Laycock-de Normanville overdrive, which was fitted to the car tested, is an optional extra and operates on third and top gears only. It is allied with a 4.1 to 1 rear axle ratio, which confers an overdrive ratio of 3.19 to 1, whereas in standard form the final drive is 3.91 to 1.

Whilst many buyers will prefer to pay extra for the overdrive, the standard ratios would probably allow maximum speed to be reached more quickly and thus more often. During the road test it became standard practice to use first gear from rest, and to change up to second immediately the car was moving; normal third was engaged at approximately 40 m.p.h., and it was then simply a matter of flicking the facia-mounted overdrive switch to obtain overdrive third, a ratio which embodies a useable speed range between 15 and 90 m.p.h.

After accelerating in this ratio, little was gained by reverting to normal top (with simultaneous movements of gear lever and overdrive switch), and it soon became customary to shift from overdrive third to overdrive top. Downward changes depended upon circumstances—either lever engagement of overdrive third, or an electric selection of normal top. There was almost imperceptible lag during the engagement of overdrive. Upward changes are made—and

The six-cylinder Healey is recognizable by the new-styled radiator grille and the air inlet vent on the bonnet top. The flashing signals are incorporated in the side lights

indeed are much smoother—if the throttle is kept open, as recommended by the makers. Half the pleasure of driving a high-geared car is lost if the gear box ratios and control are unsatisfactory. With 23.18 m.p.h. per 1,000 r.p.m. in overdrive top, the Austin-Healey is quite high-geared, but its gear box scores full marks on both counts and one welcomes excuses to use it.

With hood and side screens erect, the 100 Six proved to have about the same mean and one-direction maxima as its predecessor, when tested by *The Autocar* in September of 1953, but the car under review had covered only a nominal mileage, and might well improve on this when more fully run-in. It is understood that the same car, subsequent to

The doors, now wider, open almost at right angles; entry into the driving seat is easy; and reasonably so even when the all-weather equipment is in position. There are wide, deep map pockets in each door

The bonnet top is hinged at the rear and its lock is supplemented by two safety catches. Pancake air cleaners are fitted to the S.U. carburettors. On the right of the engine the distributor is easy to reach, and the sump breather pipe is led via the rocker cover to the rearmost air cleaner

our test, lapped the M.I.R.A. circuit in 2 min 15 sec (107 m.p.h.); and it is worth recalling that the four-cylinder car, which was the subject of our 1953 test, achieved a mean speed of 111 m.p.h. and a best speed in one direction of 119 m.p.h., after the windscreen had been removed and an aero screen and tonneau cover substituted. The 100 Six would doubtless react equally well to the same treatment. Although it has, on paper, some 12 b.h.p. in hand over the four-cylinder car, it weighs over three hundredweight more, and the acceleration figures are not quite so good. This may also result from differences in the torque curves of the two engines, and in the gear box ratios, the earlier car having a three-speed box with overdrive. Thus, although 80 m.p.h. from a standstill in 22.6 sec is creditable enough, the earlier car was more than 4½ sec quicker.

The combination of an unladen weight of 22 cwt., high gearing and a reasonable power-to-weight ratio provides the essentials for fast motoring with a moderate fuel consumption. In addition, it is difficult to drive this car to the stage where the crew become physically tired; it has, in fact, the traditional Seven League Boots. The suspension and road-holding are a combination of old and new, as is now expected with a modern sports car. There is little or no heeling over or tyre squeal on fast corners, and the ride is unexpectedly smooth, especially so on Continental *pavé*.

One is conscious of slight firmness only when travelling over indifferent surfaces with the tyres at the high pressures recommended for sustained fast cruising speeds. Steering characteristics are neutral as near as no matter, and one is able, on sharp bends, to promote a degree of oversteer at will by intelligent use of the throttle pedal. There is a satisfactory amount of self-centring action.

The clutch action is faultless; full throttle starts produced no slip, and at all times the engagement was smooth. The

Spare wheel and battery occupy much of the luggage boot. The locker lid is prevented from damaging the hood by a retaining wire cable. Separate reflectors are housed in streamlined fairings above the rear lamps. A light behind the bumper illuminates the rear number plate

pendant pedal is set at a comfortable angle, and only average pressure is called for. The three pedals seem unnecessarily close together, and it was not possible to indulge in " heel and toe " gear changes. Brake pedal pressure is light, except for full energy stops, and the brakes are adequate to the usable maximum speed. They are not prone to fade or grab. The parking brake lever is close to the driving seat, but causes no interference with the driver's movements, and is very efficient.

The general comfort of the car is praiseworthy, except that the leather-trimmed seat cushions are rather too short to support the thighs adequately, and shallow, so that the driver becomes rather conscious of the seat frame beneath after travelling some 200 miles. Backrests, which hinge forward to give access to the rear seats, are a little flimsy, and do not provide the stiff lateral support which one expects in this type of car. The angle of the backrests, however, is excellent, and they are tapered to allow plenty of elbow room.

As compared with the previous model, there is more foot room for the driver, and it is no longer necessary for him to rest the left foot on the clutch pedal. The layout suits a tall driver better than a short one, for the relationship between seat and pedals is such that a short person, having adjusted the seat so that he can reach the pedals comfortably, will find himself too close to the steering wheel.

The short, rigid gear lever, which protrudes from the left side of the gear box cover, is easy to reach and delightful to use. The movements between gears are short and precise, and the box is mechanically very quiet. The crew sit well down in the car, and there is excellent weather protection. The windscreen is a fixture, whereas the previous screen could be lowered along the scuttle to decrease frontal area during high-speed runs; and there are improved, rigid-framed sidescreens with sliding Perspex panels.

Raising and lowering the hood is a rather long and involved procedure. It would be impossible to raise the hood in the event of a sudden shower without the crew getting wet, and this would be more than ever true if the driver were travelling alone and had to do the job himself. Once up, however, it is extremely taut, and the leading edge of the hood is particularly safely secured to the top of the windscreen frame. With hood and sidescreens erect, the car is commendably quiet up to 80 m.p.h.; above this, wind noise becomes much more evident and conversation correspondingly more difficult.

AUSTIN-HEALEY 100 SIX

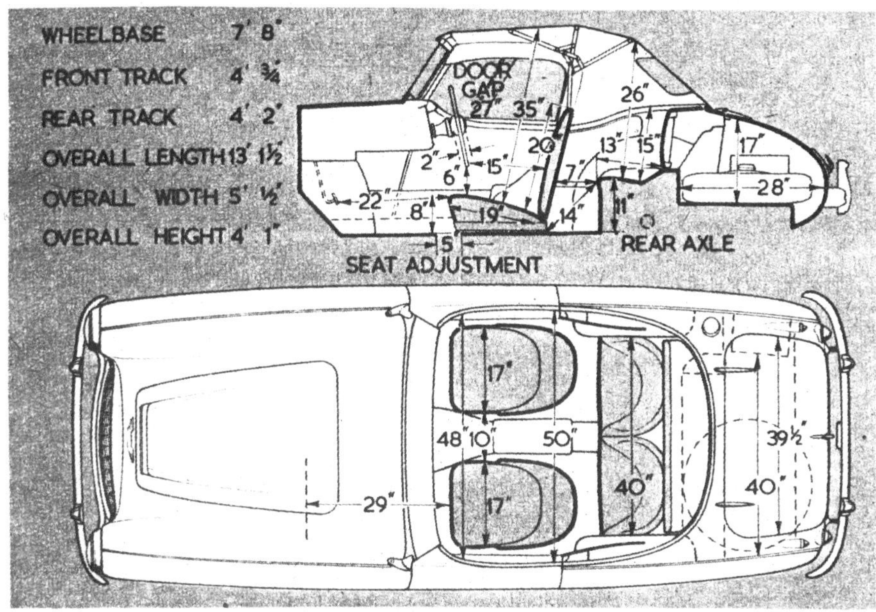

Measurements in these ⅛in to 1ft scale body diagrams are taken with the driving seat in the central position of fore and aft adjustment and with the seat cushions uncompressed

DATA

PRICE (basic), with occasional four-seater body, £762.
British purchase tax, £382 7s.
Total (in Great Britain), £1,144 7s.
Extras: Heater £23 5s inc. P.T.
Overdrive: £69 15s inc. P.T.
Wire wheels and Road Speed tyres £46 10s inc. P.T.
ENGINE: Capacity: 2,639 c.c. (161 cu in).
Number of cylinders: 6.
Bore and stroke: 79.4 × 89.0 mm (3.125 × 3.5in).
Valve gear: overhead valves and pushrods.
Compression ratio: 8.25 to 1.
B.H.P.: 102 at 4,600 r.p.m. (B.H.P. per ton laden 81.1).
Torque: 142 lb ft at 2,400 r.p.m.
M.P.H. per 1,000 r.p.m. on top gear 18.08.
M.P.H. per 1,000 r.p.m. on overdrive 23.18.
WEIGHT: (with 5 gals fuel): 22 cwt (2,478 lb).
Weight disbribution (per cent): F, 49; R, 51.
Laden as tested: 25¼ cwt (2,803 lb).
Lb per c.c. (laden): 1.06.
BRAKES: Type: F, two-leading shoe; R, leading and trailing.
Method of operation: F, hydraulic; R, hydraulic.
Drum dimensions: F, 11in diameter; 2¼in wide. R, 11in diameter; 2¼in wide.
Lining area: F, 95 sq in. R, 95 sq in (151.8 sq in per ton laden).
TYRES: 5.90—15in.
Pressures (lb per sq in): F, 20; R, 23 (normal). F, 26; R, 29 (for fast driving).
TANK CAPACITY: 12 Imperial gallons.
Oil sump, 12 pints.
Cooling system, 20 pints (plus 1 pint if heater is fitted).
TURNING CIRCLE: 35ft 0in (L and R).
Steering wheel turns (lock to lock): 2¼.
DIMENSIONS: Wheelbase: 7ft 8in.
Track: F, 4ft 0¾in; R, 4ft 2in.
Length (overall): 13ft 1½in.
Height: 4ft 1in.
Width: 5ft 0½in.
Ground clearance: 5½in.
Frontal area: 16.6 sq ft (approximately) with hood up.
ELECTRICAL SYSTEM: 12-volt; 51 ampère-hour battery.
Head lights: Double dip; 42—36 watt bulbs.
SUSPENSION: Front, independent with coil springs and wishbones, anti-roll bar. Rear, half-elliptic leaf springs and Panhard rod.

PERFORMANCE

ACCELERATION: from constant speeds.
Speed Range, Gear Ratios and Time in sec.

M.P.H.				*3.19 to 1	4.1 to 1	*4.25 to 1	5.46 to 1	7.84 to 1	12.61 to 1
10—30	..	..	..	—	7.7	—	5.8	4.2	3.4
20—40	..	..	..	10.2	7.7	7.6	5.8	4.0	—
30—50	..	..	..	10.6	8.0	7.8	5.8	4.9	—
40—60	..	..	..	11.8	8.3	8.1	6.5	—	—
50—70	..	..	..	12.6	8.8	8.7	7.9	—	—
60—80	..	..	..	14.7	10.6	10.7	—	—	—
70—90	..	..	..	19.2	15.3	16.0	—	—	—

*Overdrive.

From rest through gears to:

M.P.H.		sec.
30	..	4.3
50	..	9.3
60	..	12.9
70	..	17.5
80	..	22.6
90	..	32.3

Standing quarter mile, 18.8 sec.

SPEEDS ON GEARS:

Gear		M.P.H. (normal and max.)	K.P.H. (normal and max.)
O.D. Top	(mean)	103	165
	(best)	107*	172
Top ..	(mean)	98.5	158
	(best)	101	162
O.D. 3rd ..	..	80—95	129—153
3rd ..	..	60—73	97—117
2nd ..	..	40—50	64—80
1st ..	..	24—31	39—50

*See text, page 684

TRACTIVE RESISTANCE: 16 lb per ton at 10 M.P.H.

TRACTIVE EFFORT:

	Pull (lb per ton)	Equivalent Gradient
Top	244	1 in 9.1
O.D. Third	402	1 in 5.5
Third	464	1 in 4.7
Second...	579	1 in 3.7

BRAKES (at 30 m.p.h.):

Efficiency	Pedal Pressure (lb)
49 per cent	30
66 per cent	50
79 per cent	75
85 per cent	130

FUEL CONSUMPTION:
23.3 m.p.g. overall for 941 miles (12.12 litres per 100 km).
Approximate normal range: 20-27 m.p.g. (14-10 litres per 100 km).
Fuel, first grade.
WEATHER: Cloudy, slight headwind, dry tarmac surface.
Air temperature 58 deg F.
Acceleration figures are the means of several runs in opposite directions.
Tractive effort and resistance obtained by Tapley meter.
Model described in *The Autocar* of September 28, 1956.

SPEEDOMETER CORRECTION: M.P.H.

Car speedometer:	10	20	30	40	50	60	70	80	90	100
True speed:	13	20	29	38	48	58	68	78	87	96

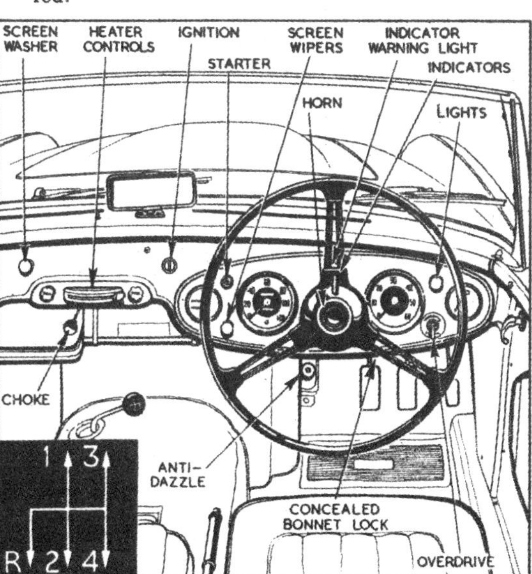

Visibility with the hood up is excellent, but the height of the rear view mirror above the scuttle is insufficient to make full use of the large rear window panel. One is not conscious of any draughts in the car when closed; in fact, after some miles of fast driving, the cockpit is apt to become rather too warm, even when the fresh-air intake is opened. The two rear seats are suitable for small children, and it is possible for an adult to sit across the car. He would, however, find his head well above the windscreen level, and with the hood erect would be unable to sit upright.

Provision of these seats has restricted the volume of the luggage locker, which now also houses the spare wheel and battery, and it is virtually impossible to stow even a small suitcase. The wisdom of placing the battery there also seems questionable. The occasional seats, moreover, have a central hump which likewise prevents a suitcase from fitting there, and this lack of properly shaped luggage accommodation might prove a severe handicap for the many who will be driving their Austin-Healeys on trans-Continental marathons. Such inadequacy of baggage space calls for the use of an external rack, but a more satisfactory solution might be to arrange external stowage of the spare wheel when it is necessary to carry extra luggage.

Stowage for small articles in the cockpit is provided by a deep pocket in each door and a shelf below the left side of the facia panel. Part of this shelf is, somewhat un-expectedly, occupied by the screen-wash bottle. Locking of the doors is rather awkward, for the left door locks with the ignition key, and the right by means of a small interior catch. It would be better if this arrangement were reversed, or if both doors could be locked by the key, since it is none too easy for the driver to move over the central gear box hump and handbrake.

The instrument panel is well laid out, and the dials easily read and well lit. There is no rheostat switch, but the lighting is not strong enough to annoy the driver, nor is there any reflection in the windscreen. In full ahead and dipped positions the head lamps earn good marks, and the twin high-frequency horns have powerful notes. The wind-screen wipers are efficient, and clear a reasonable area of the screen. The ribbed tonneau cover is exceptionally neat, and can be used with the driver only in the car. An improved feature is that the fuel tank filler is now on the outside of the body rather than inside the locker, and that it can take the full flow from a garage pump; the cap, however, proved difficult to release or replace.

The Austin-Healey 100 Six is fast, safe, efficient and easy to drive. It is equally well suited to the elderly owner who has no intention of travelling at 100 m.p.h., but enjoys driving for its own sake and prefers it with a breath of fresh air, and to the younger sportsman to whom speed and acceleration mean almost everything. Any who seek even more performance than the car offers in standard form will know that the engine has a considerable untapped reserve, and that the car as a whole is exceptionally tough.

The Bonneville Salt Flats, Utah, 1956, with the modified six-cylinder Healey Hundred in the foreground and the supercharged streamliner (which exceeded 200 m.p.h.) in the background – Donald Healey, the driver, is on the right of the group in the foreground.

More Power for Austin-Healey

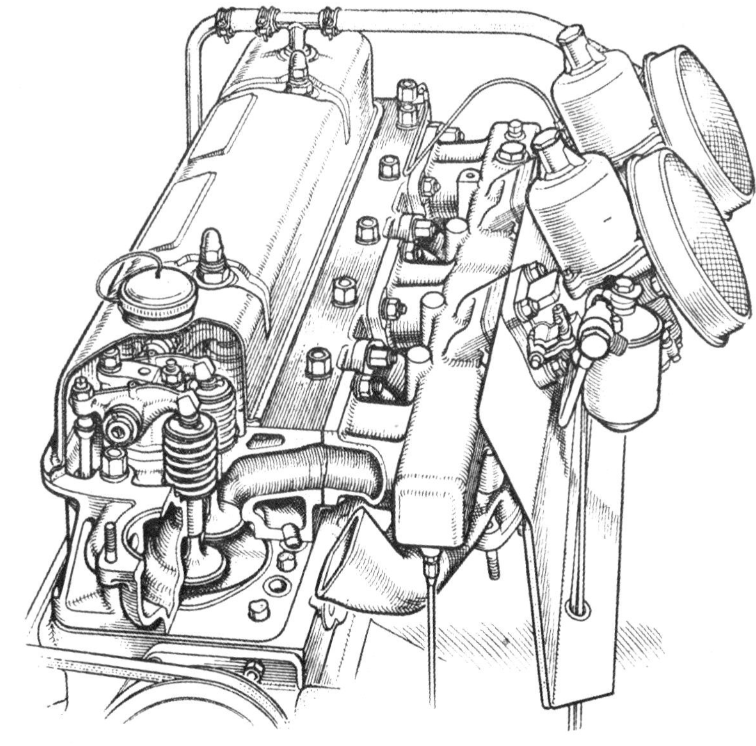

New porting of the Austin-Healey cylinder head and detachable inlet manifold

BRITISH MOTOR CORPORATION announces that following development work, an improved cylinder head assembly with an 8.5 to 1 compression ratio is being fitted to the six-cylinder C series engine used in the Austin-Healey 100 Six. The previous engine had the inlet manifold cast integrally with the cylinder head, and gas flow was restricted to a certain extent. The engine now develops 117 b.h.p. at 4,750 r.p.m.; previous output was 102 b.h.p. at 4,600 r.p.m. Maximum torque is increased from 142 lb ft at 2,400 r.p.m. to 149 lb ft at 3,000 r.p.m. Study of the power curves will show that output is increased throughout the speed range but the greatest improvement is at the top end.

Separate inlet ports are formed in the new head. These are $1\frac{15}{32}$in diameter at the valve throat, and $1\frac{5}{16}$in diameter effectively at the manifold face; there is a tapered zone increasing the size to $1\frac{1}{2}$in diameter to assist matching with the inlet manifold. The centre line of the port is 15 deg from the horizontal, and leads in an uninterrupted curve into the combustion chamber. No. 1 and No. 6 exhaust ports have rectangular outlets at the manifold face, but have the same area as the remaining four exhaust ports which are $1\frac{7}{16}$in diameter. The shape of the exhaust ports at each end of the head is determined by the positioning of the cylinder head studs. Two separate exhaust manifolds are used, as previously, and these have individual pipes to the silencer, from which there are twin exhaust outlets.

Valve head sizes have increased slightly, the exhaust from 1.420 to 1.562in diameter and the inlet from 1.688 to 1.75in diameter; the seat and stem tip of the exhaust valves are stellited for extra life. The stem diameter remains the same at 0.342in. The shape of the combustion chambers has not been altered to any appreciable extent.

The aluminium alloy inlet manifold has the six ports cast in pairs, and it is offset in the longitudinal plane so that the carburettors are level when the engine is in the chassis. A wall is cast in the manifold between the centre ports; in this wall is a $\frac{7}{16}$in diameter balance hole to correct mixture surge, acting in the same manner as an external balance pipe. Two hot-spots are formed beneath the carburettor intakes.

There are tappings on the top of the manifold at the rear for vacuum servo and screen washer attachments. Also at each end, on the underside of the mani-

fold, a small vent is located to allow excess fuel to drain away.

Twin S.U. $1\frac{3}{4}$in HD6 carburettors are fitted at a 30 deg angle; a heat shield is placed between them and the exhaust manifolds. These carburettors are of the fully enclosed diaphragm type, and the location of the float chambers prevents fuel starvation during extreme acceleration.

The new cylinder head should suit the characteristics of the Austin-Healey. Earlier models had a good top gear performance at low engine speeds; this has not been sacrificed, but the top end performance will be noticeably improved by the 11 per cent increase of power.

These modifications have resulted in an increase of price, which becomes £817 basic (previously £762); purchase tax in the United Kingdom adds £409 17s, making a total of £1,226 17s (£1,144 7s).

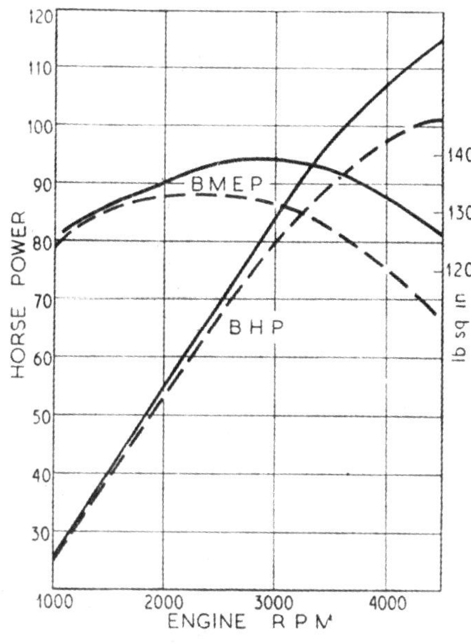

Power curves (right) showing the increase in output over the former engine (dotted); below: the current model

Rally Healeys

Above. The Sears-Garnier Austin-Healey, lying second in its class, stops at Belley in France during the 1958 Tulip Rally.

Right. Pat Moss' and Pauline Mayman's Austin-Healey on a typical forest stage of the 1962 R.A.C. Rally.

AUSTIN-HEALEY

One-litre Sports Car with Integral Structure and Quarter-elliptic Rear Springs

FOR some months past, persistent rumours of a new small sports car under development by B.M.C. have circulated amongst those with trade and sporting interests in such a vehicle. Most of these legends suggested a new M.G.; in fact, the mystery car now described is designated an Austin-Healey, for the good reason that it owes its conception to the Healey design office in Warwick.

From this stage Longbridge took over, and the new Healey was "productionized"—that is, its constituents and layout were adapted where necessary to simplify their production and assembly in very large numbers. Two prototype cars were next made by Austins, who did the initial type-testing; then the whole project was handed to the M.G. team at Abingdon, to develop further, and ultimately to assemble.

Announcement of this new car—the Sprite—was delayed until the production line at Abingdon (where its larger stablemate, the Austin-Healey 100-Six, is made also) was flowing freely; during the past several weeks, large numbers of these little sports cars have been completed and despatched to distributors in this country and overseas.

Essential factors in a project of this nature are, of course, interrelated weight and price. Excess weight of material increases cost and decreases road performance, and to ensure that the Sprite should be competitive with its rivals in these respects, a light integral structure of body and chassis has been adopted.

This description requires qualification, in that very few of the outer body panels are stressed. For instance, the bonnet, front mudguards, lamps and radiator cowl are combined in a single unit, hinged on the scuttle in front of the windscreen to give unimpeded access to the power unit, steering and suspension components. Indeed, two experienced fitters can complete an engine change in about 20 minutes. Incidentally, these body and chassis units are made by Pressed Steel at Swindon, then rust-inhibited and painted at the Morris works near Oxford before they arrive at Abingdon.

At the front of the chassis is a very substantial boxed structure, including a wide cross-member outrigged to carry the front suspension and steering mechanisms, and to provide a firm lock-mounting for the rather heavy bonnet. A secondary cross-member bridging this main member braces the upper spring pads of the front suspension. Two boxed longerons, parallel with the chassis centre-line, connect the forward cross-member with a second one approximately in line with the forward door hinges. Behind this the long body sills and the propeller shaft tunnel unite with the floor to support a raised, transverse structure carrying the rear suspension spring and torque link mountings, and the Armstrong lever-type dampers. Two L-shaped members of top-hat section run beneath the front seats from the central cross-member to this rear structure, to help support the weight of the luggage boot, spare wheel and fuel tank.

A full-width scuttle superstructure integrates with the forward ends of the body sills to add frame stiffness, and is arranged to absorb some front suspension loads by the provision of a bracing strut at each side, connecting with the front cross-member.

There is no exterior boot lid because the panel is stressed, and its contents must be reached from behind the seats—a manœuvre rendered difficult because the floor of the boot is swept up locally to clear the axle casing. Stiffening plates welded into each rear-wheel arch give added support to the overhung tail.

The scuttle is formed in the shape of separate boxes around each occupant's legs at either side of the engine compartment, which extends slightly into the cockpit. This structure is extended upwards to carry the bonnet hinges, windscreen frame and facia.

For the front suspension, standard Austin A.35 coil spring and wishbone components are used, in conjunction with lever-type Armstrong hydraulic dampers. Only the lower arm of each suspension assembly is, in fact, a wishbone, the single upper arm being also the lever of the damper, the body of

Prominent head lamps and a simple radiator grille give the new Austin-Healey Sprite an almost animate expression. The bonnet and front wing assembly is hinged just forward of the windscreen. The doors are opened by interior handles

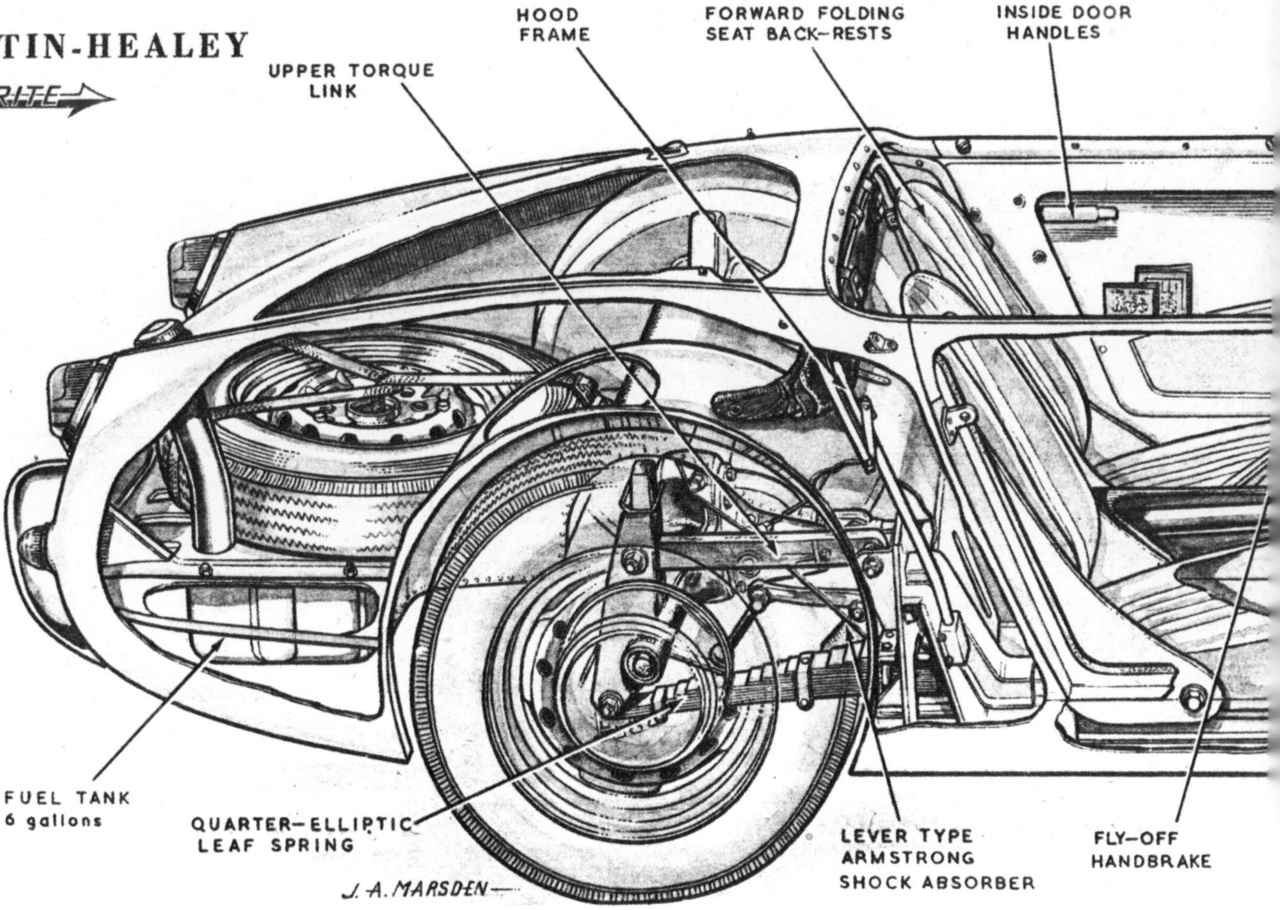

which is bolted to an upward extension of the front cross-member. Morris Minor type rack-and-pinion steering is fitted of which the rack forms the centre of a three-piece track-rod. Although the ratio gives 2¼ turns of the steering wheel from lock to lock, this is much higher than would appear at first sight, the short wheelbase (6ft 8in) giving the car a very compact turning circle.

Rear suspension details are of particular interest, in view of the reversion to quarter-elliptic leaf springs—a feature of the famous Austin 7 which was in production for most of the years between the wars. This system, with its spring anchorages well ahead of the rigid axle, concentrates suspension stresses within a very short frame. Incidentally, the new Healey might well be considered a successor to those small sporting versions of the Austin 7, the Speedy and Nippy, which were produced up to 1937.

Each spring has 15 leaves, and its "free" length—between its mounting bracket and attachment to the axle—is 16in. It is located by four studs and one dowel; the front two are fitted studs and pass through holes in the spring leaves, while the rear two straddle the spring; the dowel is placed at the approximate centre of the four studs and also passes through all the spring leaves. Each pair of studs is threaded into a bridge stepped to fit over the upper spring leaf, and a pressed steel

Above: There are individual bucket-type front seats, and elbow room is generous. The facia is trimmed in plastic material and the instrument layout is simple and neat. Below: A three-piece Vibak panel gives excellent rearward vision and admits plenty of light to the interior. A section of each sidescreen folds upwards for reaching the door handle. Access to luggage and the spare wheel is from behind the folding seat squabs

plate of $\frac{1}{8}$in thickness spreads the load by sandwiching the car frame between the base of the spring and the clamping nuts.

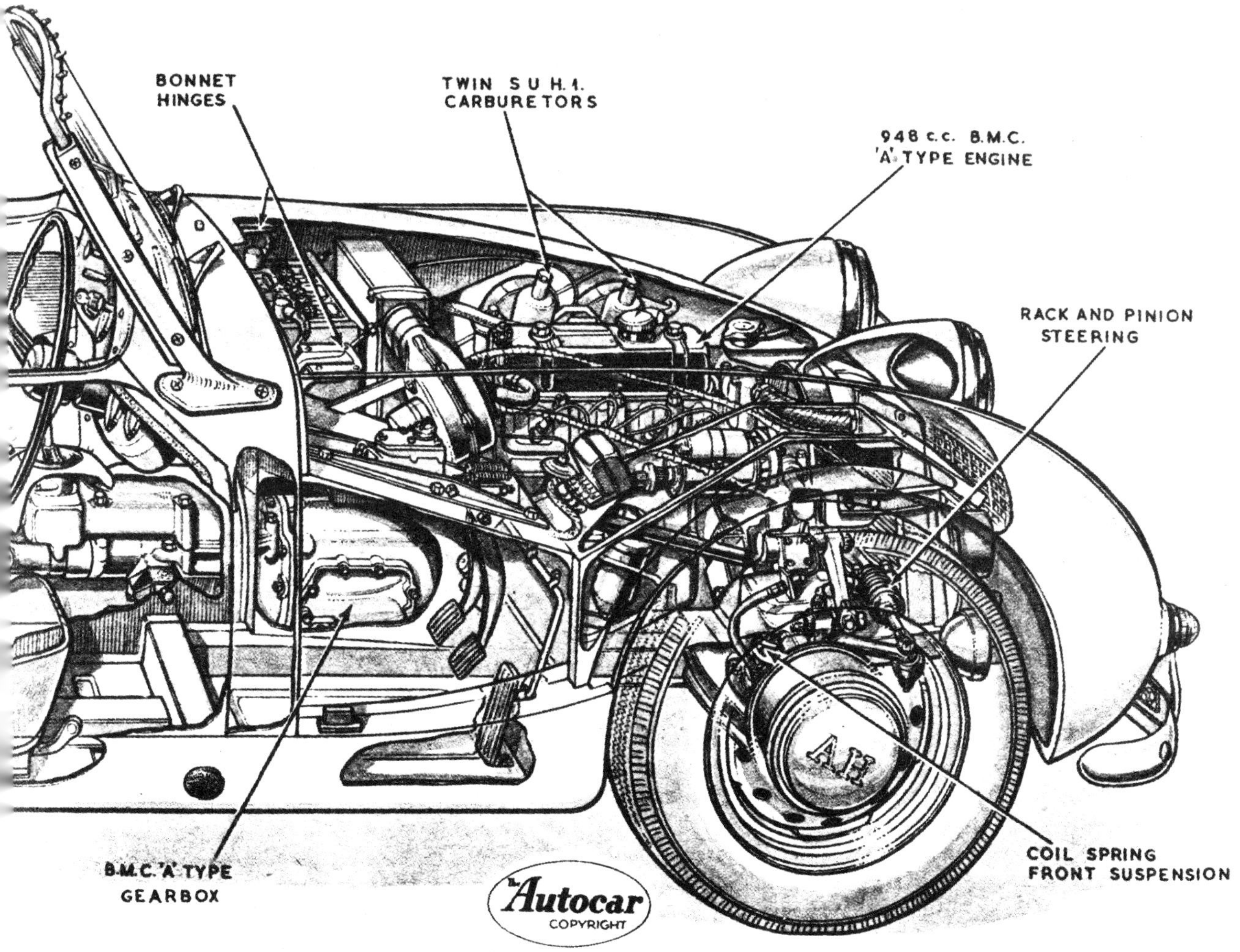

Each spring eye is formed from the two main leaves and carried below the axle centre line in a bracket welded to the axle casing, this bracket also extending above the axle tube to locate the rearmost eye of the upper torque link. These links are fabricated from channel steel pressings welded to form a box-section. They are mounted at each end on rubber bushes, so that lateral location of the axle is governed entirely by the springs. A rubber bump stop is attached to the top of this axle bracket by split-pins passing through it, and rubberized canvas straps limit rebound movement.

Braking is by a conventional Lockheed hydraulic system having two-leading shoes in the front drums, leading-and-trailing in the rear; a cable and rod hand-brake linkage, with its compensating gear, is anchored to the axle casing and operates in the wheel cylinders by the cam action of pivot levers. Although the brake shoes are only $1\frac{3}{16}$in wide, the drum faces are much wider than this, perhaps to allow braking effort to be stepped up when the car is tuned above standard performance.

Under the bonnet is that admirable and exceptionally tough B.M.C. A-type four-cylinder engine of 948 c.c. capacity, with pushrod-operated o.h.v. and heart-shaped combustion chambers. For the Sprite it is fed by two S.U. $1\frac{1}{8}$in carburettors set at a slight angle to the horizontal, and protected by individual

The rear axle is located by its quarter-elliptic springs and torque links; rubber blocks and flexible straps limit its vertical travel. Inset is the right spring fixture, with two fitted bolts passing through it, two straddling it, and a central dowel

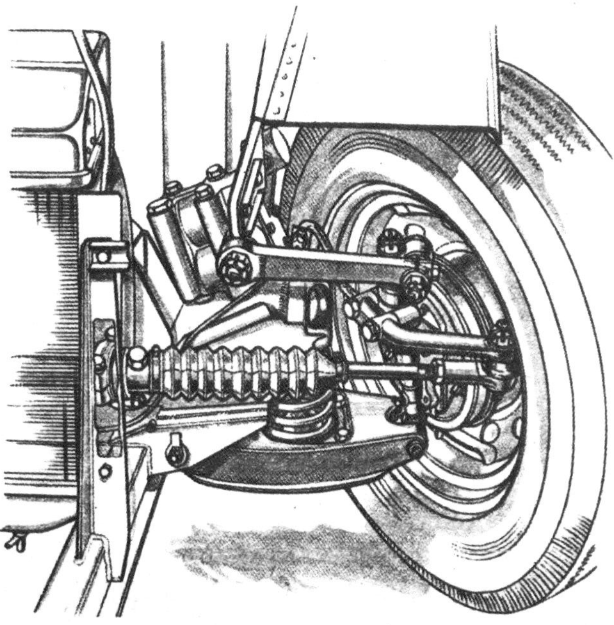

Front end details (right) include rack-and-pinion steering, coil spring and wishbone suspension and Armstrong lever - type dampers

This exhibition "chassis" shows how the main structure is self-supporting without the outer body panels. Heating and ventilation equipment is optional

Vestigial front mudguards are revealed with the bonnet opened. It is locked shut by horizontal sliding bolts and a T-handle

AUSTIN-HEALEY *Sprite*

Cooper air filters. The A.C. mechanical fuel pump, incidentally, is new to Abingdon. The exhaust valves have Stellited seats and the valve springs are special, but the compression of 8.3 to 1 is identical with those for the Austin A.35 and Morris Minor.

In this form the unit develops 43 b.h.p. (nett) at 5,000 r.p.m., and the makers claim a top speed in the early eighties, a 0-60 m.p.h. figure of about 22sec, and fuel consumption between 30 and 45 m.p.g., depending on driving methods. The gear box is as fitted to the Minor and A.35, with the remote-control lever sprouting from the transmission tunnel. Hydraulic operation and extra-strong release springs characterize the Borg and Beck clutch.

Final drive ratio of the conventional hypoid rear axle is 4.2 to 1, and the rear track of 3ft 8¾in accords with that of the A.35—the casings being similar except in the arrangements for spring mountings. The exhaust pipe, suspended from rubber-in-shear brackets, passes under the axle and terminates in a Burgess straight-through silencer.

Turning now to body details, one is struck immediately by the width of the cockpit, which is, in fact, more spacious than that of the M.G. A. Comfortable bucket seats give good lateral support, and are trimmed in P.V.C.-coated material over foam rubber on the cushions, rubberized horsehair on the backrests. The latter fold forward to give access to the spare wheel and luggage.

The hood, in P.V.C.-coated fabric, it attached to the upper screen rail and to the tail panel by fasteners of three different types. When not required, it folds neatly out of sight behind the seats, and is secured by straps beneath the lip of the luggage boot —one section of the hood frame being first dismantled, folded and stowed in special sockets. The sidescreens are attached to the doors by screws with knurled heads. Interior door handles only are fitted, which entails placing a hand through a flap in the sidescreen to open the door from outside. Since the hood can be unfastened easily from outside, the car cannot be locked.

A wide beading of polished aluminium puts a neat finishing touch to the boot's leading edge and the door tops, but the facia and its surround are sheathed in matt plastic material to avoid creating reflections in the screen. Instruments comprise a speedometer (with trip and total mileage recorders), petrol gauge, and combined water thermometer and oil pressure gauges. There

As specially developed for the Sprite, the 948 c.c. B.M.C. engine has two S.U. carburettors and develops 43 b.h.p. (nett) at 5,000 r.p.m.

are small lamps to indicate dynamo discharge, head lamp main beams and signal flashers, the latter operated by a switch which is not self-cancelling.

The head lamp dipping switch is foot-operated, and among the listed extras are a tachometer, heating and demisting equipment, screen washer, tonneau cover and a front bumper (standard on export cars). When the heater is fitted, it feeds air to the occupants' legs through trap doors in each side of the central engine and transmission housing.

There is a choice of five bright colours for the Sprite— cherry red, white, blue, primrose and dark green, and a variety of contrasting trims to go with them. In each case, the hood is available only in black.

At £678 17s including tax, this new Austin-Healey is the cheapest four-cylinder sports car listed, which is a considerable achievement in view of its mechanical merit and standards of both finish and equipment. It is many years since the name of Austin was associated with a small sports car of this nature, and there is certainly a large market awaiting it.

SPECIFICATION

ENGINE

No. of cylinders	...	4 in line
Bore and stroke	...	62.9 × 76.2mm (2.48 × 3.0in)
Displacement	...	948 c.c. (57.87 cu in)
Valve position	...	o.h.v., pushrods
Compression ratio	...	8.3 to 1
Max. b.h.p. (gross)	...	48 at 5,000 r.p.m.
Max. b.h.p. (nett)	...	43 at 5,000 r.p.m.
Max b.m.e.p. (nett)		136 lb sq in at 3,300 r.p.m.
Max. torque (nett)	...	52 lb ft at 3,300 r.p.m.
Carburettor	...	2 S.U. H.1
Fuel pump	...	A.C. mechanical
Tank capacity	...	6 Imp. gal (27.3 litres)
Sump capacity	...	6⅞ pints (3.34 litres)
Oil filter	...	Tecalemit or Purolator (renewable element)
Cooling system	...	Pump, fan and thermostat
Battery	...	12 volt 43 amp hr

TRANSMISSION

Clutch	...	B. and B. 6¼in dia (hydraulic operation)
Gear box	...	Four speeds, synchromesh on 2nd, 3rd and top, central lever
Overall gear ratios	...	Top, 4.22; 3rd, 5.96; 2nd, 10.02; 1st, 15.31
Final drive	...	4.22 to 1

CHASSIS

Brakes	...	Lockheed hydraulic
Drum dia., shoe width		7in; 1¼in
Suspension: front	...	Independent coil springs and wishbones
rear	...	Quarter-elliptic springs and trailing links
Dampers	...	Armstrong lever-type hydraulic
Wheels	...	Pressed steel
Tyre size	...	5.20—13
Steering	...	Rack and pinion
Steering wheel	...	16in
Turns, lock to lock	...	2½

DIMENSIONS

Wheelbase	...	6ft 8in (203 cm)
Track: front	...	3ft 9¾in (116 cm)
rear	...	3ft 8¾in (114 cm)
Overall length	...	11ft 0⅜in without front bumper (337 cm)
		11ft 5¼in with front bumper (349 cm)
Overall width	...	4ft 5in (135 cm)
Overall height	...	4ft 1¾in (126 cm)
		3ft 8⅛in (112 cm), hood down
Ground clearance	...	5in at exhaust pipe (13 cm)
Turning circle: right	...	31ft 2½in (9.5 m)
left	...	32ft 1½in (9.8 m)
Kerb weight	...	1,328 lb (602 kg)

PERFORMANCE DATA

Top gear m.p.h. per 1,000 r.p.m.	...	15.4
Torque lb ft per cu in engine capacity	...	.89
Brakes surface area swept by linings	...	110 sq in

PRICES

Basic ... £455; Purchase tax ... £223 17s; Total ... £678 17s
Extras: Heater-demister, £20 16s 3d. Radio, £25. Front bumper, £6. Tonneau cover, £6. Tachometer, £4 10s.

Proof that the styling of the original Austin-Healey was good lies in this illustration of the current model, largely unaltered and still modern and attractive

Autocar ROAD TESTS

Austin-Healey 100-Six

THE British Motor Corporation continues to develop and improve the largest of its sports cars, without departing to any great extent from the basic design. The latest version of the Austin-Healey 100-Six has more power than the model last tested by this journal in November 1956. The consequent gain in performance, achieved without detracting from the exceptional flexibility and smoothness of the C series six-cylinder engine, has been brought about by a modified cylinder head with a separate light-alloy inlet manifold to which are fitted two semi-downdraught SU HD 6 carburettors.

Separate inlet ports are formed in the cylinder head, and the valve head sizes are increased slightly compared with those of the earlier units. The nett result of these top changes to the engine has been to increase the power output by 11 per cent. While the increased performance is more noticeable high in the speed range, the engine also pulls strongly and without temperament below 2,000 r.p.m. The aerodynamic lines of the coachwork together with the flexibility in top gear have made Austin-Healeys economical in terms of fuel consumption; the present version maintains that reputation.

Because the torque at low engine speeds is high, the driver is not much aware of the relatively low top r.p.m. limit by sports car standards. The red normal maximum line on the rev. counter is placed at only 4,800 r.p.m. and while the engine is smooth and free revving up to this limit, it is plain that it is not anxious to exceed about 5,200 at any time.

It is a car which adapts itself readily to the mood the driver may be in; if the need or inclination calls for " press on " methods, the Austin-Healey will respond in an extremely willing fashion, covering long distances in the shortest possible time without the crew feeling they have had to do a major part of the work. The Laycock-de Normanville overdrive, an optional extra, operates on third and top gears, and as overdrive top gives a little over 23 m.p.h. per 1,000 r.p.m., high speed cruising is a comparatively restful matter. An electrical switch linked to the throttle protects the transmission from snatch, by preventing downward changes from overdrive to direct drive on the overrun—that is, with a closed throttle.

At home and on Continental roads, the driver finds real benefit from the extra power developed as a result of the new cylinder head, and the increased acceleration is particularly appreciated on British roads. The car tested showed an improvement of 1.7sec from 0-60 m.p.h. and 6.5sec from 0-90 m.p.h., as compared with the earlier design.

The speedometer needle can be kept on the 100 m.p.h. mark for mile after mile; the o/d top gear consumption is then between 20 and 22 m.p.g. At the high speeds which are well within the car's performance, the fuel capacity of 12 gallons is barely adequate, and owners who use this car for long journeys may wish for more than four hours' safe cruising range.

First thing in the morning in warm weather the choke was needed only momentarily, and the car pulled away at once with very little hesitation. Premium (not super) petrol suits the engine, but there was pinking when inferior Continental premium was used. with the hard top in place, some fumes were apparent.

Here the Healey is in open form, with hood folded and the semi-rigid rear part of the tonneau cover in position

Austin-Healey
100-Six . . .

The C series engine is notable for its smoothness at all speeds. There is, however, a prominent exhaust note from the twin tail pipes in the upper half of the r.p.m. range when accelerating. Even so, it is a simple matter to drive through crowded streets without attracting unwelcome attention. The car will trickle along with the traffic without the need for constant gear changing. But, like all cars of its type, it is more at home when it can stretch its legs.

Excellent clutch operation with a light pedal load and a smooth take-up (free from slip even during our arduous standing start acceleration tests) helps gear changing. The position of the short, stiff gear change lever is a little unusual, as it faces the driver at an angle from the left side of the gear box cover. It requires a rather long but natural reach; there is no lost movement, and the driver is able to make quick, crisp changes. First gear is normally used for starting from rest. It was found advantageous in most circumstances to use the overdrive in conjunction with normal gear changes, especially as overdrive third, though close in ratio to top, is an excellent traffic gear.

The overdrive control switch is placed on the right side of the facia and can be reached easily and quickly. Reaction is immediate.

Acceleration is unexpectedly lively in third gear, from a speed as low as 30 m.p.h. After a short experience of the car, it was decided that a favourable technique is to change up into third at approximately 40 m.p.h. and next into overdrive third.

The gear ratios are well suited to the performance of the car and the characteristics of the engine; at no time does a driver feel in need of another ratio, nor bothered by a superfluous one. Full-throttle changes could be made without protest from the overdrive mechanism; the whole of the transmission system of the car tested was commendably quiet, and appeared to be fully capable of dealing with the extra power produced by the six-port cylinder head.

Suspension and road holding of all Austin-Healeys have been well fitted to their role of fast sports-touring cars. The springing is flexible enough to absorb shocks transmitted by the surfaces of minor roads, and only when the tyres are inflated to high-speed pressures is some firmness noticed;

this is apparent only at speeds below 50 m.p.h. The ride over rough, rutted surfaces is particularly good; shocks are heard more than felt. It was found that ease of steering was affected to a considerable degree by the tyre pressures, and the recommended 20 lb front and 23 lb rear for normal driving made the steering feel unduly heavy at slow speeds. An increase of 3 lb on these figures gave a noticeable improvement for everyday journeys. The steering becomes rather heavy towards full lock.

When travelling fast the 100-Six steers best if the wheel is held lightly. This is especially apparent on heavily cambered roads abroad. A firm grip becomes tiring, and the directional stability is not improved if the driver is tensed—the Austin-Healey is much better when given its head under these conditions.

There is light but sufficient self-centring action; on the whole the steering has no bias towards under- or over-steer. When the car is cornered fast, particularly on smooth, wet tarmac, the back will swing slightly. Tyre noise and body roll are very limited; but directional stability may be affected by a strong cross wind when travelling fast.

Driver comfort on a winding road would be improved if the seat backrest were a little more rigid, but the shape and angle of the backrests are good, and movement of the driver's arms is not interfered with.

An owner who was a little on the short side would undoubtedly have to modify the pedal positions, for with the seat set forward to enable him fully to depress the pedals, he is placed uncomfortably close to the steering wheel. The pedals are not set squarely below the steering wheel, but the driver soon gets used to the angled attitude. As with so many sports cars, the pedals are very close together. Some drivers would also modify pedal levels to permit heel-and-toeing—a great advantage in this class of car. A long-legged driver would wish for more support under the thighs from the rather shallow seat cushion.

In spite of these few limitations of the driving position, all-round visibility is good. The screen pillars are slender (there is no window frame, as such), a tall driver is seated

A plastic cover fits over the battery, which is secured in the right-hand corner of the luggage compartment; a master switch forms a valuable anti-theft device. The lid of the compartment is supported in the open position by a hinged strut

low enough to avoid any beetle-browed effect, and the large, curved Perspex window in the back of the moulded glass fibre hard-top provided ample vision for reversing or watching faster traffic coming up astern. Unexpectedly on a car of this price range, it is necessary to use a spanner to adjust the position of the passenger seat.

With a car such as the Austin-Healey, which at times can be travelling faster than it appears to be, it is more than ever necessary to have an adequate, fade-free braking system. Although much prominence has been given to the use of disc brakes for fast cars, the drum brakes as fitted proved entirely suitable. Pedal pressure for all normal check braking is light, and there is a good, responsive feel to the brake. The car can be driven fast on roads unfamiliar to the driver, as the system provides powerful four-square stopping power. In the course of 1,000 miles of testing, pedal travel increased considerably. The hand-brake lever is close to the driving seat but not uncomfortably so; it has an easy movement and the action is powerful.

The detachable hard-top has many advantages. It does not detract from the appearance of the car and does not turn the cockpit into a sound box; wind and road noise are negligible. The advantages of having available saloon car protection from the elements are many. In heavy rain the fitting is completely watertight, and only at slow speeds does the windscreen mist up when it is raining. Sliding Perspex side windows are supported in detachable light-alloy frames secured firmly to the doors. A light-coloured roof lining is fitted, and with the compartment closed up, there is a snug, cosy air about the interior. The ability quickly to remove the hard-top is appreciated.   It is secured to the top of each screen pillar by an over-centre clip, and a large hook tensioned by a wing nut is used to clamp down each side behind the door openings. Removal or replacement is a matter of only a few minutes. The only criticism one has of the hard-top as fitted to the Austin-Healey is its cost, which does appear to be rather high.

The normal hood and supports are supplied in addition, and are concealed behind the backrest of the rear compartment. Attachments of the framework for the hood are ingenious, but on the road test car the unfolding movements were very stiff and difficult to achieve at first. One of the two over-centre clips had to be reassembled before it could be used. It is necessary first to engage the rigid front frame of the hood with a lip attached to the top of the screen frame; the rear skirt of the hood is then secured by spring fasteners. The attachment of the fasteners caused some difficulty even in warm sunshine when the material was pliable; it is likely to be a lengthy job on a cold, wet day. Agreed, the alternative would be a less taut, less attractive hood.

With hood and detachable sidescreens in use, there is naturally more wind noise and flapping than with the hard-top, but certainly not to an exceptional degree. With hood alone, the front seat occupants are well protected by the fixed screen, and there is little buffeting; the same is true when the car is entirely open. No change in handling can be

detected open and with hard-top but, as is normally the case, the fitting of the hard-top increases the maximum speed by two or three m.p.h.

In addition to the hood a good tonneau cover, stiffened behind the seats, is provided. This covers the complete compartment, and is divided down the centre so that the passenger compartment only may be enclosed.

The interior of the body is particularly well finished, roomy and free from uncomfortable projections.   The shallow facia is covered with leathercloth, and a plated strip round the instrument panel enhances the appearance. Instruments are well placed, and easily read from the driving seat. No rheostat is fitted to the panel lighting, but it is not over-bright, and allows the instruments to be read at night without dazzle. The curved upper portion of the facia prevents reflections on the windscreen.

A built-in heater was fitted to the test car—this is an extra piece of equipment. In the enclosed space it provides a more than adequate amount of hot air, and demisting is effective; extra supplies of cold air can be introduced by opening vents placed above the foot wells. The driving mirror is well placed, and the self-parking screen wipers clean most of the screen area. A screen wash was fitted.

For a car which is likely to be used for long distance touring, luggage accommodation in the tail is disappointing. The spare wheel and battery occupy a large proportion of the available space, and as there is no particular provision for storing tools, these seem best kept in the shallow depression at the front of the locker. However, the car is primarily a two-seater, and so some extra luggage can be accommodated behind the front seats. The shape of the emergency seats, with their dividing hump, does place a limitation on the amount of baggage to be carried here.

The bonnet opening provides plenty of room for normal maintenance, and components are readily reached. The crankcase breather is vented via the valve cover to the rear carburettor air cleaner

As these occasional seats are suitable only for very small children (with the hard-top in position, no adult can be accommodated there) it would be preferable to eliminate the seats altogether and provide fuller luggage space. This the manufacturer intends to do.

Is is reasonably easy to get in and out of the car, as the doors open at right angles to the body. Only the left door is fitted with an exterior lock—useless anyhow, because the Perspex sliding windows cannot be locked.

Progress at night is helped by an ample beam from the head lamps and the high-frequency horns carry well.

Hitherto, Healey hard-tops have been obtainable only from independent suppliers. The provision of a removable hard-top enables the competition-minded owner to enter events in either the sports or *gran turismo* class—and the higher power provided by the latest engine increases the chances of success. Of the criticisms made above none is of a serious nature. More than ordinary attention has been given to comfort and alternative weather protections, with the result that fast motoring can be enjoyed in any climate —and by drivers of any age—without the necessity to affect "enthusiast" clothing. Equally important, this latest Healey offers its performance with no more than modest running costs.

AUSTIN·HEALEY 100·SIX

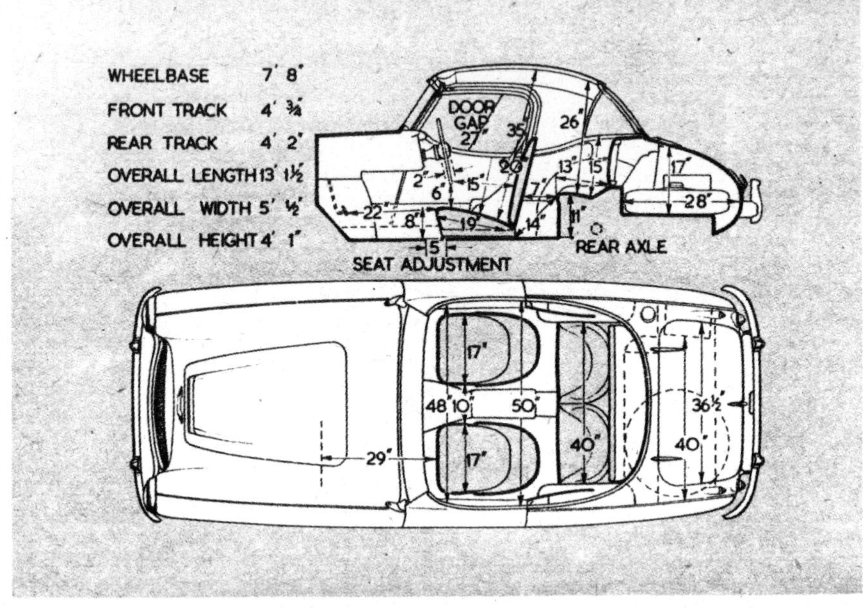

Measurements in these ¼in to 1ft scale body diagrams are taken with the driving seat in the central position of fore and aft adjustment and with the seat cushions uncompressed

— DATA —

PRICE (basic), with standard body, £817.
British purchase tax, £409 17s.
Total (in Great Britain), £1,226 17s.
Extras: Hard-top £90. Road Speed tyres £9.
Heater £23 5s. Overdrive £69 15s. Wire wheels, £37 10s.

ENGINE: Capacity: 2,639 c.c. (161.1 cu in).
Number of cylinders: 6.
Bore and stroke: 79.4 × 89 mm (3.125 × 3.5in).
Valve gear: overhead, pushrods and rockers.
Compression ratio: 8.25 to 1.
B.H.P.: 117 (gross) at 4,750 r.p.m. (B.H.P. per ton laden 107.5).
Torque: 149lb ft at 3,000 r.p.m.
M.P.H. per 1,000 r.p.m. on top gear, 18.0.
M.P.H. per 1,000 r.p.m. on o/d top, 23.28.

WEIGHT (with 5 gal fuel), 21¾ cwt (2,436 lb).
Weight distribution (per cent): F, 49; R, 51.
Laden as tested: 24½ cwt (2,761 lb).
Lb per c.c. (laden): 1.04.

BRAKES: Type: F, two-leading shoe; R, leading and trailing.
Method of operation: hydraulic.
Drum dimensions: F, 11in diameter; 2¼in wide. R, 11in diameter; 2¼in wide.
Lining area: F, 94 sq in. R, 94 sq in (172.8 sq in per ton laden).

TYRES: 5.90—15in.
Pressures (lb sq in): F, 20; R, 23 (normal).
F, 26; R, 29 (for fast driving).

TANK CAPACITY: 12 Imperial gallons.
Oil sump, 12 pints.
Cooling system, 20 pints.

TURNING CIRCLE: 35ft (L and R).
Steering wheel turns (lock to lock): 2¾.

DIMENSIONS: Wheelbase: 7ft 8in.
Track: F, 4ft 0¾in; R, 4ft 2in.
Length (overall): 13ft 1½in.
Height: 4ft 1in.
Width: 5ft 0½in.
Ground clearance: 5½in.
Frontal area: 16½ sq ft (approximately).

ELECTRICAL SYSTEM: 12-volt; 51 ampère-hour battery.
Head lights: Double dip; 42-36 watt bulbs.

SUSPENSION: Front, independent, coil springs and wishbones, anti-roll bar. Rear, live axle, half-elliptic leaf springs, Panhard rod.

PERFORMANCE

ACCELERATION:

Speed Range, Gear Ratios and Time in sec.

M.P.H.	3.18 to 1*	4.1 to 1	4.24 to 1*	5.46 to 1	7.85 to 1	12.6 to 1
10—30				5.5	4.0	3.0
20—40	10.3	7.5	7.1	5.3	3.8	—
30—50	10.5	7.4	7.1	5.4	—	—
40—60	10.7	7.6	7.3	5.9	—	—
50—70	10.8	7.9	7.7	6.6	—	—
60—80	13.2	9.1	8.9	—	—	—
70—90	16.2	11.4	11.0	—	—	—
80—100	20.1	18.0	—	—	—	—

*Overdrive.

From rest through gears to:

M.P.H.	sec.
30	3.6
50	8.2
60	11.2
70	14.8
80	20.1
90	25.8
100	37.7

Standing quarter mile, 18.1 sec.

SPEEDS ON GEARS:

Gear	M.P.H. (normal and max.)	K.P.H. (normal and max.)
O/D top (mean)	110.8	177.3
(best)	111.0	177.6
Top (mean)	100.0	160
(best)	100.0	160
O/D 3rd	80—93	128—159
3rd	60—70	96—112
2nd	32—48	51—77
1st	20—30	32—48

TRACTIVE EFFORT:

	Pull (lb per ton)	Equivalent Gradient
Top	300	1 in 7.4
Third	390	1 in 5.7
Second	555	1 in 3.9

BRAKES (at 30 m.p.h. in neutral):

Efficiency	Pedal Pressure (lb)
39 per cent	25
61 per cent	50
75 per cent	75
86 per cent	120

FUEL CONSUMPTION:
21.2 m.p.g. overall for 1,007 miles (13.6 litres per 100 km).
Approximate normal range 18—26 m.p.g. (15.5—11.0 litres per 100 km).
Fuel, Premium grade.

WEATHER: Dry, sunny, slight cross breeze. Air temperature 65-70 deg F.
Acceleration figures are the means of several runs in opposite directions.
Tractive effort and resistance obtained by Tapley meter.
Model described in *The Autocar* of 29 November 1957.

SPEEDOMETER CORRECTION: M.P.H.

Car speedometer	10	20	30	40	50	60	70	80	90	100	110	118
True speed	12.5	21	30	40	50	60	70	80	90	98	105	110

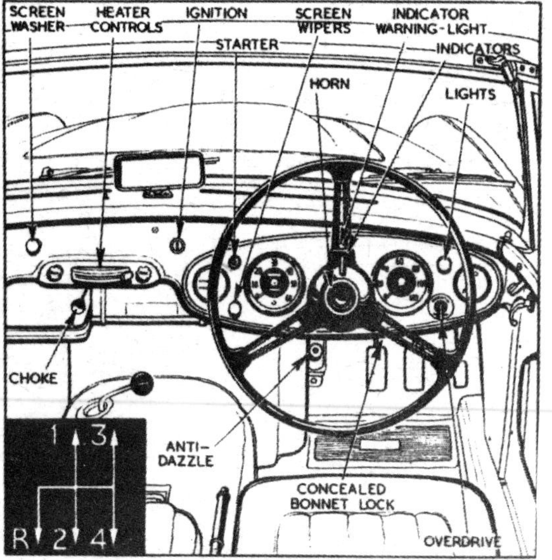

The front bumper and overriders are extras on the economically priced Sprite. A jacking point is provided at the foot of the scuttle on each side

Autocar ROAD TESTS

Austin-Healey Sprite

THE days-old advent of the Austin-Healey Sprite is the more welcome because, during recent years, there has been no quantity-produced, true sports model of approximately 1-litre capacity. The advantages of the Sprite's conception are several; for while acceleration and speed at first glance seem modest, the character, behaviour, economy of operation and, not least, the low initial cost combine to make a very rewarding total.

As used in the Sprite, the A series B.M.C. engine has twin S.U. carburettors and extra strong valve springs, and a number of modifications have been made to valves and bearings to ensure that the unit will stand the 50 b.h.p. gross output claimed. With a lower weight (at just over 13 cwt ready for the road) and smaller frontal area than any other B.M.C. model using the A series engine, and with a smooth under-floor surface, the Sprite proves to be a nippy performer for its engine size. The standing quarter-mile figure of 21.7sec, for example, is less than that of many 1½-litre family cars and, indeed, bettered by only 0.5sec even by the M.G. Magnette stablemate. Similarly the mean maximum speed of 80 m.p.h. will hold off the challenges of very many larger-engined saloons. The performance alone of the Sprite shows that the model is much more than a runabout.

As the car is specifically intended to provide enjoyable, sporting motoring at low cost, the financial aspects of the model are particularly important. The basic price of £455, making a home market total with purchase tax of £668 17s, is a good start. To complement this is a minimum m.p.g. figure of 33, with more than 40 m.p.g. readily obtainable when the car is driven in more leisurely fashion. In addition to the choice of engine, wide use has been made of B.M.C. components with resultant economy not only in initial cost but in the price of service and repairs.

The Sprite is at its most satisfying on winding roads, on which its exceptionally good roadholding can be appreciated to the full. With but 2¼ turns of the wheel from lock to lock, the Morris Minor type of rack and pinion steering is very precise; at first it feels almost over-sensitive, any trace of heavy-handedness resulting sometimes in the car weaving slightly. But the driver needs to be no more than reasonably sensitive himself to acquire the right touch; this accomplished, the way in which the Sprite goes round corners is a delight—a small movement of the wheel gives sufficient, instant response, and a precise line is held right through the bend. Unexpected bumps do not catch car or driver by surprise, always provided that he does not tighten his grip on the wheel. On wet roads the car remains predictable and safe. The structure as a whole is extremely rigid; even on rough surfaces there is, for example, no trace of scuttle shake.

A clear indication of the superiority of the Sprite in this respect over most family cars—and several sports cars, too —is provided when the little car is on the tail of one of them on a twisty road. During the test this occurred several times, and even while the car ahead was being driven near the limit of its adhesion, the Sprite remained as unruffled as a sphinx. The ride is firm to the point of being a little harsh, in feel not unlike that of sports cars of the classic era. This does not adversely affect road-holding, and the level ride enables long journeys to be completed with a

Luggage accommodation is within the one-piece rear section. Winking indicators are mounted beneath the tail-stop-lamp assemblies

Austin-Healey Sprite . . .

With hood up and sidescreens in place the car remains pleasantly proportioned. All-round visibility is satisfactory

minimum of fatigue. The bucket seats are well shaped, except that some extra support for the lower part of the back would effect an improvement, as also would greater rigidity in the backrests.

The 948 c.c. engine revs easily up to its 6,000 r.p.m. maximum; attainment of this high engine speed is owed in part to the extra strong valve springs used in this tuned version. However, it is not well served by the gear ratios. First is the natural choice for starting from rest, and while second can be used for the same purpose, this ratio would be better if changed to give higher gearing. The maximum speeds on the three indirects are 23, 37 and 63 m.p.h. The gap between the second and third gear maxima is therefore 26, while between first and second it is only 14. A slightly higher first and adoption of an appreciably higher second would be welcome, although it is realised that the present choice, which results from the use of standard B.M.C. parts, helps to keep down the price. Third and top gears serve their purpose well, and the extra power has not resulted in lack of flexibility.

A well-placed, stubby central lever permits very fast shifts of ratio to be made. The synchromesh on the upper three ratios copes amply with the potential speed of the change, and the performance of the box as a whole adds to the fun of driving this little car. A stronger safety spring against reverse would make a small improvement. On the car tested the change across the narrow gate from second to third could be affected by catching the opening to the reverse slot; and when changing from third to top as quickly as possible it was necessary to avoid using much pressure to hold the lever to the right, for fear of touching reverse itself. These criticisms appear more serious on paper than they proved to be in practice; they did not slow accurately executed changes. Clutch take-up is just right; the unit will transmit power promptly for fast getaways from rest, while being amply smooth to meet the needs of town driving. To obtain lively performance the gear box needs to be used freely, and the revs kept high. For fast long-distance cruising the Sprite's engine naturally is noticeably busy.

The transmission was quiet, with little sound from the gear box on any ratio, and a silent axle. The sports engine is naturally the major factor in noise build-up, but the volume of sound was considerably less than that of many other sports cars. The Sprite can be driven very quietly in built-up areas, and at speed on the open road the rather pleasant exhaust note is not excessively loud.

During the test the exhaust down pipe sheared just below the point at which it is clipped to the manifold. The break was in such a position that a replacement was needed, made up of the complete pipe and silencer assembly. Examination suggested that the silencer and pipe mountings could be modified to reduce the strain at the manifold union.

High maximum r.p.m., regularly used, are frequently synonymous with heavy oil consumption. Not so the Sprite tested; at the end of its period with *The Autocar* the dipstick reading showed that the level was down to the extent of less than half a pint.

With the hood up there is an appreciable amount of wind roar at relatively high speeds; when the hood is down there is less noise, but a fair amount of buffeting by the back draught which results from the size and shape of the generously proportioned screen. The hood and sidescreens fit quite well in their almost new condition, and they proved more effective than their appearance might suggest. In very heavy rain, amounting on occasion to a torrential downpour, very little moisture got past the hood and screen joints,

Engine accessibility is slightly restricted by the modest opening of the bonnet assembly. In tuned form the A series B.M.C. engine has twin S.U. carburettors, but the compression ratio is unchanged. The front suspension is by coil springs and wishbones

Ease of entry and exit, even with the hood in place, is good for a small sports car.   The dials for rev counter and speedometer are directly in front of the driver.   There is a grab handle for the passenger, and a deep pocket in each door

Austin-Healey Sprite . . .

and none at the top of the screen, on which the hood fits snugly.

High quality p.v.c. is used for the hood, which incorporates a large area of clear plastic at the rear, divided into three sections. Erection and dismantling are unusually quick and easy for this type of superstructure, and the design of the hood irons, and their positive location when in use or stowed away, are most ingenious. With the hood up, the strip of p.v.c. under the main section of the rear window interferes with visibility through the mirror, sharply cutting down the range.

The brakes stood up well to fast driving; maximum retardation, checked from 30 m.p.h., proved to be 0.86g, and only the exceptional severity of repeated test applications from high speed caused any appreciable loss of efficiency. The brakes stopped the car four-square, and the pull-up hand brake lever, conveniently placed between the seats, was absolutely positive.

In the design of the cockpit the needs of driver and passenger have been well met. The pedals, gear lever and steering wheel are satisfactorily placed in relation to the driving seat, although some drivers would prefer to be a little farther from the wheel. Through the wheel can be seen the rev counter and speedometer, the latter having a trip as well as total mileage recorder. Between these dials is the tell-tale light for the non-cancelling turn indicators. There are gauges for oil pressure, water temperature and fuel level. With the exception of the limit placed on rearward vision by the hood, all-round visibility is good when the car is closed or open. The Sprite is easy to place on the road, but a slightly higher seating position would improve the driver's vision of the far front wing. The wipers cover an adequate area of the screen, and work efficiently.

Luggage accommodation is unusually arranged, the compartment being reached from within after the backrests of the seats have been folded down. Its shortcomings are accounted for by the competitive price, and the extra rigidity provided by the one-piece, non-opening rear end. Stowage and removal of luggage and the spare wheel are not ideally simple, and oddments, once let loose in the cavity, are difficult to retrieve. However, with the use of soft bags the total volume of luggage which can be carried is greater than one would expect in a sports car of this size. There is a space between the seats and the luggage compartment proper which can take casual accoutrements, and even a young child for short journeys (owing not so much to the

shape as to the childish liking for wriggling into unpromising crannies).

Entry and exit are at least up to average sports car standards, although when the hood is up the technique calls for sitting down first, then swinging in the legs. Opening the doors from the outside when the sidescreens are in place is not easy, particularly if the entrant has only one hand free. This is partly because the door handles, which are mounted internally, are rather low and have to be pushed down. The passenger has a grab handle on the facia. Sufficient head room is provided when the hood is up, and elbow room is ample. The upper edges of the doors are horizontal and high in relation to the seating position; this makes hand signalling a little more clumsy than in most sports cars.

Mounting of the head lamps above the bonnet line, dictated partly by the minimum height regulations in the U.S.A., detracts from the symmetry of the coachwork, but the extra height is welcome at night. The range is adequate on main beam and satisfactory on dip. The horn does no more than fulfil legal obligations.

For access to the engine the whole bonnet assembly, complete with lamps, swings up on to two positive supports which are engaged automatically; a third support can be engaged manually for additional safety. The lock and safety catch are not easy to reach, and lifting the heavy assembly would be made less difficult if some sort of hand hold were

The luggage space is reached by folding down the backrests of the seats.   The mounting of the hood irons is ingenious: the higher slots take the stems when the hood is to be erected

Austin-Healey Sprite . . .

provided. Under the bonnet is further panelling to protect the engine from road dirt; the sections running over the road wheels make useful platforms for tools and small parts. Accessibility for routine checks and adjustments is affected by the limited bonnet opening.

A fully exposed fuel tank filler on the rear decking, near one of the tail lamps, takes the full flow from a garage pump without blowing back. The 6-gallon capacity gives a cruising range comfortably in excess of 200 miles, with a minimum total range of little less when the car is driven really hard.

There is an unusually long list of optionally extra items, some of which were fitted to the car tested. They include such components as front bumper and overriders, rev counter, screenwashers, locking petrol filler cap, and tonneau cover.

The little Austin-Healey Sprite has the sort of charm that grows with acquaintance. It exhibits so many pleasant characteristics on the road, does much more—and does it better—than the specification suggests, and shows every indication of providing many miles of lively motoring at very low operating cost.

AUSTIN-HEALEY SPRITE

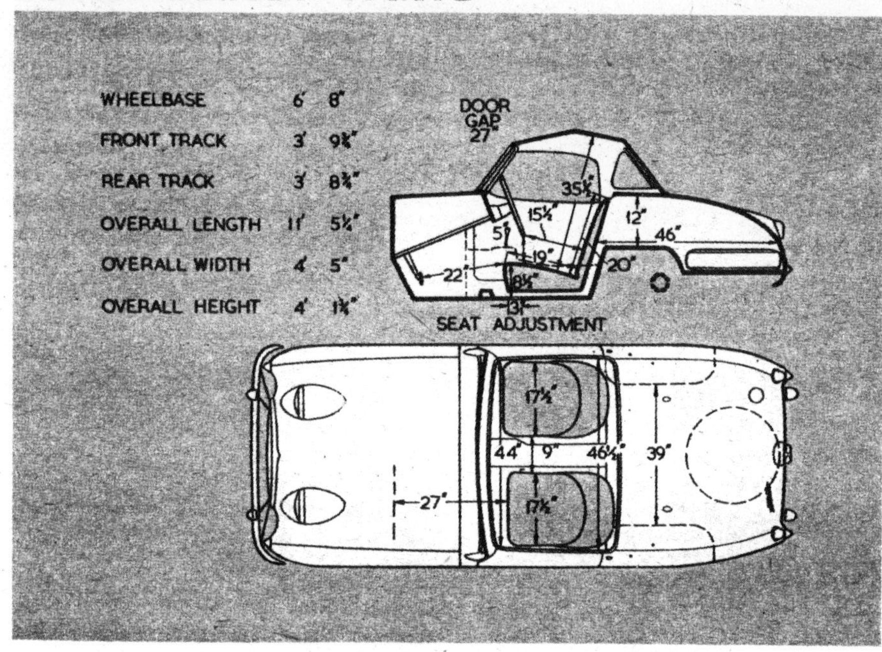

Scale ⅛in to 1ft. Driving seat in central position. Cushions uncompressed.

—— DATA ——

PRICE (basic), with two-seater body, £445.
British purchase tax, £223 17s.
Total (in Great Britain), £668 17s.

Extras:	Basic			U.K. tax		
	£	s	d	£	s	d
Heater and demister ..	13	17	6	6	18	9
Radio	16	13	4	8	6	8
Rev. counter	3	0	0	1	10	0
Front bumper and over-riders	4	0	0	2	0	0
Windscreen washer ..	1	10	0		15	0
Six-ply tyres ..	4	15	0	2	7	6
Laminated windscreen	2	15	0	1	7	6
Fresh air unit	4	0	0	2	0	0
Tonneau cover ..	4	0	0	2	0	0

ENGINE: Capacity: 948 c.c. (57.8 cu in).
Number of cylinders: 4.
Bore and stroke: 62.9×76.2 mm (2.5×3.0in).
Valve gear: o.h.v., pushrods.
Compression ratio: 8.3 to 1.
B.H.P. 45 (nett), 50 (gross) at 5,500 r.p.m.
(B.H.P. per ton laden 62.2 gross).
Torque: 52 lb ft at 3,000 r.p.m.
M.P.H. per 1,000 r.p.m. on top gear, 15.4

WEIGHT: (with 5 gals fuel), 13¼ cwt (1,463lb).
Weight distribution (per cent): F, 54; R, 46.
Laden as tested: 16⅛ cwt (1,799 lb).
Lb per c.c. (laden): 1.9.

BRAKES: Type: Lockheed.
Method of operation: hydraulic.
Drum dimensions: F, 7in diameter; 1⅛in wide. R, 7in diameter; 1⅛in wide.
Lining area: F, 30.7 sq in. R, 30.7 sq in (76.6 sq in per ton laden).

TYRES: 5.20 × 13in.
Pressures (lb sq in): F, 18; R, 20 (normal).

TANK CAPACITY: 6 Imperial gallons.
Oil sump, 6 pints.
Cooling system, 10 pints.

STEERING: turning circle:
Between kerbs 31ft 1⅛in.
Between walls 32ft 5in.
Turns of steering wheel from lock to lock 2¼.

DIMENSIONS: Wheelbase: 6ft. 8in.
Track: F, 3ft 9¾in; R, 3ft 8¾in.
Length (overall): 11ft 5¼in.
Height: 4ft 1¾in.
Width: 4ft 5in.
Ground clearance: 5in.
Frontal area: 13.3 sq ft (approximately).

ELECTRICAL SYSTEM: 12-volt; 43 ampère-hour battery.
Head lights: Double dip; 42-36 watt bulbs.

SUSPENSION: Front, independent, coil springs and wishbones. Rear, quarter elliptic, anti-roll bar.

—— PERFORMANCE ——

ACCELERATION:
Speed Range, Gear Ratios and Time in sec.

M.P.H.	4.22 to 1	5.96 to 1	10.02 to 1	15.31 to 1
10—30..	—	8.6	4.9	—
20—40..	12.7	8.3	—	—
30—50..	12.3	9.2	—	—
40—60..	17.2	12.7	—	—

From rest through gears to:

M.P.H.	sec.
30	5.3
50	13.7
60	20.9
70	35.6

Standing quarter mile, 21.7 sec.

MAXIMUM SPEEDS ON GEARS:

Gear			M.P.H.	K.P.H.
Top	(mean)		80	128.7
	(best)		81	130.4
3rd	.. ..		63	101.4
2nd	.. ..		37	59.5
1st	.. ..		23	37.0

TRACTIVE EFFORT:

	Pull (lb per ton)	Equivalent Gradient
Top	187	11.8
Third	290	7.6
Second.. ..	425	5.1

BRAKES (at 30 m.p.h. in neutral):

Pedal load in lb	Retardation	Equivalent stopping distance in ft
25	0.30g	101
50	0.71g	42.5
75	0.86g	35.1

FUEL CONSUMPTION:
M.P.G. at steady speeds

M.P.H.	Top
30	54.0
40	54.0
50	42.0
60	35.5
70	30.0

34 m.p.g. overall for 1,284 miles (8.3 litres per 100 km).

Approximate normal range 33–34 m.p.g. (8.6–6.4 litres per 100 km).

TEST CONDITIONS: Weather: dry, stiff breeze, air temperature 70 deg. F.
Road surface, dry tarmacadam. Fuel, premium grade.
Acceleration figures are the means of several runs in opposite directions.
Tractive effort obtained by Tapley meter.
Model described in *The Autocar* of 23 May 1958.

SPEEDOMETER CORRECTION: M.P.H.

Car speedometer:	10	20	30	40	50	60	70	80	85
True speed:	10	20	28	38	47	56	66	74	79

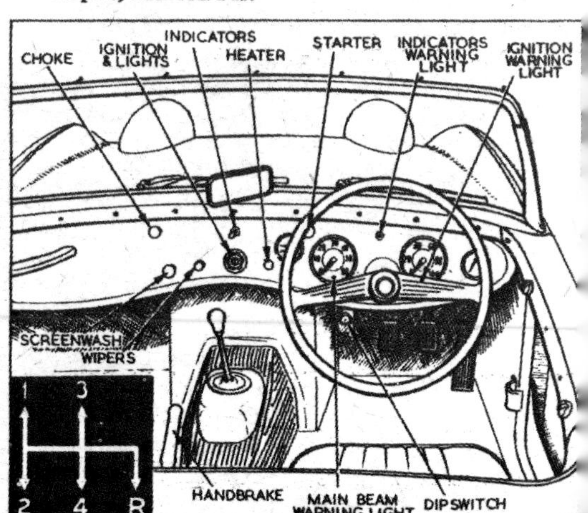

The Austin-Healey 100, first of the 'big Healeys', was so named because it could reach speeds in excess of 100 m.p.h. (the production cars had a top speed of 102 m.p.h.).

FOP 9

The Austin-Healey 3000 Mark III was the fastest of
the production 'big Healeys' with a top speed of
123 m.p.h.

Used Cars on the Road

1952 HEALEY ABBOTT CONVERTIBLE

Basic price new	£1,670	0 0
Total price new	£2,599	0 0
Price secondhand	£545	0 0
Acceleration (see text)		
Standing quarter mile		20.9
Petrol consumption		20-26 m.p.g.
Oil consumption		2,000 m.p.g.
Mileometer reading		10,747
Date first registered		March, 1952

Provided for test by Swanmore Garage, Ltd., 1176-1180, Christchurch Road, Boscombe, Bournemouth. Telephone: Southbourne 43344-5.

With its new fawn hood and maroon paintwork, the external appearance of the Healey is both smart and attractive. Doors and the hood are a good fit, and there are few draughts

FOR some motorists—usually enthusiasts—the reason for buying a car from the second-hand market is not necessarily one of cost, so much as to obtain a specialist, individual car, of which production has run out. Such a car is this Healey, powered by the four-cylinder 2½-litre Riley engine, and featuring a neat convertible body by Abbott. As a used car it still has—at a price—a great deal to offer, and continues to be an attractive vehicle for which there is a keen following. Unfortunately, not all of the salient characteristics of the model are still to be discerned in this example, though the car's body condition reveals very little deterioration.

A complete respray in maroon has just been carried out, and apart from one or two small dents in the aluminium panelling the bodywork is excellent. Mild rust and scratching mars the bumpers, but other parts of the chromium are in good condition, and the general effect of the exterior is impressive. This is partly owed to the fitting of a new hood of beige p.v.c. material which, incidentally, is well sealed, and is so easy to raise or lower that it is scarcely necessary to get out of the car to do so.

In both front and rear compartments the carpets are fairly new, and there is evidence that the leather of the seats and door trim has been treated with one of the proprietary dressings. Again the general effect, also in maroon, is extremely good; and the additional credit of clean and unmarked wood on the facia and window surrounds adds up to a commendably good all-round appearance for a six-year-old car. Excessive sag of the driving seat, such that drivers of average height need to sit on a cushion to see out of the car, is the only detracting feature.

It was typical of the efficient Riley power unit—with its side camshafts, short pushrods and hemispherical combustion chambers—that the engine always started first time, the choke was never needed during the mild weather of the test, and that there was no tendency to stall during the warming-up period. From little more than tickover to well above 4,000 r.p.m. it pulls strongly and gives the car a fair turn of speed. Unfortunately the speedometer has stuck at just over 100 m.p.h., and now starts its readings from there, so it was not possible to carry out the usual acceleration tests which in the normal way (on used car tests) are measured against the car's speedometer after correction. Nevertheless, 3,400 r.p.m. in top gear (equivalent to 70 m.p.h.) may be reached quickly, and although the maximum was not investigated, the Healey's speed potential should extend to a true 100 m.p.h. The time taken for the standing quarter mile was within two seconds of that for the model when tested new.

Pulling hard, the engine causes a fair amount of vibration, but the level of mechanical noise is low even at high revs. As a result of leakage from the silencer there is more exhaust noise than there should be. A slight gear whine is audible in bottom, though the other ratios are quiet. The central change is pleasant to use, and the ratios of the gear box—also by Riley—are well chosen for optimum performance. The synchromesh is still effective on the three upper ratios.

Two respects in which the car's behaviour is below par are the steering, which has become heavy and lacks precision, and the brakes, which require very heavy pressures and do not have the power necessary to match the available performance. The hand brake has scarcely any effect at all.

Deficiencies in the steering control are compensated to some extent by very good directional stability and the reassuring behaviour of the car in fast cornering. The suspension is very firm, and this gives rise to many squeaks and rattles from the coachbuilt body on rough surfaces. There are coil springs and trailing links all round, with a solid axle at the rear; the dampers are effective still, and there is no pitching or wheel bounce.

There is no clue to the total mileage which the car has covered. All that can be said is that it must, of course, be considerably higher than the figure recorded above.

A windscreen washer, of which the jets need tightening and adjusting, two wing mirrors, an effective but noisy recirculatory heater, and a Lucas " flamethrower " spot lamp are the accessories on the Healey. This last item is out of action, and when the car was received for test one rear lamp was not working, and the head lamps were in need of adjustment. The right trafficator is broken and the hand throttle is not working.

All of the tyres are well worn, but it is understood that two new ones are to be provided before sale. A jack and wheelbrace comprise the toolkit, and there is a starting handle.

In a sporting car of this sort, most of the effects of a limited degree of wear can be tolerated without hardship, particularly where only noise is concerned. Lack of precision in the controls of the car, however, is a different problem, and attention to the brakes and steering is essential if the high speed ability of the Healey is to be enjoyed. Most owners would also need to re-upholster the driving seat and raise it an inch or two.

At the beginning of this report it was mentioned that the car has a lot to offer at a certain price. The figure quoted—£545—certainly seems high for this sort of vehicle. But it is only fair to point out that in relation to the cost when the car was new this represents an extremely favourable rate of depreciation—over £300 a year.

At some time there has been a radio in the facia above the steering column, but this has now been removed, and the hole is covered by painted cardboard. Among the minor controls are a switch for the 1½-gallon petrol reserve, a hand throttle (not functioning), and an ignition retard knob

1960 MODELS

Austin Healey 3000 with 2.9-litre Engine

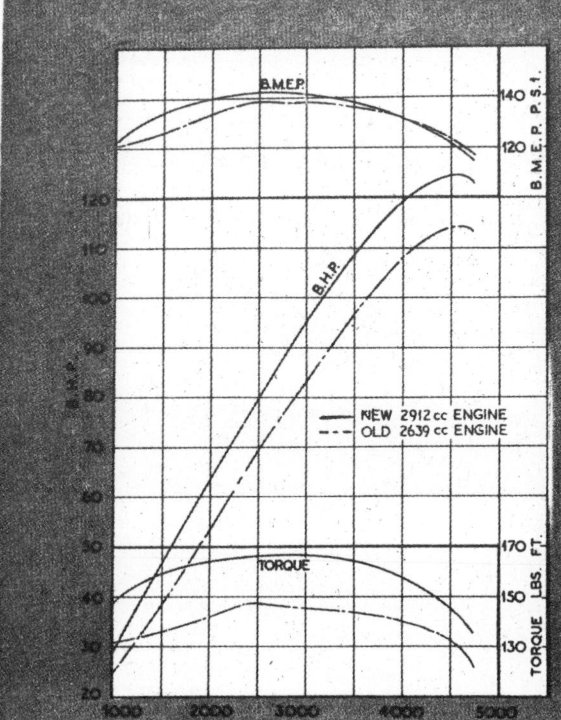

Net performance curves for the new engine compared with those for the previous one

DESIGNED by Donald Healey, the larger Austin Healey sports car has enjoyed continuous success since its introduction in 1952. First models were fitted with a four-cylinder, 2.6-litre Austin engine; four years later, the B.M.C. C-series six-cylinder unit was substituted, the car then being designated the 100-Six.

Towards the end of 1957 a new cylinder head, having separate ports and fed by a separate, light-alloy inlet manifold was introduced, and the improved gas flow increased power output from 102 b.h.p. at 4,600 r.p.m. to 117 b.h.p. at 4,750 r.p.m. The C-series B.M.C. engine has now been increased in capacity from 2,639 to 2,912 c.c. by enlarging the bores, and the net power output goes up to 124 b.h.p. at 4,600 r.p.m. This increase in engine capacity will be welcomed by competition-minded owners since the make will now be able to compete on more favourable terms in the international class D for cars having an engine swept volume up to 3,000 c.c.

A new casting has been designed for the combined cylinder block and crankcase; the cylinder bores have been increased from 79.4 to 83.36 mm, while the crankshaft stroke remains unchanged at 89 mm. To accommodate this increase in bore size the coolant passages between numbers 1 and 2, 3 and 4 and 5 and 6 cylinders are siamesed. At the same time the crankcase has been stiffened at the flywheel end by the addition of external webs. Flat-topped pistons are fitted, and the compression ratio is raised from 8.5 to 1 to 9.0 to 1.

In addition to these changes, the C-series engines have been improved in detail since our last description, published on 29 November, 1957. Among modifications which have occurred at intervals since that date have been alterations to the crankshaft damper, elimination of a reduced diameter section of the inlet valve stems, and the use of a gear-type oil pump in place of the previous rotor-type.

Main differences between the engine as used in the Austin Healey 3000 and those for other six-cylinder B.M.C. models are the six-port cylinder head, used in conjunction with separate inlet manifold, and semi-downdraught HD6 S.U. carburettors.

A thermostatically controlled auxiliary carburettor for cold starting is fitted; polythene hose is used for sections of the fuel pipe line, and an S.U. electric pump feeds the carburettors from a 12-gallon tank.

To cope with the extra torque from the new engine, stronger transmission gears are fitted, as well as a new 10in diameter single-plate Borg and Beck clutch which has a friction area of 78 sq in, compared with 66 sq in of the previous 9in-diameter unit.

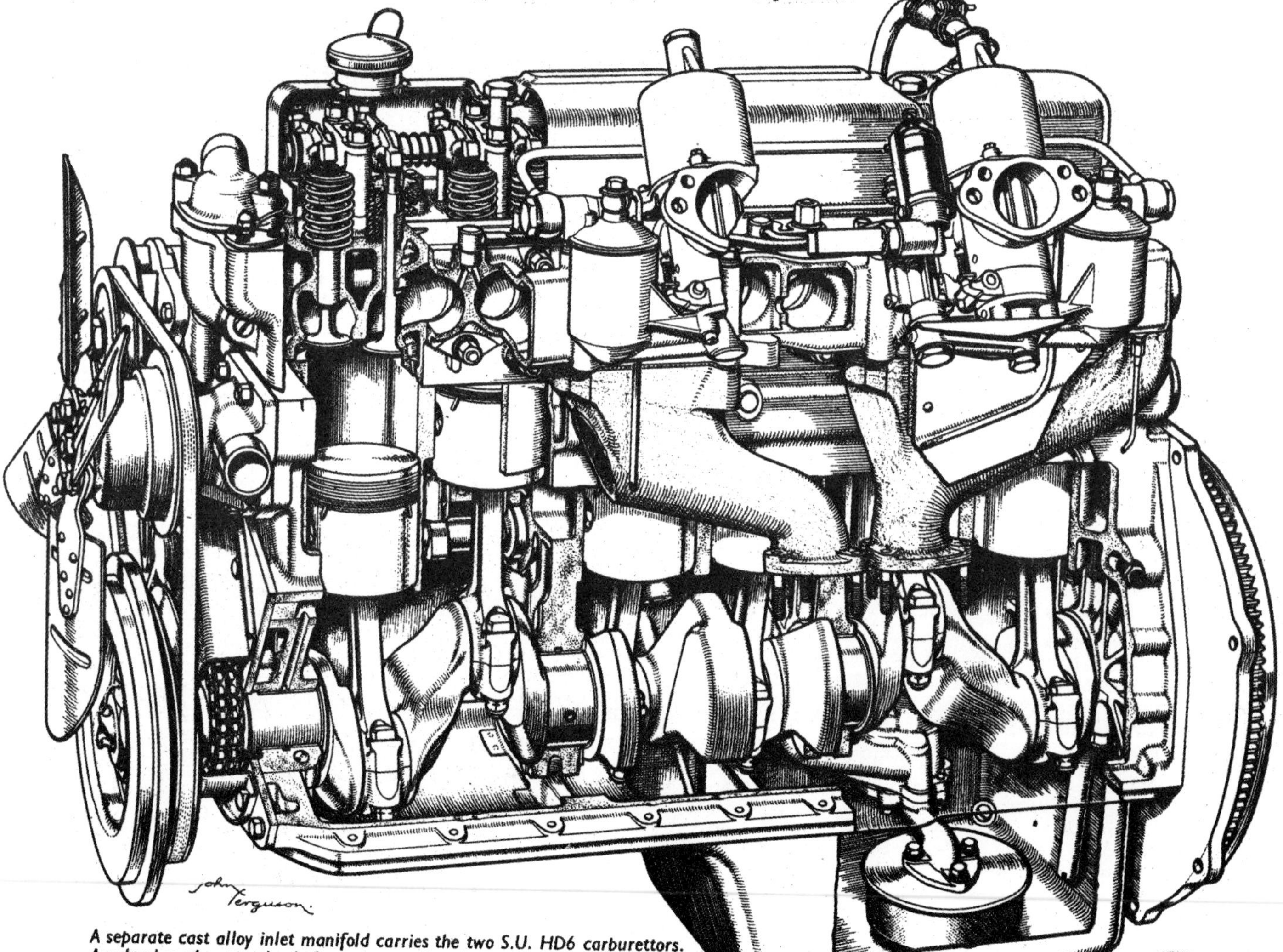

A separate cast alloy inlet manifold carries the two S.U. HD6 carburettors. A nylon breather pipe leads from the top of each float chamber, and a small diameter metal pipe is attached to each end of the manifold to carry away any excess fuel. Twin exhaust manifolds lead into a single silencer

The latest Austin-Healey can be recognized by the type number on the radiator grille and a glimpse of the disc brakes through the wheel spokes

IN general appearance the larger Austin-Healey has changed but little, since its successful Earls Court debut in 1952. Most of the changes made have been mechanical, and particularly in respect of the power unit. Three years ago the original 2.6-litre four-cylinder engine was replaced by a six-cylinder, and this has now been developed to its present size of 2.9 litres. Girling brakes again deal successfully with the higher speed capabilities of the latest model, and now 11in diameter discs at the front enable faster average speeds to be maintained without the bogey of brake fade to worry the driver.

These cars always have had a capacity for covering long distances in an effortlesss manner. Improved acceleration, particularly above 70 m.p.h., and appreciable increases in maximum speeds have resulted from the use of the larger engine. Compared with the last Road Test of a six-cylinder Austin-Healey which was fitted with a 4.1 to 1 axle ratio—than of the 3000 is 3.9 to 1—there is a cut of 4.9sec in the time from 0 to 100 m.p.h. Acceleration in the gears pays more generous dividends from the 50-70 m.p.h. range and upwards; over that range, in overdrive third, top and overdrive top, there are reductions of 0.7, 0.6 and 1.3sec on the last model's times. As the engine speed rises the times are cut further, and in the same gears between 70-90 m.p.h. the times come down by 1.1, 1.0 and 3.2sec. In the 80-100 m.p.h. range in top gear and overdrive top improvements of 4.1 and 3.4sec are recorded.

A noteworthy achievement is the gain in maximum speeds. In overdrive top there is an increase of 5 m.p.h. to 116 m.p.h., while in normal top the speed has gone up from 100 m.p.h., recorded by the 100-Six in May 1958, to no less than 110 m.p.h. for the new 3000 model. These figures are a good indication that the 2.9-litre engine is well able to deal with the extra weight and higher final drive gearing of the latest Austin-Healey.

None of the low-speed characteristics of the engine has been lost, and it pulls well on a light throttle; in town traffic the car can be driven quite comfortably in overdrive third and top gears, when low engine speeds are accompanied by an unobtrusive exhaust note. Most starts from rest can be made in second gear, even when fully loaded, and first is required only on gradients to get the car rolling.

Well-mannered as the car is when hemmed in by brick and concrete canyons, it makes a driver impatient to be outside city limits where the full performance can be savoured. Cruising speeds are entirely dependent upon road conditions, and on a Continental motorway 100 m.p.h. can be main-

tained without any mechanical distress. If time is a factor on a cross-country route, the engine responds willingly to every demand from the driver and it can be taken up to the normal limit mark for engine speed cf 5,200 r.p.m. time after time without protest. Above 3,900 r.p.m. there is a fair amount of intake roar and fan noise.

The new engine has a compression ratio of 9.03 to 1, compared with the previous 8.25 to 1, and it does not take kindly to the premium grade petrol available on the Continent. Pinking when pulling at low engine speed, and excessive running on when the engine was switched off were evident during the testing abroad. The engine operated satisfactorily on British premium fuel, although care was needed to avoid pinking when pulling hard in top gear; many owners will prefer to use super premium grade. The fuel tank holds only 12 gallons and so refuelling stops are fairly frequent.

One of the optional extras fitted to the test car was a Laycock-de Normanville overdrive operating on third and top gears. This works with the efficiency and silence one has come to expect of the unit, and it is a valuable adjunct to the normal transmission. Its use keeps engine speed down, not only assisting economical fuel consumpiion but minimizing use of a revolution range where the exhaust note may become tiring to the occupants of the car. A control switch is placed on the right of the facia where it is quickly reached. Changes into and out of overdrive are snatch-free and immediate, and

Accessibility of all units likely to require routine attention is good. A single reservoir feeds fluid to the brake and clutch operating cylinders. A gauze air filter is fitted to each carburettor

Both sidescreens are secured to the doors by strong wing nuts: the screens are a good fit, and the windscreen pillars cause a minimum of obstruction

Austin-Healey 3000 . . .

the whole of the transmission unit stands up well to full throttle test requirements. A larger clutch has been fitted to deal with the extra power of the 2.9-litre engine, and the gear teeth have been strengthened.

Clutch operation is light and there is a smooth take-up, with no slip evident during standing start acceleration tests. There is no doubt that the times taken for these tests, up to 70 m.p.h. at least, could have been improved upon if the gear change had not been so stiff, and if the rear wheels had maintained contact with the ground on initial take-off. As soon as the clutch was fully home and power applied, each time a test start was made, it was difficult to avoid axle hop.

The new gear ratios are well suited to the performance of the engine and car. Third and top, with their overdrive ratios, are pleasantly close, but not too much so, and acceleration in second and third is of the " kick-in-the-back " variety, care being necessary on wet roads to avoid wheel spin with full throttle.

Little difference has been made to the steering or suspension of the car by the extra weight compared with that of the previous model. The greater percentage is still on the rear axle and the car handles well. On wet roads, with the Dunlop Road Speed tyres inflated to 20 lb front and 23 lb rear, the back of the car is apt to swing when cornering. Steering characteristics in all normal circumstances are neutral; self-centring action is adequate without being forceful. In general the car is directionally stable providing a guiding hand rather than a firm grip is kept on the steering wheel; there is no sign of instability at maximum speed. On bad road surfaces there was some kick-back reaction at the steering wheel.

Tyre pressures are quite critical and the car handles best, two-up, with 23 lb sq in front and 26 lb rear—an increase of 3 lb on the makers' recommendation. For the high speed runs on an *autoroute* these pressures were increased by a further 6 lb front and rear.

The suspension is well damped, and firm enough to ensure that the car does not roll when cornering fast. Continental pavé can be uncomfortable if the tyre pressures are set only a few pounds above the lowest recommended. Ground clearance is limited, and " colonial " sections of road must be tackled with caution.

It was said of the drum brakes fitted to the last Austin-Healey tested that they proved entirely suitable. This may be repeated for the front disc, rear drum equipment of the 3000 model. The total test mileage amounted to over 1,500 miles, and at all times the brakes were excellent. On several

occasions when they were applied very hard at speeds in excess of 100 m.p.h. they retarded the car safely and surely.

For maximum results pedal pressures are rather high; normal check braking, however, is well within the capability of a woman driver. Servo assistance is not fitted, and providing the pedal pressures do not increase with use and wear it would not be necessary. The hand brake is efficient and the lever, between the driving seat and propeller shaft tunnel on right-hand drive cars, is easy to operate.

A number of points criticized on earlier models remain unchanged and, therefore, appear perhaps even more prominent and undesirable in a car which is basically very good. Driver comfort, for example, is marred by lack of room around the pedals; it is difficult to clear the throttle pedal when braking. The seat adjustment, pedal travel and steering wheel position suit a long-legged driver but not one of smaller stature who, in order to reach the pedals, must sit much too close to the wheel. The seat back rests, which tip forward to give access to the rear cockpit, are well raked and comfortable, but are not laterally stable. The seat cushions become " thin " after more than a 100-mile drive, and a tall driver lacks support under the thighs.

Most of the test driving was done with the hard top in position, and the performance figures were taken with the car so equipped. It is certainly a very desirable, if somewhat expensive piece of equipment; in some ways it improves the appearance of a car which is good-looking without it; it provides a warm, snug interior at night, and proved to be watertight. It is light in weight and is easily fitted to or removed from the car; there are four securing points.

The conventional folding hood, which is standard equipment, provides almost equally good protection, at the cost of more wind noise when driving fast. In order to make it neat and well fitting, no more material has been used than was necessary, and erection during a sudden rainstorm proved to be neither quick nor simple to an admittedly inexperienced crew. The same sliding Perspex side screens are used in conjunction with either hard top or hood; they are strong and well made, and fit well in the door apertures. There is no means of locking the car, and if it is left unattended for any length of time, valuables must be removed or locked in the boot.

Visibility in all directions from the driving compartment is good, the screen pillars are commendably thin, the top of each wing can be seen, and head room with hard top or hood erected is not stinted for driver or passenger. It is not really practicable for an adult to sit in the rear cockpit of the closed car, as even a child is not comfortable in this position, with its restrictions on height and leg room.

In comparison with photographs of the Austin-Healey 100 road tested by *The Autocar* in September 1953, there is very little difference to be seen in the layouts of the original production car and the latest version—another indication that the general design was satisfactory from the start. Leathercloth covers the facia, and the instruments are grouped in pairs on each side of the steering column. At night the panel lighting is sufficiently bright without causing dazzle, although there is no rheostat control. Recessed in the lower centre of the panel are the heater and demister controls.

In rain the screen of the closed car fogs up quickly, but the blower fan deals effectively with this without a great deal of noise. Self-parking screen wipers work well, and are helped by a simple form of screen washer. The water container for this is located in a hole in the shelf below the facia, where it not only occupies valuable space but is awkward to replace after filling. There is a strong grab handle in front of the passenger seat, and an ashtray sunk into the top of the propeller shaft tunnel has a sensible lid to prevent ash being blown about the car. Tucked away underneath the left side of the facia is the choke control. The bonnet release is even more elusive, to the right of the steering column behind the panel.

Powerful head lamps are essential for a fast car, and the 3000 is well equipped. There is a foot-operated dip switch which is easy to reach. Flashing direction indicators are combined with the parking and brake lights so that they are white and red, a system which does not find favour in many

European countries where amber coloured flashers are preferred.

Luggage accommodation is very limited, as the spare wheel and the battery take up a large proportion of the space in the locker. Normally, with the car used as a two-seater the space behind the front seats can be used for stowage. When the optional extra rear seats are not fitted two 6-volt batteries are placed forward of the rear axle beneath the floor and the spare wheel fits into a recess, leaving more room for luggage. A battery master switch is a useful item of standard equipment; it is in the right-hand corner of the luggage locker and provides a measure of security when the car is left unattended.

Roadside wheel changing involves the use of an old-fashioned screw-type jack, whose tedious operation would be annoying on a wet dark night. Every 1,000 miles 14 chassis points require grease gun lubrication, in addition to the checking of various oil levels.

The latest Austin-Healey maintains the reputation of a good quality, fast sports-touring car which its predecessors established; its original styling has not dated and the new performance will make it even more competitive.

AUSTIN-HEALEY 3000

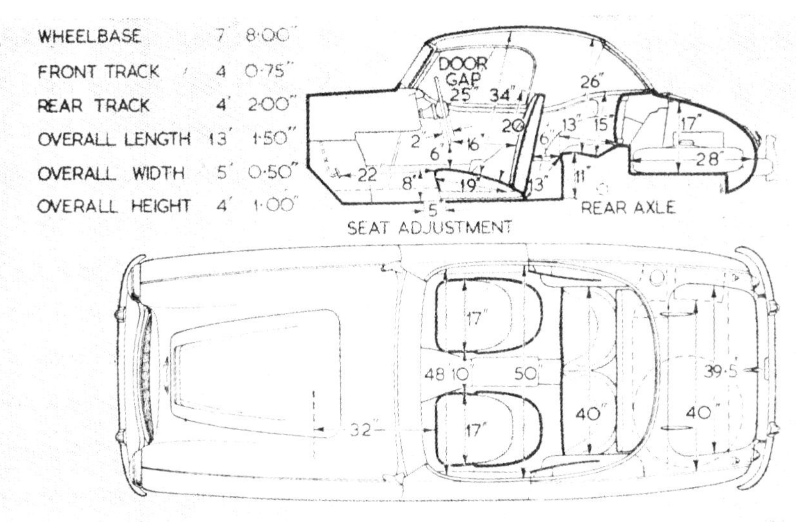

Scale ⅛in to 1ft. Driving seat in central position. Cushions uncompressed.

PRICE (basic), with four-seater body, £829. British purchase tax, £346 10s 10d. Total (in Great Britain), £1,175 10s 10d. Extras (with tax): Radio £34 Heater £21 19s 2d, Overdrive £66 8s 2d, Wire wheels £35 8s 4d, Hard top £85.

ENGINE: Capacity: 2,912 c.c. (177.7 cu. in.). Number of cylinders: 6 in line. Bore and stroke: 83.36 × 88.9 mm (3.3 × 3.5in). Valve gear: overhead, pushrods and rockers. Compression ratio: 9.03 to 1. B.H.P. nett 124 at 4,600 r.p.m. (B.H.P. per ton laden 97.4). Torque: 175 lb ft at 3,000 r.p.m. M.P.H. per 1,000 r.p.m. in top gear, 18.94. M.P.H. per 1,000 r.p.m. in O D top, 23.1.

WEIGHT: (with 5 gals fuel), 22.5 cwt (2,513 lb). Weight distribution (per cent): F, 47.3; R, 52.7. Laden as tested: 25.5 cwt 2,849 lb). Lb per c.c. (laden): 0.97.

BRAKES: Type: Girling, disc front, drum rear. Method of operation: hydraulic. Drum dimensions: R, 11in diameter; 2.25in wide. Disc diameter: F, 11.25in; Swept area: F, 228 sq in; R, 155.5 sq in (301.5 sq in per ton laden).

TYRES: 5.90 × 15in Dunlop Road Speed. Pressures (lb sq in): F, 20; R,23 (normal); F, 20; R, 26 (with full load).

TANK CAPACITY: 12 Imperial gallons. Oil sump, 12 pints. Cooling system, 20 pints.

DIMENSIONS: Wheelbase: 7ft 8in. Track: F, 4ft 0.75in; R, 4ft 2in. Length (overall): 13ft 1.5in. Width: 5ft 0.5in. Height: 4ft 2in with hood up. Ground clearance: 4.5in. Frontal area: 16.7 sq ft (approximately).

ELECTRICAL SYSTEM: 12-volt; 57 ampère-hour battery. Head lights: Double dip; 50-40 watt bulbs.

SUSPENSION: Front, independent coil springs, wishbones and stabilizing bar. Rear, half-elliptic leaf springs and Panhard rod.

ACCELERATION (mean):
Speed Range, Gear Ratios and Time in sec.

M.p.h.	3.21 to 1*	3.91 to 1	4.2 to 1*	5.12 to 1	8.03 to 1	11.45 to 1
10—30	—	—	—	5.4	3.6	2.8
20—40	9.0	6.8	6.5	5.1	3.5	—
30—50	9.0	6.8	6.5	5.2	—	—
40—60	9.0	7.1	6.6	5.6	—	—
50—70	9.5	7.3	7.0	6.1	—	—
60—80	10.3	8.4	8.2	—	—	—
70—90	13.0	10.4	9.9	—	—	—
80—100	16.7	13.9	—	—	—	—

*Overdrive.

From rest through gears to:

30 m.p.h.	..	3.5 sec.
40	.. ..	5.6
50	.. ..	8.0
60	.. ..	11.4
70	.. ..	14.3
80	.. ..	18.9
90	.. ..	24.8
100	.. ..	32.8

Standing quarter mile, 17.9 sec.

MAXIMUM SPEEDS ON GEARS:

Gear		m.p.h.	k.p.h.
O.D. ..	(mean)	114.0	183.3
	(best)	116.0	186.5
Top ..	(mean)	108.0	173.6
	(best)	110.0	177.0
O D 3rd ..	..	98.0	157.7
3rd ..	.. ..	78.0	125.5
2nd ..	.. ..	49.0	78.8
1st ..	.. ..	34.0	54.7

TRACTIVE EFFORT (by Tapley meter):

	Pull (lb per ton)	Equivalent Gradient
O.D.	240	1 in 9.3
Top	316	1 in 7.0
O D 3rd	325	1 in 6.8
3rd	424	1 in 5.2
2nd	625	1 in 3.6

SPEEDOMETER: Accurate.

BRAKES (at 30 m.p.h. in neutral):

Pedal load in lb	Retardation	Equivalent stopping distance in ft
25	0.22g	135
50	0.38g	79
75	0.60g	50
100	0.76g	39
120	0.90g	33.6

FUEL CONSUMPTION (at constant speeds):

Speed	Direct Top	O.D. Top.
30 m.p.h.	30.5 m.p.g.	35.4 m.p.g
40	27.5 ,,	33.0 ,,
50	23.2 ,,	29.8 ,,
60	21.0 ,,	25.0 ,,
70	19.6 ,,	22.4 ,,
80	18.3 ,,	20.5 ,,
90	16.6 ,,	18.6 ,,
100	—	16.4 ,,

Overall fuel consumption for 1,200 miles, 20.0 m.p.g. (14.12 litres per 100 km). Approximate normal range 17—25 m.p.g. (16.6—11.3 litres per 100 km.) Fuel: Premium grade.

TEST CONDITIONS: Weather: dry, cloudy. 10-20 m.p.h. wind. Air temperature, 65-70 deg. F.

STEERING: Turning circle:
Between kerbs, 33ft 11in R.H.; 36ft 11in L.H. Between walls: 35ft 2in R.H.; 38ft L.H. Turns of steering wheel from lock to lock, 3⅛.

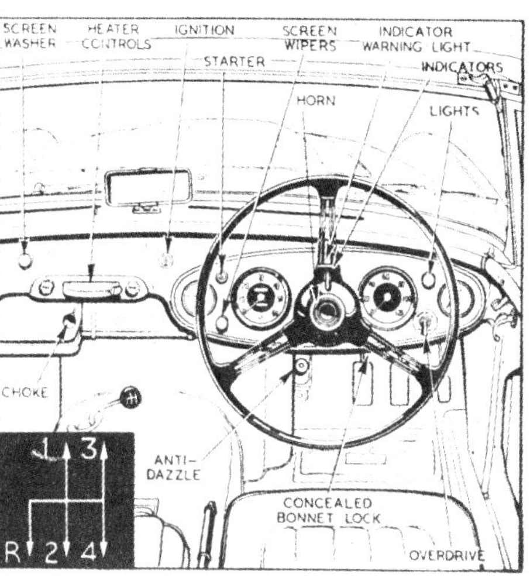

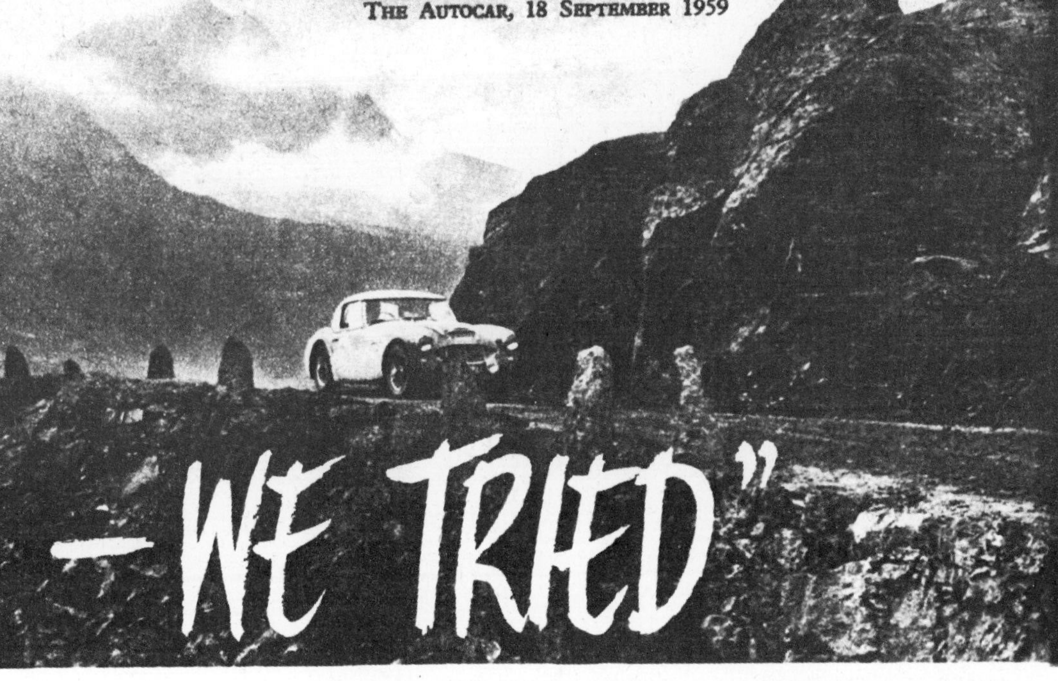

Its exhaust note echoing around the mountain tops, the Austin-Healey storms the notorious Gavia Pass

"WELL —WE TRIED"

By PETER GARNIER

IF you subscribe to the "Don't-let's-have-dog-tired-bleary - eyed - rally - drivers - tearing - around - the - roads-at-racing-speeds" school of thought you will not approve of this; but you can comfort yourself with the thought that it didn't happen here. It all began last March, after our Tulip Rally efforts with an Austin-Healey had been blessed with a certain amount of success, and in a flush of enthusiasm I said "Yes" to Jack Sears' suggestion "Let's try and persuade old Marcus to enter a team of Healeys for the Liège." I didn't think a great deal more about it until Jack 'phoned, some time later, to say that Marcus Chambers, B.M.C. Competitions Manager, had decided to enter a team of four cars, and that we were to drive one of them. He followed this news with the thought that he, for one, was going into training, and hadn't I better do the same? With ghastly visions of giving up smoking . . . bread . . . potatoes . . . going for runs . . . I got down to the business of working out the route, and marking up maps.

Bearing in mind the fact that, after four nights without sleep, the brain is incapable of making decisions—let alone working out complicated sums—a great deal of time was spent on this side of the job. The times of arrival at every town of note on the route, both at the set average and the highest permitted average, were worked out and entered in a book; and every section of map which involved tricky navigation was enlarged photographically and pasted in, opposite the relevant list of place names, with the route indicated in red.

Finally, on the last day of August, our four scarlet Austin-Healeys, with their white hard tops, took passage to Liège—accompanied by John Gott and Ken James, Jack and myself, Gerry Burgess and Sam Croft-Pearson, and Peter Riley and Rupert Jones.

Essentially a Rally for Rally Drivers, the Liège has few inhibitions; it sets out to be as tough and as fast as the traffic regulations of the countries through which it passes will allow. This year these were Belgium, Luxemburg, France, Austria, Germany, Italy, and Yugoslavia—the seven providing a total of some 3,200 miles, to be covered in 92 hours, without official allowance for either sleep or food. Before the event the organizers, the Royal Motor Union of Liège, reckoned that not more than 20 of the 106 entries would survive. In fact, 14 of the 97 starters did so; it was not a bad estimate.

The method of starting the cars is unusual—and typical. Instead of the usual practice of sending them off singly, at intervals of one minute, they send them off in threes, at intervals of three minutes. When there's a very tight section ahead every second counts, and a quick getaway is important—and when the section is dusty it is vitally important to get away before the other two cars, so that you will not travel in a permanent dust cloud. Thus, at each of the significant controls, the crowds of spectators were treated to a series of single-row, Grand Prix grid-starts, with the appropriate accompaniment of squealing tyres and high-revving engines.

Leaving the start soon after 11 p.m. on the Wednesday night, we were soon faced with a sort of "London Rally" night navigation section on small lanes around Clervaux—and, thanks to a thorough reconnaissance the day before, made no mistakes. Even at this early stage, however, four cars were penalized, two were too late to qualify, and four were put out by accidents or mechanical failures . . . Not much more than 50 of the 5,025 kilometres completed, and six cars already out.

The thought that we were through this initial pitfall gave us confidence, and the "tummy butterflies" (more like dragonflies in my case), which always seem to accompany the early stages of these events, disappeared. We trundled on into Austria and Germany, in company with Peter Riley and Rupert Jones in their Healey, taking turns to sleep. Early dawn saw us at the side of the Karlsruhe-Neu Ulm *autobahn*, eating a picnic breakfast and celebrating my birthday with a "drop of the hard stuff" from Peter's medical chest. This first day passed comparatively easily, including a rapid climb of the Stelvio, which was wet and slippery—and on which a further 36 cars incurred penalties; by now, 88 were still in the Rally, 50 of them unpenalized.

At Tarvisio, just before the Yugoslav frontier, we were met by Marcus Chambers and the B.M.C. mechanics—Tommy Wellman, Duggie Hamblin, Roy Brown, Brian Moylan, and John Giles—who were standing by in case any of us were in trouble. Though the rules state quite firmly that "organized assistance" is forbidden, I doubt if there's a single works team these days that doesn't organize assistance throughout the route.

We crossed, via the Predil Pass, into Jug-land (as we called it) late on the Thursday night—and in no time everything we possessed was covered with a fine, French-chalk-like dust. It found its way into everything; our hair became pale grey, like our eyebrows, eyelashes, and the hairs on our arms, too. The roads were appalling—dust and loose stones, on a relatively hard surface, made cornering particularly dicey.

Some of the sections were so tight that it meant driving flat-out; to go slower, and try to save the car, would have meant heavy penalization, so we had to keep going and hope for the

Two of the Healeys pause on their way towards Yugoslavia, while their crews bathe in the mountain stream below

best. Many were the punctures and burst tyres; Gerry Burgess used up both his spares, and a few people had wheels collapse.

After a couple of hours of driving through dust against the setting sun, we emerged from the Federal Peoples' Republic, without regret, late on the Friday evening—via the rough and rocky Moistrocca Pass, on which we incurred a penalty of one minute. We were in good company, however, as 31 cars lost points on this horror. By this stage, we had lost a total of three minutes; we were equal eighth, the best-placed British car.

Surprisingly, we still felt comparatively fresh—largely, I think, because of a resolute determination that no one should say that

Personal story of a Nearly Successful Austin-Healey in the Liège-Rome-Liège

" Sears and Garnier can't take it." It is astonishing how, when you've spent only one night out of bed, and know that's the lot, you feel very, very tired; yet, when you know you have had four nights out, and there's still one to come, you manage to convince yourself you're feeling fine. Again, we found the mechanics at Tarvisio, waiting for their " chicks "—and, again, there was virtually nothing for them to do on our long-suffering Healey. As a team of four cars we were still intact.

Unfortunately, the team wasn't to survive for long. John Gott's car missed a turning while one of the crew slept, and, before discovering the mistake, carried on too far to make good the time lost. Gerry Burgess crashed during the descent of the Gavia—fortunately without going over the edge of this hair-raising pass. Peter Riley completed the climb with time to spare, but our Healey *just* scraped home within the limit for non-penalization.

For some time we followed Rupert Jones across Italy while Peter slept. Our progress was mighty slow—far too slow for the time we had in hand. I tried to chivvy him on by following very close—but, every now and then, on would go his brake lights. Luckily, after an hour or two of this, Peter woke up, took over, and we all hurried on, making up lost time. At the next control I asked Rupert—"The Bishop" as we called him—why he had been going so slowly. "Well, didn't you see all those level crossings? " he asked. " I couldn't go blinding across them—particularly as the gates were closed! " In fact, I don't think we crossed the railway once; after that he decided to resort to keep-awake pills, which did the trick.

By now some 24 cars remained from the original 97. The run through Italy into France should have been without incident —but for the fact that we ran out of road and buckled the two left-hand wheels. It wasn't a serious excursion, but I do recall thinking, as we took to the bank, "Well, that's phase 1 completed; I wonder where phase 2 will finish up." Luckily the car jumped back on to the road again. At Allesandria we changed the wheels—or rather, David Higham's ever-present Dunlop mechanics did—and went off none the worse. We each took our first keep-awake pill.

We crossed into France by the Col de Larche, and ran through Barcelonnette towards the first of the final night's horrors

Breakfast-time on the Karlsruhe-Neu Ulm autobahn: Peter Riley, Rupert Jones (" The Bishop "), and Jack Sears

—a timed section from Digne to La Morte for which the organizers claimed a distance of 172 km, and for which they allowed a time of 172 minutes. This tallied nicely with the fact that, in the regulations, it stated that nowhere in France would the set average speed exceed 60 k.p.h. Unfortunately, however, the distance was nearer 199 km, making a set average of near enough 70 k.p.h. We tried a short cut, to bring down the distance—and, therefore, the average. But the short cut, though clearly marked as 4.5km on the map, and given the road number of D53, had ceased to exist; it had become submerged beneath a reservoir, so far as we could discover. By the time we emerged from this detour and reach La Morte, we had expended 25 of our total allowance of 30 minutes' lateness. A fuel stop in Grenoble accounted for a further four minutes—so that, as we embarked, somewhat dispirited, on the series of very, very fast sections from St. Jean-en-Royans, we had but one minute to play with.

Off we went, jinking, twisting, accelerating hard, braking hard, the Healey's exhaust note echoing around the darkened mountains as we flew through what seemed an unending succession of identical earthy, stony *lacets*. It seemed we were going to do it, but suddenly we ran into cloud. We crawled at 10 m.p.h., eventually stopping to remove the side screens. When we finally returned to St. Jean we had lost a further five minutes— four above the maximum. We were out of the rally with only the final, easy day's run to Spa ahead of us. Just in case the organizers should decide to scrub the Digne-La Morte section, because of the distance discrepancy, we carried on with the rally, keeping to schedule. This sting-in-the-tail had further whittled down the field; 14 cars remained and Pat Moss and Ann Wisdom, Peter Jopp and Les Leston, too, had been excluded by the distance trouble.

We ran on northwards . . . hopefully, running in convoy with Peter Riley's Healey which was the sole survivor of our four cars, and Pat Moss' Austin A.40. A couple of controls before the finish we stopped at a garage and washed the cars and ourselves. If we weren't still in the rally at least we'd put up something of a show; the two scarlet cars looked magnificent, burbling along through Belgium's green countryside.

Anyhow, the organizers didn't scrub the Digne-La Morte section, and it was all part of the fun of the Liège. If the French authorities won't allow a set average of over 60 k.p.h., the only thing to do is state that the distance is less than it really is; only by that means can you sort out the men from the boys. As a result, it is one of the best rallies in the calendar.

There wasn't much between us and disaster on the Vivione Pass

Austin-Healey Sprite Hardtop

Most of the exterior brightwork is chromium plated, but the new Weathershields sidescreens have a polished metal frame

WITH its enviable position as the cheapest British production sports two-seater, the Austin-Healey Sprite would not have to be particularly outstanding to enjoy a keen following. Very good it is, though—and it offers so many attractive features in its design, construction and behaviour on the road, that it is easy to understand how it has become so popular in the short time since its introduction in June last year. Now, useful improvements have been made for the comfort of its occupants and for the car's utility as an all-weather vehicle in winter and summer. Thus, it is available in detachable hardtop form, and the flimsy sidescreens are replaced (on the hardtop version) by an improved design. Our Road Test of the earlier Sprite appeared in *The Autocar* of 20 June 1958.

Constructed of resin-bonded glass fibre, with a large wrap-round rear window of Perspex, the hardtop is not heavy, and it was found possible to fit or remove it single-handed. Its fittings are ingenious, and even without previous experience it was a simple matter, taking only two minutes, to remove it. At the front it is secured to the windscreen top rail by two "crocodile" clips, released by raising their chrome handles, which lie flush with the hardtop in grooves. The back is secured by two bolts and wing nuts, locating in slots beside the seats. It was only for replacement of the hardtop that assistance was appreciated, to ensure that the rear securing bolts did not scratch the paintwork, or the shiny metal rail which surrounds the driving compartment to the rear of the facia.

The hardtop may be added retrospectively to existing Sprites without any modifications to the car, since its securing bolts fit into the normal hood-stay slots. In this case the hardtop—as supplied by the Donald Healey Motor Company—costs £46 10s including sliding sidescreens of slightly different construction. This price shows a reduction in comparison with the listed price of £49 11s 8d when the hardtop is ordered with the new car. The explanation given by B.M.C. for this discrepancy is that full purchase tax is not charged on an accessory ordered after delivery; so buyers will benefit if they purchase the hardtop as an afterthought.

A first-class fit results with the hardtop in position, and draughts are eliminated almost completely. There is no leakage in heavy rain, but a considerable noise increase is noticed at speed, in comparison with the open or the hood-up conditions. Exhaust boom and wind roar combine to make the car decidedly noisy at more than 60 m.p.h. which, although forgivable on a sports car, will perhaps be unwelcome to the class of motorist who will specify the hardtop for protection against the elements.

Engine noise contributes to this above about 65 m.p.h., but at lower speeds it is unobtrusive. The engine is exceptionally willing to rev.; the driver wishing to obtain the best from the car takes advantage of this, and finds that on a fast run the rev. counter spends much of the time above the 4,000 r.p.m. mark. Throughout the range, and particularly at low speeds, it is noticeably smooth. However, it lacks torque until it is revving fairly freely. Starting is immediate, the choke being necessary only for a cold start and for the first minute or two of running to prevent hesitation and misfiring. The warm-up is slow.

The overall consumption of just over 40 m.p.g. is extremely creditable, including, as it does, considerable use in London traffic and consistent hard driving. It is only in the most unfavourable conditions that the worst figure of 36 m.p.g. is achieved; most owners will readily obtain up to 45 m.p.g.

Well-placed within natural reach of the driver's left hand, the gear lever is remarkably light and precise to operate. The synchromesh is not easily beaten even in the fastest movements of the lever. In these respects the gear box earns praise, but the choice of ratios is less satisfactory. Second gear in particular is too low, and the maximum speed difference between bottom and second gears is only 12 m.p.h. Third gear could also be higher—for a car of this character a readily usable maximum of at least 60 m.p.h. should be available in this ratio.

In relation to the Sprite tested last year, the acceleration is comparable, and shows a slight gain at the higher

Removal of the hardtop or the hood to the fully open condition takes only two minutes. The hood and its supports stow neatly out of sight

Austin-Healey
Sprite Hardtop . . .

With the hood up, the flexible wrap-round rear window allows an unobstructed view when the car is being manœuvred. The sidescreens have been removed for this view

speeds. This suggests that the hardtop shape offers less wind resistance than the hood—borne out by an increase of 5 m.p.h. in the best top gear maximum speed. If the Sprite is considered more as an open two-seater than as an out-and-out sports car—which is perhaps a more pertinent description of it—the acceleration may be considered quite adequate.

Clutch operation is smooth, and the pedal pressure is light. Although there is little pedal travel, the take-up is not abrupt, and there is no clutch spin even under full-throttle standing starts.

On first acquaintance with the Sprite the remarkably positive rack-and-pinion steering comes almost as a surprise, particularly to anyone accustomed to the more "woolly" steering layouts which are fitted to many cars of less sporting character. If the driver clings too rigidly to the wheel his own involuntary movement caused by the motion of the car is sufficient to affect the directional stability. A sensitive and gentle hold on the wheel gives the best control, and the complete lack of free play is appreciated. As the car is driven the steering is appreciated more and more; it

Quite an effort is required to raise the bonnet and front-wings unit, but when it is up, self-locking stays hold it securely and accessibility of all components is unusually good. It is only when working on the engine for some time that a higher locking position for the bonnet, or forward hingeing, would be appreciated

remains light and quite free from road shocks even when rough surfaces are taken fast. It is relatively high-geared, and on the open road almost imperceptible movements of the wheel are adequate to hold the car straight. Perhaps because of this precise steering, the slight tail wander which results from the quarter-elliptic rear springs is noticed more than it would be otherwise. The slight changes of direction which occur are easily corrected, however, and the car is little affected by cross-winds. At low speeds the steering remains light, and the car's good lock makes manœuvring easy.

Average British road surfaces do not show up weaknesses in the suspension, but when the Sprite is driven at all fast on rough or unmade roads there is a great deal of firm, almost violent, vertical movement. It seems that the wheel travel permitted by the suspension is too restricted for bad surfaces, and the rear suspension in particular bottoms unduly readily. A shortcoming of this kind is not a serious fault on such a car, however, and for normal road work a commendably level and well-damped ride is provided.

Among the best features of the Sprite is its extremely high standard of cornering. In hard cornering on an uneven surface there is a tendency for the back of the car to "hop out," giving a momentary oversteer situation. When this occurs the car's movement as a whole is so small, and its recovery so quick, that the driver has no need to compensate with the steering. The balance of the Sprite on cornering is near perfect, and this is the sort of car on which the driver may easily get out of trouble after he has grossly misjudged the speed at which a given corner may be taken. In these extremes the very slight tendency to oversteer helps the driver, and is in no way vicious or progressive. Thus, on dry roads the limit of adhesion leaves a considerable margin of safety at the highest speeds at which the car is likely to be driven, and in the wet one may still make violent manœuvres without too much apprehension about surface conditions. Heavy application of the brakes on wet roads will lock the wheels, and it is also possible in these conditions to provoke wheelspin in the lower gears, but liberties may still be taken with the Sprite without any feeling of lack of control.

Dependable brakes add to the overall safety factor, and the hand brake, with readily accessible lever to the left of the transmission tunnel, will hold the car firmly on a 1 in 3 gradient. Reference to the data panel shows that the maximum deceleration figures are not as high as one might expect; they are influenced by the need to avoid wheel lock, which occurs fairly readily during heavy brake applications, even on dry roads. In normal use, however, the brakes are well up to the job of stopping the car from its around 70 m.p.h. cruising speeds, and prolonged spells of hard driving do not cause fade.

Good all-round visibility, little reduced by the hardtop, is a feature of the Sprite. The windscreen wipers are self-parking, and they clean a large area of the screen. Although the driver feels—and is—very low on the road, so that the wheels of a bus or lorry tower above him, his view is un-obstructed. To the front, a little of the bonnet, and the tops of the head lamp bodies, are visible from the driving seat. Rearward visibility also is good, but the interior mirror is mounted so near to facia level as to be of little use. It scarcely satisfies the demands of the Construction and Use regulations, and during the later stages of the Road Test it had to be replaced by a suction-mounted mirror attached to the windscreen.

For tall drivers some modification to the seat mounting would probably be helpful, to lower their eye-level and prevent the car from seeming rather beetle-browed. The fore-and-aft seat adjustment is adequate for the longest legs, and there is space for the driver's left foot off the clutch, resting lightly on the dip-switch. There is also sufficient space to the right of the driving seat for the driver to sit comfortably without finding that his elbow is nudging against the door.

An accessory fitted to the test car was the fresh-air heater, which has a powerful delivery and warms the car quickly after a night in the open. A facia control is pressed to admit air to the heating element. Distribution is controlled by hinged flaps on each side of the heater unit. To demist the windscreen only, both flaps are closed. At low speeds, when there is little ram effect, a fan may be brought into action by turning the facia knob to the right; the fan may be switched on only when the air control is pressed fully home. In warm weather the delivery of hot water to the element can be switched off by a tap under the bonnet, so that the heater may be used to admit unheated fresh air when required.

Reference was made earlier to the ingenious design of the new hardtop, but the folding hood of the Sprite also has been improved; considerable thought has gone into the new design, and this is one of the easiest sports car hoods to manipulate. The hood detaches altogether from its stays, the main supports of which fit into slots at each side of the seats. The rear hood rail engages with two shaped chrome hooks, and there are Lift-the-dot fastenings around the quarters. At the windscreen the hood clips over the top rail, and is secured by two press-stud fasteners.

Hood tightness is ensured by spring loading in the vertical supports of the framework, and to simplify the business of erecting the hood the springs can be compressed and locked, and then released after it has been secured. Little more than a minute is needed to fit or remove the hood; and when it is removed its stays fold behind the seats, and the material stows away in a wallet provided with toolkit.

Further improvement on the new Sprite is offered by the Weathershields sidescreens which, unfortunately, are standard only with the hardtop. On non-hardtop models there is an extra charge of £3 15s plus £1 11s 3d tax, and the cost is higher still if they are not specified at delivery—some allowance being included in the price for the saving on the standard screens.

They have a rigid, bright metal frame which is surrounded by rubber strips to ensure a reasonable seal when the hardtop or the hood is in position. The windows are of Perspex, and the rear section is arranged to slide forward; that on the test car was extremely stiff on the passenger side. The sidescreens fasten to the door by two large screws which can be undone readily, using a coin as a screwdriver. Access to the car from outside is gained by sliding forward one of the windows and reaching in to the small handle protruding forward from the latch. There is, of course, no way of locking the Sprite, and as there is no lockable boot or facia compartment, the owner must take a chance with any possessions left in the car.

Interior comfort owes much to the well-designed seats, which provide good support in the right places and extend fairly well under the thighs. In cornering, the driver and passenger are firmly located laterally. A touch of austerity is given by the simple interior fittings and furnishings. The uncluttered facia layout is somewhat plain. Floor mats are of moulded, ribbed rubber. The interior of the hardtop is not covered, and has the appearance of unfinished glass fibre. Full width, open door pockets are provided on each side, and generous accommodation for luggage is available to the rear of the seats. Stowage is difficult, however, and if small odd-

The interior layout and finish is plain but neat. The steering wheel is small enough not to obstruct forward visibility, and all controls come conveniently to hand. Provision is made for addition of a radio

ments find their way to the back of the luggage space the owner must crawl in to locate them. The most worth-while improvement which could now be made to the Sprite would be the provision of a separate luggage compartment with exterior lockable lid. A small grab handle is provided on the left of the facia for the passenger.

Steady readings are given by the speedometer and the optional extra rev counter—a unit which one might expect to be standard on such a car. There is a thermometer and oil-pressure gauge, but no ammeter—a reasonable omission. The gauge for the six-gallon fuel tank is fairly accurate. For a small car, the toolkit of the Sprite is unusually generous—including a simple jack, wheel-nut spanner, and a few hand tools. The jack lifts either side of the car, and it engages with an unobtrusive slot in the door sill, which is vertically below the windscreen, and covered by a rubber plug when not in use. There is no provision for a starting handle; there are no ashtrays on the car, and no reversing lamp is fitted. Such economies are reasonable with the Sprite, and form part of the general policy of keeping the price to a highly competitive minimum. In view of this it was a mild surprise to find under the bonnet an extra stay

The hardtop seats on rubber and fits snugly, leaving little space for draughts to enter the interior. The amber winking indicator lamps at the rear are protected only by the standard equipment overriders

Austin-Healey Sprite Hardtop . . .

near the radiator—in addition to the double rear self-locking stays—for holding the bonnet in the open position. This does not provide any extra lift to the open bonnet, and there is little use for it. Prospective buyers are reminded that the front bumper and overriders are also listed as optional extra equipment. Without them, the side lamps in particular would be very vulnerable.

In its new improved form the Austin-Healey Sprite is even better value than before, and continued popularity may be expected for it. The combination of first-class roadholding and steering, and good brakes, in a car of not startling all-out performance, makes the Sprite potentially extremely safe. Although more adequate protection against the elements is now available on the standard car, the option of the hardtop will no doubt appeal to many—in particular to those who must park their car in the open through the winter months.

AUSTIN-HEALEY SPRITE HARDTOP

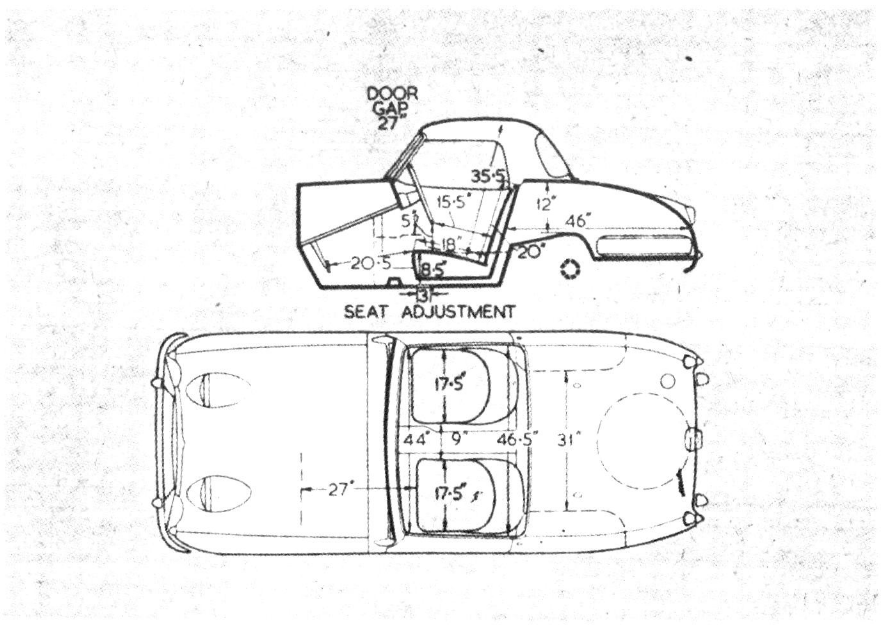

Scale ⅛in to 1ft. Driving seat in central position. Cushions uncompressed.

PERFORMANCE

ACCELERATION TIMES (mean):
Speed range, Gear Ratios and Time in Sec.

M.p.h.	4.22 to 1	5.96 to 1	10.02 to 1	15.31 to 1
10—30	—	8.7	5.1	—
20—40	11.8	8.3	—	—
30—50	11.9	8.7	—	—
40—60	15.1	—	—	—
50—70	19.2	—	—	—

From rest through gears to:

30 m.p.h.	6.0 sec.
40 „	10.2 „
50 „	14.9 „
60 „	23.7 „
70 „	33.4 „

Standing quarter mile 22.3 sec.

MAXIMUM SPEEDS ON GEARS:

Gear		M.p.h.	K.p.h.
Top	(mean)	84.1	135.2
	(best)	86.0	138.4
3rd		58.0	93.3
2nd		35.0	56.3
1st		23.0	37.0

TRACTIVE EFFORT (by Tapley meter):

	Pull (lb per ton)	Equivalent gradient
Top	225	1 in 9.9
Third	315	1 in 7.0
Second	490	1 in 4.5

SPEEDOMETER CORRECTION: M.P.H.

Car speedometer	10	20	30	40	50	60	70	80
True speed	10	19	28	38	48	57	67	77

BRAKES (at 30 m.p.h. in neutral):

Pedal load in lb.	Retardation	Equiv. stopping distance in ft.
25	0.21g	144
50	0.37g	82
75	0.77g	39

FUEL CONSUMPTION (at steady speeds):
Direct top

30 m.p.h.	58.8 m.p.g.
40 „	55.9 „
50 „	51.3 „
60 „	44.9 „
70 „	38.4 „

Overall fuel consumption for 1,452 miles, 40.3 m.p.g. (7.02 litres per 100 km.).

Approximate normal range 38-46 m.p.g. (7.4-6.1 litres per 100 km.).

Fuel: Premium grade.

TEST CONDITIONS: Weather: Dry, still. Air temperature, 53 deg. F. Model described in *The Autocar* of 23 May 1958.

STEERING: Turning circle:
Between kerbs, L, 31ft 0.5in; R, 30ft 1in. Between walls, L, 32ft 4.0in; R, 31ft 4.5in. Turns of steering wheel from lock to lock, 2.3.

DATA

PRICE (basic), with hood, sidescreens, rear overriders, spare wheel and tyre, £445.
British purchase tax, £186 10s 10d.
Total (in Great Britain), £631 10s 10d.
Extras:

	Basic £ s d	U.K. Tax £ s d
Radio	£18 0 0	£7 10 0
Heater	£13 17 6	£5 15 8
Hardtop	£35 0 0	£14 11 8
Rev. counter	£3 0 0	£1 5 0
Tonneau cover	£4 0 0	£1 13 4
Front bumper and overriders	£4 0 0	£1 13 4

ENGINE: Capacity, 948 c.c. (57.82 cu in).
Number of cylinders, 4.
Bore and stroke, 62.9 × 76.2mm (2.478 × 3.0in).
Valve gear, o.h.v., pushrods.
Compression ratio, 8.3 to 1.
B.h.p. (net) 42.5 at 5,500 r.p.m. (B.h.p. per ton laden 52.1).
Torque, 52lb ft at 3,200 r.p.m.
M.p.h. per 1,000 r.p.m. in top gear, 15.4.

WEIGHT: (with 5 gals fuel), 13.31 cwt (1,491lb).
Weight distribution (per cent): F, 54; R, 46.
Laden as tested, 16.31 cwt (1,827lb).
Lb per c.c. (laden), 1.92.

BRAKES: Type, Lockheed, two-leading shoe (front), leading and trailing (rear).
Method of operation, hydraulic.
Drum dimensions: F, 7in diameter; 1⅛in wide. R, 7in diameter; 1⅛in wide.
Lining area: F, 30.6 sq in; R, 30.6 sq in (75.2 sq in per ton laden).

TYRES: 5.20 × 13in Dunlop four-ply tubeless.
Pressures (lb sq in): F, 18; R, 20 (normal).

TANK CAPACITY: 6 Imp. gallons.
Oil sump, 6 pints.
Cooling system, 10 pints.

DIMENSIONS: Wheelbase, 6ft 8in.
Track: F, 3ft 9.75in; R, 3ft 8.75in.
Length (overall), 11ft 5.25in.
Width, 4ft 5in.
Height, 4ft 1.75in.
Ground clearance, 5in.
Frontal area, 13.3 sq ft (approximately).

ELECTRICAL SYSTEM: 12-volt; 38 ampère-hour battery.
Head lamps, double dip; 42-36 watt bulbs.

SUSPENSION: Front, independent, coil springs and wishbones. Rear, quarter elliptic leaf springs with radius arms.

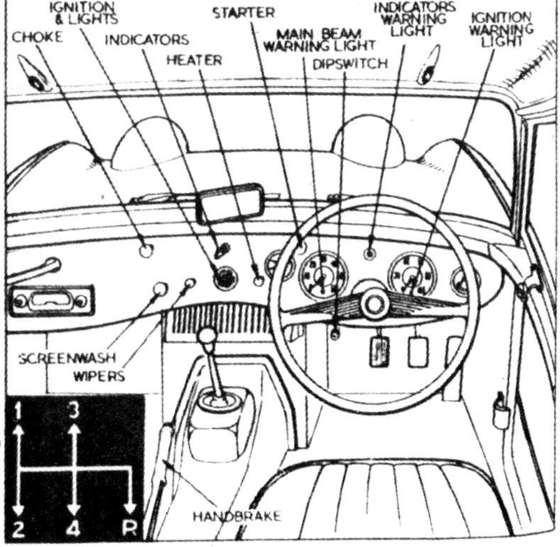

The Tulip Rally

Right. Jack Sears taking part in the final eliminating tests of the 1959 Tulip Rally, held in pouring rain. The Austin-Healey, which he shared with Peter Garnier, all but lapped its sole remaining opponent, a DB 2/4 Aston Martin. It went on to win its class and take eighth place overall.

Below. The Morley brothers in their Austin-Healey lead Pat Moss and Ann Wisdom in a similar car through the streets of Clamecy on the first day's run of the 1960 Tulip Rally. The Morley brothers won the previous year's rally.

BONNET FOR SPRITES

THERE have been many enquiries from readers who are interested in the modified head lamp arrangement on the Austin-Healey Sprite, illustrated in our Geneva Show report, published in *The Autocar* of 18 March. This modification in which the head lamps are built into the wings as on the Austin-Healey 3000, is carried out locally by the Swiss agent, Emil Frey AG., Werdmühlestrasse 11, Zurich, 23, Switzerland, to whom enquiries should be made.

From the original bonnet must be removed the hinges, radiator grille, struts, lock and head lamps, and instructions are provided with the new bonnet for fitting these units to the new shell. Emil Frey claim that the change-over takes about four hours. They add that at present they can supply these bonnets from stock, but that there is a considerable demand for them. The price is 500 Swiss francs, plus 66 francs packing and freight. The total of 566 francs is equivalent to about £47, and import duty would add some £15.

THIS IMPROVED bonnet assembly for the Austin-Healey Sprite aroused much interest when it was illustrated in our Geneva Show report, and details of its availability have now been obtained (see left)

Spritely Speedwells

TAKE CLASS RECORDS

SPEEDWELL took over to Belgium last week an Austin-Healey Sprite G.T. coupé and a special bubble-topped streamliner, to make some officially timed high-speed runs; these took place on the rather blustery morning of 13 April, on a stretch of the Antwerp-Liège motorway. Graham Hill, director of Speedwell Performance Conversions, Ltd., did four runs with the G.T. coupé, two in each direction over the kilometre. These were all that was required to attain the target speed—110.9 m.p.h. Considering that the car used is the one which has been raced so successfully by Venner-Pack, and has received little attention since the beginning of the season, this was an extremely meritorious performance.

George Hulbert then took out the fully streamlined car designed by himself and Frank Costin; because of breakdowns in the timing apparatus, and the need for small modifications to the cockpit to prevent the driver from being affected by fumes, not so many runs could be made as it was hoped, before the road was opened again. On a methanol-based fuel, a mean time of 128.78 m.p.h. was recorded; when this fuel was replaced by a nitro-additive mixture, a run at 132.2 m.p.h. was achieved. After four runs, two each by George Hulbert and Graham Hill at around the 132 m.p.h. mark, there was insufficient time left, unfortunately, for experiments with larger tyres. Since the engine speed went above the power peak with the smaller tyres, it is safe to assume that the odd mile an hour or more could have been obtained with a higher overall ratio, provided by larger tyres. Both cars collected their respective Belgian National Class records.

Considering that the B.M.C. EX.219 International G class record car—also based on a Sprite—achieved, in blown form, 146.95 m.p.h., for an hour, this Speedwell venture, with only a minute proportion of the B.M.C. resources, is indeed praiseworthy. What is more, basically the body and chassis are still Austin-Healey Sprite.

The future of this special is still undecided, but one can safely assume that it will not remain idle.

Figures for the fastest runs made by both cars, and which when ratified will stand as the new flying kilometre, Belgian National Class G records, are:—

Speedwell Streamliner 132.2 m.p.h. (212.8 k.p.h.); Speedwell G.T. Coupé, 110.9 m.p.h. (178.5 k.p.h.).

In spite of difficult conditions caused by a brisk cross-wind, both Sprite G.T. Coupé and Streamliner appeared remarkably stable. This photograph shows the special streamlined Sprite at speed on the timed kilometre

Healeys in Competition 1960

Above left. The Morley brothers in Austin-Healey No. 1 almost lead the field, in both senses, during the R.A.C. International Rally.

Above right. Making his first ever climb of the Rest-and-Be-Thankful stage during the R.A.C. Rally, John Sprinzel clocked 1 min. 18·2 sec. in a modified Sprite.

Right. Jack Sears in an Austin-Healey 3000 leads John Dalton's Sprite through the Esses during Le Mans. Sears retired around 2 am with big end trouble when lying in twenty-second place.

Below. Winner of his class in the closed car race, Hawkins swings his Austin-Healey Sprite wide of Foden, who has spun and applied opposite lock to recover, in a similar car at Tetts Corner, Aintree.

A strong Italian influence is apparent in the rectangular air intake treatment. The basic model does not have the bumper shown in this photograph. Sealed beam headlamps are standard on home and export models

WITH the introduction of their Austin-Healey Sprite in May, 1958, the British Motor Corporation no doubt had young people mainly in mind as customers. An open two-seater, small and economical to run, its initial cost was kept low and its good handling qualities quickly earned it a name for safety.

In standard form the performance was insufficient perhaps to justify the name sports car but the sporting character of the car was obvious. Latent possibilities in engine power and handling soon encouraged enthusiasts to tune and otherwise improve Sprites until they could enter national and international competitions with marked success. In rallies, tuned Sprites have proved true successors to the M.G. Midgets and Austin Seven specials of earlier days. Donald Healey's plans have been fully justified by the array of awards in sporting events during the last three years, and good commercial judgment on the part of the manufacturers has also been confirmed by the popularity of the Sprite in export markets.

Now the familiar, rather pert-looking Sprite is to be replaced by an improved and completely rebodied Mark II version which not only has a more svelte appearance but better acceleration, slightly higher top speed and much greater convenience for everyday use. The total home market price of the new model will be barely £10 more than the model superseded.

The most obvious changes for the Mark II Sprite are the completely restyled bonnet and grille, squared up and rather reminiscent of those of its attractive close relative, the Innocenti 950, assembled in Italy. The headlamps are incorporated in the wings. At the rear the bodywork provides a reasonably large boot with lid, and increased stowage space behind the seats. The restyling includes squared off wheel arches and vestigial fins, rounded off by moulded lamp covers.

Reflecting the ever-increasing weight of opinion in favour of safety belts, the body shell of the car has been modified to provide anchorages for seat belts of an approved type.

When the Sprite was originally conceived, the intention was to fair the headlamps into the combined bonnet and wing structure. Unfortunately, late in the development stage it was discovered that the designed height of the lamps did not comply with certain American state laws. Various schemes to retract the lamps into the bonnet top were considered but rejected on the score of unreliability and cost; the alternative, which was adopted,

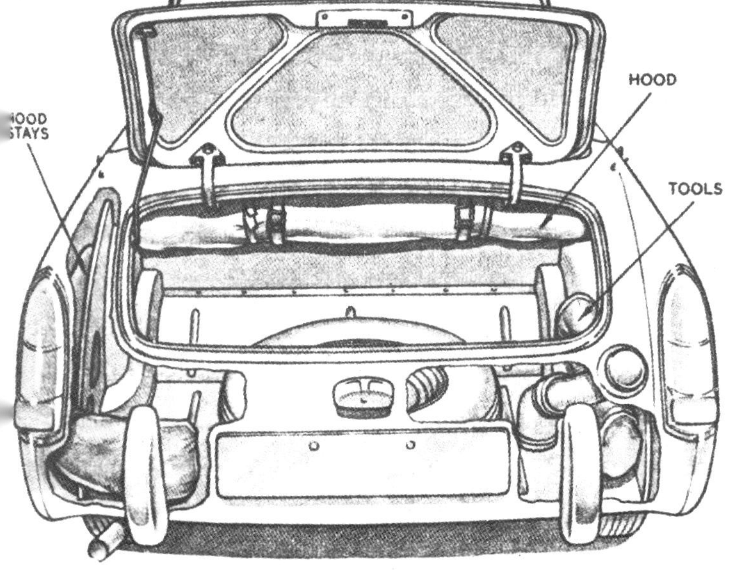

Left: Plenty of accessible space is provided in the new, separate boot. The spare wheel is retained by a setscrew. Below: Added space behind the seats could be used either for luggage or for accommodating a child. On top of the wheel arches can be seen the safety belt attachment points

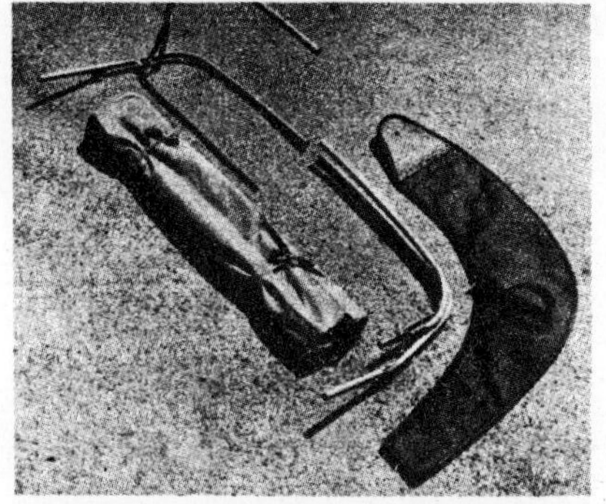

The hood is much easier to erect than this picture of the component parts suggests. The boomerang-shaped protective bag normally holds the hoodsticks

Austin-Healey
SPRITE II...

was to mount the lamps in their now familiar "pop-eyed" position.

Although there were initial misgivings about this, the sterling qualities of the little car made so many friends for it that this slightly unusual appearance soon became accepted as a characteristic. Certainly they were good lamps to drive behind, and were easily removed for sporting events.

On the Mark II car the whole front end and bonnet structure has been re-engineered, and the front wings now form a welded-on extension of the scuttle, tied together at their forward ends by a horizontal pressed panel and the front vertical panel incorporating the radiator grille. The new hinged bonnet gives good access to the engine and its accessories; only the front suspension will be more difficult to approach, although not more so than with other conventional cars.

On the original Sprite, the rear body panel was a stressed member, joining the rear wheel arches of the car. While this was a light and strong solution from an engineering point of view, it made access to the luggage space beneath it difficult because the spare wheel and any baggage had to be inserted between the backs of the seats and the front edge of the panel. In the course of the car's life there have been frequent demands for a more convenient means of loading luggage. In the Mark II Sprite an 8in. wide panel with internal bracing does the load-bearing duty of the original rear panel, and a boot lid is provided for access to the luggage space. Additionally, the cockpit length

has been increased by almost a foot, so that there is now a space behind the seats for more baggage or even a small child.

Although the length of the car appears greater because of the new front wing and headlamp treatment, in fact it is no more than before. The body improvements have brought an increase in all-up weight of 59lb, the maker's total weight being 1,525lb as compared with 1,466lb. Compensating for this, the maximum power of the engine has been increased from 42.5 b.h.p. net to 46.5 b.h.p. at 5,500 r.p.m., and the point of maximum torque is lowered from 3,300 r.p.m. to 2,750 r.p.m.

This increase in power follows four detail changes in engine design: flat-

Iliffe Transport Publications, Ltd. 1961

DICK ELLIS

topped, solid-skirt pistons with three compression rings and one oil control ring replace the older concave top split-skirt type; a redesigned camshaft gives a longer inlet valve opening time; inlet valve diameters are increased from 1·095in. to 1·156in., and twin 1¼in. S.U. HS2 carburettors replace the original 1⅛in. ones. An innovation is the provision of twin air filters of Cooper paper element type which have cold air intakes.

Lowering the point of maximum engine torque has made it possible to close-up the gearbox ratios, bottom gear now being 13·5 to 1 instead of 15·32; second gear is raised from 10·02 to 8·08 to 1, and third gear from 5·96 to 5·73 to 1. The rear axle ratio and top gear remain unchanged. With the new ratios and higher engine revolutions, maximum speed in third gear exceeds 60 m.p.h. and in second 40 m.p.h.

No changes have been made to the Sprite's suspension. At the front coil springs are used, in conjunction with pressed steel wishbones below and with the damper arms forming the upper links. At the back are 15-leaf quarter elliptics, with blades 1·75in. wide, which serve also to locate the rigid axle laterally. Parallel with the springs are longi-

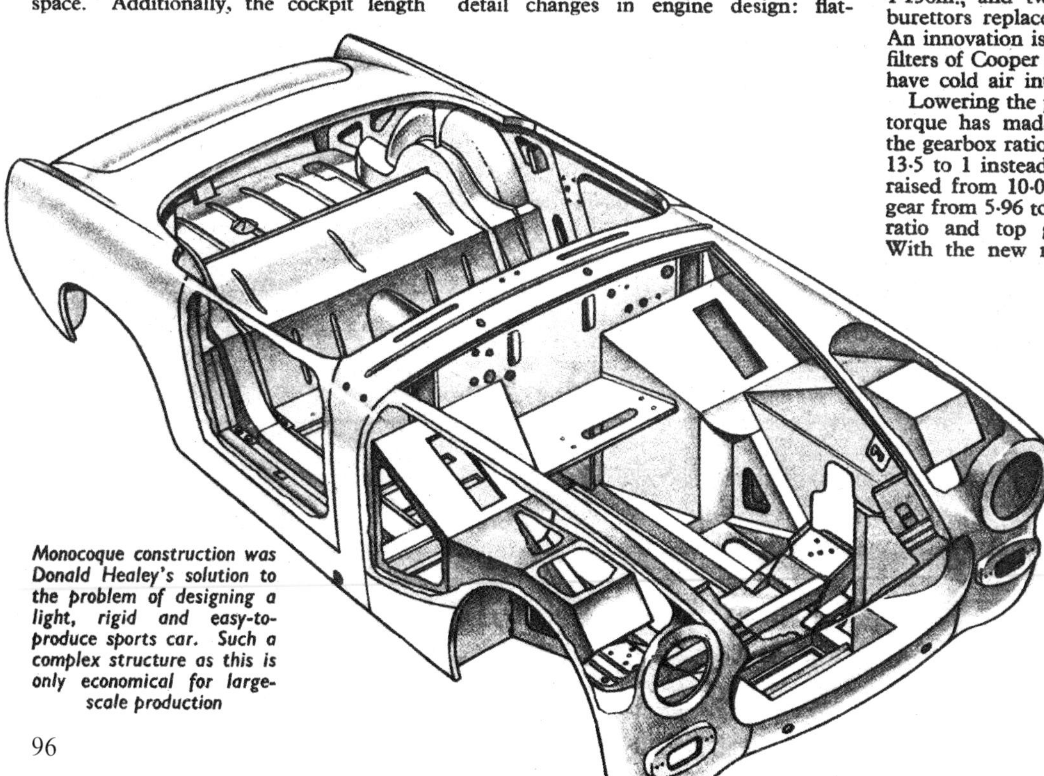

Monocoque construction was Donald Healey's solution to the problem of designing a light, rigid and easy-to-produce sports car. Such a complex structure as this is only economical for large-scale production

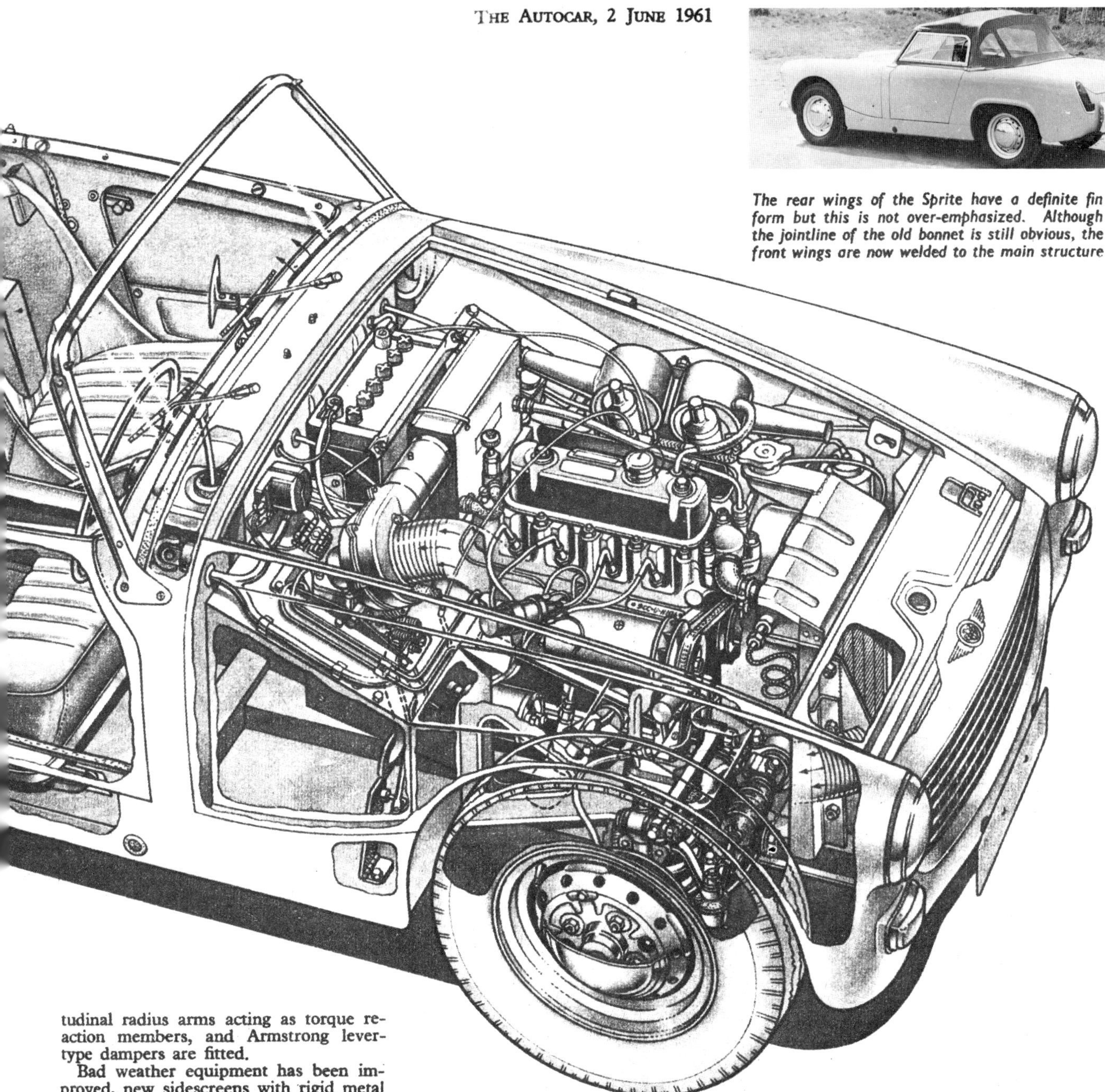

The rear wings of the Sprite have a definite fin form but this is not over-emphasized. Although the jointline of the old bonnet is still obvious, the front wings are now welded to the main structure.

tudinal radius arms acting as torque re-action members, and Armstrong lever-type dampers are fitted.

Bad weather equipment has been improved, new sidescreens with rigid metal surrounds being a standard provision. The hood folds away into two separate packages, the hood fabric into a neat roll and the hood sticks into a protective case. Both items normally are stowed in the boot.

Minor changes to the interior appointments make for greater convenience in use. For example, on the instrument panel toggle lever switches replace the push-pull type, and the high beam warning light is fitted into the speedometer instead of being located separately in the facia or in the optional rev. counter. Sealed beam headlamps are also a standard fitting.

In keeping with previous policy, the basic model will be offered at as low a price as possible—£641 9s 2d, inclusive of £189 9s 2d purchase tax. The de luxe version, with heater-demister unit, bumpers, overriders, adjustable passenger seat, revolution counter and screenwasher, costs approximately £14 more, the exact price being £655 12s 6d. The range of extras is listed on page 885.

With its much better layout and appearance, and its enhanced performance, the Sprite should make a very favourable impression on overseas markets, for which all initial production will be reserved.

SPECIFICATION

ENGINE

No. of cylinders	...	4 in line
Bore and stroke	...	62·94 x 76·2mm (2·48 x 3·0in.)
Displacement	...	948 c.c. (57·8 cu. in.)
Valve position and operation	...	Overhead, pushrods and rockers
Compression ratio	...	9 to 1
Max. b.h.p. (gross)	...	49·8 at 5,500 r.p.m.
Max. b.h.p. (net)	...	46.5 at 5,500 r.p.m.
Max. b.m.e.p. (net)	...	138 p.s.i. at 2,750 r.p.m.
Max. torque (net)	...	53 lb. ft. at 2,750 r.p.m.
Carburettors	...	Two S.U., type HS2
Fuel pump	...	AC-Delco mechanical
Tank capacity	...	6 Imp. gallons (27 litres)
Sump capacity	...	6·5 pints (3·7 litres)
Oil filter	...	Full flow
Cooling system	...	Pump, fan and thermostat
Battery	...	12 volt, 43 amp. hr.

TRANSMISSION

Clutch	...	Single dry plate 6·25in. dia.
Gearbox	...	Four speeds, synchromesh on 2nd, 3rd and top; central control
Overall gear ratios	...	Top 4·22; 3rd 5·73; 2nd 8·08; 1st 13·50; reverse 17·36 to 1.
Final drive	...	Hypoid; ratio 4·22 to 1

PERFORMANCE DATA

Top gear m.p.h. per 1,000 r.p.m.	...	15·37
Torque lb. ft. per cu. in. engine capacity	...	0·92
Brake surface area swept by linings...		110 sq. in.
Weight distribution	...	F. 52·7 per cent; R. 47·3 per cent.
Kerb weight	...	1,525lb, 13½ cwt (692 Kg.)

The *Autocar* road tests

Austin-Healey SPRITE Mark II de Luxe

In its new look form, the Sprite has lost that surprised expression that has been the joy of cartoonists

JUST three years ago the British Motor Corporation introduced the Austin-Healey Sprite; it was welcomed immediately as the first effort since the 'thirties by a British manufacturer to market a small, quantity-produced, low-priced sports car. Its continued success has shown that the manufacturer judged his market correctly, but the Sprite Mark II, which now replaces it, seems likely to enjoy a still wider popularity. Certain improvements have greatly increased the amenities of this hitherto rather stark little car.

Naturally, the first question likely to be asked is what improvements have been made. Basically the car remains unchanged, the chassis and mechanical components being identical to those of the earlier model. The power unit is the B.M.C. 948 c.c. A-type engine. Modifications include the raising of the compression ratio from 8·3:1 to 9·0:1 (the lower ratio is still available), an increase in the inlet valve diameter and the adoption of double valve springs; the camshaft and ignition distributor are also new. Air cleaners of a different pattern are fitted to the twin S.U. carburettors which have been increased in size from 1⅛in. to 1¼in. These changes have so altered the power curve that the engine now develops 46·5 b.h.p. nett at 5,500 r.p.m. instead of 42·5 b.h.p. at 5,200 r.p.m. A detailed description with drawing appears on page 97.

More important, however, than the increased power output are the changes that have been made to the bodywork. It is, in fact, an entirely new body shape. The very fact that several firms are selling differently styled bonnets for the Mark I car—as it will now be called in retrospect—shows that hitherto for reasons of either æsthetics or efficiency, not everyone liked the shape of the old Sprite. Gone now are the bulbous headlamps protruding above the bonnet, and no longer does the whole front body assembly hinge upwards for access to the engine and forward chassis components. The bonnet lid now consists of a small panel, the headlamps are faired into the wings, and the radiator grille has become squarer and larger.

Behind the passenger compartment, which is the same size as before, the tail has become less rounded and—most important of all—a locking exterior lid has been provided for the luggage boot. All of the main dimensions on the Mark II Sprite are about the same as its predecessor.

The Autocar received for test a de luxe version of the new Sprite; in this form it costs about £14 more than the standard model, but has several items of additional equipment—a rev counter, windscreen washers, bumpers and overriders, and fore-and-aft adjustment on the passenger's seat. It is noteworthy that the luxury model is £13 cheaper than the Mark I when it first appeared in 1958, although costing some £23 more than the Mark I at its final price.

How does the Sprite in its new guise differ in performance and handling? Before considering the performance figures obtained, it should be mentioned that this new car is 59 lb heavier than the previous model. Also, no owner need worry about the increase in engine power affecting reliability—a special-bodied Sprite with a much more highly tuned engine averaged 85·62 m.p.h. for the 24 hours of the Le Mans race last year. It seems reasonable to contrast the Mark II directly with its forerunner, since many potential owners will be particularly interested in such a comparison. The results of *The Autocar's* Road Test of a hard-top model in November 1959 make a suitable yardstick. They are, however, not directly comparable since the

Strapped against the front wall of the boot are bags containing the tools, the hood and its frame. The spare wheel is secured to the floor

Mark II Sprite has a close-ratio gearbox as standard; it was previously available only as an optional extra. This gearbox has higher ratios for first, second and third, and the maximum speeds in the indirects for the Mark I and the Mark II respectively are: 23-28 m.p.h., 35-46 m.p.h., 58-68 m.p.h. The increase in outright maximum speed is purely fractional but the standing start acceleration figures are greatly improved. From a standstill the new car covers the quarter-mile in 21·8sec as compared with 22·3sec, and 60 m.p.h. can now be reached in 19·8sec—3·9sec less. There is a parallel saving in time up to 70 m.p.h. This level of performance continues until around the 75 m.p.h. mark, after which it falls away and above 80 m.p.h. speed is gained rather slowly.

Although the standing start figures are thus appreciably better than those previously recorded, a similar improvement could not be shown on the 20 m.p.h. interval speed figures in the individual gears. A combination of greater weight and higher gearing in the indirects increases the necessity to make considerable use of the gearbox to keep the engine speed within the high power range, if the best performance is to be obtained. This does not imply, however, that the engine is intractable and, indeed, it pulls as willingly as ever at low crankshaft speeds, and seems smoother than the units fitted to some earlier Sprites.

All the listed performance figures were taken with the hard top in position. When a maximum speed run was made with the car open but with the sidescreens in place the fastest speed attained was reduced by over 6 m.p.h.

As well as the slight increase in weight there has been a small change in its distribution. There is proportionately less weight on the front wheels than previously. This has not appreciably altered the handling characteristics of the car, although it has probably aggravated the tendency of the rear wheels to steer the car when cornering. It is characteristic of this type of suspension that the flattening of the outer rear spring and the arching of the inner one bring the axle out of line with the chassis and create a mild oversteer. As the car is straightened after a corner the reverse effect is also noticed.

Softer Ride

Nearly everyone who drove the car thought that the springing felt softer than previously, although according to the makers no changes have been made.

Perhaps the additional weight reacting against the springs, results in a slightly greater suspension movement. As might be expected, however, the ride can still definitely be described as firm and the car handles best on smooth roads. Cornering on rough surfaces causes the rear wheels to bounce outwards and the rear axle struck its bump stops rather too easily on rough roads.

Although the above remarks might give the impression that the car did not handle particularly well, in fact it could be thrown about with almost complete abandon. One of the greatest assets while treating it in this way is the very direct and sensitive steering with which the suspension's peculiarities can soon be countered. On the test car the rack and pinion mechanism of the steering was a little sticky due to its built-in friction damping, but this is merely because it was new. Experience with other cars having this type of steering gear has shown that it will loosen up perfectly after a few thousand miles have been covered. Accordingly, on the test there was practically no self-centring.

There is no doubt that the new gear ratios have improved the versatility of the car—this particular box, however, was not a good example of its kind. The selector lever was easy to move when the oil was cold but became rather stiff when it warmed up. Synchromesh, on the upper three ratios, was only beaten by the fastest changes. First gear was not always very easy to engage when the car was stationary. The unit was noisy in all gears—especially on the overrun.

It is almost impossible to get something for nothing, and hand in hand with the improved performance goes an increase in petrol consumption. The overall figure for the 1,086 miles of the test was 33·2 m.p.g. and three pints of oil were added to the engine. A hard cross-country run

of over 100 miles with the car open resulted in 28·7 m.p.g. and the best return observed, when 50 m.p.h. was rarely exceeded, was over 43 m.p.g. Running costs have also been increased since the manufacturers now insist that 100-octane fuel be used with this 9 : 1 compression ratio engine. When checking the fuel consumption rate at constant speeds the figure at 30 m.p.h. was found to be no better than at 40 m.p.h.—presumably a result of the carburettor needles that provide a relatively rich mixture at low speeds for clean pick-up. When in a hurry on a long journey one had to replenish the six-gallon petrol tank with irritating frequency.

Most main road bends can be rounded by the Sprite at its natural cruising speed, and it is on minor roads that the brakes receive most punishment. For ordinary road use the effectiveness of these brakes must be related to the car's acceleration; it was only when using full performance on twisty roads that any signs of fade became evident. For check braking the pedal pressure seems a little high, and from near-maximum speed the brakes feel less effective than the figures would seem to indicate. In fact the retardation figures are outstandingly good. A proper fore-and-aft balance of weight must partly account for the maximum figure of 0·98g obtained. The handbrake lever is mounted to the left of the transmission tunnel and held the car on a

To enter the car the Perspex window is slipped forward and the interior handle operated. The wheel trims are an optional extra

Once inside, the interior of the Sprite is surprisingly roomy. The radio mounted below the passengers' grab handle is most useful when waiting in traffic jams. It is difficult to hear when on the move

The last few inches of the exhaust pipe are chromed. A lockable petrol filler cap is an optional extra. The handbook gives detailed instructions for folding the hood to avoid damage

1-in-3 test hill without being pulled to the ast notch. The car could not move off from this incline.

For the price, the standard of finish and bodywork detail is high and there was almost complete freedom from rattles. An irritating one was made by the side-screen flapping against the windscreen when the car was open. The bonnet lid of this car vibrated at any speed, but inspection showed that a slight modification or re-positioning of the rubber stops would probably cure this. Without doubt one of the greatest improvements is the alteration of the boot for external access—a feature that everyone has clamoured for since the Sprite was first introduced. That the car now has a completely lockable compartment greatly increases its potential for touring abroad. On the floor of the boot is the spare wheel, but this does not occupy an excessive amount of room, and the capacity is good for such a small car.

There is space for a little extra luggage behind the seats and here it was also found possible to seat two small children. For maps, torches and other miscellaneous items the door pockets are extremely commodious.

Except behind the seats, where it is carpeted, the floor of the passenger compartment is covered with rubber matting. The side-screens are well made and have neat sliding Perspex panes. They are not as rigid as they might be and with the hardtop in place the right-hand one was inclined to lean out when the car was moving fast. The basic car is sold with a Vynide hood which is mounted over a tubular frame. This frame is spring-loaded in its sockets so that the hood can be fitted without straining and then be stretched taut by releasing the spring. At the second attempt one person managed to unpack the hood from the

boot and fit it completely in under four minutes. Removing it takes a similar length of time.

Both the hardtop and the tonneau cover are extras. The hardtop was worn during most of the test and made the interior both snug and draughtproof. It is even easier to fit and dismount than the hood and is light enough for one person to handle, although a woman would probably be grateful for assistance. Provided with the tonneau cover is a rail to prevent luggage slipping off the shelf.

As would be expected the amount of noise varied according to whether the car was open or closed, with hood or hardtop. It is at its noisiest with the hardtop mounted but one could overcome this by lining the glassfibre interior. Mark I Sprite owners will feel perfectly at home in the cockpit of the latest model; the facia layout and driving control positions remain almost identical. Main differences are the independent switch for the head and side lamps (away from the ignition switch) and the fitting of a high beam tell-tale light in the speedometer face. All the instruments are simple and easy to read.

Well Placed Controls

Particularly praiseworthy in such a small car is the layout of the pedals, and the heel-and-toe technique can be performed without need to twist the ankle to any awkward angle. Twice during the test the throttles stuck open for no apparent reason. There is plenty of room to rest the left foot off the clutch pedal. The foot-operated dip-switch is easy to find, but it is surprising how often, with a relatively low-powered sports car, the need to dip and to change gear coincide. Illumination from the headlamps, which are the latest sealed-beam type, is such that they impose no limitation on fast night driving.

To open the bonnet a toggle below the facia is pulled; when open the new lid gives access only to the engine. Items needing frequent checking can be reached without difficulty. Light struts hold the boot and bonnet lids open. Particularly good on this car was the fresh air heater and ventilator which provided large quantities of hot or cold air as required. Flaps either side of the transmission cover directed the airstream to the screen or interior. The temperature could be regulated very accurately but it was impossible to stop the air flow completely, the control on the facia apparently needing adjustment.

The car is offered in a cheap basic form and a large list of optional extras is available—nearly all of them were fitted to the car on test. Individual owners can select those that best suit their pocket and purpose, but the heater and tonneau are almost indispensable, and the hardtop can be particularly recommended. A cigar lighter is very useful in an open car and the twin horns could always be heard. B.M.C.-approved accessories in this car were the combined

With the new bonnet lid, inspection of the battery has been made an easier task. As well as the main bonnet release, there is a safety hook which fastens in the loop at the bottom right corner of the picture

lap-straps and diagonal belts, but the anchorage points for these are now fitted on all Sprites.

Visibility when the car is open is good. With the hardtop or hood in position, however, even a person of medium stature found difficulty in seeing much to the side. The mirror was mounted too low for a reasonable view through the hardtop rear window.

A rather meagre tool kit is provided with the Sprite—especially since this is the type of car that many owners like to tinker with. Servicing requirements are moderate—there are 12 greasing points, and a number of other places requiring lubrication every 1,000 miles.

It would appear that many of the criticisms—certainly most of the complaints mentioned in previous *Autocar* Road Tests of the Sprite—have been remedied with the introduction of the Mark II. It does everything its predecessor did with a little more refinement—it is, therefore, a very worthy successor.

AUSTIN-HEALEY SPRITE II

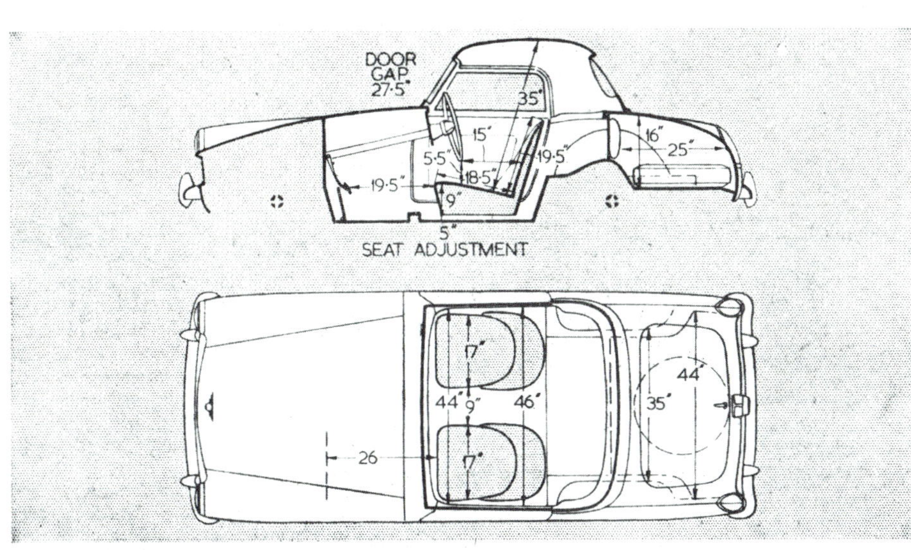

Scale ¼in to 1ft. Driving seat in central position. Cushions uncompressed.

——— DATA ———

PRICE (basic), with open two-seater body, £462.
British purchase tax, £193 12s 6d.
Total (in Great Britain), £655 12s 6d.
Extras, inc. p.t.:
  Radio £29 7s 11d.
  Heater £17.
  Hardtop £49 11s 8d.
  Laminated windscreen £3 17s 11d.
  Cigar lighter £1 11s 2d.
  Locking petrol cap 17s 9d.
  Tonneau cover, rail, and bag, £6 7s 6d.
  Wheel discs £15 17s 9d.
  Twin horns £1 11s 2d.

ENGINE: Capacity, 948 c.c. (57·9 cu. in.).
Number of cylinders, 4.
Bore and stroke, 62·9 × 76·2 mm (2·478 × 3·00in.).
Valve gear, overhead, pushrods.
Compression ratio, 9·0 to 1.
B.h.p. (net) 46·5 at 5,500 r.p.m. (b.h.p. per ton laden 55·5).
Torque, 53 lb ft at 2,750 r.p.m.
M.p.h. per 1,000 r.p.m. in top gear, 15·37.

WEIGHT (with 5 gal fuel): 13·75 cwt (1,540 lb).
Weight distribution (per cent): F, 51·4; R, 48·6.
Laden as tested, 16·75 cwt (1,876 lb).
Lb per c.c. (laden), 1·97.

BRAKES: Type, Lockheed hydraulic.
Drum diameter and lining width: F and R, 7in. diameter; 1·25 in. wide.
Total swept area: F and R, 110 sq. in. (131 sq. in. per ton laden).

TYRES: 5.20—13in.
Pressures (p.s.i.): F, 18; R, 20 (normal). F, 20; R, 22 (fast driving).

TANK CAPACITY: 6 Imperial gallons.
Oil sump, 6·5 pints.
Cooling system, 10 pints.

DIMENSIONS: Wheelbase, 6ft 8in.
Track: F, 3ft 9·75in.; R, 3ft 8·75in.
Length (overall), 11ft 4in.
Width, 4ft 5in.
Height, 4ft 1·75in.
Ground clearance, 7in.
Frontal area, 13·3 sq. ft. (approximately).
Capacity of luggage space: 11·5 cu. ft. (approximately).

ELECTRICAL SYSTEM: 12-volt; 43 ampère-hour battery.
Headlamps: 42 watt bulbs.

SUSPENSION: Front, coil springs and wishbones, lever-type dampers.
Rear, live axle, quarter elliptic leaf springs and radius arms, lever-type dampers.

——— PERFORMANCE ———

ACCELERATION TIMES (mean):

Speed range, m.p.h.	4·22 to 1	5·8 to 1	8·08 to 1	13·5 to 1
10—30	—	9·8	6·2	—
20—40	14·4	8·9	6·1	—
30—50	14·2	9·5	—	—
40—60	16·6	11·3	—	—
50—70	19·2	—	—	—
60—80	31·7	—	—	—

From rest through gears to:

30 m.p.h.	..	5·7 sec.	
40 "	..	9·0 "	
50 "	..	13·8 "	
60 "	..	19·8 "	
70 "	..	29·4 "	
80 "	..	51·8 "	

Standing quarter mile 21·8 sec.

MAXIMUM SPEEDS ON GEARS

Gear		m.p.h.	k.p.h.
Top	(mean)	85·3	137·3
	(best)	85·5	137·6
3rd	.. ..	68	109
2nd	.. ..	46	74
1st	.. ..	28	45

TRACTIVE EFFORT (by Tapley meter):

	Pull (lb per ton)	Equivalent gradient
Top	195	1 in 11·4
Third ..	280	1 in 7·9
Second ..	370	1 in 6·0

BRAKES (at 30 m.p.h. in neutral):

Pedal load in lb.	Retardation	Equiv. stopping distance in ft.
25	0·14g	216
50	0·36g	84
75	0·64g	47
100	0·88g	34
110	0·98g	30·9

FUEL CONSUMPTION (at steady speeds in top gear):

30 m.p.h.	50·0 m.p.g.	
40 "	51·3 "	
50 "	46·0 "	
60 "	39·2 "	
70 "	35·6 "	

Overall fuel consumption for 1,086 miles, 33·2 m.p.g. (8·5 litres per 100 km.).
Approximate normal range 28–45 m.p.g. (10·1–6·3 litres per 100 km.).
Fuel: Super Premium.

TEST CONDITIONS: Weather: Dry and sunny. No wind.
Air temperature, 60 deg. F.
Model described 2 June, 1961.

STEERING: Turning circle:
Between kerbs, R, 30ft 0in.; L, 30ft 9in.
Between walls, R, 31ft 4·5in.; L, 32ft 1·5in.
Turns of steering wheel from lock to lock, 2·25.

SPEEDOMETER CORRECTION: M.P.H.

Car speedometer	..	..	10	20	30	40	50	60	70	80	90
True speed	..	..	10	19	29	38	47	56	66	75	84

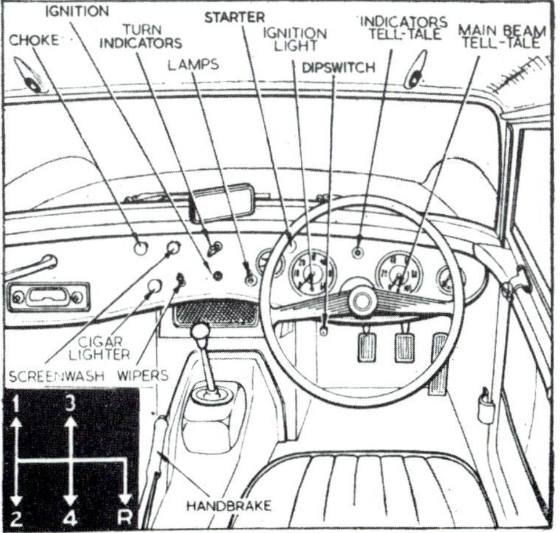

IMPROVING THE PERFORMANCE OF POPULAR CARS

Above: The car which was tested competes at an International Silverstone meeting with Australian, Paul Hawkins, at the wheel. Below: Not after the fire . . . but it shows the lengths to which competitors go to remove all surplus weight

SEBRING SPRITE

ALTHOUGH many different conversions of standard production cars come the way of *The Autocar* Road Test staff, few have been so internationally famous in competition motoring as the Austin-Healey Sebring Sprite. This car, perhaps, only just falls within the category of a conversion, since the modifications are extensive enough for it to be regarded as a separate model. Although based on the normal Sprite, it has been built in sufficient numbers for the car to be recognized and homologated as a Grand Tourer by the international authorities.

It is available in a number of different forms, depending on the uses to which the owner wishes to put it. The actual car tested belonged to John Sprinzel and has covered many hundreds of racing miles—some of them with Stirling Moss at the wheel.

Few distinguishable Sprite features remained. The B.M.C. A-type engine had been modified extensively—a formula Junior crankshaft, lightened flywheel, flat-top solid skirt pistons, oversize inlet valves and 11 to 1 compression ratio being among the changes. The fan had been removed, but a full-flow oil cooler helped to keep the temperature down. Mounted immediately behind the driving seat were two S.U. petrol pumps

PERFORMANCE

From rest through gears to:			Sebring Sprite	Mark 2 Sprite
40 m.p.h.	..	..	5·8 sec	9·0 sec
50 ,,	..	..	7·6 ,,	13·8 ,,
60 ,,	..	..	10·8 ,,	19·8 ,,
70 ,,	..	..	14·1 ,,	29·4 ,,
80 ,,	..	..	20·2 ,,	51·8 ,,
90 ,,	..	..	27·8 ,,	—
Standing quarter mile			17·8 sec	21·8 sec
Second Gear				
10—30 m.p.h.	..		5.6 sec	6.2 sec
20—40 ,,	..		4·0 ,,	6·1 ,,
30—50 ,,	..		4·3 ,,	—
Third Gear				
30—50 m.p.h.	..		5·7 sec	9·5 sec
40—60 ,,	..		5·7 ,,	11·3 ,,
50—70 ,,	..		6·5 ,,	—
Top Gear				
40—60 m.p.h.	..		8·6 sec	16·6 sec
50—70 ,,	..		9·5 ,,	19·2 ,,
70—90 ,,	..		14·2 ,,	—

Maximum Speed in Gears
Gear:

Top (mean)	100 m.p.h.	(7,200 r.p.m.)	85.3	m.p.h.
(best)	100 ,,		85·5	,,
Third ..	73 ,,		68	,,
Second	51 ,,		46	,,
First	31 ,,		28	,,

Modifications under the light-weight bonnet had been carried out in a workman-like style, and accessibility to all components is outstandingly good

SEBRING SPRITE . . .

for supplying the twin 1¼in. S.U. carburettors; a nine-spring competition clutch transmitted the torque. A power output of 80 b.h.p. at 7,000 r.p.m. is claimed.

The gearbox was the close-ratio unit now fitted as standard equipment to the Mark II Sprite. Normally the Sebring Sprite has a 4·55 : 1 rear axle ratio, but on the car tested a 4·875 : 1 axle ratio was installed. This was the ratio employed at Brands Hatch, where the car had been racing a few days before it was collected for test. Suspension changes consisted of heavy-duty shock absorbers at the front with an anti-roll bar, and adjustable dampers at the rear. Wire wheels and 5·20—13in. R5 Dunlop covers were fitted. The front drum brakes had been replaced by 8·5in. diameter discs.

The bodywork had been extensively lightened; the bonnet was constructed from glass fibre and an aluminium hardtop of streamlined shape covered the passenger compartment. All the interior trim had been removed, and the battery shifted from under the bonnet to a position just forward of the rear axle. With the spare wheel on board and the 12-gallon fuel tank half-full, the car weighed 11·75 cwt, almost 2 cwt lighter than a standard hardtop Sprite. The weight distribution was almost exactly 50 per cent fore and aft.

First impression after opening the door, which was done by inserting a hand through a small sliding pane in the side-screen and lifting an interior catch, is one of bareness and exposed wiring. The whole of the facia had been removed and the only instruments fitted were an electronic tachometer, an oil pressure gauge, a water thermometer and a petrol gauge.

Switches for lamps, ignition, starter and windscreen wiper were mounted on the central console which covered the gearbox and flywheel. Both the road and the rear axle are visible through gaps in the floor on either side of the battery box.

The first thing that one notices as soon as the engine starts, which it always did very easily, is the noise. Even the most hardened extrovert would be embarrassed by the amount of exhaust noise from this car. It is almost impossible to avoid it, however carefully one drives. In town the car was a slight nuisance, as it was inclined to overheat and even the soft plugs started to misfire. It also became very warm in the cockpit and one sat in a mist of Castrol-R fumes—very intoxicating for the diehard enthusiasts. Surprisingly enough, the engine was remarkably tractable, and one could potter along at relatively low engine speeds. Full power from the engine was not available under 5,000 r.p.m., but it then continued right through to 7,000 r.p.m. Rather fierce for road use, the clutch was much as one would have expected on a competition car.

On the open road, if one could submerge the feeling of being anti-social, the car was immense fun to drive. Hard when travelling slowly, the suspension and ride greatly improved with increased speed. The small bucket seats held their occupants securely. Steering was light, direct and positive, the rack and pinion mechanism being very well run in. Gone was the " darting " feeling experienced with many Sprites and directional stability was excellent. While cornering the good balance of the car made the steering almost completely neutral and gave considerable confidence.

What of the performance? John Sprinzel had asked that the engine speed be limited to 7,200 r.p.m. In practice it was found that the engine started misfiring if this speed were exceeded. With the lower rear axle ratio incorporated it was possible to achieve 7,200 r.p.m. in top gear with remarkable ease, even up a slight incline. This engine speed represented about 100 m.p.h. Acceleration, therefore, not maximum speed, is the interesting feature of this car. In the performance table, the figures obtained are set out alongside those of the recently tested Mark II Sprite. A standing quarter-mile of 17·8sec is extremely fast, as is 0-80 m.p.h. in 20·2sec. In racing trim, with only one person aboard and no road test equipment, these figures naturally would be even better.

The disc brakes fitted on the front of the car are an obvious must for the Sebring Sprite. With these there was never any fade when stopping from high speeds frequently and consecutively.

Total price of the equipment fitted to this car is £650, and there is no reason why the modifications should not be made to a second-hand Sprite. In this case, for just over £1,000 one can have an extremely worth-while racing or rally car to distinguish itself in any international company. Its successes have been widespread and varied, and last year one finished third in the most gruelling of all rallies, the Liège-Rome-Liège, and its name results from regular class victories at Sebring.

The Mosses, brother and sister, sprint across the track to jump into their Sprites at the start of the Sebring four-hour Grand Touring car race earlier this year

The *Autocar* road tests

Detail modifications—including radiator grille and the air intake on the bonnet top— have been made, but the basic outline of the "big" Healey remains much the same as when it was introduced in 1952. In certain ways, the Healey preserves earlier British sports car traditions

AUSTIN-HEALEY 3000

WHEN the Healey 100 made its début at the Earls Court Show of 1952, fitted with the four-cylinder 2·6-litre engine used in the Austin A.90 Atlantic coupé, it was clear that the car was destined for a successful competition career. However, one doubts whether anyone foresaw its becoming, eight years later, one of the most successful rally cars in the world, winning outright the tough Liège-Rome-Liège and Alpine rallies. Except for detail changes, the clean, attractive lines of the car have remained very much the same. Mechanically, the changes have centred largely around the power unit, the Austin-Healey 100 becoming the Austin-Healey 100-Six in 1957, when the four-cylinder engine was replaced by a six of similar capacity.

Three years later it became the Austin-Healey 3000, when the capacity was increased to 2,912 c.c., and this year the Mark 2 was introduced. Apart from a restyled radiator grille, the latest car is fitted with three 1½-in. HS4 S.U. carburettors in place of the two 1¾-in. HS6s of the previous model, together with a redesigned inlet manifold and a new camshaft giving higher lift to the inlet valves and a longer dwell to the exhausts. All this has brought the production car allegedly into line with the specification of the successful competition cars used by the B.M.C. Competitions Department. Thus, through the years, the engine output has increased from the 90 b.h.p. of the Healey 100 to the 132 b.h.p. of the Mark 2 Austin-Healey 3000, with the weight increasing from 1,960lb to 2,526. The b.h.p. per ton figure, therefore, has been increased only from 102 to 117.

First impressions of the car are that it is comfortable, has plenty of leg room, is moderately well appointed, and

Central pull-up handbrake, all-black finish, near-vertical steering wheel, and full instrumentation—this is very much a "competition" cockpit

The engine compartment is packed, yet everything that matters—carburettors, hydraulic reservoirs, distributor and radiator cap—are readily accessible. The screenwash bottle is mounted inside the cockpit

Austin-Healey 3000 . . .

is immensely strong and rigid. Also, it has a pleasant, long-legged feeling of being able to lollop along all day at a cruising speed of 90 m.p.h. or more with very little effort.

The cockpit is very well arranged and is finished throughout in black leather, or leather-cloth where wear is light. The driving seat on the car tested was hard and seemed to have inadequate upholstery; this, together with one or two other points, suggested that the 10,000 miles indicated in the speedometer window had been fairly strenuous ones. For a tall person the forward visibility is excellent; but, with the seat so compressed, a shorter driver had his view interrupted by the top of the large steering wheel. The instruments are comprehensive and well set out, while all the "driving" controls are within comfortable reach. Instrument lighting is good, without being so bright as to worry one, though there is no rheostat control. The screen pillars are slim and the extremities of both front wings are seen easily, so that placing the car in heavy traffic is no problem.

The hard-top was draught- and water-proof, making the interior of the car snug and warm. This is an optional extra, costing £60, the conventional soft hood being standard equipment; with either in position, the occasional rear seat(s) can be used only for short runs, headroom being decidedly cramped. Rigid, aluminium-framed transparent plastic sidescreens are fitted, the rearmost panels of which slide forwards. There is no method of locking the driving compartment, and no lockable glove locker, so that valuables should not be left in the car. By turning off the battery master-switch in the boot, and locking the boot lid, the car can be made secure against a thief in a hurry.

Large pockets are provided in the doors, and there is a parcels shelf above the foot-well on the passenger's side. This would be much more useful if it did not house the screenwash bottle, for which there is no room in the very full engine compartment. The heating-demisting system is most efficient, as is the fresh-air cooling system, and one

is no longer worried by the high cockpit temperatures found in earlier models of this car. The range of seat adjustment for both passenger and driver is considerable, and desirable if the rear seats are to be used. However, if one sets the driving seat to achieve a "straight-armed" position, the pedals become out of reach, despite the provision of an adjustment in steering column length of around 3in. The situation is not improved by the unusually long travel in the clutch pedal and gear lever. Adding to the impression that the particular car tested had seen a very active life was the fact that the synchromesh was practically non-existent, particularly on top gear.

The hand-brake is of the pull-up type, conveniently placed between the front seats. When the car is travelling forward it is extremely efficient, and will apply the rear drum brakes with sufficient force to lock the rear wheels; it will also hold the car from running forwards on a 1-in-3 test hill. Surprisingly, however, it will not prevent the car from running backwards on the 1-in-4 test gradient.

Cold Starting

With use of the choke, the engine starts quickly and easily from cold, though it reaches its working temperature somewhat slowly. It does not appreciate a diet of premium-grade fuel, on which it pinks and tends to run-on after being switched off. With the compression ratio of 9·0 to 1 this is scarcely surprising, and both faults were eliminated by using super-premium fuel. It is extremely smooth and flexible, and has plenty of torque at low speeds. It will pull the car away in top gear without hesitation or snatch from the surprisingly low speed of 8 m.p.h., so that it is able to trickle through traffic happily in third gear. It is reasonably quiet and unobtrusive up to 3,000 r.p.m., but above this speed there are some intake roar and roughness.

The clutch is light in operation, and very smooth in take-up; there was no prolonged slip when the standing-start figures were taken, nor when full-throttle changes were made, and it had no trouble in moving the car off quickly and cleanly on a 1-in-3 test gradient. The Laycock-de Normanville overdrive, which is available as an optional extra and was fitted on the test car, works on top and third gears. It is invaluable in keeping the engine speed down, and thus saving petrol; and it helps one to avoid the critical engine speed of 3,000 r.p.m. at which there is a noticeable resonance in the exhaust system. The transmission as a whole is very quiet, and there are no vibration periods throughout the speed range.

In general "feel" the car inspires great confidence, being undoubtedly very safe indeed and entirely without whims or idiosyncrasies. It has excellent directional stability, and will hurry along at 100 m.p.h. or more "hands off," without any desire to wander off-line. It has a slight—and de-

Very much an "occasional four-seater," the Healey offers limited space for rear passengers; headroom beneath the hard-top is cramped

The rear bumper wraps round to give good protection. Ground clearance is limited below the exhaust pipe where it runs beneath the rear cross member. The hard-top is optional

sirable—understeering characteristic; and, except when speeds are so high that the engine has run out of power, it is always possible to help the tail round by means of the throttle. If the rear wheels do begin to slide—which they will do fairly easily at the manufacturers' recommended high-speed tyre pressures of 26 p.s.i. front and 29 rear— the response to opposite lock is immediate, the car quickly straightening up. So "right" does the handling feel that one gets the impression that it would be difficult even for an inexperienced driver to get into any serious trouble. The steering is light though one would prefer slightly higher

Luggage space, if the rear seats are to be used for passengers, is strictly of the "toothbrush-and-pyjamas" variety, though when the car is used as a two-seater—as it normally would be on long runs—there is plenty of space behind the front seats

gearing than its present 3¼ turns from lock to lock. Self-centring action is pleasantly strong.

Second gear is too low, maximum speeds in the gears being 34, 48, 77, and 106 m.p.h.—and 98 in overdrive third. The gear-change is precise, and smooth in operation. In taking the standing-start acceleration figures it was difficult to avoid wheelspin on the initial take-off, even on a dry road, and in the wet one had to be decidedly gentle with the throttle.

Although surprisingly soft, the suspension is sufficiently damped to avoid much roll when the car is cornering fast, and ride comfort is excellent. Not only does it iron out the normal, main road long-frequency irregularities completely, but it rides well over the shorter bumps, such as

potholes. Very little road noise is transmitted to the interior of the car. On a rough, pavé-type surface, however, the occupants are bounced about to some extent at slow speeds, though the ride levels off as the speed is increased; on such surfaces there is reasonably little outward patter of the wheels on cornering. On the washboard test surface, the whole body structure of the car was amazingly stable, confirming the impression that it is very rigidly built. Coupled with the safe handling characteristics of the Healey, the first-class ride makes it a very restful car for long-distance travel.

Reliable Brakes

From start to finish the brakes inspired great trust, giving plenty of "feel," always pulling the car up in a straight line, and never showing signs of fade, even after repeated stops from high speeds. The car has always been sound in this particular aspect; of the drum brakes fitted to the car tested in 1953 it was said that they were "entirely suitable," and the same was said of the rear drums and front discs of the car tested last year—equipment which the Mark 2 also uses. A brake servo was not fitted to the car tested, though this is available as an optional extra, and pedal pressures were therefore somewhat high, as shown by the meter readings. Due to the angle of the pedal, however, or the relative positions of the seat and brake pedal, one never appeared to be pressing particularly hard; it seems that the use of a servo is scarcely justified, even if the car is to be driven exclusively by a woman.

There are several points about the car which, though in keeping with its honest-to-goodness, no-frills character, seem somewhat out of place in a £1,200 car in 1961. There are, for example, no automatic supports for the bonnet or boot lid when they are open; instead one has to reach for their props and fit them into the slots provided. The doors are stiff to open, due to the use of friction-damper-type devices to stop them from swinging shut; and wheel-changing involves the use of an old-fashioned screw-up jack and the business of groping underneath the car for a suitable jacking point. The forepart of the hardtop is sensibly padded, to protect the occupants' heads—yet, proud of the padding, protrude potentially dangerous sharp clips which secure the roof to the windscreen. If the Austin-Healey were an out-and-out competition car one would readily forgive a lack of concessions to creature comforts, but it is essentially a fast sports-tourer, at least in its production form.

Luggage accommodation is rather meagre, the spare wheel and battery occupying most of the boot. For long-distance touring, however, when carrying space is at a premium, the car must in any case be regarded as no more than a two-seater, and the compartment behind the front seats will take a substantial amount of baggage. The fuel tank capacity is 12 gallons, giving the car a range between fill-up stops of about 200 miles. The lighting equipment is in keeping with the performance, the headlamps giving a powerful enough beam almost for the daytime cruising speeds to be maintained. They are foot-dipped by a switch alongside the clutch, where the left foot normally rests. This space, in fact, is larger than it needs to be—and the pedals could with advantage have greater separation; it would be difficult to drive the car wearing wide shoes.

Though there are a few points of criticism, the Mark 2 Austin-Healey is a good quality, strongly built sporting car with great charm and an amazing aptitude for hard work. It has a lively performance in standard trim, a performance to which the figures achieved by this far from new car scarcely do justice; almost all of them are appreciably down on those recorded by its predecessor, road-tested last year. The general quality of finish, and attention to detail is first class, except for those points mentioned. That it is capable of giving a much enhanced performance—for those who seek it—is shown by its remarkable run of successes in International rallies.

AUSTIN-HEALEY 3000

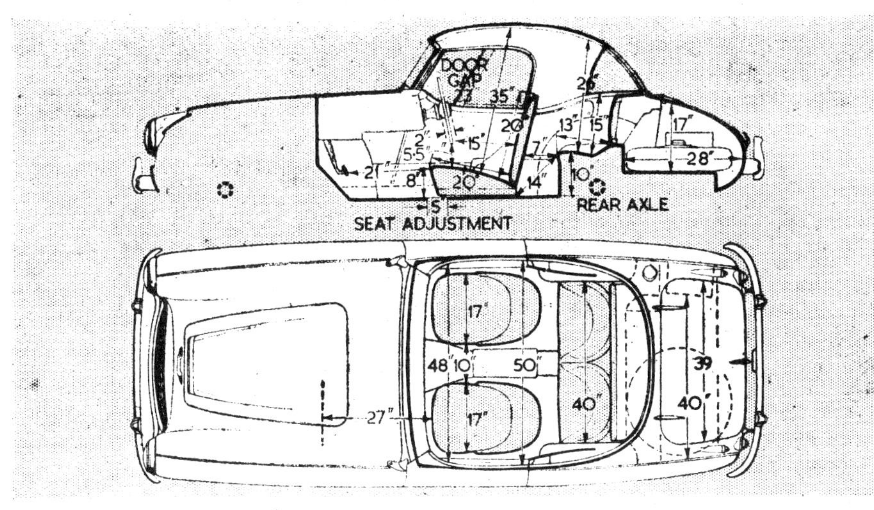

Scale ¼in. to 1ft. Driving seat in central position. Cushions uncompressed.

PERFORMANCE

ACCELERATION TIMES (mean):
Speed range, Gear Ratios, and Time in Sec.

m.p.h.	3·21* to 1	3·91 to 1	4·2* to 1	5·12 to 1	8·05 to 1	11·26 to 1
10– 30	—	—	—	7·0	4·1	3·5
20– 40	11·0	8·6	7·9	6·2	4·0	—
30– 50	11·3	8·3	8·1	6·2	—	—
40– 60	11·2	7·8	7·9	6·3	—	—
50– 70	13·1	8·9	8·8	7·6	—	—
60– 80	13·6	10·0	9·7	—	—	—
70– 90	15·0	13·2	13·9	—	—	—
80–100	18·5	17·5	—	—	—	—

* Overdrive

From rest through gears to:

30 m.p.h.	..	3·7 sec.
40 "	..	6·2 "
50 "	..	9·3 "
60 "	..	11·5 "
70 "	..	15·6 "
80 "	..	22·0 "
90 "	..	30·0 "
100 "	..	36·9 "

Standing quarter mile 18·8 sec.

MAXIMUM SPEEDS ON GEARS:

Gear			m.p.h.	k.p.h.
O.D. Top	(mean)		112·5	181·1
	(best)		115·0	185·1
Top	..	..	106	170
O.D. 3rd	..	..	98	158
3rd	..	..	81	130
2nd	..	..	50	80
1st	..	..	37	60

TRACTIVE EFFORT (by Tapley meter):

	Pull (lb per ton)	Equivalent gradient
O.D.	.. ..	260	1 in 8·6
Top	.. ..	340	1 in 6·5
O.D. Third	..	355	1 in 6·4
Third	..	445	1 in 5·0
Second	..	670	1 in 3·2

BRAKES (at 30 m.p.h. in neutral):

Pedal load in lb	Retardation	Equiv. stopping distance in ft
50	0·31g	97
75	0·47g	64
100	0·72g	42
125	0·84g	36
130	0·94g	32·1

FUEL CONSUMPTION (at constant speeds):

	Direct Top	O.D. Top
30 m.p.h.	30·5 m.p.g.	31·3 m.p.g.
40 "	27·2 "	30·0 "
50 "	25·1 "	28·0 "
60 "	23·3 "	26·0 "
70 "	21·2 "	24·2 "
80 "	19·1 "	23·3 "
90 "	15·0 "	18·0 "
100 "	11·0 "	15·1 "

Overall fuel consumption for 1,223 miles, 17·7 m.p.g. (16·0 litres per 100 km.).

Approximate normal range 13–20 m.p.g. (21·7—14·1 litres per 100 km.).

Fuel: Super premium grades.

TEST CONDITIONS: Weather: Damp surface.
0–5 m.p.h. wind.
Air temperature, 55 deg. F.
Model described in *The Autocar* of 2 June, 1961.

STEERING: Turning circle:
Between kerbs: L, 34ft 4in.; R, 35ft 4in.
Between walls: L, 35ft 4in.; R, 36ft 4in.
Turns of steering wheel from lock to lock, 3·25.

SPEEDOMETER CORRECTION: m.p.h.

Car speedometer: ..	10	20	30	40	50	60	70	80	90	100	110	120
True speed: ..	9	19	28	37	47	57	66	75	84	94	106	115

DATA

PRICE (basic), with four-seater body, £829.
British purchase tax, £381 3s 11d.
Total (in Great Britain), £1,210 3s 11d.
Extras (inc. p.t.): Radio, £35. Heater, £22 12s 1d. Overdrive, £69 7s 3d. Hard-top, £87 10s. Wire wheels, £36 9s 2d.

ENGINE: Capacity, 2,912 c.c. (177·7 cu. in.)
Number of cylinders, 6.
Bore and stroke, 83·36 × 89·0mm (3·28 × 3·5in.).
Valve gear, overhead, pushrods and rockers.
Compression ratio, 9·0 to 1.
B.h.p. (net), 130 at 4,750 r.p.m. (b.h.p. per ton laden 100·7).
Torque (net), 167 lb. ft at 3,000 r.p.m.
M.p.h. per 1,000 r.p.m. in top gear, 20·9; in overdrive, 23·1.

WEIGHT (with 5 gal fuel): 22·8 cwt (2,555 lb).
Weight distribution (per cent): F, 48·8; R, 51·2.
Laden as tested, 25·8 cwt (2,891 lb).
Lb per c.c. (laden), 0·9.

BRAKES: Type, Girling, disc front, drum rear, hydraulic.
Disc diameter: 11·25in.
Drum dimensions: 11in. diameter; 2·25in. wide.
Swept area: F, 228 sq. in.; R, 155·5 sq. in. (297 sq. in. per ton laden).

TYRES: 5·90—15in. Dunlop RS5.
Pressures (p.s.i.): F, 20; R, 23 (normal); F, 26; R, 29 (fast driving).

TANK CAPACITY: 12 Imperial gallons.
Oil sump, 12 pints.
Cooling system, 20 pints (plus 1 pint if heater fitted).

DIMENSIONS: Wheelbase, 7ft 8in.
Track: F, 4ft 0·75in.; R, 4ft 2in.
Length (overall), 13ft 1·5in.
Width, 5ft 0·5in.
Height, 4ft 6in.
Ground clearance, 4·5in.

ELECTRICAL SYSTEM: 12-volt; 50 ampère-hour battery.
Headlamps, 50–40 watt bulbs.

SUSPENSION: Front, wishbones and coil springs, anti-roll bar.
Rear, live axle, half-elliptic springs and Panhard rod.

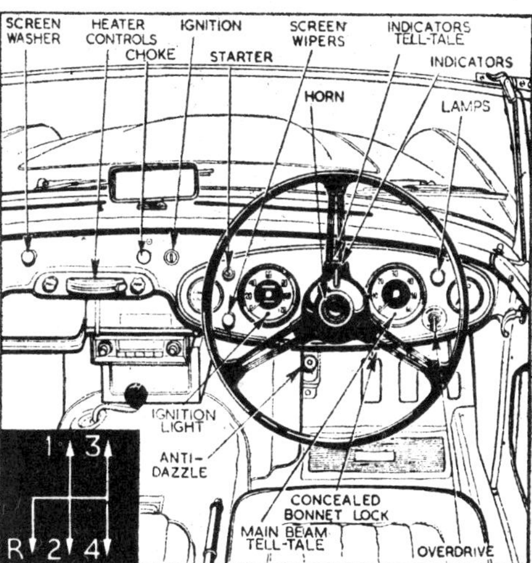

Into Battle 1961

Above left. Le Mans: the Stoop-Bekaert Austin-Healey leads a Fiat-Abarth, a couple of D.B.-Panhards and an Aston Martin. The Healey retired, with $2\frac{1}{2}$ hours to go, when lying fifteenth.

Above right. Pat Moss and Anne Wisdom and the Morley brothers' cars negotiate the streets of Ville, near Nancy, on the Tulip Rally. The Healeys performed well, coming first and second in their class.

Right. Pat Moss accelerates her Austin-Healey 3000 out of the hairpin on Rest-and-Be-Thankful during the R.A.C. Rally.

Below left. The Siegle-Morris Austin-Healey 3000 passes through Brookhouse, near Lancaster, during the R.A.C. Rally.

Below right. John Gott struggling with dusty and unmade roads, in Yugoslavia, in the Liege-Rome-Liege Rally.

AUSTIN-HEALEY 3000
Sports Convertible

IN keeping with the current trend in sports car body design, the British Motor Corporation announce the Austin-Healey 3000 Sports Convertible as a replacement for the well-established 3000 Mark II model. Retaining the same body lines as that model it offers greatly enhanced weather protection. As a result of minor engine changes, the low speed behaviour of the car has been brought into line with its new role without, however, detracting appreciably from its top end performance. An internal re-arrangement of the gearbox has reduced the effective dimensions of that unit, resulting in slightly more toeboard space.

A new windscreen with a stout, chromium-plated frame is the main apparent change to the appearance of the car. The line of the screen bottom rail is continued along the top of the doors by the use of a stainless steel moulding—a trick which raises the waist line. Plated quarter-vent frames are functional as well as adding to the area of bright metal work; they have channels in their rear edge for the new curved side window glasses, which are frameless and wind down flush with the tops of the doors. Conventional window lifts are employed, with the handles set well forward on the doors, clear of the occupants' knees.

Internally, little is altered except that trim pads with map pockets replace the door compartments of the earlier model. There is also slight loss of width across the rear compartment because of the wider boxes required to house the more complex hood frame. The main trim change is in the upholstery material itself, which is a new porous, leather-grained plastic. This covering retains its flexibility in a wide range of temperature conditions. The upholstery is in a choice of colours to contrast with the main body paint.

Folded, the hood does not drop below the main body level but makes a neat line along the rear deck and should help to reduce back swirl of wind at speed. Although it is necessary to get out of the car to stow the hood neatly, it can be lowered from the driving seat by un-fastening two over-centre clasps which hold it to the screen rail, and pushing it back with one hand. The hood frame is sturdy without being complicated and the covering, in stout black plastic, is suffi-ciently flexible to pull tight without wrinkles.

While enthusiasts may not approve of the reversion to two 1·75in. HS6 S.U. carburettors on basically the old inlet manifold, maximum power is reduced by only 1 b.h.p. With this change goes an improved torque curve which is now substantially flat between 2,800 r.p.m. and 3,700 r.p.m., a figure of 158lb./ft. (equal to a net b.m.e.p. of 135 p.s.i.) being

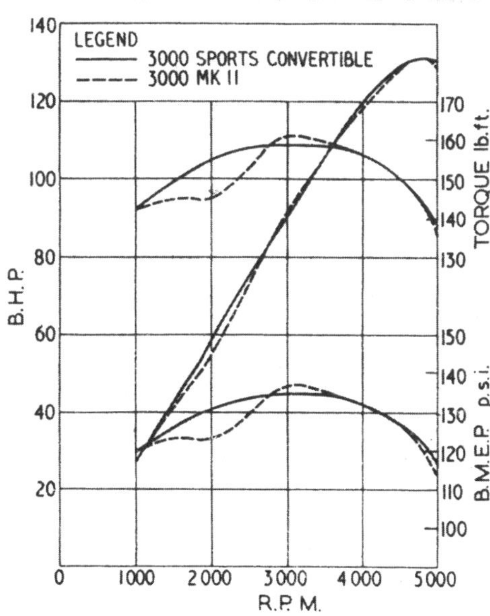

Left : Induction layout, using two 1·75in. HS6 S.U. carburettors in place of three 1·5in. instruments. It gives better accessibility for tuning, and two units are more easily synchronized

Comparative performance curves of the new and old engines, torque has been improved without significant top-end power loss

Left: Furled, the hood stands proud above the rear deck and forms a windbreak. The hood cover is standard equipment. Right: Introduction of wind-down windows has meant that the large door lockers of previous 3000 models have been lost in accommodating the window winding mechanism. However, map pockets are retained on both doors

Above: A useful feature in hot climates is the ability to roll down the rear window and obtain a flow of cool air through the car. The flexible clear plastic light is attached internally with press studs. Right: Suitable for one-man operation, the new hood is sturdy and neat. The heavy sponge rubber window seals can be seen along the edge of the frame

maintained within this range. Moreover, greater flexibility at very low speeds is claimed, and it was certainly possible to drive an early production model at less than 10 m.p.h. in top gear. Among the detail changes is a camshaft with slightly reduced dwell.

An engineering change, which considerably reduces the complication of the remote gear-change mechanism, has been a redesign of the gearbox casting to bring the selector mechanism to the top of the box. Previously this was at the side, a relic from the time when the gearbox was common to a B.M.C. model with steering column change. Apart from bringing the gear lever to the centreline of the car, the gear casing is narrower, permitting an increase of 0·75in. in toeboard width. A further improvement in this vicinity is that the transmission cover material has been changed to glass-fibre reinforced plastic, resulting in reduced heat transfer into the driving compartment.

To improve handling, the front roll stiffness has been increased by the incorporation of stiffer front springs and harder damper settings.

The incorporation of so many minor changes has had a marked influence on the character of the car. A brief run in an early production model confirmed that the level of refinement is noticeably higher because of greatly improved flexibility and increased quietness, and very little bite has been lost. The impression of refinement is owed partly to extra attention to soundproofing generally and in particular to the sound damping of the new door trim pads and side window glasses. At the moment production is concentrated on cars for the export market; however home buyers should not have too long to wait. As a result of these improvements, the basic price has increased by £36, or £49 10s with tax.

PRICES	Basic £	U.K. List £		s	d
Austin-Healey 3000					
Sports Convertible..	865	1,190		7	9
Extras :					
Wire-spoke wheels			34	7	6
Radio			33	0	0
Heater			21	6	3
Servo brakes			13	15	0
Tonneau cover			13	15	0
Overdrive			64	9	1

Two tremendously fast works Austin-Healeys arrive at the Spa Francorchamps Grand Prix circuit during the 1962 Tulip Rally. The Morleys, in the car in the foreground, came first in their class.

Austin-Healey 3000 Mk. III

PRICES

	Basic	Total (inc. P.T.)		
	£	£	s	d
Austin-Healey 300. Mk. III Sports Convertible	915	1,106	3	9
Extras (including P.T.)				
Overdrive		£60	8	4
Wire wheels		£30	4	2
Fresh-air heater		£18	14	7
Adjustable steering column		£2	8	4
Tonneau cover		£12	1	4
Leather upholstery		Price not available		

A YEAR and a half ago the Austin-Healey 3000 became a sports convertible with added comfort and refinement as its main features. To-day B.M.C. go further along these lines by announcing the Mark III version with a more luxurious interior, better exhaust silencing and a 12 per cent increase in power. To cope with the extra performance, servo brakes are standard equipment. Externally the car is unchanged, but the price in Britain has been increased from £1,046 to £1,106.

The most obvious difference in the interior of the car is the facia design, now changed from the functional lay-out of earlier models to a symmetrical arrangement of wooden panels with a central console merging with the transmission tunnel. In front of the driver, on the walnut-veneered panel, are the speedometer and an electronic rev coun-ter, visible through the spring-spoked steering wheel, and also the petrol gauge, water thermometer and choke control. On the passenger side is a glove box with a lockable lid.

Ignition and other switches are on a small strip on the console with the heater controls above them. Below the switch panel is a standard radio aperture and the speaker grille, blanked off when a radio is not fitted. Lower edges of the facia are finished with a plated bead, and the console is covered in black leather-cloth.

The same arrangement of separate bucket seats at the front and miniature bucket seats for children in the back is retained. But the appearance of the trim is improved by fluting the centre panels of the seats with a new embossed Ambla two-way stretch leathercloth, giving the appearance of hand-tooled leather. Real leather upholstery is available at extra cost.

Suitcases and large objects carried on the back seats of earlier 3000s balanced precariously on the uneven platform provided by the half-seats. Now those owners who normally travel two up will appreciate the new design of the rear seat backrest, which is made to double out forwards to form a large, flat, carpet-covered platform over the rear seats. Two sturdy bolts underneath its forward edge hold it firmly in place. A further addition is a small companion-box built into the armrest between the front seats.

Two engine modifications have increased power output from 136 b.h.p. (gross) at 4,750 r.p.m. to 154 b.h.p gross (148 b.h.p. net) at 5,250 r.p.m. One is a camshaft with longer dwell, which besides providing better cylinder filling has the advantage of giving the tappets an easier time. Secondly, the two 1·75in. HS6 S.U. carburettors fitted to the Mark II Healey have been replaced by a pair of larger HD8 2in. instruments. While the main gain in power has been at the top end of the speed range, it will be seen from the power curve that torque, which determines the accelerative ability, is much

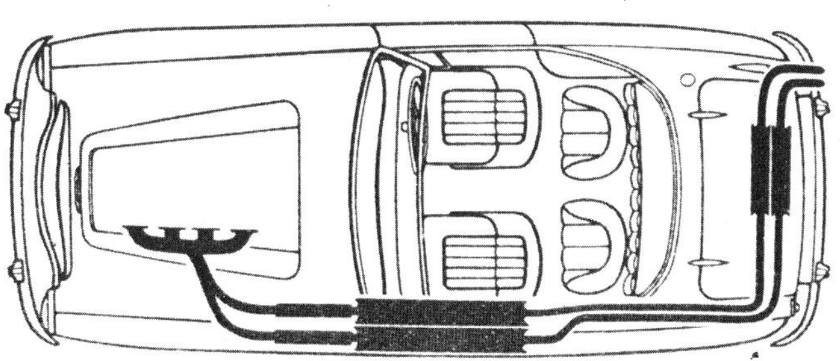

Layout of the new dual exhaust system

Below: New facia with walnut panels and centre console.

Right: Only external engine change is ths substitution of larger S.U. carburettors

improved above 1,700 r.p.m. or 35 m.p.h. in top gear.

A short drive in a Mark III showed that the reduced exhaust noise increased the impression of power. In fact, the new dual exhaust system, made necessary by impending restrictions in the U.S.A. which could well be extended to this country, absorbs no more power than the old system. The gross power output figure was achieved with the new exhaust system fitted on the test bed but without fan and dynamo. Dual cast-iron manifolds are used and flexible down pipes lead the gases to a pair of straight-through silencers mounted amidships outside the left chassis side member. The dual tail pipes then follow the line of the side member and turn across beneath the tail of the car, where the gases pass through dual expansion boxes.

A further improvement, which gives lighter clutch operation, is the adoption of a 9·5in. Borg and Beck diaphragm spring clutch. This modification was actually introduced some time ago to bring the Austin-Healey 3000 into line with other B.M.C. cars fitted with the C-series engine.

These changes confirm the Austin-Healey 3000 Mark III as a comfortable, high-speed touring car which will hold its own with most things on the road. The ruggedness of this model is a by-word—it is the only British model ever to have won the destructive Liège-Rome-Liège Rally—and its lines have a quality which should appeal to a buyer who likes to keep a car for several years.

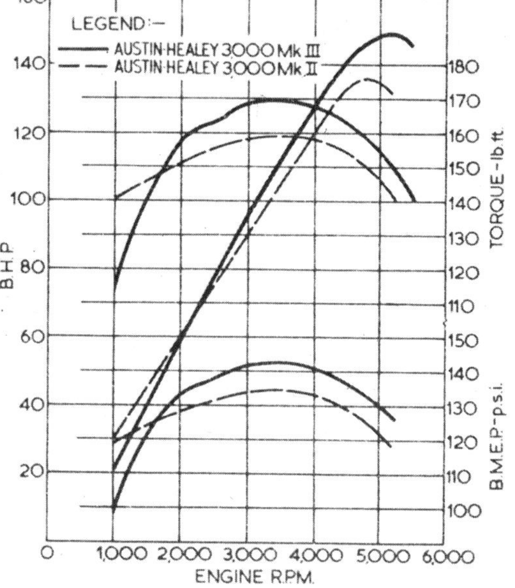

Gross performance curves for the new engine compared with the old

Specification

ENGINE (front-mounted, water-cooled)
No. of cylinders ... Six in-line
Bore ... 83·4mm (3·28in.)
Stroke ... 89mm (3.5in.)
Displacement ... 2,912 c.c. (178 cu. in.)
Valve operation ... Overhead, pushrods and rockers
Compression ratio 9·0 to 1
Max. b.h.p. (net) ... 148 at 5,250 r.p.m.
Max b.m.e.p. (net) 140·2 p.s.i. at 3,500 r.p.m.
Max torque (net) 165·2 at 3,500 r.p.m.
Carburettors ... Twin S.U. HD8
Fuel pump ... S.U. electric
Tank capacity ... 12 Imp. gallons (54·5 litres)
Sump capacity ... 12·75 pints (10 litres)
Oil filter ... Tecalemit or Purolator full-flow
Cooling system ... Centrifugal pump, fan and thermostat, pressurized to 7 p.s.i.
Battery ... 12 volt, 57 amp. hr.

TRANSMISSION
Clutch ... Borg and Beck diaphragm spring single dry plate, 9·5in. dia.
Gearbox ... Four-speed, synchromesh on 2nd, 3rd and top; central floor change.
Optional Laycock de Normanville overdrive

Overall gear ratios		Standard	Overdrive
OD Top		—	3·14
Top		3·55	3·91
OD 3rd		—	5·12
3rd		4·11	4·74
2nd		7·73	8·05
1st		10·21	11·26
Rev		13·13	14·54

Final drive ... Hypoid bevel 3·55 (3·91 with OD)

CHASSIS
Brakes ... Girling hydraulic, vacuum servo-assisted. Front discs, 11·25in. dia.; rear drums, 11in. dia.; 2·25in. wide shoes
Suspension: front Independent, coil springs and wishbones, anti-roll bar
Suspension: rear Live axle, half-elliptic leaf springs, Panhard rod
Dampers ... Armstrong lever arm type
Wheels ... Ventilated steel disc, 4in. wide rims
Tyre size ... 5·90—15in.
Steering ... Cam and peg
Steering wheel ... Three-spoke, 17in. diameter
Turns, lock to lock 3

DIMENSIONS
Wheelbase ... 7ft 8in. (234cm)
Track: front ... 4ft 0·75in. (124cm)
Track: rear ... 4ft 2in. (127 cm)
Overall length ... 13ft 1·5in. (400cm)
Overall width ... 5ft 0in. (152 cm)
Overall height (unladen) ... 4ft 2in. (127cm)
Ground clearance (laden) ... 4·6in. (12cm)
Turning circle ... 35ft 7in. (10·8m)
Kerb weight ... 23cwt (2,548lb—1,145kg)

PERFORMANCE DATA
Top gear m.p.h. per 1,000 r.p.m. 20·72 (23·01 OD)
Torque lb. ft. per cu. in. engine capacity ....0·93
Brake surface swept by linings......... 383·5 sq. in.
Weight distribution: F, 49·3 per cent, R, 50·7 per cent.

Timo Makinen and Paul Hawkins competing in the
1965 Targa Florio.

Following pages. This is a prototype of the planned
4-litre Healey 3000 Mark IV. The power unit was a
Rolls-Royce engine built and developed for Leyland.
The Mark IV project reached an advanced stage but in
the face of US safety regulations the 3000 was
discontinued in 1968.

Aaltonen and Ambrose on their way to winning the 1964 Marathon. The photographs below show the engine and special side exhaust (fitted after 1965) that were part of the 3000's success in rallies.

Competition Healeys in 1963

Left. Eric and Donald Morley pass through Blankenheim in their Austin-Healey 3000 on the way from the Nürburgring test during the Tulip Rally.

Below. Timo Makinen winds the Austin-Healey round Paddock Turn in sleet and snow in a display rally organized by the British Racing Sports Car Club for the BBC at Brands Hatch.

The M.G. Midget II in standard form and the Austin Healey Sprite III, with optional wire wheels

Austin Healey Sprite Mk. III and

MORE POWER, WIND-UP WINDOWS AND NEW REAR SUSPENSION

LATEST figures released by the British Motor Corporation for Austin-Healey Sprite and M.G. Midget production well exemplify the popularity of British small sports cars. Since 1958, 110,000 of these closely related models have rolled off the production line at Abingdon-on-Thames, helping to make this traditional home of M.G. cars the largest factory in the world devoted to the production of sports cars.

About 85 per cent are exported, mainly to the United States, and it is to satisfy the demand from this market for more creature comforts and to bring the cars into line with the character of the MGB, that the M.G. Midget Mark II and Austin-Healey Sprite Mark III models have been introduced. There has been particular resistance to detachable sidescreens in America, and the rising sales of rivals with wind-up side windows have no doubt encouraged B.M.C. to incorporate this feature in these latest models. At the same time the cockpit layout has been rearranged and restyled, to make it more luxurious and easier to "work" in.

Power output is especially important to enthusiasts, and besides cylinder head and exhaust manifold modifications, which increase maximum power to a genuine 59 b.h.p. (net) at 5,750 r.p.m., a stiffer crankshaft is fitted to reduce vibrations. For these improvements, the modest price increase of £24, including purchase tax, seems well justified.

Modifications to the cockpit layout have made both models into refined roadsters with a high standard of finish. Seat trim style is unchanged

Extra power from the engine has been obtained by increasing the size of the inlet valves by 0·06in. and by modifying and reshaping the siamesed inlet tracts to reduce the "uvula" which separates the ports. At the same time, the compression ratio has been raised to 9 to 1, although an 8·3 to 1 compression ratio engine is available for countries with low octane petrol.

A new cast-iron, four-branch exhaust manifold, similar in shape to that of the MGB, has been adopted to replace the older type inherited from the Austin A.35. The new manifold eliminates the double bend in the down pipe and is responsible for one of the extra horsepower of the latest engine. Crankshaft main journals have been increased in size from 1·87in. to 2·0in., while a minor change has been the abandonment of the engine driven petrol pump in favour of an S.U. electric unit.

Rear suspension has been completely revised by the adoption of half-elliptic leaf springs. It has always been a problem to make quarter-elliptic springs of the old design with a combination of low rate and sufficient lateral rigidity to locate the back axle accurately. Moreover, the whole weight of the rear of the car was carried on an anchorage point only 4in. long, requiring long, heavy channel section stiffeners to spread the loads through to the structure. The result was always a compromise resulting in a hard ride and undue roll stiffness at the rear, with a consequent tendency for the car to be very sensitive on steering.

The new springs give a better ride, and the old tendency for the car to "dart" has been eliminated without any loss of steering accuracy. The fourblade, half-elliptic springs are anchored at the forward ends in brackets, and

Neat and practical, the new instrument panel has the two main dials angled inwards slightly

PRICES

	Basic £	Total (inc. P.T.) £ s d
M.G. Midget Mk. II	505	610 15 5
Austin-Healey Sprite Mk. III	515	622 17 1

Extras (including P.T.)

Tonneau cover and rail	£5 8 9
Hardtop	£48 6 8
Fresh-air heater	£14 10 0
Wire wheels	£30 4 2

M.G. Midget Mk. II

at the rear are shackled to a plate bolted to the floor by way of the box section members which reinforce the boot floor.

With this half-elliptic rear springing the unsprung weight of two heavy axle brackets needed for the former quarter-elliptic parallelogram layout is eliminated, plus half the weight of the radius arms and approximately one third of the weight of the thick, wide, quarter-elliptic spring. It has been possible also to eliminate much of the body stiffening required by the old layout.

Thus the total weight saving all but makes up for the extra weight of the door glasses and window lifts, and the all-up weight of the latest cars is only 6lb more than that of their predecessors.

More prospective owners will welcome the change to wind-up windows, which in no way detract from the sporty appearance of the cars and yet add greatly to their general convenience. To fit wind-up glasses into the relatively thin doors of the Sprite and Midget without a major body redesign has called for curved side glasses. The gain is all on the side of the owner, for whom adequate elbow room is retained without any increase in external body width.

Small swivelling quarter vents with non-locking catches are standard equipment and a new, more rigid windscreen frame with full height cast aluminium pillars is fitted to provide a firm sealing abutment for the doors. A thin tie rod between the top and bottom rails of the screen frame prevents it "opening up" when the hood is tensioned and also provides a mounting for the driving mirror which was previously located on the scuttle, where it created a blind spot.

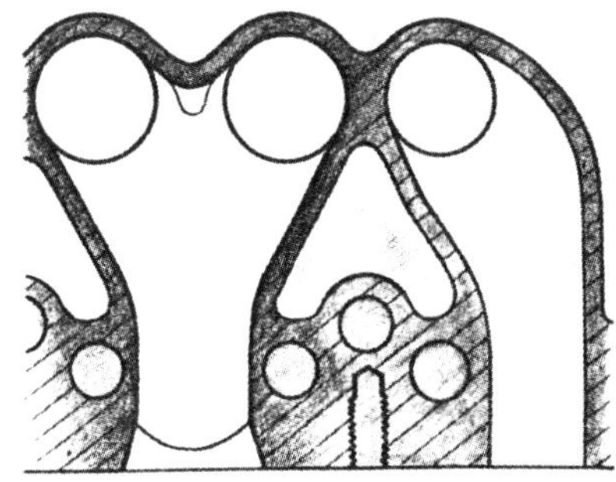

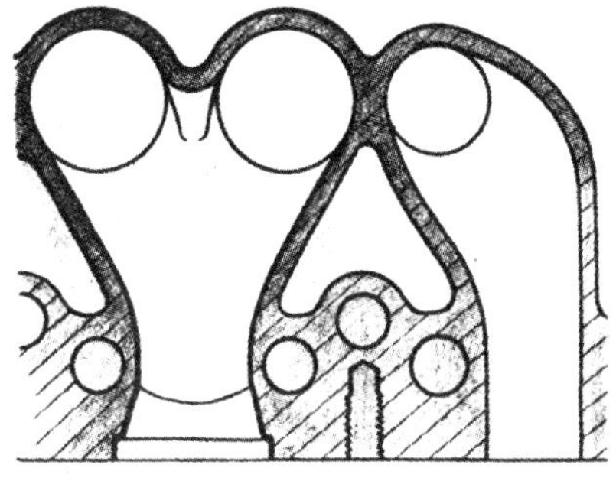

Section of the cylinder head through the ports. Above is the previous pattern, and below is the new head with better breathing capacity

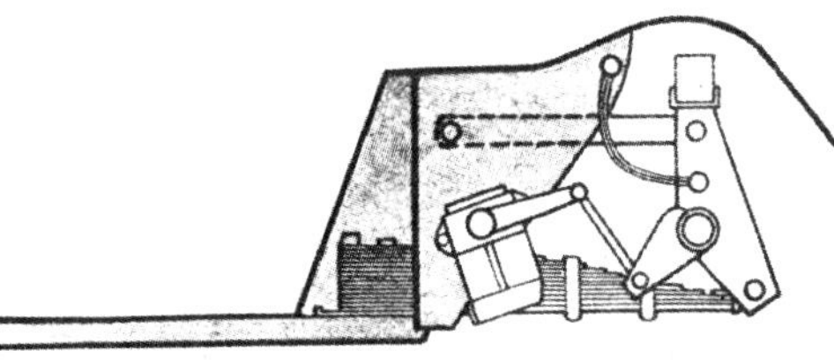

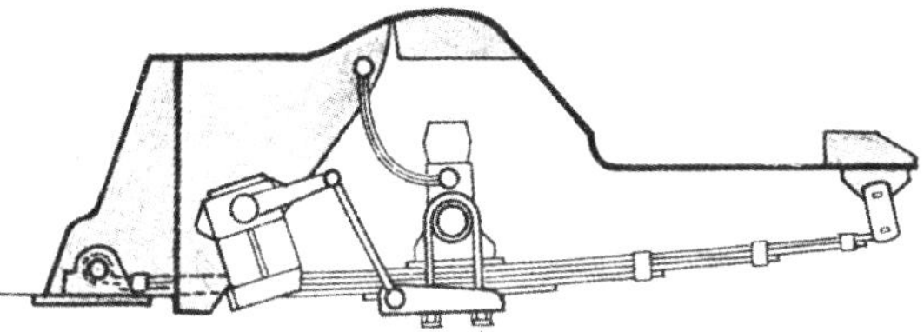

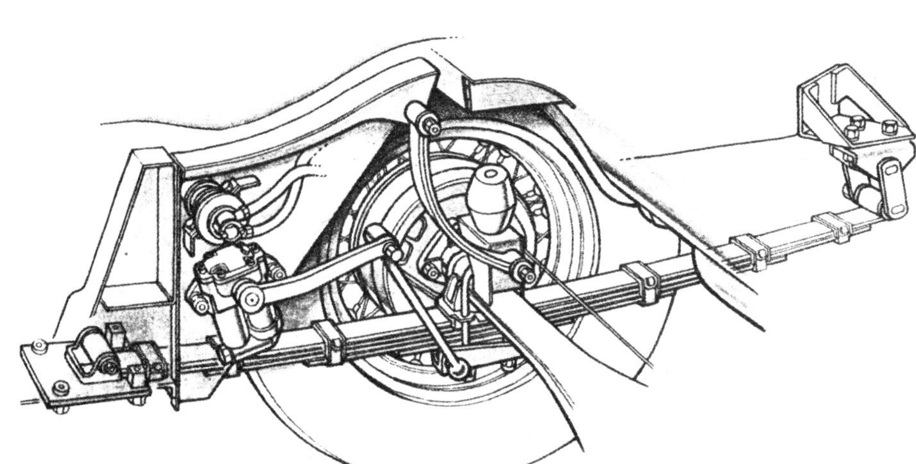

The previous type of rear suspension with quarter elliptic leaf springs and radius arms is shown in the upper left diagram. Better axle location, reduced unsprung weight and improved handling result from the new layout

ENGINE

No. of cylinders	4 in-line
Bore	64·6mm (2·54in.)
Stroke	83·7mm (3·30in.)
Displacement	1,098 c.c. (67 cu. in.)
Valve operation	Overhead, pushrods
Compression ratio	9·0 to 1 (Optional 8·3 to 1)
Max. b.h.p. (net)	59 at 5,750 r.p.m.
Max. b.m.e.p. (net)	140 p.s.i. at 3,250 r.p.m.
Max. torque (net)	62 lb. ft. at 3,250 r.p.m.
Carburettor	Twin S.U. HS2
Fuel pump	S.U. Electric
Tank capacity	6 Imp. gallons (27 litres)
Sump capacity	6·5 pints (3·7 litres)
Oil filter	Full-flow with renewable element
Cooling system	Pressurized system centrifugal pump, fan and thermostat
Battery	12 volt, 43 amp. hr.

TRANSMISSION

Clutch	Borg and Beck hydraulically operated, single dry plate, 7·25in. dia.
Gearbox	Four-speed, synchromesh on 2nd, 3rd and top. Central floor change
Overall ratios	Top 4·22; third 5·73; second 8·09; first 13·51; reverse 17·32
Final drive	Hypoid bevel, ratio 4·22 to 1

CHASSIS

Brakes	Lockheed hydraulic. Front discs, 8·25in. dia.; rear drums, 7in. dia.; 1·25in. wide shoes.
Suspension: front	Independent, coil springs and wishbones, Armstrong telescopic dampers
rear	Half-elliptic leaf springs, lever arm dampers
Wheels	Steel disc, 4 studs, 3·5in rim.
Tyre size	5·20—13 Dunlop tubeless Gold Seal Nylon C.41
Steering	Rack and pinion
Steering wheel	Three-spoke, 17in. diameter
No. of turns, (lock to lock)	2·25

DIMENSIONS

Wheelbase	6ft. 8in. (203 cm)
Track: front	3ft. 9·75in. (116 cm)
rear	3ft. 8·75in. (114 cm)
Overall length	11ft. 4·25in. (345 cm)
Overall width	4ft. 5in. (135 cm)
Overall height (unladen)	4ft. 1·75in. (126 cm)
Ground clearance (laden)	5in. (13 cm)
Turning circle	31ft. 2·5in. (9·5 cm)
Kerb weight	14cwt (1,566lb—714kg)

PERFORMANCE DATA

Top gear m.p.h. per 1,000 r.p.m.	15·37
Torque lb. ft. per cu. in. engine capacity	0·92
Brake surface swept by linings	190 sq. in.
Weight distribution	F. 52·4 per cent; R. 47·6 per cent

SPRITE and MIDGET . . .

A new type of Wilmot Breedon anti-burst lock is a safety feature. It ensures that the door cannot fly open in a crash. The inside handle is recessed into the door trim

The main effect of the latest cockpit layout is to give it a designed look, rather than the appearance of having been assembled from a number of un-related components. The new facia is handsome and practical, with the matching trip speedometer and electronic rev counter angled inwards to fall on the arc of focus of the driver's eyes. Both are clearly visible through the unobstructed upper half of the new three-spoke spring steering wheel, which has a cowled column incorporating the trafficator switch.

The instrument panel is a steel pressing taking up two-thirds of the width of the facia, and on the left-hand section (right hand for left-hand-drive cars) the fuel gauge and a combined oil pressure gauge and coolant thermometer are mounted. This section of the panel also provides a mounting for the electrical switches, choke and heater controls and screenwasher plunger. The whole of the panel and facia is finished in black crackle enamel, surmounted by a padded leathercloth roll which is extended along the tops of the doors.

On the passenger side a crushable, fibreboard parcels shelf with a padded edge provides stowage for maps and small oddments, and would collapse safely in the event of accident. The floor and transmission tunnel are covered in good quality pile carpet, and this has bound edges and rubber heel mats for both occupants.

Road Impressions

A short run in an M.G. Midget verified that the ride has been very much improved, and has a great deal in common with that of the larger MGB. The wider location base for the rear springs has allowed the manufacturers to put more rubber into the shackles. This makes for a quieter running as well as a better ride. Final drive vibration which was felt in older models is noticeably absent. Handling is particularly pleasant, light and predictable, and the necessity on certain surfaces to drive with the fingertips has gone. Particularly noteworthy is that there is ample elbowroom with two large people on board.

The Austin-Healey Sprite and the M.G. Midget were introduced as cheap, small sports cars suitable for young people to cut their motoring teeth on with safety and economy. In their latest guise they have in no sense drifted away from this precept, but rather have widened their scope, because of the comfort and convenience offered by improved suspension and weather protection, so that they now appeal to older enthusiasts looking for a small, lively car for everyday use.

Visibility is not impaired with the hood up and there is good wind protection with it removed and side windows raised

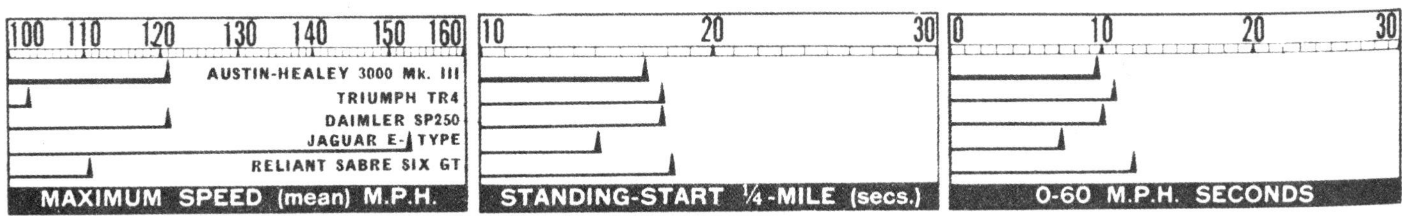

Austin-Healey 3000 Mk. III CONVERTIBLE 2,912 c.c.

SUN-CAPPED Dolomites and the distant roar and squeal of one of the works rally cars scrambling its way up the Gavia pass—this perhaps is the image that some people have of the big Austin-Healey at work. But there is a world of difference between those frequent winners, the former Spartan works rally cars, and the over-the-counter product of today—the 3000 Mk. III

For as long as many of us care to remember there has been a big Healey in the price lists. The car has been through several variations of engine size, but now, like an ageing but still beautiful dowager, repeated face lifts can no longer wholly hide the ravages of time and progress.

For many years a change in the model of the Healey has been marked with either the subtraction or addition of a carburettor; however, the Mk. III continues with two S.U. carburettors for the Series C 2,912 c.c. engine, with diameter increased by 0·25in. to 2in. With the new carburettors and a camshaft of improved design the power output of the engine has been raised from 137 b.h.p. at 4,750 r.p.m. to 148 b.h.p. at 5,250 r.p.m. Although this comparatively unsophisticated six-cylinder engine must now be very near the end of its development, it seems to have gained in flexibility and is virtually free from any temperament.

Provided full use is made of the choke, starting from cold is good. The engine takes a long time to warm through and

spits back through the carburettors if pushed at all hard before it is warm. The all-too-frequent trouble of running-on still persists and could only be prevented by opening the throttles wide as the ignition was switched off.

Although the big Healey has never been a noisy car in standard form, the latest design of exhaust system, with two silencers on the left side of the car and a further two set transversely under the boot floor, cuts the noise down to almost saloon car level at anything but near-peak engine

PRICES	£	s	d
Sports Convertible	915	0	0
Purchase tax	191	3	9
Total (in G.B.)	1,106	3	9
Extras (including P.T.)			
Overdrive	60	8	4
Wire wheels	30	4	2
Fresh air heater	18	14	7
Telescopic steering column	2	8	4
Seat belts (each)	5	5	0

How the Austin-Healey 3000 Mk. III compares:

	MAXIMUM SPEED (mean) M.P.H.	STANDING-START ¼-MILE (secs.)	0-60 M.P.H. SECONDS
AUSTIN-HEALEY 3000 Mk. III			
TRIUMPH TR4			
DAIMLER SP250			
JAGUAR E-TYPE			
RELIANT SABRE SIX GT			

Make · AUSTIN-HEALEY   Type · 3000 Mk. III (2,912 c.c.)
(Front engine, rear-wheel drive)

Manufacturers : Austin Motor Co. Ltd., Longbridge, Birmingham

Test Conditions

Weather ... Dry and sunny with 0-5 m.p.h. wind
Temperature .... 9 deg. C. (48 deg. F.)
Barometer .... 29·6in. Hg.
Dry concrete and tarmac surfaces.

Weight

Kerb weight (with oil, water and half-full fuel tank)
          23·5 cwt (2,604lb-1,180kg)
Front-rear distribution, per cent F, 52; R, 48
Laden as tested ......26·5 cwt (2,940lb-1,333kg)

Turning Circles

Between kerbs ...... L, 35ft 0in.; R, 34ft 10in.
Between walls ...... L, 36ft 3in.; R, 35ft 10in.
Turns of steering wheel lock to lock 3

FUEL AND OIL CONSUMPTION

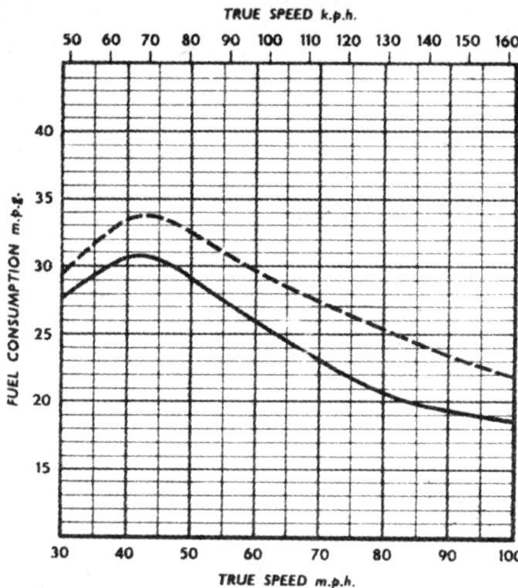

FUEL ....Super premium grade
(101 octane RM)

Test Distance ....1,583 miles

Overall Consumption ...... 20·3 m.p.g.
(13·9 litres/100 km.)

Estimated Consumption (DIN) 24·9 m.p.g.
(11·4 litres/100 km.)

OIL: SAE 10W30 ... Consumption 1,600 m.p.g.

HILL CLIMBING AT STEADY SPEEDS

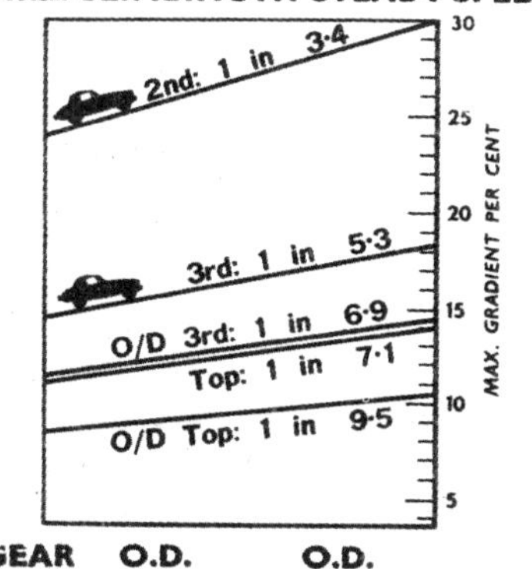

GEAR	O.D. Top	Top	O.D. 3rd	3rd	2nd
PULL (lb per ton)	235	310	340	410	635

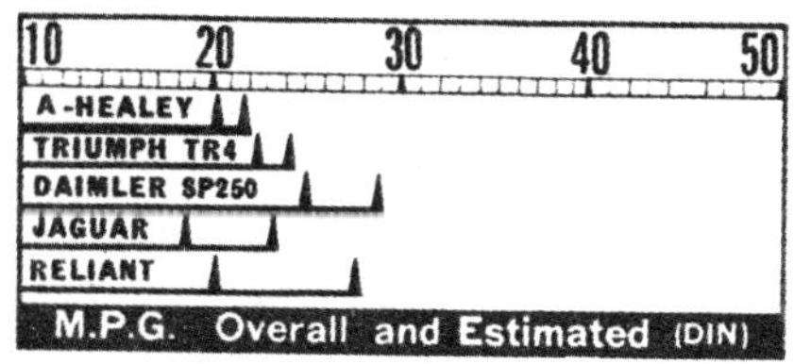

MAXIMUM SPEEDS AND ACCELERATION TIMES

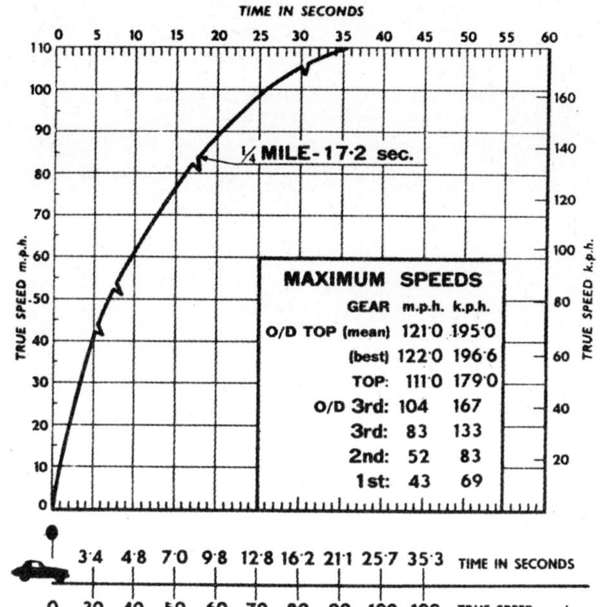

	3·4	4·8	7·0	9·8	12·8	16·2	21·1	25·7	35·3	TIME IN SECONDS
0	30	40	50	60	70	80	90	100	100	TRUE SPEED m.p.h.
	28	40	48	58	70	80	93	104	114	CAR SPEEDOMETER

Speed range, gear ratios and time in seconds

m.p.h.	O.D. Top (3·14)	Top (3·91)	O. Third (4·74)	Third (5·12)	Second (8·05)	First (11·26)
10—30	—	—	—	6·1	4·2	3·0
20—40	—	7·5	6·6	4·1	3·2	2·8
30—50	9·3	6·8	6·3	5·4	3·4	—
40—60	8·7	6·9	6·8	4·9	—	—
50—70	10·7	7·9	7·3	5·5	—	—
60—80	12·1	8·1	7·8	6·4	—	—
70—90	13·6	9·0	8·2	—	—	—
80—100	15·7	9·9	9·0	—	—	—
90—110	18·2	14·2	—	—	—	—

BRAKES	Pedal load	Retardation	Equiv. distance
(from 30 m.p.h. in neutral)	25lb	0·23g	131ft
	50lb	0·72g	42ft
	75lb	0·81g	37ft
	100lb	0·92g	32·8ft
Handbrake		0·37g	81ft

CLUTCH   Pedal load and travel—40lb and 6in.

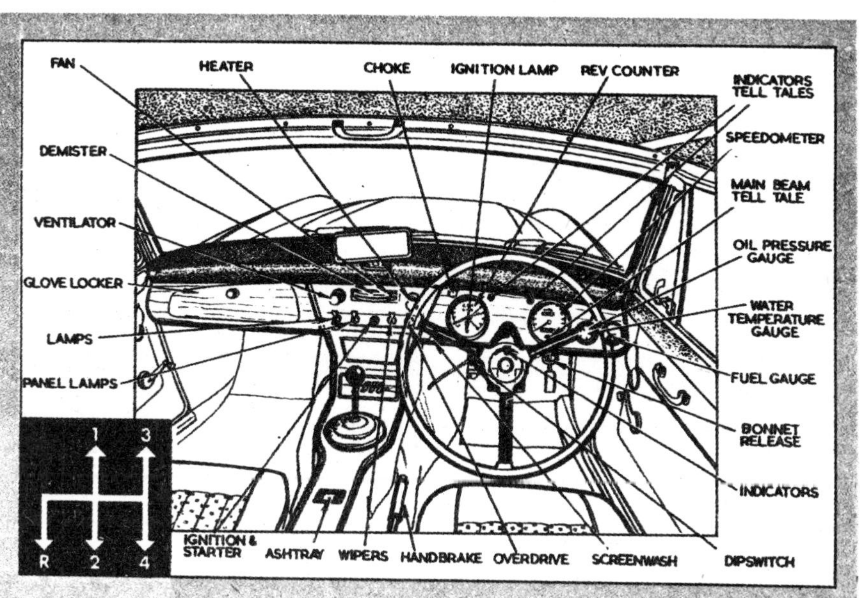

A central console, wood-trimmed facia and re-grouped instruments are new to the model; fixed quarter-light frames on the front doors can be too close to the occupants' head when getting in

revs. However, the car still suffers from very limited ground clearance and over rough roads one has to put up with bangs and thumps when the silencers touch bumps on the surface.

The test car was fitted with the optional extra Laycock de Normanville overdrive, working on third and top gears. With overdrive, a lower back axle ratio is used—3·91 in place of the normal 3·55 to 1 ratio. While this does make the car extremely flexible in the upper ratios at low engine revs, it tends to emphasize the large gap between second and third gears, with their respective maximum speeds of 52 and 83 m.p.h. Overdrive third gear produced a maximum of 104 m.p.h., direct top 111 m.p.h. and overdrive top gave a mean maximum speed of 121 m.p.h. Overdrive, operated by a switch on the facia, engages very smoothly indeed; to return to direct drive the engine has to be pulling before an inhibitor switch will release the overdrive. This prevents jolts in the transmission.

In practice, very high averages can be maintained on main roads by using just direct and overdrive top gears, the car wafting along at around the 90 mark with no more than 4,000 r.p.m. on the rev counter.

The big Healey's take-off from standstill is impressive. Without tyre squeal or wheel-spin, it reached 30 m.p.h. in 3·4 40 in 4·8, 60 in 9·8 and 100 in 25·7sec. At maximum revs—5,250 r.p.m. in this case—the combined noise of engine, cooling fan, unsilenced carburettor air intakes and exhaust reaches almost Grand Prix levels and on the maximum speed runs the scream of wind round the windows and hood adds to the din. Prolonged motorway driving at very high speeds becomes tiring for this reason.

Clutch Improved

Later models of the Austin-Healey 3000 Mk. II were fitted with diaphragm spring clutches but this was the first model of the make we have been able to drive fitted with one. The pressure is light—only 40lb—and the length of travel and smoothness of engagement are more like those of a touring car than a 120 m.p.h. sports car. Effective, rather heavy synchromesh makes gear-changing a bit slow on the upper three ratios and it is almost impossible to get into first gear while on the move without crunching. The position of the gear lever is such that one has to use a cranked elbow action to make changes, but this soon becomes quite a natural movement.

The years of competition and development have certainly improved the car's handling. For normal motoring, the car has slight understeer, but when time is short, the right foot can turn this into an accurately controllable power oversteer. When cornering hard the driver has to beware of

Left: The back of the rear seat folds forward to make a good luggage platform—which is needed as the boot (right) is much taken up by spare wheel, battery and hood covers

The unmistakable lines of the big Healey still suggest potency. The small upper rear "lamps" are reflectors

bumps in the road, which can throw the car off course with unexpected force. In the wet, an unwary jab on the accelerator can bring the tail of the car skating round and a good deal of caution has to be used on corners.

We were unable to test the car's handling on our special *pavé* track for fear of wiping off the exhaust system, but on a rough side road, the short suspension movements and firm damping make the car twitch about unless the driver concentrates on holding direction. The steering itself is heavy at low speeds, but once the car gets on to the open road it becomes a good deal lighter. At near-maximum speed, the car controls very well and holds a straight course.

Although a vacuum servo is standard equipment on the Mk. III models—it was an extra on the previous model—the brakes still feel heavy, but they are very powerful. Heavy braking from high speeds is accompanied by slight weaving; this never builds up to anything near dangerous proportions, but is nevertheless disconcerting. The pull-up handbrake, located between the driving seat and transmission tunnel held the car easily on a 1-in-3 hill, from where take-off was of the "rocket" variety, with spinning wheels.

Driving Position

In its appointments the Austin-Healey 3000 Mk. III is now more of a touring car than a sports car. The new panel design and the trim are attractive, almost luxurious. In these days of straight-arm steering, the driver of the big Healey has to get used to the old Vintage bent arm position again, with the huge 17in. diameter steering wheel only a matter of inches from his chest. On the test car the telescopic steering column (an extra) was fitted. If it had put the wheel 3in *nearer* the facia it would have been more help. The pedals are small and set close together. If space and layout allowed the pedal group to be brought back three inches and the seat moved back a similar distance, the driving position would be far more comfortable. The seats are rather small and hard, with cushions that "set" after a few miles. At the end of a long drive you are glad to have a good stretch to restore the circulation.

The "traditional" British love of wood has extended to this Healey and the dashboard has walnut veneer on its two outer panels. The centre of the facia now extends downwards to form a central console with the deep transmission tunnel. There are spaces in this console for a radio and loudspeaker.

A comprehensive set of instruments is grouped behind the steering wheel and comprises a speedometer, with total and trip mileage recorders, rev counter, combined oil pressure and water temperature gauge and fuel gauge. While driving, this last instrument swings freely between full and empty as soon as the tank contents have dropped to about

three-quarters full. In the centre of the facia are four identical switches in pairs on each side of the ignition-starter switch; they control driving and panel lamps, and screenwipers and overdrive. A differently shaped toggle for the O.D. switch would make it more easily identifiable; at

Not a spare inch is wasted under the bonnet; the lid still has to be propped open with a stay

night it is easy to flick the wrong switch and start the single speed wipers working instead of selecting overdrive. A single quadrant control adjusts the temperature of the heater, distribution of flow between the car and windscreen being adjusted by two flaps set high under the back of the dashboard.

There is a large lockable cubby in the facia and a non-locking glove box on the transmission tunnel, with a padded top to form an armrest for driver or passenger. Two small seats for children are fitted in the back, and an adult, sitting sideways, could be packed in for short trips. The backrest of this seat folds forward and is held by two substantial bolts to form a large luggage platform, with a lip on the leading edge to prevent suitcases sliding forward. This platform is really valuable because the boot is mainly occupied by the spare wheel and battery and can hold only one small grip and some odds and ends. Now that winding windows are fitted and a hardtop is offered, B.M.C. ought to provide locks for the doors. They do provide a battery master switch in the boot which cuts off all current—including the side lamps for parking at night. A prop rod has to be slotted into a catch to hold the boot open.

In these days of international conformity over direction indicators, the big Healey still uses the side and tail lamps as indicators and at night they can be confusing to following traffic if one is braking and indicating at the same time. Twin horns with an impressive volume are fitted.

The well-fitting hood was rain-tight and did not flap at high speeds; it is held down on to the screen rail by two over-centre clips with ominously sharp projections. The convertible type hood can be folded back easily and in a matter of seconds, and a hood cover is provided. Fresh-air ventilation can be greatly increased in warm weather by un-zipping the whole of the back window and folding it down. In summer, the car still suffers from too much heat coming through from the engine and to help overcome this a cold air vent is fitted under the dash—on the left-hand side.

This car is much faster than the Mk. II version, and is more economical, averaging 20·3 m.p.g. overall. Commuting and a series of fast, short runs, where maximum revs were frequently being used, dropped the consumption to 18·7 m.p.g.; on everyday motoring, the fuel consumption is around the 22 m.p.g. mark. The 12-gallon fuel tank filled easily, without any blow back. During the 1,583 miles of testing eight pints of oil were used, but the car had been fitted with new piston rings shortly before it was handed over for test and probably they were still bedding-in.

Under the bonnet, the husky six-cylinder engine fills every inch of available space, with wires and cables running everywhere. The screenwasher bottle, which used to be inside the passenger cockpit, has now been moved under the bonnet. The lid is held shut by two safety catches and is held open with a stay.

Despite some dated features, the big Healey is still terrific fun to drive. Tractable, capable of an immense amount of hard work with reasonable economy, it will still have its devotees long after production has ceased.

Specification: Austin-Healey 3000 Mk. III Convertible

PERFORMANCE DATA

Overdrive top gear m.p.h. per 1,000 r.p.m. ...	23·0
Top gear m.p.h. per 1,000 r.p.m.	18·9
Mean piston speed at max. power...............	3,035ft/min.
Engine revs. at mean max. speed	5,260 r.p.m.
B.h.p. per ton laden	111·2

▼ *Scale: 0.3in. to 1ft. Cushions uncompressed.*

ENGINE

Cylinders ...	6-in-line
Bore ...	83·4mm (3·28in.)
Stroke ...	88·9mm (3·50in.)
Displacement	2,912 c.c. (178 cu. in.)
Valve gear ...	Overhead, pushrods and rockers
Compression ratio	9·0-to-1
Carburettors ...	2 S.U. HD8
Fuel pump ...	S.U. electric
Oil filter ...	Full flow, renewable element
Max. power ...	148 b.h.p. (net) at 5,250 r.p.m.
Max. torque ...	165·2 lb. ft. at 3,500 r.p.m.

TRANSMISSION

Clutch ...	Borg and Beck diaphragm spring, 9·5in. dia.
Gearbox ...	Four speed, synchromesh on 2nd, 3rd and Top; central control
Overall ratios	O.D. Top 0·82, Top 1·00; O.D. Third 1·08, Third 1·31, Second 2·06; First 2·88; Reverse 3·72
Final drive ...	Hypoid bevel, 3·91

CHASSIS

Construction	Boxed cruciform chassis, with steel and aluminium body

SUSPENSION

Front ...	Independent, coil springs and wishbones, lever arm dampers, anti-roll bar
Rear ...	Live axle, half elliptic leaf springs, Panhard rod, lever arm dampers
Steering ...	Cam and peg
Wheel dia. ...	17in.

BRAKES

Type ...	Girling hydraulic, disc front drum rear, vacuum servo
Dimensions	F, 11·25in. dia. R, 11·0in. dia., 2·25in. wide shoes
Swept area	F, 228 sq. in.; R, 155·5 sq. in. Total: 383·5 sq. in. (286 sq. in. per ton laden)

WHEELS

Type ...	Pressed steel disc standard, wire-spoked, centre-lock extra, 4·5in. wide rim
Tyres ...	5·90—15in. Dunlop RS5 with tubes

EQUIPMENT

Battery ...	12-volt 57-amp. hr.
Headlamps	36-48 watt
Reversing lamp	None
Electric fuses	2
Screen wipers	2, single speed, self parking
Screen washer	Standard, manual plunger
Interior heater	Extra, fresh air, electric booster
Safety belts	Extra, anchorages provided
Interior trim	Ambla leathercloth
Floor covering	Carpet
Starting handle	No provision
Jack ...	Screw type
Jacking points	4, on suspension
Other bodies	None

MAINTENANCE

Fuel tank ...	12 Imp. gallons (no reserve)
Cooling system	20 pints (including heater)
Engine sump	12·75 pints SAE 10W30. Change oil every 3,000 miles; change filter element every 6,000 miles
Gearbox and over-drive ...	7 pints SAE 30. Change oil every 6,000 miles
Final drive ...	3 pints SAE 90EP. Change oil every 6,000 miles
Grease ...	11 points every 3,000 miles
Tyre pressures ...	F, 20; R, 25 p.s.i. (normal driving). F, 25; R, 30 p.s.i. (fast driving)

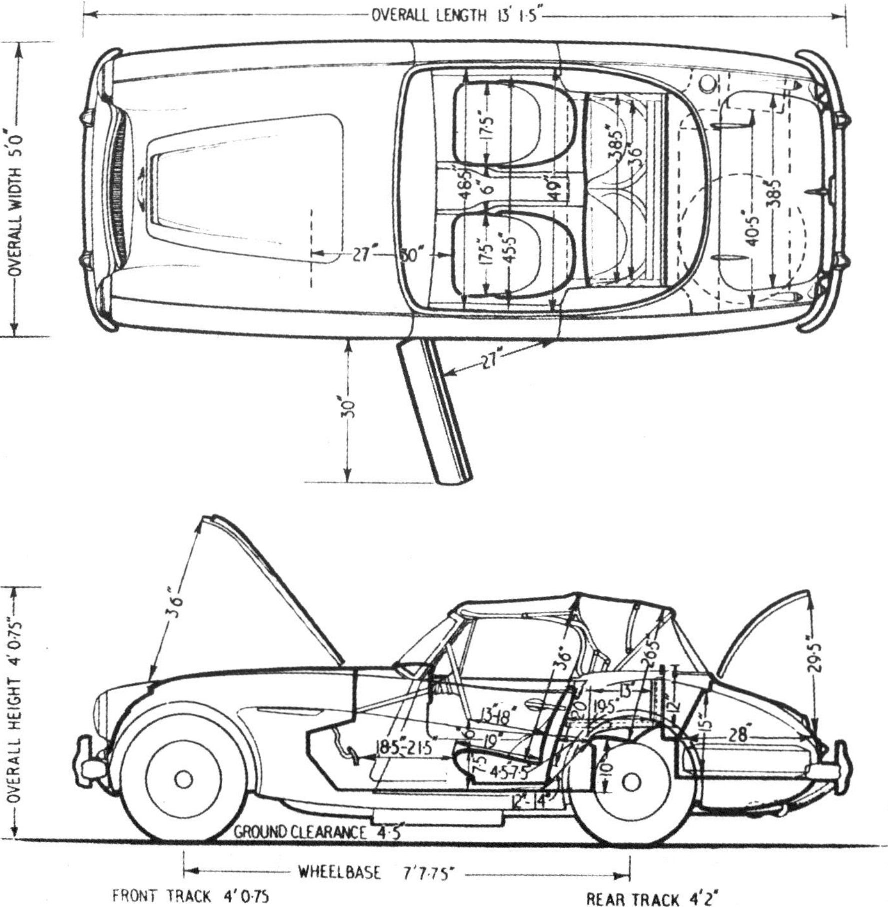

With seven lamps all fitted with iodine-vapour bulbs there is no difficulty in seeing the way at night. As rallied the two lower cornering lamps were crossed over

Rally Healey 3000

WATCHING a works Healey carve its way up the side of an Alp on a timed special stage in an international rally makes it obvious that this is a very different car from the production Mark III convertible. Everyone has known this for ages, so we felt it was high time we got our hands on one to see how the transformation is achieved and what it feels like to be behind the wheel. Stuart Turner, B.M.C. competitions manager, promised us a car after the Alpine rally and as soon as the Morley brothers' class winner got back to this country, we took it over complete with side-swiped rear wing and dust from the Dauphinois.

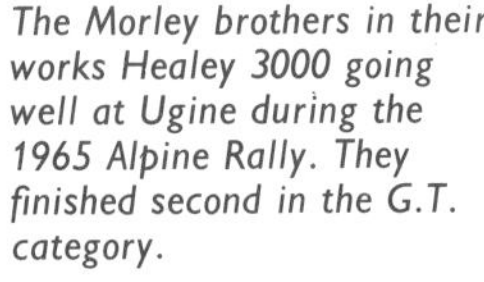

The Morley brothers in their works Healey 3000 going well at Ugine during the 1965 Alpine Rally. They finished second in the G.T. category.

PERFORMANCE CHECK FOR RALLY HEALEY 3000

Figures in brackets are for the Austin-Healey 3000 Mk. III tested in *Autocar* of 12 June 1964.
Acceleration times (mean): Speed range, gear ratios and time in seconds

m.p.h.	O.D. Top (3·54)	(3·14)	Top (4·30)	(3·91)	O.D. Third (5·05)	(4·74)	Third (6·15)	(5·12)	Second (8·08)	(8·05)	First (11·35)	(11·26)
10—30	—	—	—	—	—	—	4·6	(6·1)	3·2	(4·2)	2·3	(3·0)
20—40	—	—	6·5	(7·5)	5·1	(6·6)	3·8	(4·1)	2·5	(3·2)	—	(2·8)
30—50	8·3	(9·3)	6·3	(6·8)	4·9	(6·3)	3·4	(5·4)	2·8	(3·4)	—	—
40—60	7·9	(8·7)	5·5	(6·9)	4·7	(6·8)	3·8	(4·9)	—	—	—	—
50—70	7·4	(10·7)	5·4	(7·9)	4·4	(7·3)	3·8	(5·5)	—	—	—	—
60—80	7·7	(12·1)	5·0	(8·1)	4·7	(7·8)	—	(6·4)	—	—	—	—
70—90	7·8	(13·6)	5·3	(9·0)	—	(8·2)	—	—	—	—	—	—
80—100	7·0	(15·7)	6·4	(9·9)	—	(9·0)	—	—	—	—	—	—
90—110	8·3	(18·2)	—	(14·2)	—	—	—	—	—	—	—	—

From rest through gears to:

30 m.p.h.	2·7 sec.	(3·4 sec.)
40 ,,	4·7 ,,	(4·8 ,,)
50 ,,	6·1 ,,	(7·0 ,,)
60 ,,	8·2 ,,	(9·8 ,,)
70 ,,	10·2 ,,	(12·8 ,,)
80 ,,	12·9 ,,	(16·2 ,,)
90 ,,	16·0 ,,	(21·1 ,,)
100 ,,	19·2 ,,	(25·7 ,,)
110 ,,	23·5 ,,	(35·3 ,,)

Standing quarter-mile 15·6 sec. (17·2 sec.)

Maximum speeds in gears:

	m.p.h.		.k.p.h.	
(O.D. Top (mean):	120	(121)	193	(195
(best):	120	(122)	193	(197)
Top:	100	(111)	161	(179)
O.D. 3rd:	84	(104)	135	(167)
3rd:	70	(83)	113	(133)
2nd:	54	(52)	87	(83)
1st:	38	(43)	61	(69)

Overall fuel consumption for 1,455 miles: 13·7 m.p.g. 20·6 litres/100 km.
(20·3 m.p.g.; 13·9 litres/100km.)

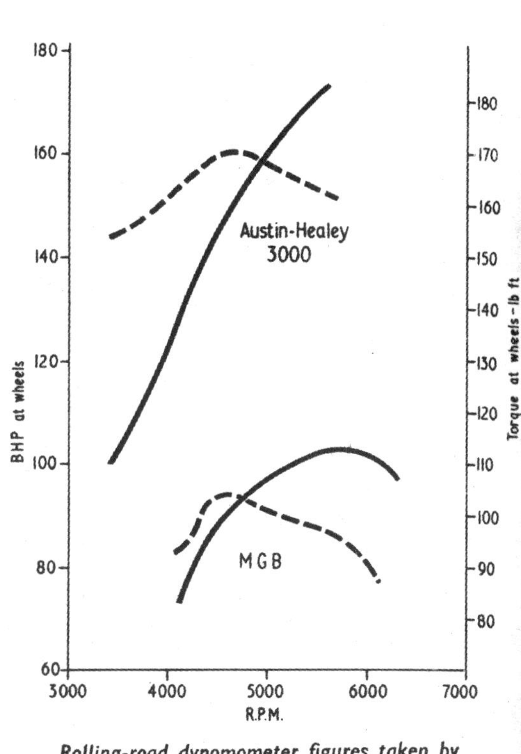

Rolling-road dynomometer figures taken by the B.M.C. competitions department for both cars. Peak power at the wheels for the Healey is 173 b.h.p. at 5,600 r.p.m. and for the MGB 101 b.h.p. at 6,100 r.p.m.

Rally Healey 3000 ...

Works rally cars are no longer taken off the production line and rebuilt very carefully. They start from scratch, in this case with the latest chassis which is upswept for extra ground clearance (originally developed for the tough Liège rally, but now standard), with ordinary front springs and heavy-duty half-elliptics at the back with no fewer than 14 leaves. A thick anti-roll bar and competition dampers (adjustable at the back) complete the suspension set-up, and a special high-geared steering rack (12-to-1 instead of 15-to-1) is fitted. Dunlop R6 racing tyres are used on standard 60-spoke wire wheels.

The braking system has entirely separate hydraulic circuits front and rear and a tandem master cylinder, each system having its own vacuum servo. Standard Girling front discs are fitted, with a similar type of disc at the back as well; all pads are competition type DS 11.

All the bodywork is made in aluminium instead of steel except for the doors. The boot lid has a hump in it so that two spare wheels can be carried and vents are cut in the side panels to let the hot air out of the engine compartment and help prevent the cockpit (and drivers) from overheating.

During preparation of the car for the Alpine a piston seized, so half the engine used for the Targa Florio was mated with the sound parts of the original one. A special aluminium head raises the compression ratio to 11 to 1, but standard size valves are retained, despite the fitting of three 45 DCOE Weber carburettors. With 95 deg of overlap the camshaft is pretty " hot " and the performance curve shows the peaky torque delivery it produces.

Rally equipment added to the cockpit consists of not much more than a Halda Tripmaster (with a metre scale that spins round like a fruit machine) and switches for the great blaze of iodine vapour lamps at the front. There is basically a four-headlamp system with two normal 7in. units for main beams and two 5in. dia. dipped beams with moulded in fairings. In the centre is a long-range Flame-thrower (modified like all the others to take a 55-watt Philips quartz iodine-vapour bulb) and down below two large Lucas fog lamps angled to give cross-over spreads for cornering.

Some very involved electrical circuits enable the spot lamp to be switched in with the main beams, so it goes out when the dip-switch is operated, *or* it can be kept on permanently. Dipped beams can be turned on *with* main beams for extra illumination, and the fog lamps have their own independent switch.

To cope with all this electrical load there is a high-output dynamo, although a small lightweight battery in the boot is sufficient, presumably because the engine is always revving hard and the dynamo charging· or at least balancing the load. The over-size reversing lamp, by the way, has an automatic switch on the gear-lever selectors.

On the Road

First problem on climbing into this one is where to put the key; everything is painted matt black and the ignition lock takes some finding to begin with. There is no choke, so it is the usual technique of pumping the accelerator for six squirts of neat petrol to flood the inlets. The song of this highly tuned six is very different from the MGB when it comes to life, much more musical and (thank heavens!) better silenced.

Donald Morley is the smaller of the twins and he does most of the driving, so the seat is set fairly well forward and does not adjust; fortunately he and I seem to have about the same leg length. One of his personal preferences is to have the overdrive switch in the gearlever knob for single-handed operation of both.

The rev counter has a thin red line at 6,000 and our only instructions were " and they mean it." This therefore was our limit, and just like the MGB the car zoomed up to

More like an aircraft than a sports car, the interior is all painted in matt black. There are electric element demisters and the overdrive switch is mounted in the large imitation wood gearlever knob

A full house with awe-inspiring gasworks. A section of the bonnet surround can be detached to get at the three twin-choke 45 DCOE Weber carburettors

max revs very easily in any gear. With the special ratios on the Healey there is in effect a nicely spaced close-ratio six-speed gearbox with almost exactly 16 m.p.h. between each ratio at peak revs.

But it is in its feel—that indefinable sense transmitted to the driver by inanimate mechanicals—that this car differs most from its production original. It is not just from things like a smooth and progressive throttle linkage and a lusty engine that really seems it could never burst or lose tune; there is an overall taut feel to the suspension and steering that we have never experienced on other Austin-Healeys. Some of it comes from the racing tyres (no wonder the top drivers use them on timed stages whenever the surface allows) but it's not quite as simple to tie down as that.

Whatever the cause it gives immediate confidence and makes one want to go straight out on a circuit and get the car *drifting*. As it was we had to make do with some pseudo rally routes around the home counties, but even so we found ourselves driving on well into the night just for the sheer exhilaration of it all.

With a flood of light boring a tunnel for miles ahead there is no need to reduce speed after dark. Thundering between hedges and grass banks one is forever at work; up through the gears, lift off for a curve, back on the throttle, into overdrive then out again, hard on the brakes for a sudden hazard, back on the throtle—that's the way it goes. In between tweaks at the wheel, stabs on the throttle and brakes, and thrusts with the gear lever (forward, back, across, up and down with the switch for overdrive), there are flicks at the light switches for better illumination or reducing the glare as a courtesy to other traffic (what are they doing here at this time of night?).

And all the time there is that pulsating beat in the ears, rising and falling as the rev counter needle springs towards the red line and then falls back as though bouncing on a rubber stop . It's a real case of *son et lumière* without the history attached, just the present as we can live it now for fun, a man's motoring that saps up adrenalin and leaves

one flushed at the end like sailing through a storm or ski-ing in a blizzard.

Living for days in the car on an international event must be exhausting, although there are a few home comforts. Inter-com sets take the strain out of conversation and help kill the noise, and there's a row of vacuum flask pockets in the passenger's door. Up in the roof a big floppy bag is the only stowage space for maps and Kleenex and glucose and cigarettes.

This is a car built with one object, to carry the Morley twins to victory in a particular type of international event. As such it has been proved successful, but in the process it has been developed into a classic competition car that behaves superbly on the road and well deserves to be classed among the all-time greats in motoring history. ∎

There was only one spare wheel in the car when we drove it, although the boot lid is modified to make room for a second. The fuel tank is bigger than standard

Rallying Healeys in 1965

Left. The Morley brothers and their Austin-Healey 3000 were fastest outright on the speed tests for the fourth successive year in the Tulip Rally. They eventually won their class outright by a large margin, and came eighth overall.

Below. In the R.A.C. Rally, Timo Makinen's Austin-Healey 3000 is push-started near the Pickering Forest special stages in Yorkshire, while Rauno Aaltonen gets back into the Cooper S. The Cooper eventually finished first overall with the Healey coming in second place.

TWO–LITRE HEALEY FOR LE MANS

Inspiration for the Healey-Climax has obviously been derived from both Lola and Matra. The body is made of Birmabright corrosion-resisting alloy which is lighter and stronger than aluminium

THE Donald Healey Motor Company, staunch supporters of the Le Mans race for many years and for the past two years entrants of the highest placed British car, are well ahead with building a mid-engined prototype powered by a 2-litre vee-8 Coventry-Climax Tasman engine for the 1968 Le Mans 24 hours.

Releasing details of the car in anticipation of the publication of the Le Mans entry list, Donald Healey emphasized that this is a private venture by the Donald Healey Motor Company and does not mark an entry of BLMC into racing. However, the choice of the Coventry-Climax engine does keep the whole project in the British Leyland Motor Corporation family. Presumably, the car will be known as a Healey-Climax. Its participation in the hot 2-litre class, dominated by Porsche, Alfa Romeo and Dino Ferraris, fulfils a personal ambition by Donald Healey to go motor racing ''properly'' again with the hope of finishing high up on the finishing list, rather than entering and running a small car powered by a hotted-up popular car engine, aimed at class or Index of Performance success. One feels that Healey deserves every support after the successes he has consistently achieved with single cars at Le Mans.

The original Healey saloon, the Silverstone Healey and the classic Healey 100 showed that Donald Healey has a nose for what the public wants in the way of sports cars.

It is significant, therefore, that in laying out this car Geoffrey Healey, who heads the Healey design office, has given it a rigid base structure built up from single-curvature sheet metal panels which could readily be reproduced as a series-production job. The principle of using a separate, unstressed body mounted on a base frame has also been adopted with this possibility in mind. On the racing car it is made from Birmabright corrosion-resisting magnesium alloy, but glass-fibre reinforced plastic would obviously be a suitable substitute for a small production run.

In the disposition of components the Healey shows both Lola and Chaparral influence, with a dash of Matra thrown in. Cooling is by twin radiators in the shoulders of the rear wings and only the engine oil radiator is located in the nose cowling. Twenty gallons of fuel are divided equally between bag tanks in each sponson with a further gallon in a collector tank, from which petrol is pumped to the engine. Provision

In the half-finished base frame, the side sponsons and the very sturdy front-end structure are shown. Note the absence of double curvatures except in the windscreen

Left: The rear suspension is conventional formula 1 pattern with all links adjustable. Right: To reduce distortion the brake discs are allowed a degree of two-way radial expansion by driving them through dogs machined in a Y-alloy distance piece mounted on the hubs

is made to carry three gallons of oil.

The design of the chassis follows the pattern set by Broadley's original Lola: large-section, light-gauge, parallel sponsons forming the two main fore-and-aft frame members, and the scuttle structure and engine bulkhead acting as front and rear cross members. A lot of thought has gone into making the scuttle torsionally rigid. The toebox is braced behind the instrument panel by a steel tube Warren girder truss, and at its forward end by a box-section frame which doubles as the front suspension support member.

Space-frame construction has been avoided as much as possible and the only tubes (other than the scuttle brace) in the main structure are two roll-over bars, one behind and one in front of the driver, the forward one supporting the rear edge of the windscreen. Deep, narrow, box-section members extend backwards from the inner faces of the main sponsons and pick up with the box-section rear suspension bulkhead which also acts as a rear engine support.

Engine and transmission

It is intended to revitalize the 1,999 cc. vee-8 Coventry-Climax engine (with which Jim Clark competed in the Tasman series) in time for the 24-hour race. No doubt the Climax engineers will de-rate the unit slightly in the way that BRM treated their vee-8s for Matra last year. However, the amount of development work carried out to make a basically five-hour engine last for 24 hours will obviously depend on the degree of approval given to the project by the British Leyland Motor Corporation. It will be recalled that this vee-8, four-valve-per-cylinder engine had a bore and stroke of 72.6 x 6mm (2.85 x 2.36in.), giving a capacity of 1,980 cc. With Lucas fuel injection into the inlet tracts, power output is 240 bhp at 9,000 rpm; 159 lbs.ft. of torque are developed at 7,500 rpm.

The torque capacity of a gearbox being a function of the weight of the car as well as of engine power output, a 4.5-litre size Hewland DG300, 5-speed box will be used. With a 3.456 to 1 final drive ratio, the car is geared to do 180 mph at 9,000 engine rpm in the indirect, 3.71 to 1 fifth gear. The drive from the engine to the box is transmitted by a Borg and Beck twin-plate racing clutch, and from the box to the wheels through

The body is well advanced and will be ready in good time for the Le Mans practice session in April

No provision has been made for a tail spoiler on the Healey-Climax. Note the recessed rear window intended to give undistorted rear vision. There appears to be a housing for a periscope in the roof

Hardy Spicer half-shafts with plain sliding splines.

Both the front and rear suspension are conventional in the Grand Prix sense. The rear hub carriers, which are fabricated from steel plate, are located laterally at their upper ends by single adjustable links with Rose joints, and at the lower ends by inverted wishbones each with one adjustable leg. Widely spaced, parallel radius arms provide fore-and-aft location. Varying the length of the upper transverse link gives a wide range of wheel camber adjustment, while shortening or lengthening the adjustable leg in the inverted wishbone controls the degree of rear wheel tow-in (or toe-out).

The double-wishbone front suspension uses forged upper triangles while the bottom member, which takes the bulk of brake torque stresses, is built up from a double-channel section lower link braced by a trailing radius arm.

The only provision made for adjustment of caster or camber angles is by means of shims.

Armstrong coil-spring and telescopic damper units are used and braking is by Girling 11.5in. dia. disc brakes. The discs on the prototype are of the solid, non-ventilated type but are mounted on special Y-alloy centres with radial dog attachments to allow for expansion and so avoid the coning and general distortion which affects disc brakes under arduous use. Dual braking circuits are of course provided with the pedal operating on a balance bar between the two master cylinders. Dunlop are to provide the tyres, and the wheels which are magnesium castings with peg drive and centre-lock fixing. Wheels are 15in. with 8.5in. rims at the front and 10in. rims at the rear.

The Healey experimental department, though small, has done sterling work for BMC over the years as a high-speed development section, achieving success at Sebring, the Targa Florio and Le Mans on a relatively small budget and with remarkably little fuss. Their experience of building high-speed cars which hang together and finish races should be a major factor in the success or otherwise of the Healey-Climax 2-litre.

Edward Eves

Cooling air is taken through intakes in the leading edges of the rear wings and exhausted from a low-pressure area in the tail. In designing the engine bed space has been left for installing an engine up to 4½ to 5 litres

NEW LOTUS ENGINE FOR JENSEN-HEALEY

A FEW weeks ahead of the launch of the exciting new Jensen-Healey sports two-seater, Lotus have released full details of the engine they are to build for it. It is the first engine to be designed by Lotus entirely and features a die-cast block, twin belt-driven overhead camshafts and four valves per cylinder. Maximum power developed from a capacity of 2 litres is 140 bhp (DIN) at 6,500 rpm.

When the engine was originally laid out it was decided to lay the cylinder axis over at 45 deg to permit the low bonnet line essential to a sports car. Four valves per cylinder, in two rows at an included angle of 38deg, were incorporated, operated by twin camshafts driven by a single cogged rubber belt. Head material is LM 25 WP aluminium alloy, gravity die casting being used. There is room between the valves for 14mm spark plugs and sintered valve seats with cast-iron guides are inserted.

At this stage in the design a suitable slave block was needed to develop the combustion chamber shape, porting and valve timing. The similarity of the Vauxhall Victor 2000 engine had not passed unnoticed, so this was adapted to form the first few prototypes. Later a gravity die cast block was substituted, incorporating an open deck and wet cylinder liners. In this respect and in the details of the tappet mechanism the new Lotus engine bears more than a coincidental similarity with the Jaguar vee-12 unit.

Rather than be different for the sake of it, bore and stroke dimensions very close to those of the Vauxhall were retained, giving a capacity of 1,973 c.c. Maximum power is developed at 6,500 rpm and the peak of the torque curve comes high up the rev range at 5,000 rpm, at which point 139 lb.ft. are developed. With a compression ratio of 8.4 to 1, 91-octane lead-free can be used.

For the British and European market, two twin-choke horizontal Dellorto carburettors will be specified, but for the USA, twin Stromberg CDSE will be substituted and without additional detox equipment the engine can comply with Federal emission requirements up to the end of 1974. The Dellorto version satisfies all known European legislation.

The announcement of the engine comes after three years development by Lotus, including some experimental racing units based on the Vauxhall block and a touring version which ran in a Lotus-owned VX 4/90 and a Bedford van. Examples of the current engine have completed 300,000 miles of road testing and 2,500 hours on the test bed.

To build the new engine, which will not be used as a replacement unit for any of the current Lotus sports cars, a new manufacturing plant has been built at Norwich at a cost of about £500,000. When full capacity is reached over 15,000 engines a year will be built, to satisfy a requirement for 10,000 Jensen-Healeys and, presumably, 5,000 units for a new Lotus model yet to be announced. Continuous-path numerical automated control is a key feature of the production line, with the facility for adding a computer later. Initial production, which will all go to Jensen, will be at the rate of 25 per week, rising to 250 per week within a year.

With its very sporting characteristics and a dry weight (with all accessories but no clutch) of 275 lb, the new engine seems ideal for the new Jensen, which will be a high-performance two-seater aimed mainly at the American market. Full details of the car are scheduled to be released in the spring and a full description with colour cutaway will be published in *Autocar* the day after it is announced. □

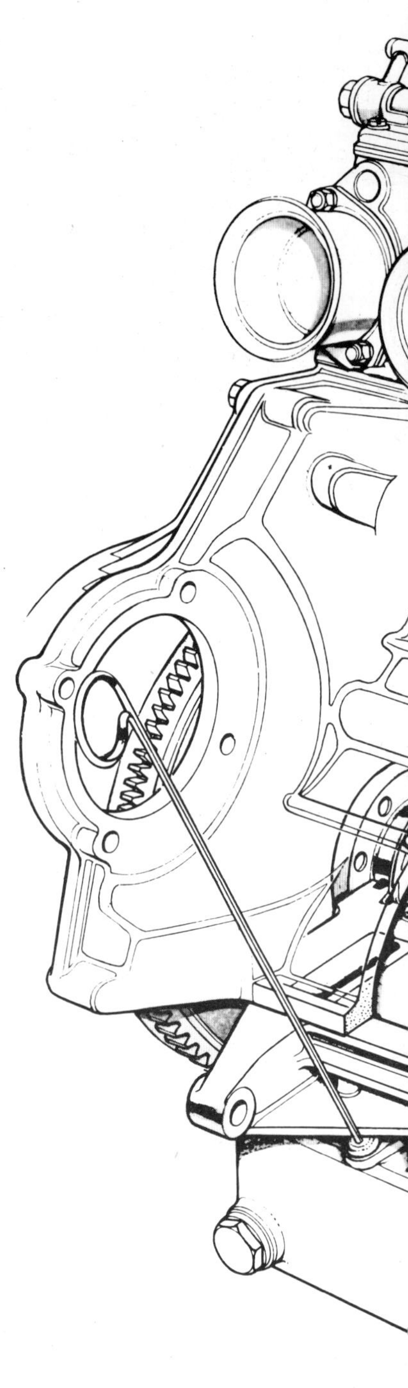

On these Marwin automatic installations blocks and heads are machined at the rate of two per hour

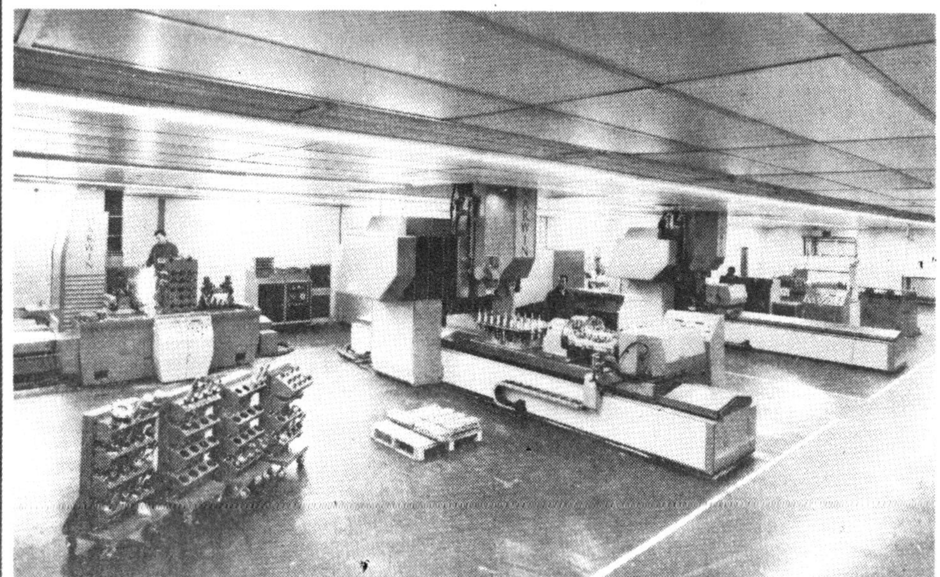

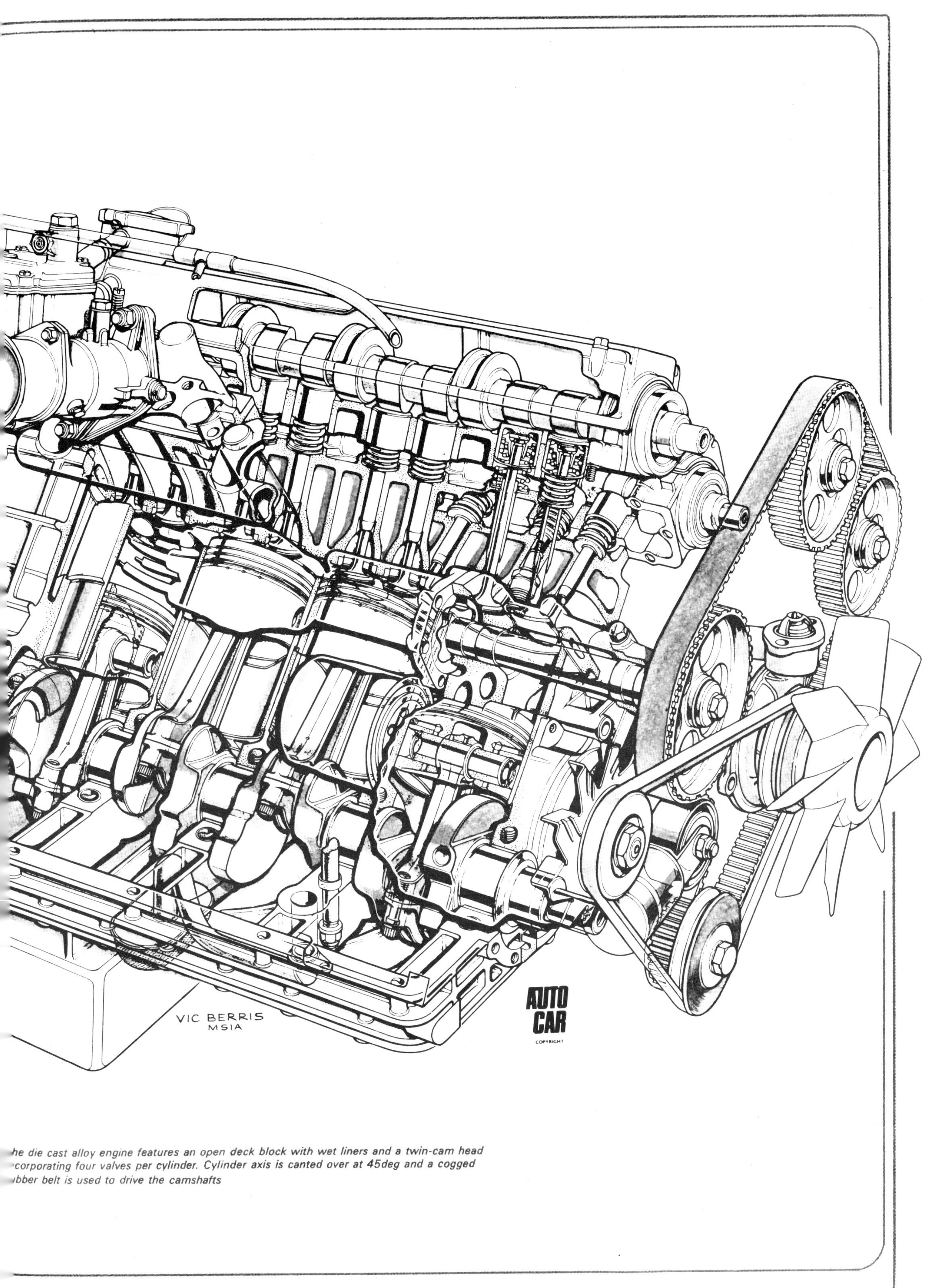

he die cast alloy engine features an open deck block with wet liners and a twin-cam head
ncorporating four valves per cylinder. Cylinder axis is canted over at 45deg and a cogged
ubber belt is used to drive the camshafts

Austin-Healey Sprite Mark IV

Above. Rear view of the latest model of the Austin-Healey Sprite.

Below. Front view of the Mark IV Sprite with American specifications.

Being the one-time driver of a Mark I Sprite, I came to the Mark IV with strong prejudices. Whether or not you liked the frog-eyed look of the original (some say genuine) Sprite, it unquestionably had very pretty lines; some wretched stylist – probably a committee of them – had descended on it, squared and flattened it, and killed its originality.

I got into it and straight away forgot all prejudice in the pleasure of sitting in almost the same snug cockpit. The seat located me, the pedals were well-placed, and the steering wheel, though rather close for fashionable straight-arm stuff, felt "right".

On the track it was very enjoyable. The 1,275 c.c. engine gave it plenty of go and there was still a lovely touch to the short gearlever, rigid but not rubbery. The same applies to the steering – first class rack and pinion, quick and light, taut and live – and the springing – firm, not rolling too much yet comfortable. Synchromesh on the top three gears was unbeatable and it was flatteringly easy to double declutch into first. Brakes were excellent, and keeping the back tyre treads flat on the road with a beam axle and half-elliptics may not be enterprising but seems to work better than simply swinging them about independently. The great thing is that it was *fun* which is all that really matters about any sports car.

M.S.

NEW JENSEN-HEALEY

Open two-seater powered by Lotus 16-valve engine with Vauxhall suspension

By Geoffrey Howard, BSc(Eng) ACGI and Edward Eves

Jensen have high hopes for their new baby, a sleek sports car destined for volume production with 80 per cent for export. Price in the UK will be under £2,000 tax paid; top speed over 120 mph; well-equipped and practical in its design.

FEW new ventures can have received more advance publicity than the exciting two-seater Jensen-Healey sports car announced this week. At one stage late last year, speculation about the power unit ran so rife that Donald Healey was almost forced to give basic details. A determination to present the car at the Geneva Show, which opens today, prior to a full-scale launch in the USA at the New York Show in April, has meant that the announcement is slightly ahead of production and the new model will not go on sale until about the end of April or early May. The target is to make 10,000 cars a year, with about 60 per cent going for export to the USA.

For the conception of the Jensen-Healey one must really look back even farther than the first idea of this particular project. Long before 1952, when the famous Healey Hundred was announced, the Donald Healey Motor Company built up a reputation for building **high-performance sports cars powered by** proprietary British and American engines. The Riley-engined Healey Silverstone and the American-engined Nash-Healey are but two of the more famous examples. With the Healey Hundred, Donald Healey hit on a commercial winner, and not surprisingly Austin (who were to supply many of the major mechanical components including engine and gearbox) took over the manufacture and the car was a considerable success for many years, especially in the USA.

At the introduction of the Healey Hundred in 1952 it was reckoned that the car would fill a gap in the American market and one of the men who were responsible for selling many, many Healeys was an American called Kjell Qvale. When the Austin-Healey 3000 (as the car became) was phased out in the face of stricter and stricter US Federal safety legislation (the tight cockpit in particular gave no room for a collapsible steering column), Kjell Qvale began planning a new model to replace it. Naturally he went first to Donald Healey, the long-established expert in the field, and they started planning mechanical layouts and sketching some styling proposals. Some time in 1968 the decision was made to use mainly Vauxhall running rear, this General Motors off-shoot being happy to supply components and to be associated with the project.

At that time the car was really not much more than a Viva GT with open two-seater bodywork. A professional stylist, Bill Townes, who designed the shape of the Aston Martin DBS, was commissioned and he produced a 0.4 scale model, which was rejected by Donald Healey and Kjell Qvale. Another stylist was consulted, and he made a 1/10th scale model of a new shape, which the partnership liked.

It was round about now that Jensen Motors found themselves in need of both a backer and a volume car that would be low priced and give a quick return on capital invested. As it happened, Jensen had built the bodies for both the Austin-Healey and the Sunbeam Alpine (the latter being discontinued for the same reasons as the Healey), so they had exactly the right experience for a new Healey project. Kjell Qvale acquired 80 per cent of the stock, appointed Donald Healey as chairman and handed the new sports car over to Kevin Beattie with a "most urgent" tag on its development.

Engineering now took over and full-scale development began. It was found that certain styling features were impractical, like a wrap-round tail that put the rear lamps too far from the body sides to be legal, so in conjunction with Bill Townes again, styling revisions were made to the outer skin. The timing of certain proposed Federal requirements, like bumpers capable of withstanding 5-mph impacts front and rear, was uncertain, so to be safe the car was designed to incorporate them, together with the other aspects already established like steering column penetration in a frontal crash, door lock and hinge strengths and even side impact intrusion resistance.

Development of the power unit proceeded in parallel tracks to meet the tightening emission standards. Vauxhall obviously were taking care

Head restraints on top of the bucket seats are standard, and bumpers front and rear can withstand a 5 mph car-to-car crash without damaging the bodywork. The boot lid can be opened only with the key and a steering lock is standard

Cast alloy wheels will be a standard fitting, but the pattern will be slightly different from those on this prototype. The large windscreen is cemented into a stainless steel frame

JENSEN—Healey . . .

of this for their own purposes, but it began to be clear that as each stage of detoxing was achieved the engine lost a bit of power, and for this sports car application the characteristics began to look all wrong.

It was then, only a year or so ago, that the search began for an alternative power unit. BMW were approached, but their production capacity did not stretch to an extra 10,000 engines a year. A prototype was built powered by the German Ford 2.6-litre vee-6 (and this involved using a higher bonnet line with radiator intake above the bumper), but again there were problems in supplying the volume of engines required. Volvo engines were considered, as was the Mazda Wankel unit from Japan, but in the end it was decided to use the new Lotus LV 220 engine which, although similar to the Vauxhall in many respects, is not based on it. Our full description of this very interesting unit, with cutaway drawing, follows in a separate section.

The attraction of the Lotus engine, apart from its obvious potential and very sporty output, mainly lay in its installation angle of 45deg (like that of the Vauxhall) and its ability to meet all the American emission requirements up to the end of 1974 at least. With such a low engine height it was possible to drop the bonnet down to meet the front bumper and put the air intake for the radiator below. This change alone reduced the drag coefficient from 0.5 to 0.42, which is that of the production car with hood up.

In production form as delivered from the new Lotus engine plant in Norfolk, the engine will develop 140 bhp (DIN) at 6,500 rpm with a peak torque of 130 lb.ft. at 5,000 rpm. The compression ratio is 8.4 to 1 and the octane requirement only 91, which permits the use of lead-free fuel. For the UK market two twin-choke 40mm Dellorto carburetters will be fitted, but for the USA, with its stricter emission control, two Stromberg CDES units will replace them. The engine has an alloy block and head, with twin camshafts operated by a cogged rubber belt. There are four valves per cylinder (like on the Ford Escort 1600 RS BDA engine) and an ignition cutout limits the maximum revs to 7,000 rpm.

As far back as 1965 Colin Chapman set in motion design studies for a full vee-8, and a four-cylinder half vee-8 with the cylinders inclined at 45 degrees to go under low bonnets. Ron Burr, one of Coventry Climax Engines' back-room boys, was engaged to lay out the basic design. Working on the thesis that the area above the cylinder head gasket is the most important the first move was to design the head and valve gear. The layout was very much influenced by Climax thinking. Walter Hassan had already established that the flow through the two inlet ports of a four-valve head was more than that through a single port of equivalent area. Later in the story there were indications that emissions of CO, hydrocarbons and oxides were much reduced with this layout. For the former reason a four-valve configuration with the valves set at the narrow angle of 38 deg was chosen from the word go.

Valve actuation by overhead camshafts and bucket tappets was a natural choice because of Lotus experience with the Mundy twin-cam head. Aluminium was chosen as a head material for reasons of thermal conductivity, weight, ease of machining and because it lent itself to diecasting. This process in itself eliminates a certain amount of machining. It is significant that the new Lotus machine shop is laid out almost entirely to deal with light alloy.

It was fortuitous that Colin Chapman spotted that the Vauxhall engine, new in 1967, had roughly the same cylinder centres as his new engine. It presented a first-class opportunity to test his new head pending the development of the Lotus bottom end. A composite Lotus-Vauxhall unit, designated 904, was fitted with Tecalemit-Jackson fuel injection and installed in the 1968 Lotus 62 GT car. In all, 12 engines were built, six being retained by the factory and six sold. Out of 19 starts they notched up seven wins, three second places and several places in the 62.

Before the 907 got into production one each of the 905 and 906 were built. The former was a touring 904 and was installed in a Viva for test purposes, the other was a high performance prototype of the 907 and is recorded as developing 200psi BMEP on the bed.

In its general conception the Lotus-Jensen-Healey incorporates the best features of a number of engines. Starting from the bottom and working upwards the crankcase is virtually half that of a vee-8, the cylinder centreline being angled at 45 degrees to the bottom face of the block which is machined across the main bearing centreline. Taking a leaf out of the Cosworth book, the main bearing caps are cast in unit with a detachable extension of the crankcase, rather like a mini-skirt. This is retained by ten 12mm studs located alongside the bearings — the normal position for main bearing cap studs — while the flange at the "waist" of the skirt is nipped to the crankcase proper by small diameter studs to ensure an oil-tight joint. They also add to the structural integrity of the whole assembly.

The main virtue of this construction is that it ties the two walls of the crankcase firmly together and reduces the tendency for them to pant and shuffle. A further help in this direction is that the crankcase proper is provided with substantial main-bearing diaphragms which separate the area above the sump into four separate chambers. Below the water jackets it is equivalent to four single-cylinder engines making for an extremely rigid construction. This must be a factor in making it possible to utilise a standard Vauxhall cast-iron crankshaft. The shaft, which has 2.5in. dia. main journals and 2.0in. crankpins, when run on Vandervell VP5 bearings has been found capable of transmitting outputs of the order of 200bhp or 200psi BMEP without failure.

Lotus have designed the forged H-section connecting-rods. They are 5.5in. between centres giving a rod to stroke ratio of 2 to 1. This "long" ratio, in combination with offset gudgeon pins, should reduce thrust effects in the angled-split main bearings. Three-ring, solid-skirt pistons with dished crowns and fully floating wrist pins are used.

Spigot type, cast-iron cylinder liners are pressed into machined bosses in the base of the open top water jackets. This construction, pioneered for large scale production by Alfa-Romeo in the Giulietta/Giulia series, is perpetuated in the 12 cylinder Jaguar engine. Ten equally spaced 12mm cylinder head studs, tapped into bosses in the bottom of the water jacket in line with the main bearing diaphragms, transmit cylinder head holding down loads directly to the main bearing caps. This arrangement provides a closed stress loop holding the engine's hat down and its trousers up.

In common with the crankcase the cylinder head is a gravity diecasting produced by the Aeroplane and Motor division of AE. This process allows the combustion spaces to be sufficiently accurately formed without machin-ing. The approximately .75in. dia. siamesed inlet ports and the exhaust ports are formed by sand-coring. Valve diameters are 1.4in. inlet and 1.25in. exhaust and the materials are 21-4N-S and EN59. Four-valve engines have the advantage that the area of valve stem in contact with the guides in relation to the valve head area is les than that of a two-valve per cylinder engine. Therefore it has not been necessary to go to the expense of sodium-cooled exhaust valves, despite the high specific output. Rather conservative valve timing with the inlets opening at 21deg before TDC and closing 71deg after BDC — the exhaust diagram is symmetrically opposite — has been chosen to reduce overlap and lessen emissions.

The lenticular-shaped combustion chambers formed by the dished piston crowns and shallow pent-roof head spaces are in line with current GM thinking. This shape — the extended nose sparking plug is in the centre — which has a narrow squish area round the periphery of the pistons, results in low emissions, of the order of 9 grams of carbon monoxide, 1.7 grams of hydrocarbons and 1.25 grams of oxides of nitrogen per mile. These results have been obtained using twin Stromberg 175CD carburettors on a water-heated manifold in conjunction with a double-retard distributor. They will satisfy the US environmental regulations until 1974. After that date further changes will have to be made to reduce NOx emissions. Engines are currently being prepared to go through the 50,000 mile durability test. European engines are fitted with twin Dellorto carburettors in unheated manifolds.

The cast-iron camshafts run directly in identical cast aluminium combined tappet blocks and cam carriers. Twin-Cam bucket tappets are used in the interest of interchangeability. They also operate directly in the tappet blocks.

Belt drive for the camshafts was a logical choice. Lotus had no long term experience of chain or gear drive which would get them quickly through development. They did know that cogged belts are very quiet, economical and do not transmit destructive torsional vibrations from the crankshaft to the camshafts. Nor do they require lubrication and they are easy to replace when worn. On the debit side they do need replacing at specified intervals. To extend the replacement period the type used are heavier than usual — 1in. wide with $\frac{3}{8}$in. pitch teeth. Drive is directly off a cogwheel on the crankshaft. Tension is maintained by an eccentrically mounted plain pulley bearing on the back of the slack side of the belt.

The camshaft-belt also drives the shaft of a combined oil-pump and distributor housing mounted on the side of the crankcase. This arrangement avoids the necessity to incorporate drive housings in the main crankcase casting, thereby simplifying the foundry work and relieving the casting of asymmetrical expansion problems which can cause distortion and friction. The separate unit is also easier to machine accurately as a separate entity.

The oil pump is mounted directly on the end of the jackshaft, pumping oil through drilled passages to the main oil gallery by way of a full-flow filter.

The cooling-water pump body is cast into the front face of the block-casting, water passing through a port cast in the cylinder jackets before being directed through ports in the head face to the exhaust valve area and inlet port area, in that order. The pump and fan — it is mounted on the same spindle — are driven by a triangulated belt drive from the crankshaft. The alternator is the third corner of the triangle.

JENSEN— Healey . . .

Transmission, chassis and suspension

Because of its shift qualities mainly, the Vauxhall gearbox was abandoned in favour of a Chrysler transmission supplied from Coventry. It is a modified version of that used in the Sunbeam Rapier H120, fitted with a revised remote control to suit the installation and a redesigned stemwheel pilot bearing with a ball-race clutch release. Overdrive is not available, but there is an installation ready should the market demand it.

In direct top the new Healey runs at 17.97 mph per 1,000 rpm which gives it a top speed of 125 mph at maximum revs, which it should easily achieve. Maximum speeds in the three indirect gears are 40, 63 and 97 mph. The final drive ratio is 3.73 to 1 and the tyre size is 185/70 SR—13in.

The chassis is an all-new sheet steel structure, not unlike that of the Austin-Healey Sprite but with a deep backbone and boxed forks at the front end to carry the engine and front subframe mounts. All plain panels are ribbed to prevent drumming and add stiffness, and the inner skins of the rear wheelarches form a vital part of the structure. At the front there is a stout tubular cross-member ahead of the engine position and all panels of the pan and bodywork are spot welded together except the front and rear wings, which are bolted on. In the main the sheet metal is of 20 swg and a torsional stiffness for the body of 2,500 lb.ft./deg has been measured. After phosphating and painting the areas exposed to the road are sprayed with bitumastic undersealing.

At the front a Vauxhall Viva sub-frame is used employing the normal Viva double wishbones and coil springs with telescopic dampers. There is no anti-roll bar however. At the rear the Viva four-link location is used for a live axle, coil springs and telescopic dampers again being used. Special springs have had to be made to give the desired ride height, but the standard Viva rates of 100 lb/in. front and 103 lb/in. rear, measured at the wheel, have proved the most suitable.

Ultimate handling has been sacrificed slightly in favour of a comfortable ride, to suit the American taste as much as the European, and there is a total wheel travel at the front of 6.5in. and 7in. at the rear. Girling monotube gas-filled dampers have given very good results on the Healey and with the aid of these the need for a front anti-roll bar has been eliminated. Slightly stiffer rubbers than those of the Viva in the rear suspension links are used and the roll axis has been lowered to give less ultimate understeer.

Viva-type rack and pinion steering is retained with just over three turns between 32 ft locks, and a GM collapsible column. A special steering wheel with moulded hand grips each side of the horizontal spokes is made to look like hand-stitched leather.

Road wheels have 5½J rims on 13in. dia. to take low profile 185/70 series radial-ply tyres. GKN are casting specially designed wheels in

The boot lid can be opened only with the key, and the space inside is good for this class of car. Spare wheel is in a cradle under the floor.

SPECIFICATION
FRONT ENGINE, REAR-WHEEL DRIVE

ENGINE

Cylinders	4, in-line
Main bearings	5
Cooling system	Water; pump, thermostat and engine-driven fan
Bore	95.2mm (3.75in.)
Stroke	69.3mm (2.73in.)
Displacement	1,973cc (120.5cu.in.)
Valve gear	
Compression ratio	8.4-to-1 Min. octane rating: 91RM
Carburettors	Twin Dellorto 40mm sidedraught
Fuel pump	SU electric
Oil filter	Full-flow, renewable element
Max. power	140bhp (DIN) at 6,500 rpm
Max. torque	130 lb.ft. (DIN) at 5,000rpm

TRANSMISSION

Clutch	8.5 in. dia. diaphragm spring
Gearbox	Four-speed, all-synchromesh
Gear ratios	Top 1.0
	Third 1.29
	Second 1.99
	First 3.12
	Reverse 3.31
Final drive	Hypoid bevel, 3.73 to 1

CHASSIS and BODY

Construction	Integral steel body and chassis unit

SUSPENSION

Front	Independent, double wishbones, coil springs, telescopic dampers
Rear	Live axle, coil springs, trailing and semi-trailing links, telescopic dampers

STEERING

Type	Rack and pinion
Wheel dia.	15in.

BRAKES

Make and type	Girling disc front, drum rear
Servo	Vacuum type
Dimensions	F 10in.dia. R 9in.dia. 1.75in. wide shoes
Swept area	F 194sq.in. R 99sq.in. Total 293sq.in. (267sq.in./ton laden)

WHEELS

Type	Cast alloy, four studs 5.5in. wide rim
Tyres—make	Dunlop or Pirelli
—type	70-series/radial-ply/tubeless
—size	185/70 HR—13in.

EQUIPMENT

Battery	12 Volt 50 Ah.
Alternator	35 amp
Headlamps	120/90 watt (total)
Reversing lamp	Standard
Electric fuses	5
Screen wipers	2-speed
Screen washer	Standard electric
Interior heater	Standard air-blending
Heated backlight	Not available
Safety belts	Extra
Interior trim	PVC seats PVC hood
Floor covering	Carpet with rubber mats in footwells
Jack	Screw pillar
Jacking points	Anywhere under sills
Windscreen	Laminated
Underbody protection	Bitumastic after painting

MAINTENANCE

Fuel tank	11 Imp. gallons (no reserve) (50 litres)
Cooling system	12 pints (including heater)
Engine sump	10 pints (5.7 litres) SAE Change oil every 6,000 miles. Change filter element every 6,000 miles.
Gearbox	3.5 pints SAE 20W/50 No change necessary
Final drive	2.5 pints SAE 90 EP No change necessary
Grease	1 point every 5,000 miles.
Tyre pressures	F 24 R 24 psi (normal driving);
Max. payload	500lb (227kg)

PERFORMANCE DATA

Top gear mph per 1,000rpm	17.97
Mean piston speed at max. power	2,960 ft/min.
Bhp per ton laden	128

SPECIFICATION

Wheelbase	7 ft. 8 in. (234 cm.)
Track—front	4 ft. 5.2 in. (135 cm.)
—rear	4 ft. 4.5 in. (133 cm.)
Overall length	13 ft. 6 in. (411 cm.)
width	5 ft. 3.2 in. (161 cm.)
height	3 ft. 11.8 in. (121 cm.)
Ground clearance	5 in. (13 cm.)
Kerb weight	2,150 lb. (978 kg.)

JENSEN— Healey . . .

light alloy, and there is room in the wheelarches for much larger section tyres and 7in. rims. Original equipment will be HR rated (safe for sustained speeds up to 130 mph) and supplied by Dunlop or Pirelli.

Girling brakes the same as those of the Viva are used, front discs being 10in. dia. and the rear drums 9in. dia. Hydraulic circuits are divided with a pressure differential switch between the two halves warning of a failure on left hand drive cars only. There is a vacuum servo. The only change necessary to adapt the Viva system was a new material for the front discs to obtain the correct balance.

Equipment and fittings

Production will be entirely of open two-seaters and there is very little room in the shell for any additional seats, should a demand for a two-plus-two eventually materialise. The well behind the seats is really only big enough to take the hood plus a couple of small grips.

The boot is quite shallow because the spare wheel is under its floor in a cradle, but the rated capacity is 6 cu.ft. The lid can be opened only with the key.

A lot of attention has been paid to making the hood a snug fit and easy to fold away neatly. Velcro burr fastening attaches the fabric to the window frames each side and the main hoops are counterbalanced to make erection less of a struggle. Triumph-type cam pegs secure the frame to the top screen rail. The screen itself is cemented into the channel and a bright metal surround bonded on top to hide the seal entirely.

Bumpers are made from 16 swg pressed steel painted black with a 20 swg stainless steel capping. They can withstand a 5-mph car-to-car impact at front and rear without the body being damaged, top-hat shaped brackets folding up around rigid chassis extensions.

Seats are covered in ventilated pvc and they follow very closely the design of those used in the Interceptor. Small head restraints are standard and backrests are adjustable. A very practical consideration is the use of carpet on the tunnel, sill sides and rear floor with rubber mats under driver's and passenger's feet. The boot floor has a plasticized felt mat, with cutout for access to the spare wheel cradle winch.

British Leyland type steering column stalks are fitted, with indicators-horn-flasher matched by a wash-and-wipe arrangement on the left. In front of the driver are a large speedometer and rev counter, together with a battery voltmeter, oil pressure, water temperature and fuel gauges. An integrated heater and ventilation system is used, with provision for boosting fresh air to facia vents. There are separate ram-air footwell ventilators.

Kerb weight for the new car is 2,150 lb with a static unladen weight distribution of 51:49. With about 125 bhp per ton laden, the performance should be very brisk indeed with a 0 to 60 mph acceleration time in 7-8sec bracket and a 0 to 100 mph time of well under 30 sec.

As soon as production is under way we hope to carry out a full road test and we shall also be adding a new Jensen-Healey to our fleet of long-term staff cars. The price has not been decided as these pages close for press, but details can be found elsewhere in our News section.

Left: Full instrumentation and ventilation is included in the fully padded facia. Right: The Lotus engine for Europe will have twin Dellorto carburettors, while for the USA Strombergs will be substituted

Below: The Viva front and rear suspension shows clearly here, and the alloy wheels depicted are the final production pattern (wheels on the preceding page are prototypes). Note the dual exhaust system

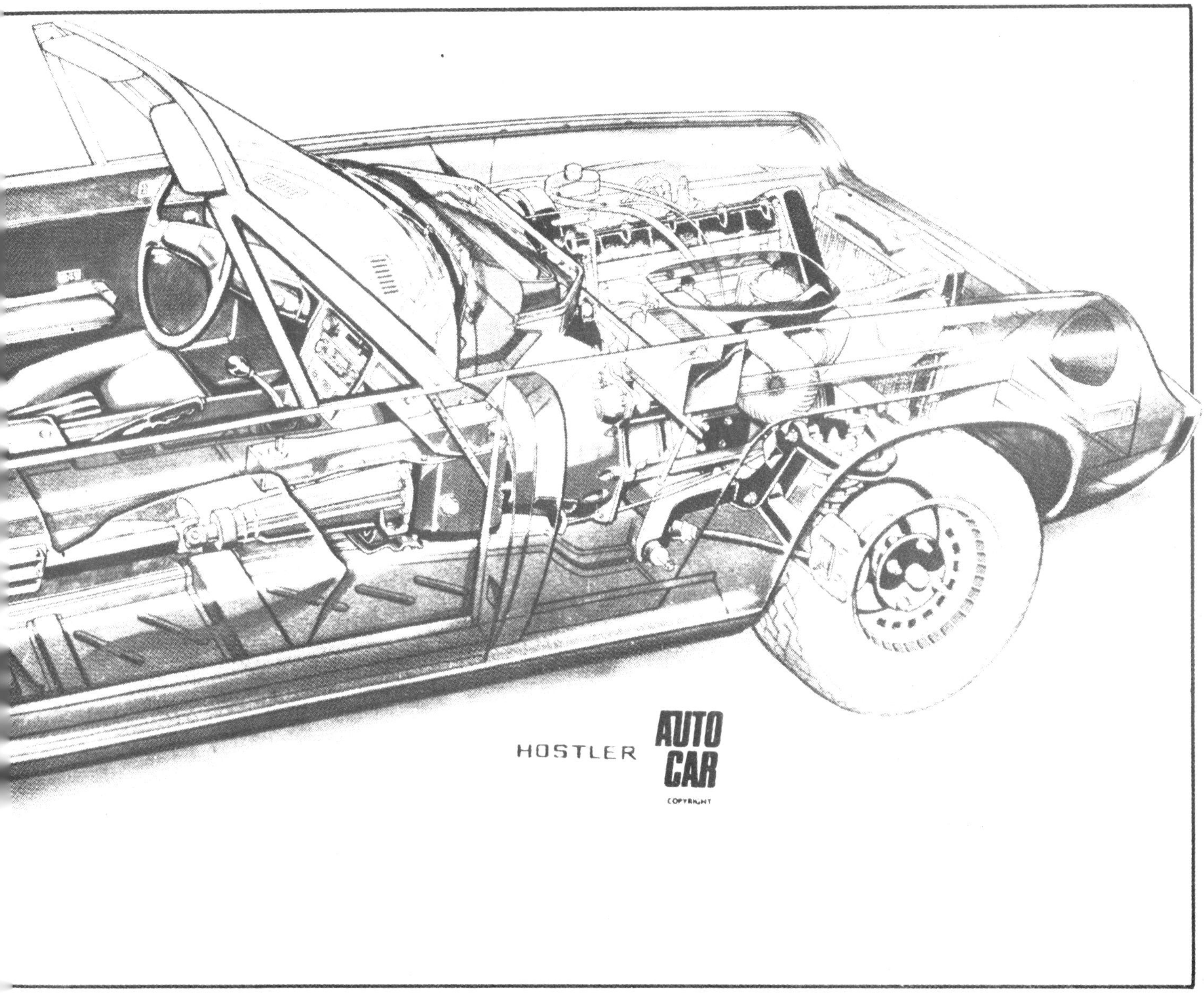

AUTO TEST

JENSEN-HEALEY

Everything a Healey should be

AT-A-GLANCE: New sports car with 2-litre Lotus engine. Excellent performance, good ride, balanced handling. Light steering and brakes. Comfortable cockpit, well placed controls. Well built open two-seater with neat hood and accessible engine. Easy to drive well and lots of fun.

BEARING in mind all the background similarities and the differences, it is amazing how closely the new Jensen-Healey has been cast in the traditional Healey mould. It is everything a British sports car should be, simple in concept, basic in construction, sporty in performance and nimble through the curves. If two slightly contrived words were used to sum up the whole car they would be "roadable" and "drivable" because this exciting new two-seater excells in both these virtues.

Since the demise of the Austin-Healey 3000 in 1968 and the unsuccessful MGC replacement for it, the sports car market both here and in the USA has been remarkably lacking in good, value-for-money two-seaters. Apart from the rather old and now too slow MGB, the little Midget, Triumph Spitfire and the TR6 (sold in America with a detuned carburettor engine to comply with emission controls), the cupboard has until now been bare. After some initial delays caused mainly by production teething problems with the new Lotus 2-litre engine, the line at Jensen is now moving steadily and building up progressively to the target output of 200 cars per week. Of these about 60 per cent will be exported to the USA and Canada, the remainder being equally divided between the home market and other overseas territories. Already over 40 Jensen-Healey dealers have been appointed and others have been selected for the future.

The new car was announced in March this year in time for the Geneva Show. It is offered only as an open two-seater, although a detachable hardtop will be available as an extra soon. The body is made of steel, integral with a pressed platform chassis, front and rear wings being bolted on for quick and cheap accident repairs. As well as being totally dipped in phosphate primer, the body is sprayed after painting with bitumastic underseal on all surfaces exposed to the road.

Suspension front and rear uses Vauxhall Viva components, modified to provide significantly different geometry and with gas-filled dampers and shorter springs to give much better wheel control and the required ride height. Cast alloy wheels with 5½J rims and low-profile radials are standard, tyre supplies coming from either Dunlop or Pirelli. Viva-type Girling brakes are used with a large vacuum servo and special front pad material to balance the front/rear braking characteristics to the weight distribution of the two-seater.

The engine is an all-new design built by Lotus in Norfolk on a new fully-automated high-speed line. It features a die-cast aluminium block and head, twin overhead camshafts driven by a cogged rubber belt and on UK and European cars twin Dellorto carburettors. For the US market, where the emission requirements are much more strict, twin Stromberg CD units are used instead. Both versions of the engine use a compression ratio of only 8.4-to-1 and run perfectly well on 91-octane lead-free fuel.

To put the Jensen-Healey in its class, it turns the scales at exactly 19 cwt with a half-full tank (4.5 cwt or about 20 per cent lighter than the Austin-Healey 3000, which had a separate chassis) and developes 140 bhp (DIN) at 6,500 rpm (compared with an optimistic claim of 148 net at 5,250 for the old 3000). The wheel-base of 92 in. is the same as that of the old Healey, but the body is 4½ in. longer and 3 in. wider. The front track is actually 4½ in. wider and there is a lot more ground clearance—always a weak point with all the big old Healeys.

On acceleration therefore the new Jensen-Healey is streets ahead of the old 3000, clocking a 0 to 60 mph acceleration time of comfortably under 8 sec, which puts it second in the comparisons behind the big-valve Lotus Elan Sprint. In this

respect it is quicker than the Datsun 240Z, the Triumph TR6 (with fuel injection) and the latest Alfa Romeo 2000 GTV. On top speed it is ahead of all but the Datsun and the Alfa (both of which have the advantage of a five-speed gearbox) and on the more revealing acceleration from rest to 100 mph it is ahead of all but the Elan by an even bigger margin (Jensen-Healey 24.7 sec, Alfa 27.7, Datsun 25.6 and TR6 29.0) Compared with the old Austin-Healey 3000, the new Jensen-Healey is no fewer than 10.6 sec quicker from rest to 100 mph.

If this were the whole story of the new engine's performance it would be impressive enough. In terms of flexibility and bottom-end pulling power it is even more extraordinary. Pottering along at only

20 mph in top, the car will pick up cleanly and quickly when the throttle is floored with a very respectable 20–40 mph time of only 7.9 sec. From 30–50 mph takes no longer and the increments continue with single figures until the 80–100 mph bracket, which still takes only 11.7 sec. This consistency shows clearly the wide and flat shape to the torque curve, which has a nominal peak at 5,000 rpm, but starts and ends at very high levels.

This ease with which high gears can be used for brisk main road overtaking and the

Below: There is so little bright-work on the Healey that it almost looks plain. The bumpers can withstand a 5 mph impact without body damage

Left: Apart from the distributor, which is totally buried, engine accessibility is good. There are twin Dellorto carburettors

JENSEN-HEALEY (1,973 c.c.)

ACCELERATION

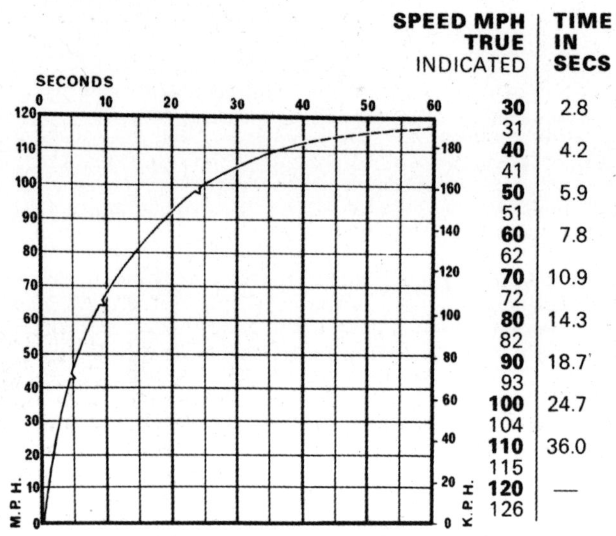

SPEED MPH TRUE (INDICATED)	TIME IN SECS
30	2.8
31	
40	4.2
41	
50	5.9
51	
60	7.8
62	
70	10.9
72	
80	14.3
82	
90	18.7
93	
100	24.7
104	
110	36.0
115	
120	—
126	

GEAR RATIOS AND TIME IN SECS

mph	Top (3.73)	3rd (4.81)	2nd (7.42)
10–30	—	7.2	4.0
20–40	7.9	5.9	3.8
30–50	7.8	5.6	3.7
40–60	8.1	5.6	4.1
50–70	8.4	5.8	—
60–80	8.7	6.2	—
70–90	9.7	7.4	—
80–100	11.7	—	—
90–110	17.8	—	—

Standing ¼-mile
16.2 sec 85 mph
Standing Kilometre
29.8 sec 105 mph
Test distance
1,096 miles
Mileage recorder
2.2 per cent over-reading

PERFORMANCE

MAXIMUM SPEEDS

Gear	mph	kph	rpm
Top (mean)	119	192	6,600
(best)	120	194	6,650
3rd	98	158	7,000
2nd	64	103	7,000
1st	41	66	7,000

BRAKES

FADE
(from 70 mph in neutral)
Pedal load for 0.5g stops in lb

1	35–20	6	45
2	35–20	7	45
3	40	8	45
4	40–43	9	45
5	40–45	10	45

RESPONSE
(from 30 mph in neutral)

Load	g	Distance
20 lb	0.28	108 ft
40 lb	0.58	52 ft
60 lb	0.93	32.4 ft
70 lb	1.02	29.5 ft
Handbrake	0.35	86 ft
Max. Gradient	1 in 4	

CLUTCH

Pedal 35 lb and 4.5 in.

COMPARISONS

MAXIMUM SPEED MPH

Datsun 240Z	(£2,309)	125
Alfa Romeo 2000 GTV	(£2,433)	120
Jensen Healey	**(£1,810)**	**119**
Triumph TR6 P1	(£1,520)	119
Lotus Elan Sprint	(£2,201)	118

0–60 MPH, SEC

Lotus Elan Sprint	7.0
Jensen Healey	**7.8**
Datsun 240Z	8.0
Triumph TR6 P1	8.2
Alfa Romeo 2000 GTV	9.2

STANDING ¼-MILE, SEC

Lotus Elan Sprint	15.0
Datsun 240Z	15.8
Jensen Healey	**16.2**
Triumph TR6 P1	16.3
Alfa Romeo 2000 GTV	16.4

OVERALL MPG

Lotus Elan Sprint	25.5
Datsun 240Z	21.4
Alfa Romeo 2000 GTV	21.1
Jensen Healey	**21.0**
Triumph TR6 P1	19.8

GEARING

(with 185/70-13 in. tyres)

Top	18.1 mph per 1,000 rpm
3rd	14.0 mph per 1,000 rpm
2nd	9.1 mph per 1,000 rpm
1st	5.8 mph per 1,000 rpm

CONSUMPTION

FUEL
(At constant speed—mpg)

30 mph	34.4
40 mph	33.9
50 mph	32.2
60 mph	26.6
70 mph	24.2
80 mph	22.2
90 mph	19.6
100 mph	17.7

Typical mpg 24 (11.7 litres/100 km)
Calculated (DIN) mpg 22.0 (12.8 litres/100 km)
Overall mpg 21.0 (13.4 litres/100 km)
Grade of fuel. Regular, 2-star (min 91 RM)

OIL
Consumption
(SAE 20/50) 1,000 miles/pint

TEST CONDITIONS:
Weather: Fine Wind: 0–7 mph.
Temperature: 18 deg.C. (64 deg.F.)
Barometer: 30.0 in. hg.
Humidity: 60 per cent.
Surfaces: Dry concrete and asphalt.

WEIGHT:
Kerb Weight 19.0 cwt (2,128 lb–965 kg)
(with oil, water and half full fuel tank).
Distribution, per cent F, 51.5; R, 48.5
Laden as tested: 22.0 cwt (2,467 lb–1,120 kg).

TURNING CIRCLES:
Between kerbs L, 33 ft 1 in.; R, 31 ft 9 in.
Between walls L, 34 ft 8 in.; R, 33 ft 4 in.
Steering wheel turns, lock to lock 3.3
Figures taken at 3,500 miles by our own staff at the Motor Industry Research Association proving ground at Nuneaton and on the Continent.

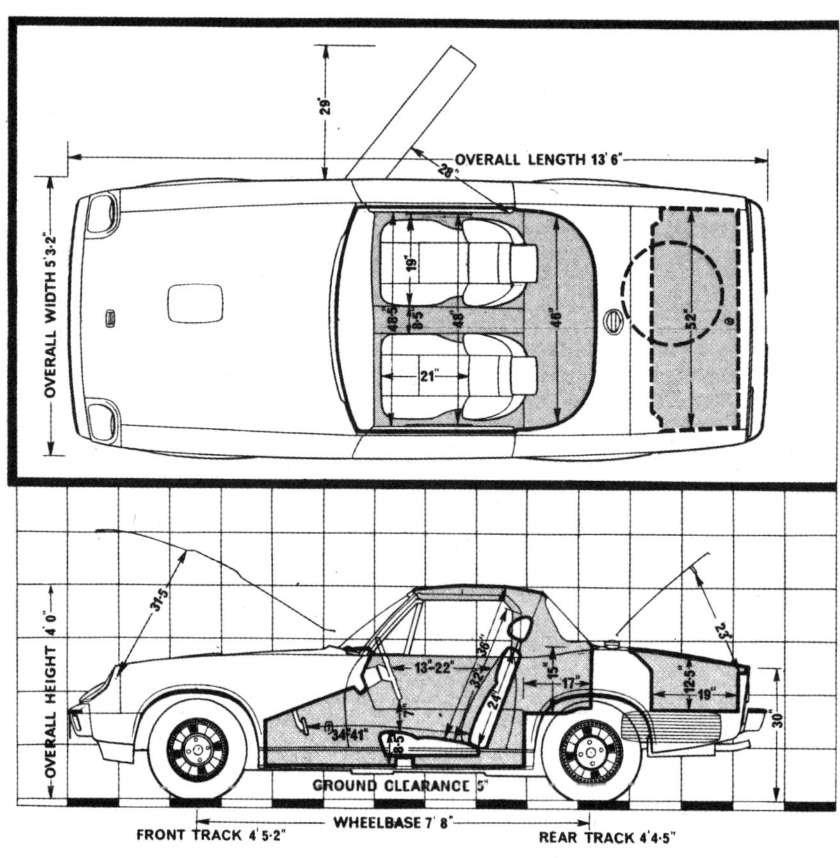

STANDARD GARAGE 16ft × 8ft 6in.

SPECIFICATION

FRONT ENGINE, REAR-WHEEL DRIVE

ENGINE

Cylinders	4 in line at 45 deg.
Main bearings	5
Cooling system	Water; pump, fan and thermostat
Bore	95.2 mm (3.75 in.)
Stroke	69.3 mm (2.73 in.)
Displacement	1,973 c.c. (120.5 cu. in.)
Valve gear	Twin overhead camshafts, cogged belt drive
Compression ratio	8 4-to-1 Min octane rating: 91 RM
Carburettors	Twin Dellorto DHLA 40
Fuel pump	SU electric
Oil filter	Full-flow, renewable element
Max. power	140 bhp (DIN) at 6,500 rpm
Max. torque	130 lb. ft (DIN) at 5,000 rpm

TRANSMISSION

Clutch	8.5 in. dia., diaphragm spring
Gearbox	Chrysler 4-speed all-synchromesh
Gear ratios	Top 1.0
	Third 1.29
	Second 1.99
	First 3.12
	Reverse 3.32
Final drive	Hypoid bevel, 3.73-to-1

CHASSIS and BODY

Construction	Integral steel body and chassis

SUSPENSION

Front	Independent, double wishbones, coil springs, telescopic dampers
Rear	Live axle, coil springs, trailing and semi-trailing links, telescopic dampers

STEERING

Type	Rack and pinion
Wheel dia.	15 in.

BRAKES

Make and type	Girling disc front, drum rear
Servo	Vacuum type
Dimensions	F 10 in. dia.
	R 9 in. dia. 1.75 in. wide shoes
Swept area	F 194 sq. in., R 99 sq. in.
	Total 293 sq. in. (267 sq. in./ton laden)

WHEELS

Type	Cast alloy, for stud fixing 5.5 in. wide rim
Tyres —make	Dunlop or Pirelli, Dunlop SP Sport on test car
—type	70-series/radial ply/tubeless
—size	185/70HR-13 in.

EQUIPMENT

Battery	12 Volt 50 Ah
Alternator	AC Delco 35 amp
Headlamps	Lucus sealed 150/100 watt (total)
Reversing lamp	Standard
Electric fuses	3
Screen wipers	Two-speed plus single-wipe provision
Screen washer	Standard, electric
Interior heater	Standard, water valve control
Heated backlight	Not available
Safety belts	Standard
Interior trim	PVC seats, PVC hood
Floor covering	Rubber mats with carpet on tunnel
Jack	Screw pillar
Jacking points	Anywhere under sills
Windscreen	Laminated
Underbody protection	Bitumastic after painting

MAINTENANCE

Fuel tank	11 Imp. gallons (no reverse) (50 litres)
Cooling system	12 pints (including heater)
Engine sump	10 pints (5.7 litres) SAE 20/50 Change oil every 6,000 miles. Change filter element every 6,000 miles.
Gearbox	3.5 pints SAE 20/50. No change
Final drive	2.5 pints SAE 90 EP. No change
Grease	1 point every 6,000 miles.
Tyre pressures	F 24; R 24 psi (normal driving) F 28; R 28 psi (fast driving)
Max. payload	500 lb (227 kg)

PERFORMANCE DATA

Top gear mph per 1,000 rpm	18.1
Mean piston speed at max. power	2,960 ft./min.
Bhp per ton laden	127

AUTOTEST JENSEN-HEALEY . . .

lusty way the engine pulls so strongly all the time are amongst the main characteristics of the new car. In this respect it recalls the original old Austin-Healey 100, which also had a four-cylinder engine and made do with only a three-speed gearbox.

Starting was at all times instantaneous on the new Healey, a little choke first thing in the morning being all that was required. Immediately the knob can be pushed back and the engine then runs sweetly without hesitation and with no flat spots. Lean mixtures in the middle of the range cause a certain amount of spitting-back and popping in the exhaust on the over-run, but the throttle response is always immediate and clean.

Clutch effort is pleasantly light and the pedal action well designed for easy and progressive operation. We were able to pull away without clutch slip on a 1-in-3 test hill and there was enough bite to spin the wheels during standing start acceleration runs. After four or five brutal getaways in fairly rapid succession there were some signs of clutch fade, so anyone contemplating competition driving would need a special heavy-duty unit with stronger clamping loads. For normal road use the standard clutch presents no problems and is notable for having nicely blended characteristics. The Chrysler gearbox is equipped with powerful synchromesh and well-spaced ratios, indirect maxima being 41, 64 and 98 mph at 7,000 rpm.

There would be little point in pretending the Jensen-Healey is a quiet car to drive; it is not meant to be particularly refined and sports car drivers, in general, like to be aware of the necessary mechanical processes going on under the bonnet. Exhaust is well subdued, however, as it needs to be under present legislation, the loudest noise being a combination of raucous induction roar and an almost harsh kind of combustion beat. In many ways the sound is like that of an old Healey 100/4, both big-fours having similar secondary tremors, but the Jensen-Healey being much better balanced though, of course. Other cars which make this kind of noise are the MGB, to a much lesser extent, the Ford Escort 1600 RS and the Sunbeam Rapier H120. Above about 70 mph wind roar takes over, drowning out all other sounds including the radio by the time the car has reached 100 mph. At its natural cruising gait of 85–90 mph the Healey is much quieter with the hood down, if you don't mind the substitution of buffeting for noise. With the side windows wound up and a cap to prevent flailing hair strands, the protection from wind in

the cockpit is very good indeed and it would be a comfortable car to drive on tour in open trim.

Our test period happily coincided with a spell of fine weather, and we mostly ran the car with the hood folded away. With the optional full-length tonneau fitted over the passenger's half of the cockpit, a driver can stay very snug on a cold morning thanks to the powerful heater. Around town it is also easy to hear the radio with the top open and without having to turn the volume up to the level where it creates a disturbance to others.

Ride and Handling

If the Jensen-Healey lags a little behind the Lotus Elan on performance, it more than makes up for this in its riding qualities. For a sports car the ride is definitely soft, and in a different class from all the other traditional British offerings. Main road bumps, uneven edges to minor roads and even the neglected kind of railway crossing are soaked up extremely well by the supple suspension which has more generous wheel travel than is normal for cars in this class. The Vauxhall front anti-roll bar has been discarded in favour of better damping and with it has gone the interference of one front wheel with the other's behaviour on bumps. There is some slight kickback through the steering on really bad surfaces, but generally this is a very good rough-road car.

The rack and pinion steering is very light, even when parking in a tight spot, and immediate in its response on the move. With just over three turns between compact 32 ft turning circles the gearing is nice and quick around town. On a motorway it takes little more than a wrist twist to change lanes at speed, yet this positive control is not spoilt by unwanted oversensitivity nor is there any tendency to dart about in cross winds.

On corners there seems to be unlimited front-end grip to pull the car round at speed, steering effort remaining light and free from "stiction" at all times. Towards the limit there is some understeer which gets progressively stronger until in the ultimate condition the front runs wide of the chosen radius, but this behaviour is well outside the normal course of things on public roads. At MIRA we just managed to provoke the other condition of slight tail-out attitude by applying full power in second gear on a very tight turn, but most of the time and at all rational speeds the handling remained neutral and beautifully balanced. On a 50 ft radius steering pad we were able to pull 0.75 g laterally before reaching the limits of tyre adhesion. The test car was fitted with Dunlop SP Sport Formula 70 radials which were more than a match for the power available and never posed any traction problems. On MIRA's

Usually the ultimate handling characteristic is one of understeer, but with enough power applied in a low gear it is just possible to get the tail out of line

dry high-mu surfaces we recorded well over 1 g retardation.

One very reassuring feature of the suspension which showed up during handling tests was the complete absence of any carry-over from one direction to the other when making quick steering movements. "Swervability" therefore is of a very high order indeed and we can think of hardly any other car we would rather be in when faced with an "avoid it or else" emergency at speed.

The brakes are very light and have a progressive action with plenty of "bite". Normal check braking calls for only 25–30 lb pedal effort and 70 lb produced a full maximum-g stop with all four wheels marking the tarmac strongly yet without skidding. During 10 stops from 70 mph in quick succession there was a slight build-up in the effort required, especially during each of the latter decelerations, and some rumbling occurred after the fifth stop, accompanied by the smell of hot linings. On the road this characteristic very rarely cropped up and overall the brakes are a perfect match for the performance. The handbrake just failed to hold the car on a 1-in-3 gradient, but it coped adequately with a 1-in-4.

Unlike many other sports cars in this size class, the Jensen-Healey is built for drivers with long legs and with big feet. It is possible to get well back from the pedals which are well spaced and have a wide clear area to rest the left foot when off the

Above: Headrests are standard and the seats are adjustable for rake. There is a drop-down box in front of the passenger and two trays in the central tunnel. Below: The boot has a good square shape with the spare wheel under the floor

clutch. The steering column is not adjustable, but it seems naturally to be at arm-stretch reach for all sizes of driver. Backrests on the seats are adjustable over a limited range of rake but the hood irons and rear shelf prevent any fully reclined provision.

Seat comfort is very good indeed, the combination of firmness for lateral support and softness for extra bump absorption being well balanced. Small head restraints are standard and these do not hamper visibility in any way. There has been no attempt to provide occasional accommodation in the rear, the car being strictly a two-seater.

In front of the driver is an oval instrument panel containing matching speedometer (with trip recorder) and rev counter, flanked by clearly visible oil pressure and water temperature gauges. Outboard of these are the fuel gauge and battery voltmeter, both somewhat obscured by the wheel rim and the driver's hands. We found the fuel gauge gave very steady and accurate readings of the level in the 11-gal tank and the rev counter on the test car was dead accurate. At maximum speed we noticed a falling off in the oil pressure after 10 or 12 miles, but this quickly recovered when we eased back on the throttle.

Two small sub-panels flank the steering column on the lower edge of the facia. That on the right contains rocker switches for lamps and hazard warning, a square-knobbed rotary panel rheostat separating them. The panel on the left is blank, ready to accept switches for any accessories. A stalk on the left of the column controls the two-speed wipers, electric washers and a single-wipe provision, like that of the Morris Marina. The righthand stalk is the usual indicators, horn and headlamp flasher combination.

Heater controls are mounted in the centre of the car, two horizontal slides taking care of temperature and distribution. A rocker switch alongside operates the two-speed booster fan, which is reasonably quiet on its slower setting. A water valve only is used to regulate temperature and its response was typically sluggish. Two eyeball nozzles in rthe facia emit cool boosted air at face level and under the scuttle each side are footwell vents with individual controls. These were moderately effective, but barely able to keep pace with the heat soak from the transmission on a hot day with the hood erect.

The hood itself is a neat piece of tailoring and it takes no more than a few minutes to fold it away or put it up. There are seven press studs in all, the remainder of the fastening apart from two windscreen rail pegs being by Velcro burr-zip strips. The unframed side windows fit snuggly against the hood aperatures and we experienced no draughts at speeds up to the maximum.

The hood is a neat fit and it proved draught-free at all speeds. From this angle the body style looks particularly attractive

Putting the roof down is very simple and there is a neat cover for the fabric and irons included as standard. A £16 extra is a full-length tonneau cover with centre zip which is a struggle to fasten, but well worth the trouble when parking overnight in the open. On the test car the centre zip proved far from waterproof, allowing rain to seep through and fill up the wells on the tunnel.

A General Motors collapsible steering column is fitted, together with a Vauxhall type steering lock which requires two hands to secure it and remove the key. Whilst this may be a useful safety feature against inadvertent locking, it makes opening the boot, which can be done only with the other key, an extra chore. Inside the boot there is quite a lot of luggage room for such a small car and the shape is sensibly square to take suitcases as easily as squashy holdalls. The spare wheel is in a cradle underneath which can be winched down with the wheelbrace.

The bonnet lid over the engine extends the full width between the front wing crowns, so with it open the engine accessibility is excellent. We would have liked the stay to have been longer, allowing a little more clearance above our heads, but that is only a small detail. Carburettors are right on top of the inclined engine where they are easy to work on but the distributor is so buried that it must be removed for attention.

With a UK price of £1,810 the new Jensen-Healey has been pitched right between the home-built offerings from British Leyland and the imported opposition from Alfa Romeo and Datsun. In this sector of the market it has very little to compete against it, so home sales are bound to do well. Overseas it will have to fight rather harder against its competitors, but on the all important qualities of performance, ride, handling and comfort, it comes out very high on our score sheets. Even the very early production car we tested felt mature and fully developed. Much more than that, it felt like a future classic, the kind of car that one day will become a collectors item.

MANUFACTURER:

Jensen Motors Ltd., Kelvin Way, West Bromwich, Birmingham.

EXTRAS (inc. P.T.)

Basic	£1,497.00
Purchase Tax	£ 313.44
Seat belt standard	
Total (in G.B.)	£1,810.44

PRICES

*Tonneau cover	£ 15.95

* Fitted to test car

PRICE AS TESTED   **£1,826,39**

Long Term Test
JENSEN-HEALEY

Engine by Lotus;
Gearbox by Chrysler;
Suspension by Vauxhall;
Development by customers?

THE TRADITIONAL British sports car may be an anachronism in 1973 but a lot of people still like them, including most of the *Autocar* staff. So when Kjell Qvale of Jensen took up Donald and Geoffrey Healey's ideas for a replacement for the Austin-Healey 3000 and created the first all-new sports car for years, we were keen to add one to our fleet of long-term test cars.

"Everything a British sports car should be", we said in our original *Autotest* (31 August 1972); the Lotus-engined Jensen-Healey had proved to be a fast, good handling, comfortable two-seater in the Healey tradition. It certainly wasn't perfect — but we *enjoyed* it, and enjoyment is surely one of the main reasons for sports car motoring. Furthermore, we thought that its specification and price were exactly right for the home market, being pitched in the middle of the £800 price gap between the mid-range British Leyland sports cars and the more exotic offerings of Lotus, Datsun and Alfa Romeo.

Now, with 10,000 miles of Jensen-Healey motoring behind us, we confess to some disappointment. We still admire the basic concept and we accept that no company, however large, can get a complex all-new product like a motor car 100 per-cent right from the word "go". But the reliability and finish of our example during its first nine months suggest that Jensen have some way to go before they can compete on equal terms with the Datsun challenge in the United States and even represent a worthwhile alternative to the longer established — and cheaper — British models in this country.

In fairness I should point out that ours is a very early Jensen-Healey — one of the first 800 to be delivered. We were among the first to place an order after the car was previewed to the Press in February last year. It was a car of obvious significance and we wanted to get one on the strength as quickly as we could. Initially, delivery was expected in September 1972 but we didn't receive the car until mid-January this year. Enquiries during the waiting period brought forth stories of a batch of engines with lubrication problems and the lack of some bought-out components which were holding up production. In addition our car had been rejected by the distributors at the pre-delivery check and been returned to the factory for a respray.

When it was delivered the car had 800 miles on the clock and had been run-in. It was thoughtful of Jensen to relieve us of the tedium of the settling-down period but, as its designated custodian, I was rather annoyed that we had not been able to start the test from scratch. It still felt rather tight and the gearbox was stiff so I decided to run it to the recommended 3,000 rpm running-in rev limit until the 1,000 mile mark. Even so I was disturbed to see puffs of smoke from the exhaust on the over-run and when accelerating from rest, and at 1,100 miles it needed a quart of oil. An oil consumption of 150 miles per pint at this early stage was cause for some concern. At this point I had to go off to the Monte Carlo Rally, a job which required a more commodious transport (a Capri 3000GXL), and while I was away the Healey's oil consumption deteriorated further

Long Term Test
JENSEN-HEALEY

Above: *Cockpit is well planned but facia finish on our car is poor. Unusual steering wheel is comfortable in use. Drop-down glove compartment is of generous size — and lockable — while plastic moulding turns transmission tunnel into useful space for oddments*

Right: *Lotus 907 engine reclines at an angle with Dell'Orto carburettors on top. Reservoirs are easy to get at but dipstick is awkward, and oil filter and distributor near impossible without dismantling*

Below: *Clean, simple lines make the Jensen-Healey attractive, if not spectacular. Headlamp surrounds are fibreglass and substantial bumpers meet US regulations*

and the car was returned to Jensen for investigation. New piston rings were tried but did not effect a cure and the eventual result was an engine change. So we re-started at 1,635 miles with the 500 miles of running-in missed before.

In other respects the car was in good order. An annoying squeak from a rear damper disappeared, and I got used to the old-fashioned scuttle shake and the plop-plop ticking of the electric fuel pump from behind the passenger's left shoulder. When it was taken to the London distributors Charles Follett Ltd., for its second 500-mile service, with it went a request to adjust the clutch and handbrake, attend to a loose window winder and replace the rusty tonneau cover clips on the doors. To my surprise it was returned with a modified distributor (there had been some instances of oil seeping past the nylon spindle seal on the earlier type) and four new sparking plugs. The tonneau clips were replaced by the same type with the same ill-fitting, unplated countersunk self-tapping screws — and after one damp night in the open they rusted again.

Not long afterwards Warren Allport was driving the car in a spell of rainy weather when the engine stopped inexplicably. After making all the usual checks and calling the RAC's assistance when he could find nothing obviously wrong, it was discovered that the fuel tank had a vapourlock, presumably because the breather pipe was blocked. Simply opening the filler cap did the trick and though no action had been taken as a result, this trouble has not recurred. Some 300 miles later I was conscious of a definite clunk somewhere in the drive-line when the clutch took up, and a metallic rattle from the gearbox area. This quickly developed into a vibration that was serious enough to discourage me from using the car. Back to Follett's — where it was discovered that the front propeller shaft universal joint was breaking up (though it had looked all right on a cursory examination). The joint was replaced under warranty but I felt that a £1.75 charge for road testing (clearly essential after a job of this type) because "it can't be reclaimed from Jensen", was unjustified.

While this trouble was being attended to a modified bonnet catch and exhaust pipe strap were installed — two of a number of modifications found to be necessary in the first few months of production. In addition, I drew attention to "bubbling" below the paint surface on the offside rear wing and after inspection by the Jensen service representative it was agreed to respray the wing and rear "deck" section. The result is a not very good colour match and some paint on the hood — which suggests that they didn't bother to put it down when they did the job.

At last it seemed to be running consistently well. Photographer Ron Easton and I decided to take it to the Belgian Grand Prix at Zolder — not a particularly long run, but one which would give us a chance to use its performance to the full, and assess its touring capabilities. The weather was good and so we were able to make the journey with the hood down. We appreciated the Healey's ability to cruise comfortably at over 100 mph; its good top gear acceleration; the good gearchange (the box is the close-ratio one from the Sunbeam Rapier H120); the relative lack of noise and wind buffeting with the hood down and the side windows up; the long-range comfort of the seats and the sensible layout of the cockpit. It was proper sports car motoring and reminiscent of a longer trip which I had made in a TR6 a few years ago; this is a compliment, since I regarded the TR as "my sort of car".

Comparisons with the Triumph, which runs the Healey close on performance, are inevitable — and show that although the Healey follows the traditional style there has been a conscious effort to bring it up to date. Instead of heavy steering and a rock-hard ride, it has saloon-type ride comfort, which is perhaps not so surprising when it uses Vauxhall Firenza front and rear sub-assemblies, albeit with springs and dampers specially tailored for the car. The way that it soaks up road imperfections like *pavé* at high speed is very impressive for a sports car with a live axle. And there is certainly no lack of roadholding, the Dunlop SP 185 70-series radials doing an admirable gripping job in the wet or dry. But one pays for it in other ways; there is more body roll than one would expect from a car of this type, and the handling is always on the side of understeer even if it is near-neutral at moderate speeds. There is a lot of feedback through the steering on bumps and surface changes and a mid-corner bump can throw the whole car off line. The result is that the handling lacks the rugged positiveness of the older cars. It is difficult to analyse. The steering (Vauxhall rack and pinion) is nice enough, light and not too low geared but there somehow isn't that initial confidence-inspiring "feel" when turning into a fast corner. On the plus side, straight-line stability is good even in strong cross-winds, ground clearance is generous (what a contrast that is to the old Healeys!) and all the controls are light enough to make this an easy car for a woman to drive.

Perhaps it is disappointing that it is so compromising, that one does not have to make a special effort to drive a special kind of car. Amidst this "mild" package one or two things remain to remind one of the tough sports cars of the past. The most remarkable is the engine, which could easily have come from the same humble surroundings as the suspension if Vauxhall hadn't lost so much power from their 2.3 in making it meet US emissions regulations; or from BMW, or Ford, if they could have supplied the right numbers of the right engines at the right time. In the end Jensen did a deal with Lotus to become the first users of the light alloy four-cylinder 907 engine which is to power the next Lotus — and is conveniently Vauxhall sized. With twin belt-driven overhead camshafts and four-valves-per-cylinder it is a more sophisticated engine than the otherwise conservative specification would seem to demand. Its power output is rated (conservatively, we are told) at 140 bhp net at 6,500 rpm, and there is the big advantage that the engine meets current emissions standards by the very proper method of efficient combustion; with a market of their own in the United States, Lotus will of course keep it in compliance with future regulations. The compression ratio for both the European Dellorto twin carburetted version and the US specification which uses two CD Strombergs is the same at 8.4 to 1; Jensen recommend the use of 3-star fuel though they say that 91 octane should be adequate.

Starting has never been a problem and the choke has not been needed; the Weber technique of "two pumps and half throttle" has always worked from cold, and there is little hesitation during the warming-up period. It is a noisy engine when it is working hard, with a good deal of induction roar, though the exhaust silencing works well. At low speeds it is unobtrusive and its flexibility is good indeed; it will accelerate smoothly and quickly from 1,000 rpm (18 mph) in top gear. Above 4,000 rpm or so the noise turns to a harsh "caminess" (not unlike the RS 1600's BDA engine, which of course shares the complexity of 16 valves operating within a light-alloy cam box) which begins to sound dangerously rough from 5,800 rpm towards the 7,000

Above left: *Putting the hood down is simple — though stowing it neatly is a chore.* **Above right:** *Full tonneau cover needs a lot of effort to fit — and more clips to locate properly.* **Left:** *Collapsed hood frame interrupts the run of inertia-reel safety belts.* **Right:** *Velcro fastening is used along hood and tonneau sides — but is not really man enough for the job.* **Below right:** *Boot is a reasonable size for a two-seater and is augmented by useful space behind seats*

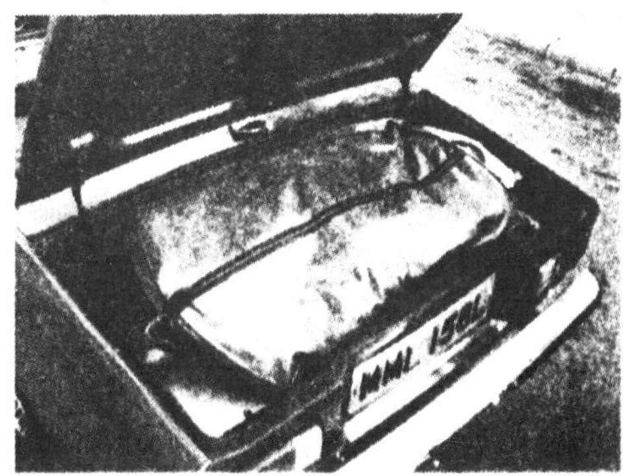

rpm rev limit. (A mechanical cut-out operates at maximum revs — 6,700 rpm in our case.) Ours has a vibration at period at 4,500 rpm in top (85 mph) which is annoyingly transmitted through the throttle pedal. A lot of the noise and harshness could probably be reduced by some simple sound insulation procedures; it can be argued however, that the archetypal sports car owner wouldn't want that. I think that I agree — if you want super stereo etc, there are plenty of fast saloons to choose from . . . .

Our fuel consumption over the Belgian Grand Prix trip worked out at 22 mpg, slightly better than the overall figure, which includes a fair amount of town running (after which, incidentally, there is occasionally some plug oiling which is quickly cleared). Less satisfactory however, was the engine's appetite for oil which had started at a barely acceptable 250 miles per pint and deteriorated by the 7,000 mile mark to less than 150 miles per pint, with the attendant clouds of black smoke from the exhaust. Once again we made the trip to Follett's Temple Fortune service department. Once again the Jensen service inspector (who judging by the assembled Jensen-Healey owners in their reception area is a pretty busy man) passed judgment. The oil control rings were to be changed for a modified type, under warranty.

Since this was its second, and presumably modified engine, I was concerned. I tackled Lotus about the oil consumption problem. Initially they had experienced difficulty in

PERFORMANCE CHECK

Maximum speeds

Gear	mph		kph		rpm	
	R/T	Staff	R/T	Staff	R/T	Staff
Top (mean)	119	117	192	188	6,600	6,500
(best)	120	119	194	192	6,650	6,600
3rd	98	94	158	151	7,000	6,700
2nd	64	62	103	100	7,000	6,700
1st	41	39	66	63	7,000	6,700

Standing ¼-mile	R/T:	16.2sec	85mph
	Staff:	16.5sec	82mph
Standing	R/T:	29.8sec	105mph
Kilometre	Staff	30.82sec	103mph

Acceleration	R/T:	2.8	4.2	5.9	7.8	10.9	14.3	18.7	24.7	36.0
Time in seconds	Staff:	2.9	4.4	6.5	8.4	11.9	15.3	20.1	27.8	38.6
True speed mph		30	40	50	60	70	80	90	100	110
Indicated speed MPH	R/T:	31	41	51	62	72	82	93	104	115
Indicated speed MPH	Staff:	32	43	53	63	73	84	94	104	114

Speed range, Gear Ratios and Time in seconds

mph	Top		3rd		2nd	
	R/T	Staff	R/T	Staff	R/T	Staff
10-30	—	—	7.2	7.6	4.0	3.9
20-40	7.9	8.3	5.9	6.5	3.8	3.5
30-50	7.8	9.1	5.6	6.2	3.7	3.7
40-60	8.1	10.4	5.6	5.9	4.1	4.2
50-70	8.4	9.8	5.8	6.3	—	—
60-80	8.7	11.1	6.2	6.8	—	—
70-90	9.7	13.4	7.4	8.3	—	—

Fuel Consumption

Overall mpg	R/T:	21.0 mpg (13.4 litres/100km)
	Staff:	20.7 mpg (13.7 litres/100km)

NOTE: "R/T" denotes performance figures for Jensen Healey tested in AUTOCAR of 31 August 1972

JENSEN-HEALEY

running-in engines due to piston scuffing. The lower piston ring was therefore replaced by one with a lower wall pressure, which solved the scuffing problem but led to higher oil consumption. Finally — and before 1,000 engines had been made — a third design of spring-expanded oil control ring was introduced which has solved the problem. During the supply difficulties when the Healey production line was starting up a number of early engines were stockpiled, and the replacement installed in our car was, it seems, one of these — hence the need for a modified distributor.

At the same time, I instructed Folletts to carry out a belated 6,000 mile service which including materials and balancing the four wheels, cost £31.65. The home mechanic would not find this a particularly daunting task as underbonnet accessibility is generally good — though replacement of the oil filter and access to the distributor (hidden underneath the carburettors) is very awkward.

I also had to ask Folletts if they could get the hood repaired, for someone had borrowed the car and lowered the hood without reading the instructions first — and in doing so had torn the press studs out of the fabric sides. Ah, the hood — now there's another throw-back to the Golden Age of Sports Cars. When it is up it is not a bad fit and reasonably draught free though there is a tendency to let in water at the top corners of the screen in heavy rain. Over about 70 mph wind roar contributes to the high interior noise level, and over 80 mph one of the rear "quarters" automatically blows open. The edges and the sides of the frame are sealed to the fabric with Velcro "touch and close" strips which are all right as long as the two surfaces fall close together but cannot bridge the gap that develops if the retaining rail at the rear isn't precisely located and do not form a strong enough joint to resist interior wind pressure at high speed. Actually, putting the hood down is not difficult, but folding and rolling up the fabric so that it stores neatly and flap-free under the little "finisher" cover is a fiddle. If there was one item that I would like to have seen the Seventies' traditional sports car have, it is a hood that is almost as quick and convenient to open and close as a sun-roof. It can be done, but the Jensen-Healey's is not even as good as that of the last Austin Healey 3000.

I gave up the uneven struggle with the first tonneau cover. There was no way that the one originally supplied could meet all of its locating clips at the same time so I asked Folletts to fix that too. I think that they supplied another one which has obviously been modified but it still doesn't fit easily, though it has stretched and now requires slightly less super-human effort than before.

The tonneau has to be a rather odd shape to cope with the seats' fixed head restraints. They are a good feature of excellent seats which are not unlike those of the big Jensens and are both comfortable and supporting. There is a generous range of adjustment and the backrests recline, so that with its sensibly placed steering wheel and pedals most people can find a driving position that is really comfortable (which is not often true of the "traditionals"). Shorter people find the seat cushion a bit low and a minor annoyance for me is the way that the hood frame scuffs the seat back when it is in the most comfortable

Soft suspension for a sports car gives good ride comfort but quite a lot of body roll. The specification does not include anti-roll bars

position and the hood is down. More serious is the way that the collapsed hood frame interrupts the run of the seat belts from the rear mounted inertia reels. Much as I appreciate the convenience of these automatic belts and would normally choose them in preference to any other, the static type would overcome the problem in this case. A red warning light on the facia — part of the party tricks required under American law — glows persistently if the car is in gear and the occupants have not buckled up.

Jensen deserve some congratulation for the thoughtful layout of the controls and instruments. The good positioning and light operation of the pedals, gear change and steering wheel have already been referred to. The various dials and warning lamps, grouped together in a hooded nacelle, are easy to read while all the switchgear is close to hand, the headlamps, indicators and horn and the washer/wipers being controlled by two Marina-type column stalks. There are two eyeball ventilators as well as footwell ducts and they work well, though the interior can get still quite hot as they have to compete with heat soak through the transmission tunnel. The heater itself is of the imprecise water-valve type.

An ingenious centre console moulding turns the top of the transmission tunnel around the handbrake into a useful space for oddments and there is a good-sized drop-down glove locker. The latter seemed so weakly attached that I was sure that it would break — but it hasn't yet. The glove box is a particularly scruffy plastic moulding, and the neat design of the facia in general is spoilt by rather poor finish; improvements have been made on more recent models, including the provision of an exterior passenger door lock — an important omission on the early cars.

Criticism of the car's finish also applies to the paintwork which shows more signs of incipient rust than we believe a car of this age and price should. We are told that improvements in this area have also been made.

To confirm that ours was now mechanically "right" we completed the first 10,000-mile instalment of this long term assessment with an 1,800 mile run to Monza for the Italian Grand Prix. Glorious weather on the outgoing journey and over the race weekend meant another open-top trip. It went well, crusing at 100 mph for hour after hour on the autoroutes (only at over 110 mph is there a slight increase in water temperature and corresponding decrease in oil pressure), and rushing satisfyingly across the winding roads of the Alps. An average of 70 mph from Geneva to Boulogne on the return confirmed its long-legged cruising ability. Fuel consumption over the whole trip was 21.5 mpg and — more significantly — the oil consumption was a satisfactory 800 miles to the pint.

Changing, as Jensen have done, from a manufacturer of low volume, high quality, cars to the much higher production of everyday cars is a big job. It is clear that the dictates of the company economists put both the car and the engine into production earlier than they would have liked from an engineering point-of-view. They admit to teething troubles. Production, at present at 110 cars per week (70 per cent go to North America) cannot keep up with the current demand, which proves that the concept of the car is right, that there are plenty of people who want just the sort of motoring that Jensen aim to provide.

We know that our experiences with an early car are not unique. Equally we are confident that both Jensen and Lotus are aware of the problems, and have done and are doing everything they can to ensure that the Jensen-Healey that you buy today is a better, more reliable machine than the one that we bought nine months ago. □

COST of OWNERSHIP

Running Costs	Life in miles	Cost per 10,000 miles
		£ p
One gallon of 3-star fuel, average cost today 37p	20.7	178.74
One pint of top-up oil, average cost today 23p	225+	10.12
Front disc brake pads (set of 4)	24,000	1.28
Rear brake linings (set of 4)	12,000	6.17
Dunlop SP70 185 HR 13 tyres (front pair)	22,500	13.60
Dunlop SP70 185 HR 13 tyres (rear pair)	22,500	13.60
Service (main interval and actual cost incurred)	6,000	36.86
Total		**260.37**
Running cost per mile:	2.6p	
Approx. standing charges per year		
*Insurance		79
Tax		25
Depreciation		
Price when new		1,959
Trade in cash value (approx.)		1,500
Depreciation (actual over 9 months)		459
Typical advertised price (current)		1,700
Approximate standing charges per year		716
Total cost per mile (based on cash value) 9.7p		

Insurance cost is based on Cornhill quotation for a 30-year-old driver, with 65 per cent no claims bonus, living in London. Restricted to approved drivers only, over 30; compulsory £50 excess and excludes personal accident and medical costs. +See text.

WESTLAND
R. HELIPORT

AUTO*TEST*

Jensen GT

**Fixed-head addition to Jensen range, based on Jensen-Healey sports two-seater
More refined; slight loss in performance because of extra weight,
but still a delightfully quick car, spoiled by unnecessary carburettor flat-spot.
Brakes excellent. Handling fair. Ride a little loose.
Practical and enjoyable.**

ALTHOUGH Jensen seemed to eschew the association, the Jensen GT is of course basically a Jensen-Healey with an elegant fixed head top. Wheelbase, track, body length and width are identical to the sports two-seater, and obviously the same handsomely shaped panels are used for the wings, front and back. But the Jensen (-Healey) GT is clearly aimed at a different sort of person, who may not care for traditional sports-car wind-in-the-hair pleasures — or discomforts. With the arrival of a young child or two, the married Jensen-Healey owner could remain faithful to the marque — which in spite of presently being still in the hands of a

receiver at the request of the management, is reported as flourishing — and cater for his enlarged family.

Taking retail prices as a basis, he will have to part with an extra £856. The Jensen GT costs £4,198, which sounds even in these inflated days a lot of money, but which turns out to be at the lower end of the car's competitors price-wise.

The car uses exactly the same power and drive units as the sports-car. With the extra glass, bodywork and more lavish interior decoration and sound insulation, it weighs 21.6 cwt, compared with the current two-seater's 20.0 cwt (which thanks to the heavier five-

speed gearbox and those vast American bumpers was 1 cwt more than the original four-speed two-seater). Not surprisingly it isn't quite as quick in acceleration from a standing start (five-speed Jensen-Healey tested 28 June 1975 acceleration times in brackets), though it performs more than well enough: 0-50 mph in 6.7 sec (6.2 sec); to 60 in 8.7 (8.3), to 80 in 14.9 (14.0); and to 100 in 27.0 (25.4). It will not comfortably achieve 110 mph within the MIRA twin horizontal mile straights as the sports-car did (in 37.4 sec), but thanks presumably to its cleaner shape aerodynamically, it returned the same 119 mph top speed on the

MIRA banking as the old four-speed (which is 3 mph faster than the five-speed test car).

Speeds in the gears are naturally the same as before — 41, 63, 86 and 109 mph respectively in the intermediates, at the engine's ignition cut-out-limited red line of 7,000 rpm. Power output is claimed as 144 bhp at 6,500 rpm (DIN) nowadays. Top speed corresponds to 6,100 rpm, so that the car is slightly over-geared in fifth. As before, and even more so in this smoother, more refined role, we would have preferred the Getrag gearbox to have the first four gears conventionally spaced, with fourth direct (giving the same gearing as fifth

Jensen GT

does now), and fifth a genuine overdrive for quieter, more economical motorway running.

The point is that the Lotus double-ohc light-alloy engine is — or rather can and *ought* to be — most delightfully flexible. It does not need close ratios, since there is a wide spread of power — or rather there is when the car is accelerating relatively slowly in top gear. The qualification about the Jensen GT's flexibility is the source of the only really irritating weakness of the car's performance. This weakness, which we first met on the five-speed sports-car, is the maddening carburettor flat-spot which you have to drive around most deliberately in ordinary road use if the car is to give its best. Accelerate from 10 mph in third gear (less than 1,000 rpm), and the engine begins to pull well, without any hint of temperament — until, at 1,300 rpm it starts to misfire, so that you have to coax it with relaxed throttle openings up to 2,500 rpm (31 mph) when it will take full throttle again and get on with the job in the delightfully lusty way one used to expect from this unit. It is the same at corresponding speeds in other lower gears.

This hole in the performance low down is embarrassing. At the traffic lights you get in other drivers' way as the car splutters, just when they have every right to expect you to depart smartly. To avoid this, one must use a lot more revs than is discreet when pulling away from a standstill, and a lot of harmful clutch-slip. For our standing start acceleration runs at MIRA, we had to let the clutch in with a bang at 5,000 rpm, in order to clear the flat-spot with wheelspin — it worked well on a private test track, but is not a practice which the owner will wish to indulge on public roads.

Compliance with the dictates of European exhaust emission regulations will be blamed; but since we have met other high performance cars which comply without spoiling their driveability, we feel sure that Jensen and Lotus between them can correct this most unsportscar-like blemish.

How about that other, more persistent failing of the Lotus engine — its roughness and vibration from 5,000 rpm onwards? It seemed, from the five-speed sports-car of last June, that a lot of this had been got rid of with the improved engine-gearbox joint, which stiffened the allegedly weak crankcase. On the Jensen GT, there is apparently a further improvement, although the engine's smoothness is not in the same class as the similarly four-cylinder'd BMW 2-litre range. How much of this is due to engine alterations and how much to obviously better insulation is not clear, but the result is pleasing.

Engine noise, mostly induction roar, is still dominant at higher speeds and when accelerating, although not at all to an unpleasant degree; at 70 mph you can still hear the wireless without having to turn up the volume too much. The car has a viscous-coupled fan now, which must help. What little wind noise there is comes from the front of the doors. Road noise is surprisingly well subdued, perhaps at slight cost to the car's absolute straight stability, which on the test car was not as good as on the sports-car; one found oneself consciously steering all the time.

The gearchange is reasonable, but not as good as one might expect — a bit too sticky. We would prefer an Alfa (or Maxi) style five-speed gate, with fifth out on the limb as it were, instead of first. In town one is forced to use first by the flat spot, and this is made more tedious when one is a little tired by the heavy spring pressure biasing the lever inwards. The box on the test car demanded that the clutch pedal be fully floored, otherwise the synchromesh into first objected audibly; it also developed some chatter during the test, and tended occasionally to baulk.

As we have suggested already, economy could probably be improved with a more definitely over-driving top gear. The overall test figure achieved reflects a lot of hard driving, and may well be bettered usefully by many owners, although that flat-spot leads to wasteful driving habits, as explained.

Handling, ride and brakes

At the weight distribution unladen at the kerb is near-ideal, with a slight rear bias — 47·8/52·2 front/-rear. There is consequently not much understeer. In fact the car starts off near-neutral, which may be an additional reason for the very slight wander mentioned already — and in spite of the addition of a front anti-roll bar, where the sports-car has none. It sticks to the road very well on those quite big 70-section radials, which on the test car were Pirelli, not Dunlop as before; both makes suit the car

The facia on the GT is finished in walnut, with padded surrounds. Speedometer and rev counter have the oil pressure and fuel tank contents gauges between them, with battery volt meter and water temperature gauges on the outside. Switches are mostly rocker type, with twist and pull ones for wash/wipe and choke. Rocker switches on central tunnel are for electric windows. Radio and stereo cartridge player are standard

Maximum Speeds

Gear	mph	kph	rpm
Top (mean)	119	192	6,100
(best)	120	193	6,150
4th	109	175	7,000
3rd	86	138	7,000
2nd	63	101	7,000
1st	40	64	7,000

Acceleration

True mph	Time secs	Speedo mph
30	3.0	32
40	4.4	42
50	6.7	52
60	8.7	62
70	11.6	72
80	14.9	82
90	20.5	92
100	27.0	102
110	—	113
120	—	123

Standing ¼-mile:
16.7 sec 73 mph
kilometre:
30.9 sec 105 mph

mph	Top	4th	3rd	2nd
10-30	—	—	9.1	5.0
20-40	—	10.3	6.7	4.2
30-50	12.0	12.1	5.4	3.6
40-60	11.8	7.1	5.2	3.9
50-70	11.1	7.3	5.4	—
60-80	11.3	8.3	6.2	—
70-90	12.7	9.1	—	—
80-100	15.5	10.2	—	—

Consumption

Fuel
Overall mpg 19.5
(14.5 litres/100km)
Calculated (DIN) mpg 24.3
(11.6 litres/100km)

Constant speed:

mph	mpg
30	33.1
40	32.8
50	31.7
60	29.2
70	26.1
80	23.8
90	20.9
100	17.5

Autocar formula:
Hard driving, difficult conditions
17.6 mpg
Average driving, average conditions
21.5 mpg
Gentle driving, easy conditions
25.4 mpg

Grade of fuel: Regular, 2-star
(91RM)
Mileage recorder: 3.2 per cent
over reading

Oil
Consumption (SAE 20/50)
1,000 miles/pint

Brakes

Fade (from 70 mph in neutral)
Pedal load for 0.5g stops in lb

	start/end		start/end
1	30	6	35-40
2	30	7	35-40
3	35-30	8	40
4	35	9	40
5	35-40	10	40

Response (from 30 mph in neutral)

Load	g	Distance
20lb	0.22	137ft
40lb	0.55	55ft
60lb	0.75	40ft
70lb	0.90	33ft
80lb	1.00	30.1ft
Handbrake	0.32	94ft

Max. gradient 1-in-3.

Clutch Pedal 35lb and 4½in.

Test Conditions

Wind: 10-15 mph
Temperature: 10 deg C (50 deg F)
Barometer: 30.0 in. Hg
Humidity: 70 per cent
Surface: Dry asphalt and concrete
Test distance: 954 miles

Figures taken at 4,500 miles by our own staff at the Motor Industry Research Association proving ground at Nuneaton.

All Autocar test results are subject to world copyright and may not be reproduced in whole or part without the Editor's written permission

Regular Service

Change	6,000	12,500	25,000
Engine oil	£3.50	£3.50	£3.50
Oil filter	£1.84	£1.84	£1.84
Gearbox oil	—	—	—
Spark plugs	—	£2.42	£2.42
Air cleaner	—	£4.69	£8.69
C/breaker	—	£0.39	£0.39
Total cost	**£26.84**	**£38.86**	**£38.86**

Interval

(Assuming labour at £4.30/hour)

Parts Cost

(including VAT)

Brake pads (2 wheels) — front	£4.02
Brake pads/shoes (2 wheels) — rear	£10.37
Silencer(s)	£42.42
Tyre — each (typical advertised)	£15.72
Windscreen	£39.43
Headlamp unit	£2.70
Front wing	£26.35
Rear bumper	£70.88

Warranty Period
One year or 12,000 miles

Weight

Kerb, 21.6 cwt/2,417lb/1,096kg
(Distribution F/R, 47.8/52.2)
As tested, 25.2cwt/2,817lb/1,278kg
Boot Capacity: 15.3 cu ft maximum

Turning circles:
Between kerbs L, 33ft 1in; R, 31ft 9in;
Between walls L, 34ft 8in; R, 33ft 4in.
Turns, lock to lock 3.3

Test Scorecard

(Average of scoring by
Autocar Road Test team)

Ratings: 6 Excellent
5 Good
4 Better than average
3 Worse than average
2 Poor
1 Bad

PERFORMANCE	4.15
STEERING AND HANDLING	4.18
BRAKES	4.82
COMFORT IN FRONT	5.17
COMFORT IN BACK	2.94
DRIVERS AIDS	4.71
(instruments, lights, wipers, visibility etc.)	
CONTROLS	4.32
NOISE	3.95
STOWAGE	3.72
ROUTINE SERVICE	2.17
(under-bonnet access: dipstick etc.)	
EASE OF DRIVING	4.07
OVERALL RATING	**4.02**

Comparisons

	Price capacity £	max power mph	0-60 sec	mpg	c.c.	bhp	wheelbase in.	length in.	width in.	kerb weight	fuel gall	tyre size
Jensen GT	**4,198**	**119**	**8.7**	**19.5**	**1,973**	**144**	**9.2**	**165.8**	**63.3**	**21.6**	**11¾**	**185.70 HR 13in.**
Alfetta GT	4,198	117	9.4	23.7	1,778	122	95	165	65	21.4	11.9	185/70-14
Datsun 260Z 2+2	4,499	120	9.9	23.9	2,565	150	102½	174	65	23.5	13.2	195/70-14
Lotus Elite 503	7,625	124	7.8	20.9	1,973	155	97.8	175½	71½	22.8	14¾	205/60-14
Reliant Scimitar GTE	4,368	121	8.9	20.8	2,994	138	99	170	66	21.8	17	185-14
Triumph Stag	4,676	115	11.6	20.6	2,997	145	100	173¾	63½	25.1	14	185-14

Jensen GT

equally well. The steering itself is never too heavy, even at tight-manoeuvring speeds, and the gearing is good, at 3·3 turns for a useful 32½ft turning circle. There is still quite a bit of roll for this sort of machine, though not too much. A Jensen-Healey feature that persists here is the relative lack of pitch damping. It lifts and bobs its nose too easily.

Ride is correspondingly not as hard as you might have expected, in spite of the live back axle; the car reacts surprisingly softly, relatively speaking, to many bumps, moving a lot, though not often uncomfortably. A bad point is the low ground clearance under the exhaust, which bottomed too easily two-up.

The brakes impressed greatly, having the right balance to achieve an indicated 1g maximum retardation without any locking of wheels, though with a lot of nose-dive. Fade resistance is good, but when we tried to repeat the best braking figure, the previously ideal brake balance had disappeared, the front wheels locking early, limiting the retardation to 0·9g. The brakes also grew a little rough — "three-penny-bit-y" — towards the end of the fade test, recovering their normal smoothness when cool again. The handbrake could not be pulled hard enough to lock the back wheels, presumably because of the weight bias, but returned a quite tolerable 0·32g, and holding the car well on 1-in-3. (Because of the flat-spot, it would only pull away on 1-in-4, however.)

Comfort and convenience

The biggest differences between this and its forebears are seen inside. In place of that needlessly American-style dashboard, there is a handsome example of walnut-veneer for the entire facia, which raises the tone of the car tremendously. Jensen are clearly proud of the transformation; inside the pull-down glove locker lid, you find a plate declaring the coachwork to be by Jensen Motors. The centre console is used to carry all minor switches, as well as the surprisingly loud-ticking Kienzle clock, the centre face-level vents, heater controls and radio. The panel is set in a foam-filled surround, which helps insulate the interior as well as improve safety.

The driving position is good, with conventionally easy stalk controls spoiled only by the usual regrettable positioning of the horn on the signalling stalk instead of in the middle of the steering wheel, and on the test car (and according to the instruction manual) the left-hand-drive layout of the stalks — signalling on the left instead of in its proper place on British cars, on the right. Another piece of regrettable left-hand-drive layout was found in the wiper arcs, which left too much screen unswept on the right, just where the driver needs clear vision.

Visibility otherwise isn't bad. There are no serious blind spots on any quarter, although the top of the

back window is a little low. A help to a different sort of vision is the delay in switching off the courtesy lamps after you have shut the doors. The windows are electrically lowered, and too slow by American standards. You can't see how far ahead or behind the bumpers obtrude, and it is easy to find oneself touching other cars when parking; the construction of the bumpers usually saves both parties any damage, however.

Jensen wisely do not claim more

Above: The hatchback styling blends well with the original sports car lines. The tailgate opens from inside the car, and the wiper parks clear of the glass

Left: Jensen do not make wild claims for their back seats in the GT. They are large enough for children, and tip forward to increase the load space

Left: With the Lotus engine canted over to the left, access to the various auxiliary equipment is good. The bonnet is not self-supporting and has to be propped open

than occasional room for children in the back seats, whose upright sections can be unbolted individually to flop forward and form a longer load deck, with a maximum length of 42¾in. inside, though a bit more is available if you include the clearance to the backs of the front seats. Bearing in mind the ground clearance problem, there is then quite a useful load space for this type of car. Even with the seats all in use, the space behind is surprisingly generous; valuables can be

hidden in a lockable place under the carpet, which is a good feature which would be appreciated on all estate cars.

Gas struts hold the framed glass tail gate open. It is unlocked from the driver's door pillar; we felt that some sort of handle would be appreciated, particularly by drivers who may try to open it when wearing gloves. As it is, you have to use your nails to start the opening. Access to the load space is reasonable, though there is a sill to lift awkward things over; talking of access, we wondered why the driver's and passenger's doors could not be allowed to open further — those on the test car made getting in and out unnecessarily awkward.

We found the heater controls too stiff, and although one could achieve the desired temperature fairly easily, response to a change of the lever's position was slow, suggesting that it uses some form of water-valve control rather than air-blending. There are through-flow vents, but they do not seem to allow enough flow without being forced to with the fan; perhaps that is why Jensen advise the driver to keep the fan on at least slow speed at all times.

The seats (in front) are superbly comfortable for most people. One tester wanted a little more lumbar support, but this was the only criticism. It was generally agreed that, in comfort, this model followed the sports-car, which has already established itself as one of the least tiring of long-distance tourers as far as accommodation is concerned.

Generally, therefore, we liked the Jensen GT very much. That flat-spot excepted, it is a very satisfying car to drive and to run, and in the majority of opinions good to look at too. It seems quite well priced, and although there are some points which need attention, they are not by any means insurmountable by a firm of Jensen's abilities. With its equally, if differently, delightful open stablemate, it should widen the appeal of the excellent small Jensens. We wish both the car and its makers well. □

MANUFACTURER:
Jensen Motors Ltd.,
Kelvin Way, West Bromwich,
Birmingham,
Warwickshire

PRICES	
Basic	£3,588.04
Special Car Tax	£299.00
VAT	£310.96
Total (in GB)	**£4,198.00**
Seat Belts	Standard
Licence	£40
Delivery charge	
(London) approx	£20
Number plates	£12
Total on the Road	
(exc insurance)	£4,270
Insurance	Group 7
EXTRAS (inc. VAT)	
Hide seat facing	£93.60
Fabric sun roof	£117.00
TOTAL AS TESTED	
ON THE ROAD	**£4,270**

World Wide COMMENT

Where now for Jensen?

A CLOSER examination of the Jensen insolvency reveals a number of factors which are puzzling rather than disturbing. First came Kjell Qvale's initial statement blaming the unions for the company's difficulties, followed almost immediately by a withdrawal of the statement. Then there is the relatively small margin between Jensen's assets and liabilities. Assets were originally stated to be £4·2 million and liabilities £4·5 million. Many companies are trading with a bigger differential than this without calling in the Receiver. Moreover suppliers report that Jensen were paying their accounts promptly right up to the end so no-one will be "taken" for a big sum.

What does come out of it is that Qvale is disillusioned with the whole project. It will be remembered that he took over the company in 1970 with the object of producing a replacement for the Healey 3000 which had accounted for a major part of the sales, and success, of his company, British Motor Car Distributors, in California. The Interceptor side of the business came as a bonus. Qvale's main object in acquiring Jensen from Brandts the bankers was to gain access to the skilled labour force and assembly shops which had produced, in their time, 90,000 Healey 3000 bodies, the Sunbeam Tiger and the Volvo P1800 coupé. It was an ideal production unit for 200 or so medium priced sports cars per week. At the same time he arranged to use the Healey name, British Leyland being in the throes of giving it up, and made a deal to buy up to 200 engines a week from Lotus. The one snag was that the factory did not belong to the company but was leased from the Church Commissioners.

In the event the most Jensen-Healeys produced in one week was 110, a figure defined by the number of Lotus engines available. At that time the workforce numbered about 1,300. Then came the oil crisis

and sales of all cars all over the world slowed down. Even before that time the Jensen-Healey price was being forced up by the increased cost of engines and labour. The price of the engine alone is now three times the originally negotiated figure.

As a consequence of the increased price and a spate of teething troubles with engines, Jensen-Healey sales slowed up even more than everyone else's to the point where in January British Motor Car Distributors had 1,000 Jensens in stock at their various US branches. By any reckoning that is at least £3 million of motor cars. Qvale acted quickly at West Bromwich and was able to cut back his labour force to 650 with pretty good co-operation from the unions. He also reduced the scheduling of the Jensen-Healey to a minimum 25 cars

per week. At the same time his sales people in the USA got down to selling off the backlog. It is now down to two hundred or so vehicles.

In the absence of comment from Qvale, who has returned to America, it seems that he was prepared to live with this situation. Unfortunately militants in the workforce seem to have been encouraged by Ministerial suggestions that if Jensen got into trouble Government help would be forthcoming. Whether this is true or not, Qvale was certainly subjected to constant niggling disputes. He also failed to get increased productivity for higher wages. The final blow came when the Church Commissioners decided to treble the rent. One can hardly blame Qvale for seeing this as the last straw and deciding to go back to his profitable American business where labour and rents are

predictable and profits large and tangible. His way of baling out by declaring the company insolvent is unusual. However it does ensure that it is taken over by competent management in the shape of the Receiver. And he had not let it run down and accumulate a backlog of debts.

It seems certain that the Receiver has decided that the company is viable for the time being and that business can continue as usual. It still remains to be seen where new capital will come from but it is certain that Jensen will be at the Motor Show as usual with a full range of models – including the Jensen-Healey roadster which is to continue in production.
*Amid the troubles at Jensen comes the sad news that Kevin Beattie, chief engineer and previously managing director, had died.

AUTOCAR w/e 29 May, 1976

Jensen— production ceases

PRODUCTION OF JENSEN CARS ceased on Friday 21 May when, as predicted two weeks ago in *Autocar*, supplies of components ran out, and the Receiver could no longer continue the assembly of cars from the parts held in stock. A statement from the company says that while the production lines have been closed down, the parts and service departments, together with the sections of the works concerned with sub-contracting work, have continued in business to serve existing owners.

This sad decision was taken against a background of frantic activity to try to put together a consortium to save the company. With time running out fast, Kjell Qvale flew into this country at the

beginning of last week to try to swing the balance with a guarantee of orders for the American market next year. However, one of the prime movers of the scheme for the consortium, Tony Good, simply could not put the deal together in time to avert the closure of the factory.

A statement on behalf of Tony Good says that efforts to put the consortium together are continuing and a decision is expected within the next two weeks. However, the task of the consortium is made more difficult by the closure, and the few manufacturing staff remaining have now left the factory. The production workers will be returning at the end of this week for their final pay settlement, and

this is the last opportunity to keep them all together. However, if rescue comes within a reasonable period it should still be possible to re-sign key people.

The closure comes at a time when Interceptor and Jensen GT sales in America appeared to have turned the corner, and it is understood that Qvale who severed his financial connection with the company late last year, when the Receiver was appointed, but remains the American distributor, had with him a guarantee of substantial orders. □

PRODUCTION RECORD

Warwick-Built Cars

Chassis Type	Total	Abbott	Duncan	Elliott	Nash	Silverstone	Sportsmobile	Tickford	Westland	Sports Convertible	Others
A	97		8	15					15		59
B	231		31	85			23		41		51
C	170	27		1				124	8		10
D	51					51					
E	54					54					
BT	50	14						36			
F	100	36						64			
N	253				253						
N Farina	151				151						
G	28									25	3
Totals	1185	77	39	101	404	105	23	224	64	25	123

Longbridge and Abingdon-Built Cars

Model	Engine	bhp/rpm	Produced from/to	Production
100 BN1 (3-speed)	2660c.c. 4-cyl	90/4000	1953-1955	10,688
100 BN2 (4-speed)	2660c.c. 4-cyl	90/4000	1955-1956	3,924
100S	2660c.c. 4-cyl	132/4700	Feb-Jul 1955	50
100M	2660c.c. 4-cyl	110/4500	1955-1956	—
100/6 BN4 (4-port)	2639c.c. 6-cyl	102/4600	1956-1957 ⟩	10,268
100/6 BN4 (6-port)	2639c.c. 6-cyl	117/4750	1957-1959	
100/6 BN6 (6-port)	2639c.c. 6-cyl	117/4750	1957-1959	4,150
3000 BN7/BT7 2-carb	2912c.c. 6-cyl	124/4600	1959-1961 ⟩	13,650
3000 BN7/BT7 3-carb	2912c.c. 6-cyl	132/4750	1961-1962	
3000 BJ7 Mk II 2-carb	2912c.c. 6-cyl	131/4750	1962-1964	11,563
3000 BJ8 Mk III	2912c.c. 6-cyl	148/5200	1964-1968	17,703
Sprite AN5 'Frog'	948c.c. 4-cyl	43/5200	1958-1961	48,999
Sprite AN6 Mk II	948c.c. 4-cyl	46/5500	1961-1962 ⟩	30,500
Sprite AN7 Mk II	1098c.c. 4-cyl	56/5500	1962-1964	
Sprite AN8 Mk III	1098c.c. 4-cyl	59/5750	1964-1966	25,905
Sprite AN9 Mk IV	1275c.c. 4-cyl	64/5800	1966-1971	21,282

Index

The Austin-Healey 'Le Mans' Sprite, based on the Sprite Mk III, was raced with some success in the mid-1960s. In 1965 Paul Hawkins and John Rhodes won their class and came 12th overall at Le Mans, while Rauno Aaltonen and C. Baker drove the car to another class win in the 12-hour race at Sebring.